THE NEW YODER

THE NEW YODER

EDITED BY
Peter Dula *and* Chris K. Huebner

CASCADE *Books* • Eugene, Oregon

THE NEW YODER

Cascade Books
An Imprint of Wipf and Stock Publishers
199 W. 8th Ave., Suite 3
Eugene, OR 97401

www.wipfandstock.com

ISBN 13: 978-1-60899-044-3

Cataloging-in-Publication data:

The new Yoder / edited by Peter Dula and Chris K. Huebner.

    xx + 338 p. ; 23 cm.

    ISBN 13: 978-1-60899-044-3

    1. Yoder, John Howard. I. Dula, Peter, 1970–. II. Huebner, Chris, 1969–. III. Title.

BX8143.Y59 N45 2010

Manufactured in the U.S.A.

Contents

Contents

Acknowledgments

Essays in this volume first appeared as follows:

Peter C. Blum, "Yoder's Patience and/with Derrida's *Differance*," in *A Mind Patient and Untamed: Assessing John Howard Yoder's Contributions to Theology, Ethics, and Peacemaking*, eds. Ben C. Ollenburger and Gayle Gerber Koontz, 75–88. Copyright © Cascadia Publishing House, 2004. Used by permission.

Peter C. Blum, "Foucault, Geneaology, Anabaptism: Confessions of an Errant Postmodernist," in *Anabaptists and Postmodernity*, eds. Gerald Biesecker Mast and Susan Biesecker Mast (Telford, PA: Pandora Press, 2000), 60–74. Used by permission.

Daniel Boyarin, "Judaism as a Free Church: Footnotes to John Howard Yoder's *The Jewish-Christian Schism Revisited*," in *CrossCurrents* 56/4 (Winter 2007) 6–21. Used by permission.

Romand Coles, "The Wild Patience of John Howard Yoder," in *Beyond Gated Politics: Reflections for the Possibility of Democracy* by Romand Coles (University of Minnesota Press, 2005), 109–38. Copyright 2005 by the Regents of the University of Minnesota. Used by permission.

Cynthia Hess, "Traumatic Violence and Christian Peacemaking" in *Brethren Life and Thought* 51/4 (Fall 2006) 201–20. Used by permission.

Acknowledgments

Chris K. Huebner, "Patience, Witness, and the Scattered Body of Christ: Yoder and Virilio on Knowledge, Politics and Speed," from *A Precarious Peace: Yoderian Explorations on Theology, Knowledge, and Identity* by Chris K. Huebner. Copyright © 2006 by Herald Press, Scottdale PA 15683. Used by permission.

P. Travis Kroeker, "The War of the Lamb: Postmodernity and Yoder's Eschatological Genealogy of Morals," in *Mennonite Quarterly Review* 74/2 (April 2000) 295–310.

Nancey Murphy, "John Howard Yoder's Systematic Defense of Christian Pacifism," in *The Wisdom of the Cross: Essays in Honor of John Howard Yoder*, eds. Stanley Hauerwas, Chris K. Huebner, Harry J. Huebner and Mark Thiessen Nation (Grand Rapids, MI: Eerdmans, 1999), 45–68.

Gerald W. Schlabach, "The Christian Witness in the Earthly City: John H. Yoder as Augustinian Interlocutor," in *A Mind Patient and Untamed: Assessing John Howard Yoder's Contributions to Theology, Ethics, and Peacemaking*, eds. Ben C. Ollenburger and Gayle Gerber Koontz, 221–44. Copyright © Cascadia Publishing House, 2004. Used by permission.

Alain Epp Weaver, "On Exile: Yoder, Said, and a Politics of Land and Return," in *States of Exile: Visions of Diaspora, Witness, and Return* by Alain Epp Weaver. Copyright © 2008 by Herald Press, Scottdale PA 15683. Used by permission. Earlier versions of the essay first appeared in *CrossCurrents* 52/4 (Winter 2003) 439–61 and then in *A Mind Patient and Untamed: Assessing John Howard Yoder's Contributions to Theology, Ethics, and Peacemaking*, eds. Ben C. Ollenburger and Gayle Gerber Koontz (Telford, PA: Cascadia, 2004), 161–86.

The editors and authors gratefully acknowledge the copyright holders for permission to reproduce copyright material.

Introduction

PETER DULA *and* CHRIS K. HUEBNER

John Howard Yoder has exerted a powerful influence over contemporary theology and ethics ever since the publication of *The Politics of Jesus* in 1972. At that time, Yoder emerged as the most articulate defender of Christian pacifism against a theological ethics guild still dominated by the Troeltschian assumptions reflected in the work of Walter Rauschenbusch and Reinhold and H. Richard Niebuhr. For most of the last thirty-five years Yoder has continued to be read in conversation with Rauschenbusch, the Niebuhrs, and other mid-century orthodoxies. But in the last decade there has been a clearly identifiable shift in the scope and focus of Yoder scholarship. A new generation of scholars has begun reading Yoder alongside figures most often associated with post-structuralism, neo-Nietzscheanism, and post-colonialism, resulting in original and productive new readings of his work. At the same time, scholars from outside theology and ethics departments and from outside of Christianity, like Romand Coles and Daniel Boyarin, have discovered in Yoder a significant conversation partner for their own work. The essays collected in this volume are some of the best examples of this shift.

The Old Yoder

We shall refer to this situation as marking the emergence of a "new Yoder" that differs in some significant ways from the "old Yoder" that captivated the work of an earlier generation. This is not to identify a shift in Yoder himself. His work was remarkably consistent over the course of a long career. Nor do we mean to suggest that this shift is absolute, that new readings of Yoder have altogether supplanted the old ones. It is not, in other words, a purely temporal shift. Old Yoder discussions can still be found. We also do not wish to suggest that it is always easy to tell which is which (still less that newer is better). And yet we think that the categories of old and new are helpful, but only if understood as broad, occasionally clumsy, generalizations. The new Yoder represents an important development in the way Yoder has come to be read in recent years. In particular, it reflects an approach to Yoder that finds it helpful to bring him into conversation with a range of dialogue partners with whom he was not himself explicitly engaged. In doing so, attention is drawn to a series of important moments in his work that tended to be obscured, or at least underappreciated, by an earlier generation's encounters with his writings. In particular, we understand the transition from the old Yoder to the new Yoder to involve three interrelated shifts.

First, essays before the 1990s tended to work within the parameters of the Christian ethics guild as set by Troeltsch, Rauschenbusch, and the Niebuhr brothers. These parameters are determined by the Troeltschian typology of church and sect. They are defined against the background of Troeltsch's claim that "the preaching of Jesus and the creation of the Christian Church were not due in any sense to the impulse of a social movement."[1] Debates in Christian ethics thus came to be divided between those who set out to translate theological convictions so that the church could make meaningful contributions to political matters and those who denied that theology could be so translated and thus set the church outside the realm of the political. Within those parameters, the Christian pacifist was presumed to be epistemologically and politically handcuffed. Faithfulness and effectiveness were assumed to name alternatives in a zero-sum game. The more faithful, and therefore sectarian, a community was said to be, the less relevant, responsible, and comprehensible to the world.[2] It is this set of assumptions that Yoder set out to

1. Ernst Troeltsch, *The Social Teachings of the Christian Churches*, 2 vols., trans. Olive Wyon (Louisville: Westminster John Knox, 1992) 1:39.

2. See, for example, Duane Friesen, *Christian Peacemaking and International Conflict* (Scottdale, PA: Herald, 1986). While not strictly an interpretation of Yoder, it is not unfair to describe Friesen's work as an attempt to demonstrate that Yoder's "politics of Jesus" can be interpreted in such a way that it makes a realistic contribution to contemporary global politics.

challenge in his most well-known book, *The Politics of Jesus*. Old Yoder essays tend to focus on his defense of pacifism against those who dismiss peace as an irresponsible sectarian ideal. These discussions often set out to evaluate the cogency of his critique of mainstream Christian ethics. They ask whether or not Yoder's theological articulation of peace is finally sectarian. In other words, they are concerned to determine whether his pacifism had political teeth, whether it is sufficiently realistic to have anything to say to the increasingly "complex" world of contemporary politics.[3]

Second, it is fair to say that this sort of engagement with Yoder was done primarily by Mennonites. While Yoder was read widely as a representative of Christian pacifism, with the exception of Stanley Hauerwas and Jim McClendon, few non-Mennonites did significant work on him. But Yoder was and continues to be an ambiguous figure for Mennonites. On one hand, he gave Mennonites a voice in the wider academy and church. But his "politics of Jesus" still seemed too "sectarian" for some Mennonites who had lived through the Civil Rights and anti-Vietnam War movements and who were eager to flex their new-found political muscles. Interpretations of Yoder often became a battlefield upon which Mennonites worked out their anxieties about what Troeltsch and others called sectarianism. In that respect, it might be suggested that old Yoder discussions often tell us as much about the extent to which Mennonite conversations were determined by the Troeltschian categories whose grip Yoder sought to loosen as they do about Yoder himself.[4]

3. The debate around the work of J. Lawrence Burkholder is representative here. See the essays collected in Rodney Sawatsky and Scott Holland, eds., *The Limits of Perfection: A Conversation with J. Lawrence Burkholder* (Waterloo, ON: Institute for Anabaptist-Mennonite Studies, 1993). The exchange between A. James Reimer and J. Denny Weaver is also of note in this regard. Put briefly, Reimer worries that Yoder's pacifism is too idealistic. He seeks to correct for this perceived weakness by turning to the categories of law and justice, on the one hand, and classic creedal statements, on the other. Weaver, by contrast, seeks to defend Yoder against Reimer's critique. In doing so, he maintains that the peace of Christ entails a rejection of creedal Christianity, which he reads as a product of constantinian accommodation. What is significant for our purposes is how both Reimer and Weaver engage Yoder against the background of a set of assumptions that fairly straightforwardly reflect the Troeltschian alternatives of church and sect. See J. Denny Weaver, *The Nonviolent Atonement* (Grand Rapids: Eerdmans, 2001); and A. James Reimer, *Mennonites and Classical Theology: Dogmatic Foundations for Christian Ethics* (Kitchener, ON: Pandora, 2001).

4. In this regard, it is perhaps not merely a coincidence that two significant figures

Third, old Yoder essays tend to be preoccupied in a rather direct and narrow way with questions of peace and violence. Indeed, they might be described as war-centered insofar as they take war and physical confrontation as the paradigmatic instances of violence. Of course, Yoder's work was heavily oriented towards issues of war and peace. But it was also an ongoing attempt to interpret and theorize what it is that the categories of peace and violence name. By contrast, old Yoder discussions often proceed as if peace and violence name fairly straightforward realities. In this regard, peace tends to function as the tail that wags the theological dog.[5] Whether intentionally or not, such an approach had the effect of leaving us with a Yoder whose discussions of war and peace lacked background and context and was therefore sometimes difficult to distinguish from what he called "liberal pacifism." This reification of peace is also reflected in the way the discussion quickly turns to the task of exploring how we can go about making the world less violent and more peaceable. In this regard, old Yoder scholarship bears a significant kinship to the fields of conflict resolution and restorative justice, not to mention the work of NGOs such as the Mennonite Central Committee.[6]

The New Yoder

Richard Rorty once wrote that it is characteristic of great thinkers that their "purpose is to dissolve the problems considered by [their] prede-

---

in the previous generation of Mennonite scholarship in theology and ethics wrote dissertations on Troeltsch. See Duane Friesen, "The Relationship Between Ernst Troeltsch's Theory of Religion and His Typology of Religious Association," PhD diss., Harvard University, 1972; and Harry J. Huebner, "The Continuity of Axiology and Epistemology: An Examination of the Presupposition of Ernst Troeltsch's Historicism," PhD diss., University of Toronto, 1981.

5. The work of J. Denny Weaver most straightforwardly exemplifies such an approach. But it is also reflected in the way Yoder has influenced a generation of Mennonite biblical scholarship, where finding a "peace theme" in some text has become a familiar move. See, for example, Willard M. Swartley, *Covenant of Peace: The Missing Peace in New Testament Theology and Ethics* (Grand Rapids: Eerdmans, 2006).

6. By way of example, see the essays collected in Duane Friesen and Gerald Schlabach, *At Peace and Unafraid: Public Order, Security, and the Wisdom of the Cross* (Scottdale, PA: Herald, 2005).

cessors, rather than to propose new solutions to them."⁷ Interestingly, Rorty's description echoes one of Yoder's early attempts to describe his own approach. Toward the end of *The Christian Witness to the State*, Yoder made the following claim: "It is normal for the newcomer to a debate which is already in process to accept the prevailing definition of terms and choose one of the existing sides, whereas the wiser approach is to question the definitions."⁸ One important trait of the new Yoder is the recognition of the way this particular form of greatness animates his work. Whereas old Yoder essays often worried that his illiberalism was too conservative, new Yoder essays tend to see him as a radical. That is, they read him as challenging the categories themselves instead of just taking up a position within the given categories.⁹

So, for example, Daniel Boyarin begins his chapter with a quote from Yoder: "Yet most of the redefinition going on in the vast scholarly literature [on the Jewish/Christian schism] still is engaged in making adjustments *within* the framework of the received schema. The corrections being made weaken that schema yet without replacing it. What this present study contributes is not another volume of details within those debates, but an alternative perspective on what the problem was and still is." A similar claim is at the heart of Peter Blum's essay on Foucault where he writes, "Yoder's strategy is interestingly similar to that of Foucault, in that he responds to questions not by answering them in their own terms, but by inquiring into where the questions come from, by showing that the frame of reference within which they are raised is not as monolithically self-evident as we might have assumed." Or Daniel Colucciello Barber: "Already it is possible to see Yoder resisting, when faced with the task of explaining the distinctive

7. Richard Rorty, *Consequences of Pragmatism* (Minneapolis: University of Minnesota Press, 1982) 40.

8. John Howard Yoder, *The Christian Witness to the State* (Newton, KS: Faith and Life, 1964) 90.

9. While Yoder articulately undermined the categories of the mid-century debates, he often did so after long essays (like *The Christian Witness to the State*) working within the terms of the old frameworks. One way to describe the shift from old Yoder to new Yoder would be as a difference in emphasis on these two aspects of his work. But once again, the division is not hard and fast. See for example, Theodore J. Koontz, "Christian Nonviolence: An Interpretation," in Terry Nardin, ed., *The Ethics of War and Peace* (Princeton: Princeton University Press, 1998), which nicely straddles this divide.

lifestyle of the community of disciples, the easily-at-hand opposition between the domain of the church and the domain of the secular."

For decades, Yoder's insistence on speaking from a particular place, his denial of the possibility of starting from scratch, left him vulnerable to the charge that his fidelity to first-century texts left him unable to communicate to a wider public.[10] The Yoderian thus bore the burden of proof in arguing that one did not have to jettison particularity in order to communicate with the wider world. This charge could take the shape of an accusation of political irrelevance or irresponsibility.

What makes the essays in this volume "new" is not so much that they agree with Yoder on this score but that they don't think the argument is a very interesting one. They simply start with the assumption that Yoder is right and build from there, asking a different set of questions and pursuing different lines of inquiry. Old Yoder essays argue about whether or not his claim that "there is no public that is not just another particular province" is somehow "sectarian." New Yoder essays take that claim for granted, and it rarely occurs to them to think of it as "sectarian" when it is already common knowledge to those reading Foucault or Deleuze.

Moreover, they find Yoder useful in exposing the kinds of violence implicit in many of the old liberal orthodoxies. Peter Blum captures this nicely when he calls the following Yoder lines, "a Nietzschean question": "We want what we say not only to be understandable, credible, meaningful. . . . We hanker for patterns of argument which will not be subject to reasonable doubt. . . . To say it another way, *the hunger for validation is a hunger for power.* We want people to *have* to believe what we say." Blum, like the other contributors to this volume, realizes that it is not just that the "public" world of universal truth was intellectually misguided, but that it was politically repressive. This intertwining of political and epistemological matters is also evident in Romand Coles's essay, "The Wild Patience of John Howard Yoder." Coles wrote, "few today offer as compelling a vision for pursuing justice and political

10. See James Gustafson, *Ethics from a Theocentric Perspective,* 2 vols. (Chicago: University of Chicago Press, 1981) 1:74. In old Yoder conversations, this issue was often framed as a debate between Yoder and Gordon Kaufman. See James Reimer, *Mennonites and Classical Theology,* Duane Friesen, *Artists, Citizens and Philosophers* (Scottdale, PA: Herald, 2000) and numerous essays of Scott Holland. In contrast, new Yoder writers do not seem to have read Kaufman.

engagements in heterogeneous societies." Against the background of Troeltsch and the Niebuhrs, such a claim was much harder to make and defend, simply because of the way the notion of "the political" was defined as an autonomous realm from which questions of knowledge were excluded. In contrast to the war-centeredness of the old Yoder, where violence was interpreted primarily in physical and narrowly political terms, new Yoder essays find in Yoder an appreciation that questions of violence and peace are as much a matter of epistemology, aesthetics, the formation of identities, etc.

It is also worth noting that new Yoder discussions tend to be conversational or dialogical in their very form. More often than not, they proceed by reading Yoder alongside some other figure, such as Foucault, Derrida, Certeau, Said, Stout, and Rowan Williams, to name just a few of the other voices to appear in this volume. Again, we turn to Romand Coles in order to illustrate the significance of this point. "What most interests me about Yoder," Coles writes, is "the way he combines bearing evangelical witness to his confessedly provincial tradition with vulnerable and receptive dialogical practices with others." Not only does Coles capture better than many what Yoder says about theology as a dialogical pursuit, he also appreciates the sense in which Yoder's own work was a series of dialogical performances. Accordingly, Coles's essay is itself an attempt to perform the kind of vulnerable and receptive dialogical engagement that he finds so powerfully exemplified by Yoder, in his case by bringing Yoder into conversation with radical democratic theory. Although the conversation partners may be different, many of the other essays included in this volume similarly approach Yoder in such a dialogical fashion.

It should be added that these essays are not first of all intended as interpretive efforts designed to make sense of Yoder's work. They do contribute to and enrich our understanding of what Yoder said. But to assume that their primary focus is with Yoder's work itself is to miss their full significance. They typically engage him in conversation as part of a larger constructive enterprise of some sort. They turn to Yoder because they have found him helpful in an attempt to explore a range of contemporary questions and concerns, many of which are not given explicit or extensive treatment by Yoder himself. For example, Coles engages Yoder because he finds in him a helpful resource for the task of articulating the sorts of insurgencies, mobilizations, and experimental practices that enable one "to envision what a more radically democratic flourishing might look like in a heterogenous world."[11] Boyarin turns to Yoder as part of his ongoing efforts to interrogate the invention of the difference between Judaism and Christianity. Barber finds in Yoder an instructive alternative to the options commonly presented in the much-debated question of "the secular." Alain Epp Weaver uses Yoder to address the Palestinian discussion of exile and return. And Cynthia Hess draws upon Yoder in order to respond to the kind of psychic violence taken up by the field of trauma theory. Moreover, some, like Gerald Schlabach, do so in ways that lead to a re-examination of some of Yoder's favorite foils, most notably Augustine and constantianism.[12] Accordingly, we think that the significance of these essays might be described as two-fold. Not only do they make Yoder's work come alive in a variety of refreshing new ways. They also serve to introduce a new range of academic voices and concerns, both theological and otherwise.

How We Got Here

One feature that might go some way toward explaining the developments associated with the new Yoder is the way in which some formative moments in his life overlapped with those associated with post-structuralism and post-colonialism. The post-colonial theorist Robert Young begins his book *White Mythologies* by saying, "If the so-called 'post-structuralism' is the product of a single historical moment, then that moment is probably not May 1968 but rather the Algerian War of Independence. . . . In this respect it is significant that Sartre, Althusser, Derrida and Lyotard, among others, were all either born

---

11. Romand Coles, *Beyond Gated Politics: Reflections for the Possibility of Democracy* (Minneapolis: University of Minneapolis Press, 2005) x.

12. See also J. Alexander Sider, "Constantinianism Before and After Nicea," in Ben Ollenburger and Gayle Gerber Koontz, eds., *A Mind Patient and Untamed: Assessing John Howard Yoder's Contributions to Theology, Ethics, and Peacemaking* (Telford, PA: Cascadia, 2004) and Charles Mayo Collier, "A Nonviolent Augustinianism?: History and Politics in the Theologies of St. Augustine and John Howard Yoder," PhD diss., Duke University, 2008.

in Algeria or personally involved with the events of the war."[13] Helene
Cixous wrote, describing her childhood in Algeria,

> I learned everything from this first spectacle: I saw how the
> white (French), superior, plutocratic, civilized world founded its
> power on the repression of populations who had suddenly be-
> come invisible. . . . I saw that the great, noble, "advanced" coun-
> tries established themselves by expelling what was "strange."[14]

There is no biographical evidence that Yoder was as affected by Algeria
as Cixous. But from the perspective of the new Yoder, it seems more
than coincidence that Yoder was working in Algeria in the late 50s.
Those post-colonialists and post-structuralists taught us that the
formation of Western politics and identity came at the expense of its
colonial others. Yoder taught us to include the Anabaptists as one of
the original colonial others. So Yoder's anti-foundationalism comes not
from a close reading of Quine or Wittgenstein, but rather, as with the
postcolonialists, from a marginalized, persecuted minority's recognition that the establishment's categories themselves worked to defend
against any possible destabilization from its others.

Whereas George Lindbeck and Stanley Hauerwas had to learn
how to occupy the space of minority and unlearn the habits of establishment, as a Mennonite Yoder was already there and so betrayed none
of post-liberalism's anxiety about the need to secure the church's ongoing survival in an increasingly secular world. In a similar way, it might
be suggested that for Yoder, "exile" was not a regrettable fait accompli
of late modernity. It was a fact of Anabaptist history. This history allowed Yoder to be way ahead of others who have blended theology with
cultural studies. Twenty years before Kathryn Tanner,[15] Yoder's critique
of *Christ and Culture*[16] dovetailed uncannily with the work of cultural

13. Robert Young, *White Mythologies: Writing History and the West* (London:
Routledge, 1990) 1.

14. Ibid.

15. See her *Theories of Culture* (Minneapolis: Fortress, 1997), and "Social Theory
Concerning the 'New Social Movements' and the Practice of Feminist Theology,"
in Rebecca Chopp and Sheila Greeve Devaney, eds., *Horizons in Feminist Theology*
(Minneapolis: Fortress, 1997) 179–97.

16. See "How R. Richard Niebuhr Reasoned: A Critique of *Christ and Culture*," in
Glen H Stassen, D. M. Yeager and John Howard Yoder, *Authentic Transformation: A
New Vision of Christ and Culture* (Nashville: Abingdon, 1996) 31–89.

studies theorists such as Raymond Williams, Stuart Hall, and Dick Hebdige.

More generally, it might be suggested that, largely because of the accidents of time and place, Yoder found himself ahead of an intellectual world that has only more recently come to cultivate spaces that allow a voice such as his to be heard. The emergence of the new Yoder surely has something to do with the way the North American academy has changed in the past twenty years. Whereas twenty years ago, religion was generally on the defensive throughout the academy, now intellectual luminaries such as Derrida and Certeau, Agamben, and Žižek, Chakrabarty and Asad, Stout and Coles, all find in religion a helpful antidote to some outworn modernist orthodoxies. In such a climate, the theologians who hoped to save Christianity by rendering it intelligible to its cultured despisers (Gordon Kaufman and James Gustafson, for example) can be of little help, while Yoder and Barth become important resources.

Finally, the role of Stanley Hauerwas needs to be mentioned in this regard. Hauerwas is responsible for introducing Yoder to a wider audience, so much so that, for better or worse, the names of Hauerwas and Yoder are often assumed to be synonymous. As Hauerwas came increasingly to be engaged alongside the kinds of figures and conversations mentioned above, partly on his own and partly by means of his kinship with the movement known as Radical Orthodoxy, many began to approach Yoder with those same dialogue partners in mind. And yet this has had the ironic effect of leading some to distance Yoder from Hauerwas. For example, in *Christ, History and Apocalyptic*, Nathan Kerr reads Yoder's radically apocalyptic conception of history against the tendencies toward historical closure he sees exemplified in Hauerwas's church. In his contribution to this volume, Kerr expands this reading of Yoder by placing him in conversation with Certeau. We do not mean to overemphasize the role of Hauerwas here, as if to suggest that his distinctive voice is always lurking in the background. Sometimes it is, and sometimes it isn't. Nor do we mean to suggest that the new Yoder is somehow an essentially anti-Hauerwasian Yoder. The authors represented in this volume would no doubt reflect a range of positions on that score. But we nevertheless do suspect that the relationship between

Hauerwas and Yoder has played a significant role in the emergence of the new Yoder.

Conclusion

To refer to all of this as the "new Yoder" in not an attempt to introduce a better or new-and-improved Yoder. It is worth noting, for example, that most of the essays collected here do not engage with the sources most foundational for Yoder himself—scripture and sixteenth-century Anabaptism. Not only is the new Yoder much more philosophical than Yoder himself was, it is more philosophical than he ever would have wanted to be. And he would no doubt have expressed hesitation with some of the projects he is associated with here. Similarly, in contrasting all of this with the "old Yoder," we do not mean to imply a negative judgment on this sort of work. After all, the old Yoder—Mennonites focused on war and spending a great deal of energy sorting through the legacy of Troeltsch and the Niebuhrs—*is* Yoder himself. That work carried on Yoder's work, continued fighting his battles and pursuing his agenda. It is just that his work also involved more than this. It is this "more" that *The New Yoder* points to. In so doing, we hope that these essays might serve to enrich and round out the kinds of questions taken up by an earlier generation's interest in the work of John Howard Yoder.

1

Judaism as a Free Church: Footnotes to John Howard Yoder's *The Jewish-Christian Schism Revisited*

DANIEL BOYARIN

At the very beginning of his posthumously published volume, *The Jewish-Christian Schism Revisited*, John Howard Yoder wrote:

> A wide stream of literature, some erudite and original, some creatively popular, has opened up the inadequacies of the traditions through which both Jews and Christians have interpreted our differences for centuries. Yet most of the redefinition going on in the vast scholarly literature still is engaged in making adjustments *within* the framework of the received schema. The corrections being made weaken that schema yet without replacing it. What this present study contributes is not another volume of details within those debates, but an alternative perspective on what the problem was and still is.[1]

Innocent (although I shouldn't have been) of Yoder's work until very recently, I have been carrying on a scholarly-ethical project for a decade and more that dogs his steps in many ways and carrying it on, as it were, from a "Jewish" perspective, that is, as one self-defined and communally located within historical Judaism and historical Jewry. Yoder's work, almost by definition, invites dialogical response.[2]

---

1. *The Jewish-Christian Schism Revisited*, ed. Michael G. Cartwright and Peter Ochs (Grand Rapids: Eerdmans, 2003) 31.

2. The very volume to which I am largely responding in this essay is a product of one such dialogue with the deceased. I shall engage in dialogue, then, with the dialogue.

Perhaps one could say that I have been (and am) inadvertently writing footnotes to Yoder. Let me begin to lay out for you my starting place in this conversation that I am about to begin. At about the time that Yoder's book was being published, I was struggling to complete a book of my own on the Jewish/Christian schism and not managing to do so. As I indicated finally in a pathos-filled preface, something seemed lifeless in the work, flaccid; I wasn't confronting the political core of the book and consequently couldn't find the desire and energy to write it (although it was 90 percent complete at the time). I realized that a piece of work that I had insisted was not political must discover and uncover its political and ethical power in order for me to find the passion that alone would let it be done. I had to discover where my passion lay, or I could not finish the book. Convinced that the passion could not be for what seemed like it might be the obvious consequence of the book, calling the Jewish/Christian difference into question, I searched elsewhere.

Although the book is called *Border Lines: The Partition of Judaeo-Christianity*, a revisionist reading of the Jewish/Christian schism, I still insisted in its preface—the preface that made it possible for me to finish the book—that the historical work was just that, history (at least of a certain sort), and that the politics of the work lay elsewhere entirely, allegorically, in my deep and ongoing concern for justice for the Palestinians.

Indeed I asserted rather loudly that:

> Why does my book want me to "come out?" Why need I tell about the love that (almost) would not dare to say its name, the love of this Orthodox Jew for Christianity? Even more grandiosely, I could pose the question (but very hesitantly, almost taking it back as I ask it), what purpose might this strange attraction play? Perhaps it has led me to uncover something: Implicitly through this scholarship and explicitly right here, I suggest that the affiliation between what we call Judaism and what we call Christianity is a much more complex one than most scholars, let alone most layfolk, imagine and that that complexity has work to do in the world, that we can learn something from it about identities and affiliations. The world that I have found in this research is one in which identities were much less sure than they have appeared to us until now, in which the very terms of identity were being worked on and worked out. Not only had there

not been the vaunted "parting of the ways," but Christianity was deeply engaged in finding its identity, its boundaries and even busily and noisily sorting out what kind of an entity it would be, what kind of an identity would it form. There was no telling yet (or even now) what the telos of the story would be. Non-christian Jews, and especially an important group of Jewish religious elites, were busy, as well, working hard to discover how to define their own borders in a discursive world being dramatically changed by the noise that Christians were making, soundings of "New Israels," "true Jews," and "heretics." "Judaism"—an anachronism—was up for grabs as well, as it were, by which I don't mean only the by now well-accepted notion that there was no normative Judaism, only Judaisms, but something more. Even rabbinic Judaism was struggling to figure out for itself what a "Judaism" is and who, then, could be defined as in and out of it. My book is a narrative of that period of struggle, of false starts and ruptures and abandoned paths during the initial phases of this site under construction. . . .

I am not, after all, a heretic from either the orthodox Christian or orthodox Jewish point of view, neither a Judaizing Christian nor a Christian Jew [a *min*], for all my attraction to Christianity and Christians. I do not choose, in any way, to be a Messianic Jew, a Jew for Jesus, or anything of that sort, but actually, to be just a Jew, according to the flesh and according to the spirit. Let me state here the obvious, the simple, the straightforward, and definitive: I do not believe that Jesus the son of Joseph of Nazareth was (or is) the Messiah, let alone do I subscribe to even higher christological glories ascribed to him as "Son of God." I am not, I think, a Jew *against* Jesus but there is no credible sense in which I could be construed as a Jew *for* Jesus either. I do not seek, of course, covertly (as sometimes Jews for Jesus do) nor overtly, to convert myself or any other Jew to Christianity, nor claim that Christianity is the true Judaism, nor preach that somehow Jews must accept John as Gospel truth.

In the wake of all that insistent denial, all that allegation of who I am not, there really was nowhere for me to go but to assume that my book was (for me) about something else. I agree with nearly every aspect of Yoder's account of the historiographical revision itself. As Yoder remarks, in the standard account, "the historical development of the first three centuries of our era ended with the presence, in many of the same places, of two separate, mutually exclusive systems (intellectual, cultural, social) called 'Jews' and 'Christians'. Therefore the standard account claims that this mutual exclusiveness must be assumed to have been inevitable, i.e., logically imperative, even when and where the actors in the story which led to that outcome did not know that yet." But, as Yoder has also written, "The new angles on the story in which recent scholarship has been so prolific modify this account in one detail or another. They leave standing the overall outline," that overall outline in which "we know perfectly well what 'Christianity' and 'Judaism' are."[3] In my own work, I retold the whole story and strikingly along the lines of Yoder's own retelling, but I still (through my baroque denial and in defiance of all logic) managed to leave standing the overall outline, of knowing perfectly well what Christianity and Judaism are, or at least that they are not each other. When my own spirit wouldn't let me call it just scholarship, I found some other explanation for it. Now, in the trail of Yoder I seek to undo the denial and ask more fully two questions that I could not confront even two years ago: What *are* the implications of such a radical revision of the history of the Jewish/Christian schism for the diaspora lives of Jews and Christians now? And, How do those implications impact on our response to the tragedy of Zionism? Do we (I) need to rethink indeed what Christianity and Judaism are? And, (II) is the refusal to do such rethinking an implacable obstacle on the way to justice and peace (for Palestine!) and does the radical reformation in any way provide for a possible way towards such a rethinking in the wake of the historical work I have done, in *some* ways more radical even than Yoder's, on the origins of the divide between something we call Christianity and something we call Judaism?

The Jewish/Christian Schism Revised

Yoder was clearly ahead of his time in his historical conception vis-à-vis the so-called separation between Judaism and Christianity. Before most of the more properly historical work had been done, he had already adopted a highly revisionist understanding of the matter; he had understood that there was no definitive form of Judaism that could claim either temporally or phenomenologically to be the one true Judaism before the rabbinical period beginning in the early third century with

3. *Jewish-Christian Schism*, 31.

the publication of the Mishna and also that Paul did not understand himself as breaking away from Judaism to found a new religion but as constituting a strand, the "true" one, as everyone else was doing, within Judaism.[4] I would go further than Yoder in fact. From my scholarly point of view, rabbinic Judaism cannot claim (historically speaking) to be the one true Judaism even long after the Mishna was promulgated. I have argued that the Mishna was part of a project to establish a Judaic orthodoxy but one that ultimately failed, such that throughout late antiquity there were various kinds of Jews, rabbinic and para-rabbinic who had as much "right" to the name "Jew" as anyone else did. Some of those Jews held religious convictions strikingly like ones that are otherwise understood as definitive of Christianity; indeed, I would assert that there is no particular theological claim or expectation that marks Christianity as "other" to the Judaism of its time, excepting, of course, the claim that Jesus of Nazareth is the one. This is not to say that I consider all Christians always as Jews. Many Christians resist and reject that name from quite early on and with rejection of the name come shifts in practice and belief that might be said, phenomenologically speaking, to define themselves out. This is analogous to the situation with the Karaites later, some of whom remain Jews till this day and others that have clearly left Jewishness entirely.

Yoder himself understood that the very project of a Jewish orthodoxy is, in large part, a response to the Christian formation of proto-orthodoxy: "We do not know *for sure* of *any* rabbi trying to drive a wedge between himself and the *nozrim* before Justin began driving his wedge between himself and the Jewish church. If Justin's need for Gentile respectability[5] had not lead [sic] him to be ready to split the church, we cannot be sure the rabbis would have reciprocated in kind."[6] Like Yoder, I too think that there were Christians who were Jews late, very late, into late antiquity, Jews who continued to hold to Logos theology, expectation of the Son of Man, and some who even believed that Jesus of Nazareth was that Son of Man. I have argued that it takes an army

4. Ibid., 32–33.

5. On which, see J. Rebecca Lyman, "The Politics of Passing: Justin Martyr's Conversion as a Problem of 'Hellenization,'" in *Conversion in Late Antiquity and the Early Middle Ages: Seeing and Believing*, ed. Anthony Grafton and Kenneth Mills (Rochester: University of Rochester Press, 2003) 36–60.

6. *Jewish-Christian Schism*, 61.

(Theodosius II's army) to pry Judaism and Christianity apart, and that is a major aspect of the Nicene project. Adam Becker adds that outside of the Roman *limes*, the separation may have been even messier and longer than inside the Empire.[7] Thus where Yoder considers the Jewish-Christian schism as a product of the second and third centuries,[8] I am more inclined to see it as a product of the fifth[9] and even then never quite a done deal. Yoder draws radical theological conclusions from his revision of the history; what theological conclusions shall I draw, in dialogue with him, from my own somewhat more radical historical revisionism?[10]

7. Adam H. Becker, "Beyond the Spatial and Temporal *Limes*: Questioning the 'Parting of the Ways' Outside the Roman Empire," in *The Ways That Never Parted Jews and Christians in Late Antiquity and the Early Middle Ages*, ed. Adam H. Becker and Annette Yoshiko Reed (Tübingen: Mohr Siebeck, 2003) 373–92.

8. *Jewish-Christian Schism*, 43.

9. See, however, ibid., 66 n. 26, gesturing towards the fifth century as well.

10. Yoder is not always as good a reader of the historiography as he could be. Thus, he imagines that in the Temple period there were already "rabbis," some of whom, "the most respected of whom," were "Pharisaical" (ibid., 48). One would have thought that his reading of Neusner would have disabused him of that anachronism. Interestingly, sharper historiography would only have strengthened his case. Another instance: Yoder allows that there is Jewish manuscript evidence from the "third century [!] that in the usage of *some* synagogues the term for 'Christians' (*nozrim*) had *by that later date* been added in the third line [of the curse of the heretics] to that for 'heretics'" (52). Talmud scholars would be only too delighted to have any manuscript evidence from the third century indeed. The earliest we do have is from the ninth century in fact. The writings of Jerome provide, however, a *terminus ad quem* in the early fifth century for this formulation. Again this only strengthens Yoder's point, not weakening it at all but a surprising inaccuracy. Well aware that the terms "Jew" and "Christian" are anachronistic, Yoder seems hardly to notice that his preferred "rabbinic" and "messianic" are at least as anachronistic in turn (54). These are not nits but neither, of course, do they invalidate the work, not by any means. Most of Yoder's historical instincts seem to me to be spot on. He anticipates (54, for one) nearly precisely the same definition of the role of Justin Martyr in making a difference between Judaism and Christianity as I have done in *Border Lines: The Partition of Judaeo-Christianity*, Divinations: Rereading Late Ancient Religions (Philadelphia: University of Pennsylvania Press, 2004) 37–73, only having left for me, as it were, the task of actually working it out in the texts. His book was published when mine was well underway at the press, and I do need to admit that had I read his work earlier mine would have seemed somewhat less innovative to me. It is a shame that his work has been so badly served by its recent editors who could easily have fixed quite a number of minor errors with respect to Judaism: e.g., confusing Yehuda Ha-Nassi (redactor of the Mishna) with Yehuda Ha-Levi (a medieval poet-theologian), an error on the order of confusing Augustine of Hippo with Augustine of

Yoder presents a remarkable and important set of reflections on the historiography of the partition of Judaeo-Christianity (my term) under the rubric of "It did not have to be."[11] His primary *ethical* (although he does not designate it such) claim is that it is a wrong to the people of the past to assume in any way that what came to be had to be that way and no way else, that a given moment of decision before a Rubicon was crossed could only have gone the way it did.[12] Historiography for Yoder means being alive intellectually (and affectively) to the indecision, the openness, to the ways in which it could have been otherwise, "in order to discern options which might have been really available if someone had had the information, or the courage, or the organization to reach them, distinguishing these from other kinds of wishful thinking and from wasteful or resentful utopias." The real point of the exercise, of course, is to find a way to change history, as it were, to go back to a moment of real decision, of real openness, when it did not have to be that way and make it otherwise, now and for our future. It is this moment to which Yoder refers as a "repentant" mode of historiography and one with which I am in deep sympathy, one that although I have always used a different sort of language for it, has been the motivating force for all my own historiographical work until now, with respect to gender, sexuality, race, Zionism. Clearly, however, I have balked at letting that be the force of the newest work, the work that—like Yoder's history-writing—undoes the naturalness, the inevitability of the production of two "religions" out of Judaeo-Christianity. Although it would seem that the whole point of writing a book subtitled, *The Partition of Judaeo-Christianity*, recalling such events as the partition of India and

---

Canterbury or Gregory of Nyssa with Gregory the Great. The editing of this volume is shockingly bad to the point of distorting the communication drastically. Thus, for one example, on 62, "*could* have happened" (emphasis original) has to be "*couldn't* have happened" for the sentence to make any sense whatever. The grossest error, perhaps, among many results in a sentence reading: "Non-cooperation, when empowered by a level of conviction that is willing to suffer, is a more powerful way to move a society than is the ballot box; it can be used defectively [sic] by minorities." This poor editing is especially unfortunate in the light of the editors' statement that they have intervened in the text to make it more readable (63, editor's note.)

11. Ibid., 43–63.

12. It will be important, I think, to read this aspect of Yoder's work in the light of Michael André Bernstein, *Foregone Conclusions: Against Apocalyptic History*, Contraversions (Berkeley: University of California Press, 1994).

of Palestine, political, even colonialist, schisms imposed from above, would appear to call the partition into Christianity and Judaism the same kind of thing and thus into question, I kept forgetting/denying that very point as I wrote the book. I need to own that consequence, difficult for me as it is.

Thus, at the same time that I acknowledge now that my own research brings me to a deconstruction of the Jewish/Christian opposition, I don't want to too easily tread there. Yoder writes that "doubting that things had to go as they did *way back when* correlates logically with doubting the rightness of how they continued to go later."[13] This strikes me as a non-sequitur. Perhaps better to say that it *permits* such doubt. Is doubting the rightness of the Jewish/Christian difference where I want to go, or is there, perhaps, some alternate way of learning from Yoder and from my own historiography, some way that moves at least some humans forward towards justice and peace without necessitating the loss of that which I take (still) to be most valuable about human cultural (including religious) diversity per se? Is there a possibility of an ethics of the preservation of that which is in some genealogical sense, mine, just simply because it is the unique cultural product of the people with whom I choose/have been chosen to be historically connected (a project with which I am not sure that Yoder is in sympathy)? To be sure, there are causes other than the defense of one's own separate identity that would render morally imperative a counter-cultural commitment, and, too, there are causes that might make the renunciation of such identity morally imperative. Is the defense of one's own separate identity ever a moral imperative of its own? For Yoder the "division" is tragic; I am sure that the division has led to tragedy and that as surely I would want to change, but I still ask whether it is necessary to undo the division to end the tragedy, or possible, perhaps, to comprehend and live it differently.

These are real, not rhetorical, questions for me, by which I mean only that I don't know the answers.

The Jewish Radical: Diaspora Ethics

I want to begin anew now by clearly articulating what it is that makes Yoder's work so different from most Jewish/Christian "dialogue." The

13. *Jewish-Christian Schism*, 45.

answer is a simple one. Yoder is listening as well as talking. Most inter-religious dialogue strikes one as folks simply trying to articulate their unchallengeable positions to each other politely, or as Yoder has put it: "The alternative to each of us having his/her own picture of the other would be to ignore each other and to limit each of us to describing only himself/herself."[14] Yoder is not interested in just describing himself; he wants genuine dialogue in which he (and the other) can be changed in the encounter; he wishes to fairly (as fairly as possible) appropriate Judaism: "So the right way forward must rather be a constructive appropriation of the other's identity."[15] He is making his own ecclesiology by learning something from Judaism and the Jews. He refuses explicitly the option (taken by many Christians, including some pacifist and some feminist Christians) of participating in "the way in which, once western Christians have had it decided for them that 'the Jews' are to serve as a foil, to be accused of whatever counter-view will serve to make the Christians look better, then 'the Jews' can be described in ways quite unjustified by the record. In the Gospel accounts Jesus is rejected by many individuals and sometimes by the leaders of groups of people, for various reasons, but his nonviolence is not given as a reason. Neither is his calling for the law to be 'fulfilled.'"[16] Yoder, I think, truly and successfully supersedes supersessionism.

This clear critical perspective leads Yoder to an entirely different account of the relationship of Judaism to Christianity than I have seen anywhere else. Rather than seeking that which differentiates Judaism from Christianity, Yoder assumes, as I do, that Jesus's Torah—as given variously in the Gospels—*was* Judaism, that is, a recognizable Judaism. (In forthcoming work, I shall be suggesting that in some respects the Gospels provide the best example we have of first-century Judaism.) Thus the politics of Jesus are seen by him as part and parcel of demonstrable historical developments within Israelite religion over the centuries between the earlier parts of the Tanakh and the first century. Israelite religion is, for him, not frozen in some ahistorical primitive state of tribal ethos in order to make Jesus new, but Jesus is read rather as "prolong[ing] the critical stance which previous centuries of Jewish

---

14. Ibid., 115.

15. Ibid.

16. Ibid., 70.

experience had already rehearsed."[17] Yoder insists that in some sense
the most authentic Judaism, or at any rate the Judaism that he frankly
and openly prefers, is what he calls the "peace tradition" within Judaism
(there is no pacifist tradition in early Judaism, but I think he is right in
insisting that there is a pietist "peace" tradition as early as Jeremiah and
continuing throughout). Where I part company with Yoder is in his
insistence, paradoxical indeed from my point of view, that the peace
tradition, the free church, must be a missionary church. He supports
this historically with a further claim, namely that prior to the promul-
gation of the Mishna, "Judaism" was indeed a missionary religion and
that only owing to fear of Christianity [!] was it that rabbinic Judaism,
which after all begins with the Mishna, was to forego missionary ideals and thus, already?, to set itself on the path of Christianizing and
ultimately Zionist Constantinianism. There are several real problems
with this formulation. The first is historical: There seems to this scholar
little data to support a notion of a Jewish mission prior to the Rabbis
that was abrogated by them. To be sure, there were many Gentiles
who attended Synagogues as Godfearers before the Rabbis, but that
does not constitute evidence of a mission. Moreover, there were many
Gentiles (Christians!) attending Synagogues long after the Mishna was
promulgated, including at Origen's Caesarea, near the very epicenter
of rabbinic power itself. Secondly, missionizing precisely does not
distinguish peace churches from other Christian, including the most
Constantinian, of churches. To be sure, mission does not necessarily
mean precisely the same thing in the "Constantinian" church that it
means in the free churches. Nevertheless, to the extent that rabbinic
Judaism constitutes a critique of missionary work, I think that that critique ought to be attended to by radical Christians as well. This Jew
finds it much easier to accept those messianic Jews who renounce any
claim, desire, or effort to convert other Jewish to their way, and while
we Jews ought to accept converts, we have wisely learned, I think, both
sociologically and theologically not to seek them. Where for Yoder it
seems that the notion of universal salvation via the seven laws given to
all people in the Noahide convenant is a defect in rabbinic Judaism, I
would see it as a theological step forward, one that was indeed encouraged by the challenge of missionary Christianity. Thus Yoder seamlessly

17. Ibid., 71.

moves from the notion that pre-mishnaic pharisaism, as represented by Rabbi Yochanan ben Zakkai, was "non-violent" in substance to an assumption that this means that it manifested a "continuing missionary openness."[18]

There are several difficulties here. First of all (and very tellingly, I think), the narrative about Rabbi Yochanan ben Zakkai to which Yoder refers is entirely a product of the Babylonian Talmud and thus entirely a part of that to which Yoder refers as "Constantinian Judaism" itself. We have no access to any information about the "real" Pharisees, other than Josephus, Philo (and Paul), and nothing that we know about them suggests that they were a peace, or, on Yoder's terms, a missionary party. In other words, I suggest, Yoder's binary oppositions break down in several ways here. Constantinianism is not the opposite of mission and being resolutely out of power is not the necessary opposite of caring for the world. Rabbinic Judaism is not the opposite to Pharisaism, but actually in many ways, the inventor after the fact of the Pharisees.

In the days and weeks since I have presented this as a lecture, several kind Mennonite scholars have written to me that I mistake the Mennonite notion of mission, Yoder's even more so. I don't think so, for he explicitly divides it from the project of rabbinic Judaism, which is, as articulated over and over again in the early rabbinic writings, in the Talmudic story of Rabbi Yochanan ben Zakkai even more, a quietist witness to G-d's presence in the world and his goodness by enacting good. The term for this practice is *kiddush Hashem*, sanctifying the name of G-d through exemplary behavior in the world, including the willingness to die for G-d, to be martyred, for which this phrase is also the name. Rather than identifying particular religious forms, then, as peace churches or Constantinian churches (Jewish or Christian), I suggest rather that we attend to Constantinianism as the temptation that lies within each of us as individuals and each of us (always) as religious organizations. Jews are enjoined by the Rabbis to avoid power but seek the peace of the city. (Of course, we fail most often on both accounts, but then who doesn't?)

From my perspective, mission is not a sign of non-violence and refraining from missionizing hardly a regression. As I wrote fifteen years ago, "The genius of Christianity is its concern for all of the Peoples of

18. Ibid., 153.

the world; the genius of rabbinic Judaism is its ability to leave other people alone. This is grounded theologically in rabbinic Judaism in the notion that in order to achieve salvation, Jews are required to perform (or better, to attempt to perform) the entire 613 commandments while non-Jews are required only to perform seven commandments given to Noah that form a sort of natural, moral Law. Jewish theology understands the Jewish people to be priests performing a set of ritual acts on behalf of the entire world. Clearly the temptation to arrogance is built into such a system, but precisely the temptation to 'Sacred Violence' that leads to forced conversion, whether by the sword, ridicule or the Pound, or de-culturation in the name of the new human community, is not."[19]

I believe that radical reformed churches and (some versions of) radical rabbinic Judaism may have much, much more in common (even in communion) with each other than I would have imagined revisiting the Judaeo-Christian schism (historically and through Yoder), but I think we also still have something to teach each other. Radical rabbinic Judaism may be able to temper the dangers of missionizing while radical reformed Christianity may provide an attractive dialogue partner for a reformed ethnocentrism that does not produce contempt for the other peoples of the world. What I had imagined as possible for the dominant versions of Judaism and Christianity may only be possible, and may indeed be possible for those who are out of control within their own traditions as well as within the world.

This brings me to explore a crucial question with respect to my own understanding and taking on of Yoder's theological project. While his work is obviously deeply, deeply congenial to me, there is an aspect that is troubling as well, one that makes it difficult for me to simply be that which Yoder would have me be as a Jew. Now it is not that I, myself, am not in sympathy, in the deepest sympathy with his political vision for Judaism, for a Judaism that is forever the repository and manifestation of a diasporic politics, the politics of a religion that is "not in charge," and thus too an anti-Zionist. My difficulty, then, is not in being the kind of Jew that Yoder would want Jews to be; my difficulty is in the assumption that this is simply what Jews ought to be if they

19. [See Daniel Boyarin, "The Subversion of the Jews: Moses's Veil and the Hermeneutics of Supersessionism," *Diacritics* 23:2 (1993) 16–35.—Ed.]

are to be Jewish. My own dilemma is between adopting a position in which I want to call for something that I perceive to be a better and *an* authentic Judaism, while not denying the right of others, even those whose position I find repugnant—and where human lives are at stake—the right to that name. This is a tricky moment, because, after all, it is precisely anti-Zionist, out-of-chargedness, diasporism to which I have been in my work and political life calling Jews, Jewry, and Judaism as well. However, I have been trying to be careful—I hope—in not defining an *essence* to Judaism, while Yoder is, I think, not careful enough. The reason for such care is, on the one hand, an ethical respect, one that I know Yoder would share, for those with whom one disagrees, even most sharply, and an unwillingness to engage in a politics of virtual excommunication; on the other hand, the reason is to avoid even the appearance of apology and triumphalism. Reading the past in an idealized way in which one assumes a pristine moment for one's own (or another) tradition is a very different, move, I think, from seeking the best in one's tradition and asserting its value even when most of one's fellows reject it. Thus, Judaism is not, in the end a free church, any more than Christianity is, and to read it as such will produce the response that I have often heard that Yoder is a romantic idealizer, but a Jew (this Jew) can hope to learn from the free church tradition in constituting a radical dissenting position as anti-Zionist, calling it the best that Jewish history and tradition have to offer us, not mistaking that with the dominant or historically essential truth. I read Yoder as not able to decide between, on the one hand, seeing in historical Jewry/Judaism an exemplum for the free church of how a dissenting community might maintain its identity and moral, critical force when it is out of political power, and, on the other, calling (tacitly, as he must) for the strengthening of a critical tradition within Judaism/Jewry. While embracing such a position with all the consequences, I am at the same time uncomfortable to be the "good Jew" for what, I hope, are obvious reasons. Is it "Judaism" and "Christianity" that will turn out to have been the schism that need not have been with all that that implies for the future, or only minority dissenters, then and now? Can there be for Yoder a messianic Judaism that does not accept Jesus? In what way, then, would it be different from rabbinic Judaism *tout court*, always messianic?

Yoder, for his part, frankly chooses the so-called "peace tradition" as the Judaism that interests him but immediately shows his awareness as well of the ethical pitfall in doing so:

> Why not let the Jews be themselves? Is it not bias for us even to have an opinion as to who 'the Jews' 'ought' to be? Or who they are? Is it not both bad historical method and bad inter-community dialogue to choose one's own picture of who the Jews must properly be, what image of Judaism one considers representative? Of course it is: but to take note of that fact is the beginning, not the end of our needing to work at the problem.[20]

I want to take the rest of my time working at this problem along with Yoder. Yoder writes obviously and frankly from one subject position, the position of a theologian of a free church, of a radical reformation church, going back to the first two centuries for a model of a time when Judaism and Christianity were not two separate entities, two religions, seeking a new kind of communion with Jews through appropriating that time, and arguing that contemporary Jews are heirs to that time as well and if they are not, then they too need a radical reformation. He argues that historically the Jewish People have through most of their history lived out (perforce or no) the vocation of a free church of a minority religion out of power with all of the critical force that such a position can be invested with. As Yoder puts it, countering a certain charge, "What goes on here is *not* that I am 'co-opting' Jews to enlist them in my cause. It is that I am finding a story, which is really there, coming all the way down from Abraham, that has the grace to adopt me."[21]

Among the singular importances and powerful originalities of Yoder's work is the argument that the dissenting radical free church is not withdrawing from the world but participating in it via non-cooperation with that which it abhors. He provides a blueprint of a principled non-being-in-charge that is nevertheless not quietist but active in its resistance to that which it finds evil in the world. Using the Jeremianic injunction to "seek the peace of that city to which God has sent you," and a somewhat idealized reading of this as the principle of the Jewish diaspora, Yoder argues that "Not being in charge of the civil order is

20. *Jewish-Christian Schism*, 113.
21. Ibid., 115.

sometimes a more strategic way to be important for its survival or its flourishing than to fight over or for the throne."[22] This is indeed very close to the political ethic of anti-Zionism, or positively put, Diasporism, that I have articulated and defended as a vision for Jewry throughout my work, sometimes in almost explicitly pacifist terms, although I think that I am not truly a pacifist.[23] He identifies as well, very vividly, "social effectiveness from below" in the ways that the Jehovah's Witnesses enlarged our notions of religious liberty, the "Old Order Amish break the stranglehold of homogeneous state education," and "Christian scientists and charismatics who believe that God heals challenge the American Medical Association medical-care cartel."[24] Indeed, "our refusal to play the game by the agreed rules may be morally more basic than our courageous wrestling with things as they are."[25] But at the same time, Yoder's missionary impetus leads him to the position (further developed by his disciple Stanley Hauerwas) that the believers should continue to be involved in public life and discourse without in any way "compromising" (Yoder's scare-quotes) "the particular identifying value commitments of a faith community, in favor of common-denominator moral language. Yet if in order to 'be involved' you commit yourself to values less clear or less imperative than your own, which are more acceptable because the 'public' out there already holds them, then your involvement adds nothing to the mix but numbers."[26] How then shall the Christian be involved in public life if she holds as a matter of faith moral positions that are particular to a particular reading of Scripture? How shall such positions be maintained in a public space of those who read Scripture quite differently and those who don't read Scripture at all?

I think that when Yoder wrote he could not have predicted that there would be a president and a political party in the United States that would be heirs to one version of the radical reformation tradition, as Yoder himself has defined it, including within its purview both Methodism and such American religious traditions as the Rapture

22. Ibid., 172.

23. Jonathan Boyarin and Daniel Boyarin, *Powers of Diaspora: Two Essays on the Relevance of Jewish Culture* (Minneapolis: University of Minnesota Press, 2002).

24. *Jewish-Christian Schism*, 174.

25. Ibid., 175.

26. Ibid., 169.

and the Bible Churches. Yoder already wrote in the 1970s that the Bible Churches were the representative form of radical reform in the United States, and now these churches are fair becoming the dominant form of Christianity in the United States as well as developing enormous political power. Could he have imagined a world in which not mainline Protestantism and Catholicism but radical dissenters from those churches were becoming the most powerful religious figures in the United States and ones with great political power as well? How can one distinguish, then, between Yoder's insistence on a mission, including his insistence that Christian involvement in public life must not compromise its particular moral values, those that are different from the majority or at least an enormous minority, from the current situation in which we see abhorrent values increasingly being imposed in the name of the Bible on those who would have none of them—such as, for instance, opposition to contraception or the dignity of same-sex love? Of course, such coercion is the very opposite of the Anabaptist tradition, but it is not logically incompatible I think with the positions that Yoder takes on scriptural truth and Christian moral witness. I am not, in any way, identifying the moral positions of the Anabaptists with those of American radical Christianity, but I am wondering about some similarities of ecclesiology and missiology that seem to an outsider to give us pause. Were the Christian Science position to become somehow dominant, not only the AMA medical cartel would be destroyed but at least arguably, medicine itself. Were the position of those who oppose homogenizing public education to become dominant (and this is less unrealistic), then one of the glories of American democracy would be demolished, one which has been the primary vehicle for social leveling such as there has been in the United States until now.

A theology and an ethic of being-not-in-charge has to confront questions of this sort as well. Yoder's work is not finished; he, alas, did not live long enough. He has given us, however, a wonderful legacy, a space I think where a Jew can really engage with Christians beyond the dialogues of the deaf called inter-faith dialogue. He profoundly has understood that "Many other Christians, embarrassed first of all about any kind of particular faith commitment in the face of the pluralistic and relativizing impact of the Enlightenment, and reinforced in their embarrassment by a sentiment of guilt for their indirect participation in 'the Holocaust', want to see Jews otherwise than as people who reject the fulfillment of God's purpose for them. They do not take this 'accepting' stance on the grounds of the fundamental kind of rethinking proposed in the present study. On the contrary, they thereby prolong and harden the tendency to see western Jewry as just one more equally valid denomination of western Protestantism."[27] Yoder's way beyond supersession is for us to begin to imagine ourselves as one thing, as one community, to disinvest ourselves in difference. And I begin to think he may be right. While I still see value in difference per se, in the maintenance of communal and cultural religious tradition, perhaps more than Yoder does, when such maintenance begins to produce so much harm in the world, then perhaps we need to let go, however painfully, of it. Perhaps, perhaps, perhaps not. I am certain that Jews cannot demand of Christians support for Israel as a condition of respect, but I am troubled, anti-Zionist that I myself am, with a gesture of "appropriation" that reads so many Jews somehow right out of Judaism. Yoder has done a more radical rethinking of a possible, once and future, relationship between Judaism and Christianity than anyone else. The questions his work raises are the questions we need to confront as we seek to reform American religion itself.

27. Ibid., 111.

2

The Christian Witness in the Earthly City: John Howard Yoder as Augustinian Interlocutor

GERALD W. SCHLABACH

Seek the peace of the city—its welfare, its prosperity, its *shalom*. After all the violence and humiliation at the hands of the nations, after all the temptations to counter-hubris and patriotic self-exaltation, after all the promise and hiddenness of a covenant-making God, after all the epiphanies and betrayals of loyalty to this God, after all the disorientation of land loss and forced exile—this was Jeremiah's last word to Israel's exiles in Babylon.[1] The social stance to which it called them was supple and manifold, requiring them both to stubbornly preserve their identity and to sufferingly serve the common good they shared even with their conquering enemy. They must be "in but not of"—long before that phrase became a cliché that is barely able to move us anymore with its rich social creativity.

And so too both Augustine of Hippo and John Howard Yoder. Intriguingly, each in his own way ended long reflections about the role of the Church in the world at this same point, exhorting Christians to follow the model of Jeremiah's exiles in Babylon. This, I will argue, is no mere coincidence. For Augustine's last word on how the "heavenly city" of Christians still on pilgrimage should live amid the "earthly city" has served Christian traditions in the West not so much as a final answer to the question of how they should order their politics within the passing societies of every age, but rather as a definitive statement of that ques-

---

1. Jer 29:7.

tion. We can thus construe Yoder's pacifist, ecclesial social ethic as a late answer—perhaps the best answer—to the very question that Augustine did so much to sharpen but ultimately left hanging: just how *are* we to seek the peace of the city, without eroding our loyalty to that better one in whose hope we move and live?

John Howard Yoder was, in other words, far more deeply embedded in Augustinian problematics and debates than we usually recognize. Even to recognize this possibility, however, the reader may need also to recognize at least a couple of three assumptions by which I will proceed. First, what is true of most "authorities" in the Christian tradition is prototypically true of Augustine, that by being pilgrims they left traces along multiple paths by which we may now construe their legacies. Second, the fidelity of one especially creative thinker to another greatly influential one may only be traceable through deep and imaginative reading, not the slavish counting of citations. And third, sometimes those with whom we argue are the ones who influence us most.

Converging upon Jeremiah

St. Augustine of Hippo has exercised such an abiding influence upon political thought in the West for a curious reason: intrinsic to his vision of human society is the insight that we can never quite set our affairs in order and never quite get our politics right. The world's best possible peace is a shadowy one; its most stable order is a tenuous one; its fullest possible justice is always only somewhat more just than current arrangements. In fact, the very effort to forge a definitive political order lies at the root of many of humanity's gravest injustices, disorders, and conflicts. For when the earthly city imagines itself to be too like the heavenly city—eternal and approaching the glory that is proper only to God—it intensifies the very conditions of human fallenness and thus invites its own falling. Inevitably if not explicitly, therefore, politics according to Augustine must always be temporal, tentative, and revisable. This leaves every generation with a remainder to rework. And that makes Augustinian political thought itself into an ongoing debate that no age, system, or ideology can definitively capture.[2] Paradoxically, it

2. For a fuller argument that the Augustinian tradition has been a resilient and

thrives upon the recognition of human limitations—but that must include the limits of any particular "political Augustinianism."[3]

If the politics Augustine charted for the earthly city is *necessarily* and *rightly* incomplete, however, the same cannot be said of Augustine's ecclesiology. Given the rigor of Augustine's critique of the Roman Empire in *City of God*, and the depth of political insight that his critique occasioned, one might have expected from him an ecclesiology at least as thorough as his political theory. If an adequate account of the life of the Church must include not just a theological metaphysic but a practicable sociology, however, Augustine's ecclesiology is elusive and suggestive at best.[4]

In a strictly theological sense, no doubt, Augustine's ecclesiology is immensely rich. For Augustine, the Church is nothing short of shared participation in God's own trinitarian life of mutual love.[5] Such communion is possible insofar as the earthy, bloody incarnation of God in Christ, together with the outpouring of love into our hearts by the Holy Spirit, heals both our divided wills and our disordered relationships.

---

living tradition precisely because of its inherent capacity for self-correction, see Gerald W. Schlabach, "The Correction of the Augustinians: A Case Study in the Critical Appropriation of a Suspect Tradition," in *The Early Church and the Free Church: Bridging the Historical and Theological Divide*, ed. Daniel H. Williams (Grand Rapids: Eerdmans, 2002) 47–74.

3. Robert Markus, in his influential *Saeculum: History and Society in the Theology of St. Augustine*, 2nd ed., (Cambridge: Cambridge University Press, 1988), may have overstated his case when he portrayed Augustine as laying the basis for political liberalism by desacralizing every temporal order. My intention is not to weigh in on the growing, revisionist debate concerning Markus's thesis, reflected for example in Mark Vessey, Karla Pollmann, and Allan D. Fitzgerald, eds, *History, Apocalypse, and the Secular Imagination: New Essays on Augustine's City of God* (Bowling Green, OH: Philosophy Documentation Center, Bowling Green State University, 1999). Still, I simply cannot imagine how Augustinian political thought can ever do without some sense of the limitations of human politics, whether or not those limitations are now construed to require political liberalism. I thus assume that the summary statements in this paragraph will reflect an uncontroverted consensus however the debate between Markus and his revisionists proceeds.

4. H. Richard Niebuhr suggested something similar when he noted in *Christ and Culture* that Augustine's *City of God* lacked an ecclesiology to match its philosophy of history. See *Christ and Culture* (New York: Harper and Row, 1956) 215–16.

5. Cf. Augustine *De Trinitate* 6.5.7, and Oliver O'Donovan's comments in *The Problem of Self-Love in St. Augustine* (1980; reprint, Eugene, OR: Wipf & Stock, 2006) 128.

If the Church remains a hospital for convalescents, and the mystery of healing renders an invisible quality to the final identities of the Church's members, that is because the Church lives in an eschatological tension between already-in-communion and not-yet-fully-transformed. In short, Augustine's ecclesiology is seamlessly integrated with his trinitarian theology with his doctrine of love with his eschatology.

In fact, Augustine's vision of the Church was not devoid of practical, sociological, or political specification either. Virtually all of Augustine's writings were "occasional" in some way, insofar as they responded to specific controversies, accusations, or pastoral challenges. Whatever else *City of God* became through its twenty-two lengthy "books," therefore, it began as a response to an accusation.[6] Roman aristocrats were saying that the reason their city had been sacked in 410 was that Christianity had weakened its citizens' virtue and diverted their devotion away from the gods. So when Augustine countered that Rome (the most immediate instantiation of "the earthly city") had slipped because it had risen too high, had deteriorated because it had overextended itself, was humbled because it had grown through imperial pride,[7] his critique came with lessons for that other society that was making its way through the earthly city. The pilgrim heavenly city that is the Church must thrive by humbling itself and glorifying God not self, nor the collective self of nation; its love cannot be for domination, but for God, neighbor, and even enemy. And though no one may mistake Augustine for a pacifist, he certainly recognized that the Church had in fact extended itself through the faithfulness of the martyrs and the witness of a people who, like the Hebrews, "was gathered and united in a kind of community designed to perform [the] sacred function of revelation" through "signs and symbols appropriate to the times."[8] This witnessing presence in the world hints at the affirmation of the Second Vatican Council that the

6. *City of God* 1.1. The translation I am quoting is Augustine, *The City of God*, translated by Henry Bettenson, with an introduction by David Knowles (Harmondsworth, England: Penguin, 1972).

7. These are themes and arguments that run throughout *City of God*, but that Augustine anticipated already in the preface to book one when he noted "how great is the effort needed to convince the proud of the power and excellence of humility," in contrast to the pride, arrogance, and lust of domination that God was surely resisting according the promise of Jas 4:6.

8. *City of God* 7.32 (quoted); 18.50.

Church itself is the sacrament of the world's salvation. It also hints at the truthful power of what John Howard Yoder called the creative minority whose presence is the "original revolution" in the world.

But by now we are *only* talking about hints. What Augustine's ecclesiology lacks is a politics or sociology to chart out how Christians are to live simultaneously in the earthly and heavenly cities, without confusing their loyalties or conflating their duties. To be sure, just as no politics for the earthly city can be definitive—given the eschatological tension of the age—likewise any polity for the heavenly city that is intermixed within the earthly must have a certain open-ended quality. After all, Christians must not only anticipate variations according to culture, history, and circumstances, but must remember precisely that they *are* on pilgrimage, never fully settled but intermixed within the earthly city, and thus still being perfected.

What we may rightly wish of Augustine, however, is that he had at least been clearer about whether and when his political commentary on the earthly city applied normatively to Christians.

A passage often assumed to settle the case may illustrate. How are we to interpret book 19 of the *City of God* in general, and the identity of "our wise man," the reluctant judge of *City of God* 19.6, in particular? The chapter begins with recognition that even in human cities that are relatively at peace, some must pass judgments upon others. For those judgments to be just, Roman jurisprudence could not imagine the interrogation of suspects without recourse to torture. But anyone informed by the best wisdom of human philosophy (the subject of previous chapters) would recognize how imperfect was the juridical process. Torturing suspects to extract the truth might prompt the innocent to lie—and all the more quickly if they too heeded the philosophers, who counseled courage to welcome death and escape the miseries of this life! Doing one's duty to preserve justice in the earthly city thus necessitated an array of tragic choices: release the innocent only after undeserved torture, execute the innocent upon false confession, or execute an actual criminal without certainty of the grounds. Because "our wise man" recognized "this darkness that attends the life of human society" without flinching, he would accept its claims, do his duty, and sit on the bench without shirking. "Here we have what I call the wretchedness of man's situation," wrote Augustine. And if the wise man was not to be called wicked, that was only because he hated the very "necessity of his own actions," was learning a further wisdom from devotion to God, and cried out for deliverance from his necessities.

To most interpreters, the lesson we should take from Augustine has seemed obvious. In the following chapter, *City of God* 19.7, "our wise man" turned "wise judge" serves as template for explaining why even the best and wisest philosopher officials will not only punish wrong-doers but wage wars, though they will wage even just wars reluctantly. But although that much is straightforward in the text, the standard interpretation goes farther than the text itself warrants. For when it makes "our wise man" into the exemplar for any politician informed by Augustinian sensibilities—and thus for any politically-involved Christian—it assumes that Augustine's purpose was to provide a normative argument rather than a description of the human predicament apart from God.

Most of *City of God* 19 is about indictment not guidance. It is one of Augustine's many and characteristic endeavors to drive his readers to despair precisely in order that they like he will look elsewhere for hope, recognize their need for God, and cry out for deliverance.[9] The first chapters of *City of God* 19 constitute the climax to a long series of similarly structured indictments that build upon each other and thus constitute the master argument of the tome: The Roman aristocrats who accuse Christianity of weakening Roman virtue are the ones who have weakened the empire by failing to match the virtues of the old Romans.[10] But the virtues of the old and founding Romans in fact had rested on vices—love of glory, praise, domination, and self—so that whatever glories they had in fact achieved in this world, "they have received their reward" and could look forward to nothing eternal (Matt 6:2, 5, 16).[11] Ancient philosophers offered somewhat better counsel about where to lodge one's hope and how to pursue the human good; of

9. On this characteristic rhetorical practice, see John Cavadini, "The Structure and Intention of Augustine's *De Trinitate*," *Augustinian Studies* 23 (1992) 103–23; John C. Cavadini, "Time and Ascent in *Confessions* XI," in *Augustine: Presbyter Factus Sum*, papers originally presented at a conference at Marquette University, November 1990, eds. Joseph T. Lienhard, Earl C. Muller, and Roland J. Teske, Collectanea Augustiniana (New York: Peter Lang, 1993) 171–85.

10. *City of God* 1.1, 1.33, 2.2.

11. *City of God* 5.12–20.

all the various philosophical sects, Platonism came closest to an answer by recognizing that we must look beyond this life for life's happiness.[12] But even they fell short by seeking their good through pride in their own efforts, rather than faith in God.[13] And if the one thing the philosophers all agreed upon was that the human good must be social, the best that human society had to offer was a "shadowy peace" still full of ills, enmity, and tragic choices.[14] Such is the panorama of misery Augustine has just finished presenting in *City of God* 19.5.

"Our wise man" of 19.6, then, was the one who had learned all these lessons—the best that Roman civic culture and antique philosophical eclecticism had to offer. He was Stoic in composure, Platonic in aspiration, and perhaps somewhere upon the threshold of Christian devotion to God, but no more than that was certain. What he should do next in his official capacity simply was not the driving point of Augustine's argument.

Augustine knew and counseled many such men, of course. He had been one, and though he had once renounced public life he later found himself re-immersed in it as a bishop. The *City of God* itself he directed to Marcellinus, a genuinely pious Christian and a Roman official in North Africa. When Count Boniface was considering the monastery— wishing deliverance from his necessities, perhaps—Augustine urged him to stay in the military, only to see his moral stature deteriorate in the following years.[15]

Such pastoral counsel often responded as much to Augustine's pragmatism as his principle, however.[16] Disjunctures between his systematic reflection and his occasional letters are as much a sign that he himself was unsettled about what "our wise man" and judge should do next, once devoted to God, as they are an authoritative template for Christian political engagement. To Boniface he wrote famously, for example, that his only objective in war should be peace, not vengeance. Yet Augustine's more systematic reflections in *City of God* 19.12 dem-

---

12. *City of God* 10.1, 19.1–4.

13. *City of God* 10.29.

14. *City of God* 19.5.

15. Augustine *Letters* 189 and 220.

16. Cf. Robert Dodaro, "Eloquent Lies, Just Wars and the Politics of Persuasion: Reading Augustine's *City of God* in a 'Postmodern' World," *Augustinian Studies* 25 (1994) 77–138.

onstrate that all creatures, even monsters, seek peace as their ultimate end anyway. So only that "only" in Augustine's counsel to Boniface is normative, and then at risk of devolving into a mere platitude. Further, even that "only" is problematic, for of all the Church Fathers, Augustine knew better than any that no one can really know one's own intentions, leaving no way to verify when one is acting justly in war.[17]

The normative guidance that Augustine did offer to worldly-wise Christians in *City of God* 19 was that they look to God for hope, look to the heavenly city for citizenship, and look at the earthly city as no better than a "captivity."[18] They should not cease to be "a society of resident aliens" drawn from many languages and cultures—not abandon therefore the status that Christians had embraced prior to Constantine.[19] The inadequate, shadowy peace of the earthly city surely had value insofar as it gave the Church time and space to grow in the worship of God, but Christians should merely *use* this earthly peace not rest in it or identify with it as their own.[20] To "seek the peace of the city" was in fact an obligation for members of the pilgriming heavenly city, but they should do so precisely as did the captive exiles to whom Jeremiah once wrote.[21] If Jeremiah's exiles were the template for Christian political engagement (and if the young Jewish men in the Babylon of the book of Daniel have a historical basis) then yes, one way to seek the peace of the city might be to work as civil servants. But unlike the Roman officials with whom Augustine corresponded, Diaspora Jews had had little trouble remembering themselves to be captives. They dare not forget that they *were* in Babylon, that resistance to imperial idolatry could never cease to be an option, and that they belonged first to God and God's people.

---

17. For a masterful argument as to why Augustine's just war theory falls apart precisely at this point, see Robert L. Holmes, "St. Augustine and the Just War Theory," in *The Augustinian Tradition*, ed. Gareth B. Matthews, Philosophical Traditions 8 (Berkeley: University of California Press, 1998) 332.

18. *City of God* 19.17.

19. *City of God* 19.17. Cf. the *Epistle of Mathetes to Diognetus* 5–6; *Shepherd of Hermas* s. 1; Clement of Alexandria, *Stromata* 6.5–6; Tertullian, *The Apology* 38; Origen, *Against Celsus* 8.75; *The Life and Passion of Cyprian* 11; Gregory of Nazianzen, *Oration* 43.49.

20. *City of God* 19.10, 19.17.

21. *City of God* 19.26.

For all practical purposes, Jeremiah's final exhortation was Augustine's last word on politics and Christian engagement in *City of God*. It does not solve but rather leaves hanging the fruitful question of *how* exactly Christians are to seek the peace of the earthly city. To take the practices of Augustine's wise but more-Stoic-than-Christian judge as our final answer to the question of how to seek the peace of the city, is to misread his larger argument, to ignore his rhetorical practices, and above all to beg the question Augustine left hanging. The "wise man" of *City of God* 19 then serves as a blank for later interpreters to fill in with whatever they have already decided to be the best wisdom of their age; his "necessities" become whatever they think they must do when they "do what they have to do" on other grounds. And if Augustine himself could only barely imagine a Christian politics that helped answer the wise man's cry for deliverance—if he himself assumed that the best his Christian friends in high places could do was act like "our wise man" and carry out their "necessities" with purer intentions and authentic grief in their hearts—that only means that he too was begging the question that Jeremiah put to *him*, even as he posed it definitively for later Christian traditions.

Now, what if a later interpreter accepted the contours of Augustine's critique of the earthly city but did more than he to explore the implications of Jeremiah's guidance for life in exile and Diaspora? What if he did at least as much to help Christian "resident aliens" remain clear about where their ultimate loyalties lie? And what if he thus identified a more complete and creative politics for the pilgriming heavenly city that is obliged to seek the peace of the earthly city? It would hardly seem remarkable for someone to describe that interpreter as deeply engaged in the Augustinian project.

Except of course that I refer to John Howard Yoder.

Diverging from Niebuhr

Reinhold Niebuhr's name appears only rarely in the last book that John Yoder prepared for publication, *For the Nations*.[22] Yet as Yoder turned to Jeremiah and Diaspora for models of constructive social engage-

22. John Howard Yoder, *For the Nations: Essays Public and Evangelical* (Grand Rapids: Eerdmans, 1997).

ment he was answering—one more time, in one more way, in earshot of still other conversations—the Niebuhrian charge that often seems to have shaped his career.[23] That charge: Christians who embrace the nonviolent ethic of Jesus might be getting Jesus right, but thus render themselves politically irrelevant and socially irresponsible.

Diaspora Judaism belied this charge. What Jeremiah had made clear when he wrote to the first exiles, urging them to seek the peace of the city, was that living in exile without political sovereignty was an opportunity for mission and constructive contribution to the good of other cultures. Though counter-cultural in one sense, it was pro-cultural and "for the nations" in another; Jeremiah's injunction could be translated far more forcefully, according to Yoder: "seek the salvation of the culture to which God has sent you."[24] Diaspora Jews down through the centuries may have done this in ways that were sometimes "grudging and clumsy" or sometimes "wholehearted and creative."[25] But doing so had depended on neither their own ability to gain access to reins of power nor their host culture's ability to comprehend on its own terms the *shalom* to which God's people were contributing.[26] Diaspora Jews had contributed more not less to Near Eastern and European societies, precisely because they repeatedly became fluent in other peoples' cultural "languages" without losing the thought world of their own

23. Long-time students of Yoder will hardly need evidence that the debate with Niebuhr, Niebuhrianism, and the assumptions that other non-pacifist Christians had held but that Niebuhr definitively articulated, run like a thread throughout his career. Mennonite students of Yoder will also recognize that the response to Niebuhr's charge had already begun in the decade or two before Yoder began writing. The following references, therefore, are only a sample of the most forthright statements recognizing the task of taking on Niebuhr, chosen because they thread back a half a century: Guy Franklin Hershberger, *War, Peace, and Nonresistance*, 3rd ed., Christian Peace Shelf Selection (Scottdale, PA: Herald Press, 1969) 236–54; John Howard Yoder, *Reinhold Niebuhr and Christian Pacifism*, reprint, 1955, A Concern Reprint (Scottdale, PA: Concern, n.d.); John Howard Yoder, *The Christian Witness to the State*, Institute of Mennonite Studies Series 3 (Newton, KS: Faith and Life Press, 1964) 5–8, noting n. 4 on p. 7; John Howard Yoder, *The Politics of Jesus* (Grand Rapids: Eerdmans, 1972) 11–25 (noting especially nn. 4, 7) 110–13; John Howard Yoder, *The Priestly Kingdom: Social Ethics as Gospel* (Notre Dame, IN: University of Notre Dame Press, 1984) 90–91, 100–101.

24. Yoder, *For the Nations*, 76 n. 60.

25. Ibid., 1.

26. Ibid., 33–34, 67–68.

particular "language" or identity.[27] While their social posture might be sectarian in some technical sociological sense, it was that very posture that gave them resources to be more rather than less socially engaged, responsible, and efficacious—in other words, to be anything *but* sectarian in the pejorative ethical sense.[28]

So even though Yoder did not set out intentionally to critique one strand of Augustinian political thought by drawing upon another, closer attention to Jeremiah's exiles showed that "our wise man's" necessities might not be quite so necessary after all. Reinhold Niebuhr was nothing if not a twentieth-century American version of that "wise man," at least according to the standard interpretation of *City of God* 19 that Niebuhr himself has helped to make seem obvious. He was worldly-wise according to the best wisdom of his age, he claimed remorse for actions that fell short of God's true peace, yet he was "tough-minded" enough to recognize his necessities and do what apparently had to be done. As such, having become a "wise judge" presiding over the court of public opinion in mid-century Protestant America and among its Washington elite, Niebuhr like the Stoic of *City of God* 19.6, provided a template for "wise" warriors to follow.[29]

For Yoder to move inadvertently closer to Augustine when he critiqued the putatively Augustinian Niebuhr on eminently Augustinian

27. Ibid., 71. Cf. John Howard Yoder, "On Not Being Ashamed of the Gospel: Particularity, Pluralism, and Validation," *Faith and Philosophy* 9 (1992) 290–91.

28. Yoder, *For the Nations*, 3–5 Yoder prepared and entitled *For the Nations* in part to clarify that is own position was less contrarian than his former colleague Stanley Hauerwas's often appeared to be. Hauerwas, after all, had published *Against the Nations*. (Cf. the hint of this purpose at *For the Nations*, 4 n. 6.) Long-time readers of Yoder, of course, know that he had regularly drawn up lists of the ways that a prophetic minority, creative minority, Abrahamic community, Jeremianic Diaspora community, or any other preferred term for a putatively sectarian group provides societies-at-large with the resources for constructive social change. See for example *Christian Witness to the State*, 18–22; "Christ, the Hope of the World," in *The Original Revolution: Essays on Christian Pacifism*, Christian Peace Shelf (Scottdale, PA: Herald Press, 1971) 203–7; "The Biblical Mandate for Evangelical Social Action," in *For the Nations*, 184–89; *Body Politics: Five Practices of the Christian Community Before the Watching World* (Nashville: Discipleship Resources, 1992).

29. For a fresh account of the role that Niebuhr played in the emerging managerial elite of mid-century America, see Eugene McCarraher, *Christian Critics: Religion and the Impasse in Modern American Social Thought* (Ithaca, NY: Cornell University Press, 2000) 64–70, 91–97.

grounds was nothing new, however. Niebuhr sometimes portrayed his own work as a recovery of Augustine's orthodox doctrine of sin and human limitation in the face of misguided liberal optimism about human perfectibility.[30] By his own admission, however, Niebuhr turned his attention only belatedly to a doctrine of grace that would correspond to his doctrine of sin,[31] while he incorporated a doctrine of eschatology only fitfully,[32] and wrote on ecclesiology hardly at all.[33] Yoder had pointed out how impoverished was Niebuhr's orthodoxy already in the early fifties.

"In spite of the appearance of the label 'neo-orthodox,'" wrote Yoder in his 1954 essay, *Reinhold Niebuhr and Christian Pacifism*, he "is far from what a historian of theology could call orthodox."[34] While countering Niebuhr's characterization and rejection of Christian pacifism in various ways in the pamphlet, Yoder insisted that the "most significant" objection to Niebuhrianism went "still deeper." Although Niebuhr's recovery of an orthodox doctrine of sin constituted a proper and largely biblical diagnosis of the human predicament, according to Yoder, it "consistently slighted" all "those Christian doctrines which relate to [God's] redemption" and point to the Bible's answer to our deepest human need. Yoder reminded Niebuhrians, therefore, of the resurrection and the "new ethical possibilities" that it opens up through grace and

30. Reinhold Niebuhr, "Reply to Interpretation and Criticism," in *Reinhold Niebuhr: His Religious, Social, and Political Thought*, ed. Charles W. Kegley and Robert W. Bretall (New York: Macmillan, 1956) 436; Reinhold Niebuhr, "Intellectual Autobiography," in *Reinhold Niebuhr: His Religious, Social, and Political Thought*, 9; Reinhold Niebuhr, *Human Nature*, vol. 1 of *The Nature and Destiny of Man*, reprint, 1941 (New York: Scribner's, 1964) 49; Reinhold Niebuhr, *The Irony of American History* (New York: Scribner's, 1952) 17.

31. Against charges that he had been preoccupied with original sin, Niebuhr wrote: "I must plead guilty to this charge in the sense that it was a long time before I paid as much attention to the Christian conception of the cure as to the diagnosis, to 'grace' as well as to sin." "Intellectual Autobiography," 10.

32. Note Niebuhr's doubts about the wisdom of having drawn on eschatological themes when he wrote the preface to a reprint of *Human Nature*, ix.

33. In *Human Destiny*, Niebuhr's longest sustained discussion of ecclesiology offered no constructive proposal but only a critique of Roman Catholicism, along with what he considered its essentially Augustinian doctrine of grace. See *Human Destiny*, vol. 2 of *The Nature and Destiny of Man*, reprint, 1943, The Scribner Lyceum Editions Library (New York: Scribner's, 1964) 138–39, 144–52.

34. Yoder, *Reinhold Niebuhr and Christian Pacifism*, 4.

regeneration. Anticipating themes in his later work, he pointed out the absence of the Church in Niebuhr's thought and corrected this omission by pointing towards ways in which that "divine-human society, the church, the body of Christ," as a "supernational society," can break with the patterns of group egoism that Niebuhr thought demonstrated the inevitability of war. Of course that break is not complete in the human society of the Church, but in 1954 Yoder was also preparing to counter positions such as Niebuhr's by stressing the need for an adequate eschatology.[35] Meanwhile, as Yoder observed in *Reinhold Niebuhr and Christian Pacifism*, "the common denominator of the above-mentioned doctrines of resurrection, the church, and regeneration is that all are works of the Holy Spirit, and the Holy Spirit is likewise neglected in Niebuhr's ethics."[36]

Though Yoder did not say so, however, a theology that took the reality of sin seriously yet continued to chart the course of a multinational society of pilgrims being transformed truly if only partially in this life through the love of God "poured into our hearts through the Holy Spirit that has been given to us"[37]—well, this was a theology that became more not less Augustinian even as it challenged Niebuhr. Ecclesiology, eschatology, pneumatology, and grace were precisely the Augustinian doctrines that Niebuhr had slighted.

Yoder's long debate with Niebuhr, on terms that were surprisingly Augustinian both early and late in his career, does not make Yoder himself him an "Augustinian," of course. Yoder could be alternately charitable and caustic about the role Augustine had played in launching the just-war tradition and consolidating the Constantinian synthesis of church and state,[38] but he surely would not have called himself an

35. See Yoder's essay "Peace Without Eschatology?" published in various versions: "If Christ is Truly Lord," in *The Original Revolution: Essays on Christian Pacifism*, Christian Peace Shelf (Scottdale, PA: Herald Press, 1971), 64; "Peace Without Eschatology?" in *The Royal Priesthood: Essays Ecclesiological and Ecumenical*, ed. by Michael G. Cartwright (Grand Rapids, MI: Eerdmans, 1994), 152–53.

36. Unless otherwise indicated, all quotations from this paragraph are from Yoder, *Reinhold Niebuhr and Christian Pacifism*, 17–19. For an explicit statement of Yoder's acceptance of "Niebuhr's real service to theology, and to pacifism, in making real the omnipresence of sin," see *Reinhold Niebuhr and Christian Pacifism*, 19.

37. The quotation from Romans 5:5 is one Augustine often cited in explicating his conception of Christian love.

38. Compare *Priestly Kingdom*, 75, where Yoder said that "Ambrose and Augustine

Augustinian. Characteristic of his life-long approach to ethical debate and ecumenical conversation alike was that very willingness he associated with Diaspora Judaism to learn other peoples' languages and engage them on their own terms, without confusing linguistic systems or endorsing his interlocutors' ethics and worldviews. A willingness to debate all comers, one after another, was Yoder's alternative to what he considered dubious efforts to build a universal theological system that might anticipate every challenge, foundation, and common principle in advance.[39]

And yet one wonders. If nothing else, the length and breadth of Yoder's debate with Niebuhrianism makes it something more than one conversation among Yoder's many. For Yoder to chart his way through such a formative debate using so many Augustinian markers would seem to result from or result in *some* kind of Augustinian formation.[40]

---

did the best they could," with *Royal Priesthood,* 89, where Augustine appears midway in a dynamic leading from Constantine to the Inquisition.

39. On this matter I can offer personal confirmation. Some months after I had finished a review essay of *Royal Priesthood,* but before its publication, I sent Yoder a copy. Although he quibbled with various points, on one matter he supplied the kind of unambiguous affirmation that most of his students will recognize as rare, when he simply wrote "well summarized" in response to the following paragraph:

> What may not have been so clear without the accumulation of reminders that Cartwright's anthology affords us is that a truly ecumenical conversation in the free church style is Yoder's alternative to theological system-building. Yoder's theological method itself is an open-ended conversation with all comers, in respect for the dignity even of opponents, and vulnerability to their insights. If one does not attempt to construct a system that will solve all problems in advance, one may nonetheless act on the very-particular yet also-universal faith that because Jesus Christ is Lord, conversation is in principle possible with persons of any particular "tribe" or tradition or ideology or position. Because *this* Lord is the lamb that was slain, one should not coerce those persons to believe using one's overarching system any more than one coerces with superior weaponry. And if unbelief is possible, so is intractable disagreement. But in principle, if the gospel is knowable and believable within any culture, so is translation and agreement across traditions. There is no way to know without the discipline of actually conversing—again and again.

See Gerald W. Schlabach, "Anthology in Lieu of System: John H. Yoder's Ecumenical Conversations as Systematic Theology," *Mennonite Quarterly Review* 71 (1997) 305–9.

40. To be sure, Yoder once remarked that the "imperatives of dialogue with majority mentalities [had] skewed" the emphasis in his own position. Does that mean if Yoder's arguments sometimes take an Augustinian shape or form, this is in fact a Niebuhrian de-formation? Some will want to say so, and yet the paragraph I am citing makes clear

Given the subtle but pervasive way that Augustine has shaped political and theological problematics in subsequent Western thought, exact
lines of influence may be too amorphous to trace in a way that will sat-
isfy skeptics.[41] In whatever way that Augustinian assumptions got into
Yoder's thought, however, they continued to surface even when Yoder
moved from critique of Niebuhrian politics to constructive proposals
for political engagement according to his own peace church tradition.

The primary audience for Yoder's *The Christian Witness to the State*
was "nonresistant Christians" who doubted that they could or should
address policy deliberations by the state at all.[42] Niebuhr had reinforced
this doubt, of course, and so *The Christian Witness to the State* constitutes
one more chapter in Yoder's engagement with Niebuhrianism—but it
is much more than that. Where Yoder worked from assumptions that
coincide with Augustine's we may safely suppose that they respond to

---

that if anything Yoder's positions would have come across as *more* orthodox and pious
if unconstrained by the parameters of debate with Niebuhrians. Yoder's remark occurs
in a one-paragraph concluding section with the title, "Back to True North;" thus I have
long wondered whether this Yoder was not leaving us a commentary on his own entire
career. See Yoder, *Priestly Kingdom*, 101.

41. If one did wish to trace a more exact genealogy of ideas, however, the place to
begin would probably be in the influence of historian Herbert Butterfield. References
to Butterfield occur occasionally in Yoder's work. In June of 1954 Yoder submitted a
book review of Butterfield's *Christianity, Diplomacy and War* (New York: Abingdon-
Cokesbury, 1953) to Guy F. Hershberger for the *Mennonite Quarterly Review* (never
published). In the cover letter he told Hershberger: "This book has made a great
impression on me, chiefly in the direction of demonstrating the lines along which
the study of history can and should contribute to the church's prophetic witness to
the state, precisely because the anabaptist (N.T.) [sic] doctrine of the State is not only
a doctrine but also a historical reality." (Guy F. Hershberger papers, Archives of the
Mennonite Church, Goshen, Ind., box 10, file 23).

What Yoder found confirmed in Butterfield's historiography was precisely what I
am arguing appears also in Augustine—a circumscribed conception of the state in
which the police function is legitimate, yet when wars "go beyond this limit [police ac-
tion] and claim ideological value or religious or philosophical sanction," they become
more harmful, hypocritical, and "rend the fabric of society more than they protect it."
As to the influence of Augustine on Butterfield, see the suggestive remark in Herbert
Butterfield, *Christianity and History* (New York: Scribner's, 1949) 3; and a more extended discussion in Herbert Butterfield, *Writings on Christianity and History*, ed. C.
T. McIntire (New York: Oxford University Press, 1978) 124–32.

42. *Christian Witness to the State*, 6.

his own desire to articulate a biblical theology, rather than to respond to the more constraining rhetorical task of meeting Niebuhr's agenda.[43]

A reader familiar with characteristic ways of thought in both Augustine and Yoder will note that Yoder's Christian witness to the state corresponds with Augustine's attitudes toward the earthly city in numerous ways:

1. Both Augustine and Yoder shared a *markedly eschatological frame of reference*, and a corresponding recognition that the present challenge for God's people is to live "between the times." Augustine's famous contrast between the earthly city and the heavenly city is not a static ontology, for the heavenly city on earth knows itself to be on pilgrimage home to the fullness of communion with God and all creatures who love God. These pilgrim people live in tension, as resident aliens, not only because they are away from home but also because the current world is a contested zone, in which the angelic citizenry of each city (the faithful and the rebellious angels) vie to direct our loves and our loyalties toward opposing ends.[44] Yoder in turn set the stage for Christian witness to the state by describing how "the present historical period is characterized by the coexistence of two ages or aeons," in which Christ is already reigning, although the powers governing the world still refuse to acknowledge that he is Lord precisely through the triumph of the cross. Still, this coexistence is not perpetual, for ultimately "the church and the reign of Christ will one day be englobed in the same kingdom."[45]

2. For Augustine and Yoder, however, eschatology was not just a question of time, but a question of space, wherein *the two societies are presently inter-mixed, yet distinguished according to their ends, loyalties and loves.* Augustine spoke of co-mixture, Yoder of coexistence. Both described the Church as societies spread around the world, across borders and cultures, united by the character of their love. What distinguished the two societies for Augustine is that the citizens of the earthly city glorify themselves, lust for domination, and love themselves

43. Cf. note 40, above.

44. *City of God* 10.7, 11.1, 15.2, 18.1, with Augustine's entire march through history closing in upon the final judgement (book 20), eternal punishment (book 21), and "the eternal bliss of the City of God" (book 22, as introduced in 22.1).

45. *Christian Witness to the State*, 8–11, 13, 17; quotations are from 8 and 17.

to the point of contempt for God—while the citizens of the heavenly city glorify God, seek to serve one another in love, and love God to the point of contempt for self. Likewise for Yoder, the distinction between Church and world was not the kind of *dualism* that would imagine that the Church could separate itself entirely from the world, but rather a *duality* based on faith and unbelief, allegiances in opposite directions, and social relationships patterned according to the contrasting logics of self-interest and Christ-like love.[46]

3. For both Augustine and Yoder, *the purpose of history and the good of the social order are never knowable on their own terms.* Augustine argued at some length that when the ancient Romans built up their empire, they were not doing what they thought they were doing. They might think they were establishing themselves through their own glorious strength and virtue, or by the power of their gods. But in fact even their virtue had vice at its base, and their gods were demons seeking the glory that belonged to God. It was the one God who was ruling for purposes that were ultimately inscrutable but surely included such ends as establishing that partial earthly peace of which believers were to make use but not trust, and providing lessons concerning virtue and vice from which believers could learn.[47] Yoder was of course more blunt: "The Christian church knows why the state exists—knows, in fact, better than the state itself." The state merely provides the "'scaffolding' service" within which the Church can evangelize. Christ's triumph is what "has already guaranteed that the ultimate meaning of history will not be found in the course of earthly empires or the development of proud cultures, but in the calling together of the 'chosen race, royal priesthood, holy nation,' which is the church of Christ."[48]

4. To be sure, nations tend to think otherwise, so in turn, Augustine and Yoder identified pride as the great problem for the state and *made*

---

46. *City of God* 1.35; 10.32, 14.1, 14.4, 14. *Christian Witness to the State*, 17, 28–31, 42, 72–73. Among the Augustine passages, note that in 1.35 Augustine's discussion of co- or inter-mixture does not imply an "invisible church" in which pacifism is scarcely imaginable because Christians look so much like non-Christians, but rather leads to pacifist possibilities, because among the enemies of the heavenly city are hidden its future citizens, who must therefore be treated patiently, until they convert.

47. *City of God* 5.11–21, but especially 5.16 and 21, and cf. 19.17.

48. *Christian Witness to the State*, 10–11, 13, 16, 17, 36, 40; quotations are from 16, 11, and 13.

thorough-going critiques of imperial presumption. The problem with the earthly city that Augustine knew best was not just that the Romans had been ignorant of God's purposes, but that they had willfully over-stretched themselves in their pride, were falling all the harder, and in the process had inflicted great suffering on other peoples. The grandeur of empire was a fragile illusion at best; look closely and imperialism turned out to be brigandage on a grand scale. The power of the gods who projected Roman values was a "poverty-stricken kind of power," scrambling for lost dominions, claiming honors proper only to God.[49] Pressing the issue, Yoder insisted that such pretension is a problem for all states, not just empires, and not just self-deifying ones that explicitly asked for worship. Certainly in every attempt to create an ideal society, rulers act on pride—"the one sin that most surely leads to a fall, even already within history." But the "universal temptation" of all states was not to neglect the policing duties God had assigned them according to Romans 13, it was to overdo the function. Thus, idolatry does not have to be explicit, nor apostasy cultic, to express "essential rebellion against God," since violent domination and nationalism are always "intrinsically self-glorifying."[50]

5. Still, even though the capacity of the state to effect true peace with justice is always limited—and to think otherwise is to invite the very pride that tends toward greater injustice—Augustine and Yoder both expect that *Christians can always call the social order and the state to do somewhat better.* Augustine's qualified appreciation for the virtues of the old Romans, despite their grounding in vices like self-glorification, implies as much. So too does his appreciation for the peace of the earthly city, even though it is but a shadow of God's ultimate peace and in fact falls short of the harmony of purpose that is possible already in this life for those who share in the love of God. Hence the Jeremianic injunction to seek the peace of the earthly city.[51] Yoder's task of explaining how a pacifist church can witness to "the social order at large" even though he could not expect it "to function without the use of force," required him to specify still more clearly why (and how) pacifist Christians can expect policies that are less violent and more just.

49. *City of God* 4.36, 11.1, 12.1, 14.3–4,13, 14.28, 15.7; quotation is from 11.1.
50. Yoder, *Christian Witness to the State*, 37–38.
51. *City of God* 5.12–15, 19.10–14, 19.17, 19.21, 19.26–27.

Christians can expect the contribution of the state to be "modest," "constantly shifting but nevertheless definable." In asking civil authorities to do their "second best" even if they cannot imagine acting according to the fullness of the gospel, pacifist Christians ask something of them that "does not cease to be gospel by virtue of the fact that we relate it to [their] present available options." Policy proposals cannot be total. But they will expose "one injustice at a time, pointing each time to a less evil way which the statesman can understand and follow;" it is thus realistic to hope for "improvement in the tolerability of the social compromise and thus in a certain sense progress."[52]

6. Finally, Augustine and Yoder stated *similar motivations for seeking the peace of the earthly city*: the aid it afforded to the mission of the Church which is the true purpose of history, and love of neighbor. "While this Heavenly City . . . is on pilgrimage in this world," wrote Augustine, "she calls out citizens from all nations and so collects a society of aliens, speaking all languages"—and so "makes use of the earthly peace." What is more, the pilgrim people places earthly peace into relationship with heavenly peace. How? By faith they already possess and live that peace which "is the perfectly ordered and completely harmonious fellowship in the enjoyment of God, and of each other in God;" in view of the fullness of that peace they perform "every good action . . . in relation to God and in relation to a neighbor, since the life of a city is inevitably a social life."[53] Yoder, while describing the state as performing a "scaffolding function" that helps the church to evangelize, emphasized that on many particulars, a primary reason for Christians to witness to the state is "the very personal and very concrete concern" that Christian have for the welfare of the neighbor, the stranger, and even the enemy.[54]

Of course, Augustine and Yoder certainly differed too. Where they did, the thought of each can sometimes push the other in ways both subtle and blunt. Take the issues that prompted Yoder's turn to the con-

---

52. *Christian Witness to the State*, 6, 7, 13, 25, 32–33, 38–39, 42, 71–73; quotations are from 6, 25, and 39. Key to Yoder's approach was the notion of "middle axioms," which he mentions on 32 and treats at greater length on 71–73. I will give greater attention to middle axioms below.

53. *City of God* 19.7.

54. Yoder, *Christian Witness to the State*, 10–11, 14, 41–42.

ceptual device of "middle axioms."[55] Yoder was sure that Christian pacifists could not appeal as traditional social ethics had done to principles that are "somehow built into the nature of man or of the social order." Convinced that God's will for human social life is only accessible in "definite and knowable" ways through Christ, they instead must translate truths known through Christ into terms that are concrete, practical and accessible to those operating from other ethical convictions. Such translations "mediate between the general principles of Christological ethics and the concrete problems of political application. They claim no metaphysical status but serve usefully as rules of thumb to make meaningful the impact of Christian social thought."[56]

"Usefully." Had Augustine employed this device of middle axioms as self-consciously as Yoder, he might have had a far easier time addressing Roman officials without becoming one himself according to the Constantinian synthesis that was solidifying throughout his career. Since Augustine would recognize in *any* truthful principle a reflection of God's created order, middle axioms must have *some* kind of "metaphysical status" for him. But this would hardly make them less "useful" to an Augustinian social ethic. For resident aliens who maintain primary loyalty to their heavenly, eschatological home, middle axioms are a practical way to negotiate the "already" and "not yet" of pilgrimage through the earthly city while contributing to its peace—and what Augustine's vision most lacks is the practical explication that would give "our wise man" somewhere to turn for guidance besides the dubious wisdom of the age.

If Yoder's thought can nudge Augustinian thought toward greater faithfulness not only to Jeremiah's injunction but to Augustine's own vision, however, Augustinianism can serve to probe Yoder's as well. For what is unclear about middle axioms, in Yoder's hands, is whether

---

55. I state the matter carefully in order to avoid what would otherwise be the laughable anachronism of expecting Augustine to have had access the same conceptual toolbox Yoder had in the mid-twentieth century. And yet it is not historically irresponsible to imagine Augustine himself thinking up a concept *like* "middle axioms." His pre-Christian career, after all, was that of a professor of rhetoric, which requires appealing to the presuppositions of diverse audiences and interlocutors in order to score one's own points. Augustine continued practicing exactly this in both his many theological controversies and his regular correspondence with government officials.

56. Yoder, *Christian Witness to the State*, 32–33.

they can ever become anything *more* than "useful"—whether, in other words, they ever dare make truth claims or instead must devolve into the truces, compromises, and contracts of a liberal pragmatism. (Such pragmatism has its own violent and manipulative proclivities, and is thus at *least* as dangerous an ally for pacifists as Augustinianism allegedly is.) Despite renouncing natural law principles built into human nature and social life, Yoder did want to affirm that "there exists a level of human values, not specifically Christian but somehow subject to Christian formative influences, where the real movement of history takes place."[57] What are those "human values?" What is that "level"? What constitutes the "human?" Logically, Yoder still needed *some* theology of creation.[58] Thankfully, Stanley Hauerwas has begun charting a way forward by arguing in his Gifford lectures for a natural theology that is not autonomous from but rather enclosed within the yet-prior claims of Christology.[59] Certainly, such a formulation need not coincide at every point with Augustine's. But finally, any development of Yoder's insight that the cross does "run with the grain of the universe" must

57. *Christian Witness to the State*, 40.

58. Although, for reasons of both principle and humility, Yoder never claimed to be a philosopher, the power of his intellectual rigor rarely left him making logical blunders. Two sentences on *Christian Witness to the State*, 29 are deeply puzzling, therefore. Yoder was arguing (correctly) that the question of whether Christian principles are relevant to the social order is misleadingly simple. As part of this argument he wrote: "Whether or not, or in what sense, non-Christians or the non-Christian society *should* love, forgive, and otherwise behave like Christians is a speculative question. The spiritual resources for making such redeemed behavior a real possibility are lacking." Paired, these two statements constitute a non-sequitur, apparently based on the confusion of "ought" (or here, "should") with the "is" of "spiritual resourcelessness." What is puzzling becomes troubling when we linger over the first sentence. If Yoder must not only be humble about specifying exactly what God's will is for a non-Christian social order (which is surely appropriate) but must refuse even to say whether God's will for non-Christians is that they love and forgive—because such a question is "speculative"—then he surely needed a more robust theology of creation. Failing to provide one only helps reinstate the case for some kind of natural law theory.

59. Stanley Hauerwas, *With the Grain of the Universe: The Church's Witness and Natural Theology* (Grand Rapids: Brazos, 2001) While drawing most explicitly on Karl Barth, Hauerwas's *With the Grain of the Universe* honors Yoder by pursuing Yoder's own hints that it is only unbelief which prevents us from seeing that the cross does "run with the grain" of all God's creation after all. For the source of that title phrase, see John Howard Yoder, "Armaments and Eschatology," *Studies in Christian Ethics* 1 (1988) 58; John Howard Yoder, *The Politics of Jesus*, 2d ed. (Grand Rapids: Eerdmans, 1994) 246.

offer a theology of creation as robust as Augustine's own, thus allowing for stronger truth claims than his use of "middle axioms" seemed to allow.

Testing the Counter-Intuitive

Of course Augustine and Yoder differed more bluntly still in their respective acceptance and rejection of Christian participation in war. If that difference is incommensurable, my purpose is not to domesticate Augustine for pacifists but to make it all the harder for non-pacifist Christians to marginalize Yoder's witness. Stated cautiously, my claim is that Yoder's pacifist ecclesial social ethic is a surprisingly Augustinian answer to the eminently Augustinian question: just how *shall* the heavenly city on pilgrimage within the earthly city seek the peace of that earthly city? Stated more strongly, my claim is that an Augustinian can be a pacifist and a pacifist can be an Augustinian.[60] Stated most strongly, my claim might be that they *must*—but I am not so foolish as to expect a single paper to establish such a claim in either direction, much less simultaneously. The moderate claim that one can be both a pacifist and an Augustinian is counter-intuitive and challenging enough. To make it imaginable is therefore response enough. It is imaginable because John Howard Yoder himself was a serious contender for, within, and not strictly over-against the Augustinian legacy.

And yet this claim will prove stronger still if the counter-intuitive intuits more than we expected. Stanley Hauerwas, in the final chapter of his *Peaceable Kingdom*,[61] has already tested the counter-intuition by showing why pacifists need something of an Augustinian spirituality in order to sustain their struggle and witness. And he has done so by

---

60. Though the purpose of this paper was not to reply to James Turner Johnson's ill-considered claim in the pages of the *Journal of Religious Ethics* that a pacifist can hardly begin to understand much less interpret Augustine, it obviously does constitute one reply. See James Turner Johnson, "Can A Pacifist Have A Conversation with Augustine? A Response to Alain Epp Weaver," *Journal of Religious Ethics* 29 (2001) 87–93.

61. Stanley Hauerwas, "Tragedy and Joy: The Spirituality of Peaceableness," chap. 8 in *The Peaceable Kingdom: A Primer in Christian Ethics* (Notre Dame, IN: University of Notre Dame Press, 1983) 135–51.

drawing on that Augustinian sensibility which Reinhold Niebuhr did properly share.

A "spirituality of peaceableness" must sustain joy, thankfulness, and hope even while training us to face the tragedy of our world—nay, our own love of self-delusion—with unblinking honesty. This was Hauerwas's conclusion as he surveyed the classic 1932 debate in the pages of *The Christian Century* between H. Richard and Reinhold Niebuhr over Japan's invasion of Manchuria.[62] At the time Richard Niebuhr remained a pacifist, unlike Reinhold, and throughout his career he would remain the more ecclesial theologian of the two brothers. Facing the sense many had at the time that nothing could be done to arrest the historical forces moving towards war in Asia, he argued that some ways of *apparently* doing nothing were theologically significant and fruitful. For they slowly planted seeds of change, while trusting God's ultimate work in history, and creating the cells for a "Christian international" throughout the nations. Such a vision was by implication a Jeremianic, Diaspora one akin to Yoder's later politics; the fact that Reinhold did not address his brother on this front might actually be a sign of his *lack* of political imagination. Instead he charged Richard with an incoherent faith because he trusted God to use the brutal forces of history to eventually bring about a just and loving social order, but would not allow Christians to use those same forces to achieve an imperfect measure of relative justice. Hope was appropriate, but must look beyond history for the fulfillment of history; Richard's mistake was to gloss over the perennial tragedy of human history.[63]

The lesson to learn from the brothers Niebuhr, according to Hauerwas, was not that we must choose between them, but that we cannot sustain "the kind of position represented by H. Richard Niebuhr . . . without a spirituality very much like that hinted at by Reinhold." Though we rarely think of Reinhold Niebuhr as providing a spirituality, Hauerwas noted, he was training us in the very spiritual disciplines we need to sustain a struggle for justice—one that is not surprised by setbacks nor deceived by relative gains. God's peace is dangerous. It ex-

---

62. H. Richard Niebuhr, "The Grace of Doing Nothing," *Christian Century* 49 (1932) 378–80; Reinhold Niebuhr, "Must we Do Nothing?" *Christian Century* 49 (1932) 415–17.

63. Hauerwas, "Tragedy and Joy," 135–40.

poses the lies upon which human beings "to a greater or lesser extent" have built all "social orders and institutions." The "normalcy and safety" we long for come in ways we prefer to repress, "at the expense of others." If in our interpersonal relationships "we 'use' even our love and those whom we love" in order to secure our needs, and if our larger circles of friendship become "a conspiracy of intimacy to protect each of our illusions" and allow us a measure of "peace," then all the more do we fear and defend ourselves against the stranger who would challenge our illusions. Unless, that is, we are hospitable to the God who is our ultimate stranger and challenger of our self-images. Unless, that is, we welcome the hope we only truly find on the far side of our human tragedy. Namely, neither can we save ourselves nor can we transform our world through violence, precisely because God has already won our peace through the cross and resurrection of Jesus. "Joy is thus finally a result of our being dispossessed of the illusion of security and power that is the breeding ground of our violence."[64]

But all of this is deeply Augustinian.[65] If Hauerwas is right, then the claim that we do not have to choose between H. Richard and Reinhold Niebuhr is interesting, but far more is at stake. What H. Richard Niebuhr got right about the hope we must live out through cells of that Christian international we call the Church, Yoder would later explain at greater length and in finer detail. What Reinhold Niebuhr got right about facing our illusions unblinkingly, Augustine was training us to do all along. Surely what matters most is that we choose the way of Jeremiah and Jesus, the gift God gave us long before Augustine and Yoder. Between these two witnesses, however, we need not choose.

64. Ibid., 141–48.

65. The current paper has demonstrated his unblinking social critique as practiced in *The City of God* and his practices of thoroughgoing self-examination are famous from his own *Confessions*. For an exposition of Augustine's analysis of friendship and the illusions by which we subtly but wrongly use our friends, see Gerald W. Schlabach, "Friendship as Adultery: Social Reality and Sexual Metaphor in Augustine's Doctrine of Original Sin," *Augustinian Studies* 23 (1992) 125–47.

3

John Howard Yoder's Systematic Defense of Christian Pacifism

NANCEY MURPHY

Introduction

Christian pacifists are often disadvantaged in debates with other Christians by not having the prestige of systematic theologians to back up their claims, showing them to be essential to Christian life and thought. However, the writings of John Howard Yoder constitute a fairly complete, systematic account of Christian theology, in which Christian nonviolence is shown to be not an optional extra for the heroic Christian, but the very substance of Christian faithfulness.

Yoder disclaimed being a systematic theologian. He believed (rightly, I think) that theology should be written in the service of the Church, addressing issues as they arise, and not driven by any philosophical or systematic motivations. However, this perspective on the nature of theology does not prevent others from looking at Yoder's many writings and perceiving the organization and coherence of the whole.

My method for displaying the systematic coherence of Yoder's theology will seem peculiar to some. I have written previously on the similarities in structure between scientific reasoning (the structure of "scientific research programs") and the structure of systematic theologies.[1] I believe it was my immersion in philosophy of science that attuned me to the sophisticated reasoning and use of evidence in Yoder's

1. Nancey Murphy, *Theology in the Age of Scientific Reasoning* (Ithaca, NY: Cornell University Press, 1990).

works. Thus, I hope I may be excused for importing jargon from philosophy of science for ordering my presentation of Yoder's thought.

Scientific Research Programs

The philosopher of science Thomas Kuhn is well known in a variety of disciplines today for his theory of paradigms and revolutions in science—the Newtonian paradigm supplanting the Aristotelian, and being supplanted in turn by relativistic physics.[2] However, it has proved surprisingly difficult to pin down exactly what Kuhn meant by a paradigm. Imre Lakatos, less well known outside of philosophy of science, has provided a much simpler and clearer account of the logical structure of science.[3] He describes the history of science in terms of competing research programs.

A research program has the following structure: It includes a core theory, which unifies the program by providing a general view of the nature of the entities being investigated. For this reason, and because the core theory is not directly testable, it is called metaphysical. For example, the ancient metaphysical theory of atomism became the core of early modern physics and chemistry.

The core is surrounded by a "protective belt" of "auxiliary hypotheses." These are lower-level theories, which both define and support the core theory. The auxiliary hypotheses are referred to as a protective belt since potentially falsifying data are accounted for by making changes here rather than in the core theory, called the "hard core" since it cannot be abandoned without rejecting the entire research program. Included among the auxiliary hypotheses are theories of instrumentation— the theories involved in the construction of experimental apparatus (e.g., electron microscopes) and needed for interpreting the data they produce.

Finally, assorted data support the auxiliary hypotheses. That is, the auxiliary hypotheses nearest the edges explain the data and are thereby

2. Thomas Kuhn, *The Structure of Scientific Revolutions*, 2nd ed. (Chicago: University of Chicago Press, 1970).

3. See Imre Lakatos, "Falsification and the Methodology of Scientific Research Programmes," in Imre Lakatos and Alan Musgrave, eds., *Criticism and the Growth of Knowledge* (Cambridge: Cambridge University Press, 1970) 91–196.

confirmed by those data; higher-level hypotheses—that is, theories nearer the center—explain lower-level theories. The core theory itself is the ultimate explanatory principle.

It would be more accurate to say that a research program is a temporal *series* of such networks of theory, along with supporting data, since the core theory stays the same but the belt of auxiliary hypotheses must be changed over time to account for new data.

A mature program also involves what Lakatos calls a positive heuristic, which is a plan for systematic development of the program in order to take account of an increasingly broad array of data. An important development in recent philosophy of science has been the recognition of the role of models in science. Scientists use a variety of kinds of models, from mathematical models to physical models of various sorts. Another way to describe the positive heuristic is to say that it envisions the development of a series of increasingly accurate and sophisticated models of the process or entities under study.

For example, the hard core of Newton's program consisted of his three laws of dynamics and his law of gravitation. Auxiliary hypotheses included initial conditions and applications of the laws to specific problems. The positive heuristic was the plan to work out increasingly sophisticated solutions for the orbits of the planets: first, calculations for a one-planet system with the sun as a point-mass, then solutions for more planets, and so on.

Yoder's Research Program

I have argued that by making appropriate substitutions we can see that theological programs have the same structure as scientific research programs. Here, doctrinal theories will take the place of scientific theories; data will come from scriptural texts, and perhaps from religious experience, from historical events, and elsewhere.[4]

The task of the rest of this essay, then, will be to show that Yoder's theology fits the form of a scientific research program. This means that we must be able to isolate a core theory—a central thesis from which all the rest of the theoretical structure (the network of auxiliary hypotheses) follows. These lower-level theories must be supported by appropriate

4. See Murphy, *Theology in the Age of Scientific Reasoning.*

sorts of data. In addition the system as a whole must show development over time; and ideally that development ought to be governed by a positive heuristic, a coherent plan for elaborations and refinements of the theoretical content.

The Hard Core

David Kelsey has written that the use one makes of Scripture in grounding theological claims depends on a prior "single, synoptic judgment" in which one attempts to "catch up what Christianity is basically all about."[5] Yoder's best-known work is *The Politics of Jesus*.[6] In the preface to the second edition he writes that the book is intended to show that the total moral witness of the New Testament texts is political.[7] I believe one could go further and say that, for Yoder, the point of the New Testament witness, *tout court*, is first of all moral and political (as opposed to metaphysical, doctrinal, mystical). I venture to sum up Yoder's program as follows:

> The moral character of God is revealed in Jesus's vulnerable enemy love and renunciation of dominion. Imitation of Jesus in this regard constitutes a *social* ethic.

I shall take this to be the hard core of Yoder's theology. In the following sub-sections I present auxiliary hypotheses that fill out the program.

Relating the Core to Ethics

The first aspect of the program that I shall examine is the line of reasoning by which Yoder's social ethic is developed and related to the description of God in the hard core.

The rationale for ethics, not only for Yoder but for many Christian ethicists, is the requirement to imitate the character of God. Yoder claims that sharing in the divine nature is "the definition of Christian

---

5. David Kelsey, *The Uses of Scripture in Recent Theology* (Philadelphia: Fortress, 1975) 159.

6. John Howard Yoder, *The Politics of Jesus*, 2nd ed., (Grand Rapids: Eerdmans, 1994).

7. Ibid., vii.

existence" and cites texts from throughout the New Testament as grounds.[8]

Because the moral character of God is revealed in Jesus, the definition of Christian existence can also be expressed as "being in Christ": loving as he loved, serving as he served. However, Yoder argues that there is only one respect in which Christians are specifically called to *imitate* Christ, and that is in taking up the cross.[9] So a crucial question is how to interpret the cross. The Christian's cross, Yoder argues, does not represent any and every kind of suffering; it is exactly the price of social nonconformity. Jesus's warning to expect persecution is a statement about

> the relation of our social obedience to the messianity of Jesus. Representing as he did the divine order now at hand, accessible; renouncing as he did the legitimate use of violence and the accrediting of the existing authorities; renouncing as well the ritual purity of noninvolvement, his people will encounter in ways analogous to his own the hostility of the old order.[10]

Yoder's arguments in elaborating his ethical views involve drawing conclusions from his core theory in conjunction with sociopolitical insights. One of the ways in which Yoder's work contrasts with that of many other Christian ethicists is in the requirement he places upon himself to draw his sociopolitical analyses themselves from Scripture.

The most significant contribution that Yoder's reading of Scripture makes to political analysis is his use of the Pauline doctrine of the "principalities and powers." Yoder raises the question: if Jesus's ministry is to be understood in political terms, where in the New Testament do we find the equivalent of the concepts of *power* or *structures* as these are used by contemporary social scientists? It happens that in the 1950s and 60s New Testament research by G. B. Caird, Hendrik Berkhof, and others began to build a body of exegetical literature turning upon a set of terms used by Paul and his school: "principalities and powers," "thrones and dominations," "angels and archangels," "elements," "heights and depths," "law," and "knowledge." In the intervening centuries many of

8. Ibid., 115. The biblical citations are: Matt 5:43–48; 6:12, 14–15; Luke 6:32–36; 11:4; Eph 4:24; Col 3:9,13; 1 John 1:5–7; 3:1–3; 4:17; 1 Pet 1:15–16.

9. Yoder, *Politics of Jesus*, 94–95.

10. Ibid., 96.

these terms were taken to apply to demons and angelic beings, and thus came to be ignored in the modern period.

Apparently, the New Testament concept of the powers developed from concepts of the alien gods of other nations in Old Testament understanding—hence there is a lingering sense of their being spiritual realities. However, the most significant function of the terms is to apply to what we would now call power structures: human traditions, the state, class and economic structures, and religious institutions, to name a few.[11]

If we can make this connection between Paul's peculiar set of powers and our contemporary concept of power structures, then we are in a position to appreciate Paul's sociopolitical theory and to see Jesus's relation to the power structures. The powers were created by God for good purposes, since human social life is impossible without them. However, they are "fallen" in the sense that they do not serve the good of humankind for which they were created, but seek instead their own self-aggrandizement. They have become idols in that they require individuals to serve them as though they are of absolute value.

Christ's role in relation to the powers was to destroy their idolatrous claims. In his public ministry he showed that it was possible to live a genuinely free life in spite of the powers. He conquered the powers through his death, in that the most worthy representatives of Jewish religion and the Roman state conspired to put him to death and thus revealed their true colors. Christ "disarmed the principalities and powers" by stripping them of their ability to create an illusion of absolute legitimacy; he made a public spectacle of them and thereby triumphed over them (cf. Col 2:15).

In the time between Christ's victory on the cross and the eschaton, the powers linger on, but their absolute sway over Christians is broken. With our Western heritage of freedom of dissent (a legacy partly of the Radical Reformation, or Free Church tradition) it is difficult for us to imagine the liberating effect that Jesus's "defeat" of the powers must have

---

11. Walter Wink has written extensively on the powers. He claims that the spiritual realities are the "interiorities" (we might say, the analogue of personalities) of sociopolitical entities. See Walter Wink, *Naming the Powers* (Minneapolis: Fortress, 1984); *Unmasking the Powers* (Minneapolis: Fortress, 1986), and *Engaging the Powers* (Minneapolis: Fortress, 1992).

had in a traditional society in which social class, gender roles, family, religion, and nation placed absolute demands on the individual.

The ethical conclusions that follow from this analysis, along with the injunction derived from Yoder's core hypothesis to follow Christ to the cross are as follows. Power structures are a reality, and they serve essential purposes in human life. However, their claims cannot be granted ultimacy because the powers are fallen. Thus, the Christian must sometimes refuse cooperation. The refusal to cooperate is a *sign* of the (truly) ultimate claim of God on human life, and helps to liberate others from slavish obedience to the powers. The cost of defying the powers, especially when it effectively undercuts their idolatrous claims, is suffering—sometimes even to the point of death. This, precisely, is the meaning of bearing one's cross.

> What Jesus refers to in his call to cross-bearing is rather the seeming defeat of that strategy of obedience which is no strategy, the inevitable suffering of those whose only goal is to be faithful to that love which puts one at the mercy of one's neighbor, which abandons claims to justice for oneself and for one's own in an overriding concern for the reconciling of the adversary and the estranged.[12]

Methodological Auxiliary Hypotheses

I have already alluded to an auxiliary hypothesis of a methodological sort that shapes Yoder's program: the requirement to make use of the sociopolitical analyses that can be found in Scripture, rather than analyses based on other sources.

Another methodological auxiliary is Yoder's systematic rejection of individualism. The ethical tradition tells us that we must choose between the individual and the social. "But Jesus doesn't know anything about radical personalism." The personhood Jesus proclaims is instead a call to be integrated into a new, healing sort of community. "[T]he idea of Jesus as an individualist or a teacher of radical personalism could arise only in the (Protestant, post-Pietist, rationalist) context that it did."[13]

12. Yoder, *Politics of Jesus*, 236.
13. Ibid., 108.

Notice that Yoder's preference for the understanding of the relation of individual to community that he attributes to Jesus, in preference to that of modern Protestantism, is an *instance* of preferring the sociological analysis of Scripture over that of other sources.

The Positive Heuristic

Lakatos invented the term "positive heuristic" in order to allow him to discriminate between scientific research programs that develop a unified vision of their subject matter from those that progress by means of accidental accretion of theoretical insights. The positive heuristic, then, is a plan, either consciously formulated or implicit, that directs the growth of a scientific research program. I have suggested elsewhere that the positive heuristic of a theological program will be the plan to elaborate the central vision in such a way as to cover all of the traditional theological loci in a manner consistent with the hard core of the program and in accordance with any other binding constraints.[14] For example, the positive heuristic of an existentialist theological program would be to reinterpret the traditional Christian doctrines in terms of the existentialist account of the nature of human existence.

The positive heuristic of Yoder's program would be the plan to interpret the standard Christian doctrines in a way consistent with his core theory and with his political reading of Jesus's ministry, and subject to the methodological assumptions just mentioned. A more thorough account of Yoder's program would also address his more technical exegetical assumptions. As mentioned above, Yoder does not intend to write as a systematic theologian, so he would disavow any such conscious plan. I argue, though, that no one could hope to promote a view of Jesus that differs so radically from the standard account without expecting it to be possible to work out the theological consequences of this view within the usual theological battle grounds (loci).

In the following sub-sections we see the fruit of this heuristic for Christian doctrine.

14. Murphy, *Theology in the Age of Scientific Reasoning*, 185–86.

Doctrinal Auxiliary Hypotheses

One way to interpret the epistemological status of theological doctrines is to see them as auxiliary hypotheses contributing to a research program in theology. Accordingly, I now proceed to examine the doctrinal positions that make up the theological content of Yoder's program.

Christology and Trinity

Yoder's accounts of the *content* of Christology and the doctrine of the Trinity are close to the historic orthodoxy of the ancient creeds and councils. Where his account differs from the standard account is in his justification of these doctrines. Both are justified insofar as they attribute to Jesus the "metaphysical" status he must have in order that the church be justified in worshipping *and obeying* him as absolute LORD. So the doctrinal affirmations are justified because they explain *why* the ethic taught by Jesus is morally binding.

> When the later, more "theological" New Testament writings formulated the claim to preexistence and cosmic preeminence for the divine Son or Word (John 1:1–4; Col. 1:15ff.; Heb. 1:2ff.) the intent of this language was not to consecrate beside Jesus some other way of perceiving the eternal Word, through reason or history or nature, but rather to affirm the exclusivity of the revelation claim they were making for Jesus. The same must be said of the later development of the classic ideas of the Trinity and the Incarnation. "Incarnation" does not originally mean (as it tends to today in some theologies of history, and in some kinds of Anglican theology) that God took all of human nature as it was, put his seal of approval on it, and thereby ratified nature as revelation. The point is just the opposite; that God broke through the borders of our standard definition of what is human, and gave a new, formative definition in Jesus. "Trinity" did not originally mean, as it does for some later, that there are three kinds of revelation, the Father speaking through creation and the Spirit through experience, by which the words and example of the Son must be corrected; it meant rather that language must be found and definitions created so that Christians, who believe in only one God, can affirm that that God is most adequately and bindingly known in Jesus.[15]

15. Yoder, *Politics of Jesus*, 99.

So the doctrine of Christ's divinity and the unity of the Son with the Father function as guarantees that no other claims can be more binding on humankind than those of Jesus. There is no other redeemer figure whose claims take precedence over those of Jesus Messiah; there can be no other source of divine revelation that contradicts Jesus's teaching. Conversely, doctrinal heresies are defective insofar as they lead to the rejection of Jesus's ethic. Ebionitic heresies (denying Christ's divinity) thereby deny his right to moral lordship. Docetism (denying the full humanity of Christ) calls into question the possibility, and thus the requirement for, mere humans to imitate Jesus's faithfulness.

Atonement, Sin, and Justification

When we come to the doctrines of atonement and justification, Christian anthropology and sin, we reach the point where Yoder's theology is most clearly divergent from the standard account of Christian doctrine. By the standard account, I mean to refer especially to Reformation and post-reformation forms of Christianity, owing much to Augustine. The features of the standard account include a doctrine of the Fall as a key to understanding human nature, a major emphasis on substitutionary atonement, and justification as imputed righteousness.

It has become common since the publication of Gustaf Aulén's *Christus Victor*[16] to speak of three types of atonement theories: the Anselmian or substitutionary theories; the Abelardian or moral influence theories; and the "classical" ransom or conflict theories, according to which the work of Christ is interpreted in terms of conflict with and triumph over cosmic evil powers. A variety of versions of the latter were developed during the early centuries of the Church: Christ as a ransom paid to the Devil; a transaction wherein God used Christ as "bait" to deceive the Devil; and a political form in which the Devil lost his rightful dominion over sinful humankind by abusing the sinless Christ.

While the classical theory clearly has New Testament support, it has been seen as objectionable because it involves the concept of the Devil, which many now take to require "demythologization." Aulén had argued that the mythological language of the conflict theory could sim-

16. Gustaf Aulén, *Christus Victor*, trans. A. G. Herbert (New York: Macmillan, 1931).

ply be dropped, leaving the theory intact. But then it is no longer clear what is meant by "cosmic evil powers."

Yoder's central understanding of atonement fits the classical model, and fills the gap left by the excision of a mythical Devil by means of the interpretation of the "principalities and powers" described above. These super-human power structures are the forces with which Jesus came into conflict, and from which he has freed humankind, both by his example (and here the moral influence theory gets its due) and by stripping them of the illusion of absolute legitimacy, precisely because their most worthy representatives abused him in his innocence. The cross has as much significance in this theory as it does in the substitution theory, but for different reasons.

Yoder does not ignore personal sinfulness, but he gives it neither the significance nor the inevitability that it has in Augustinian Christianity. His focus instead is on institutionalized sin; the remedy for it is found in freedom from bondage to the principalities and powers, and especially in the creation of a new social order, the church.

Yoder's account of justification, also, is sociopolitical.

> Let us set aside for purposes of discussion the assumption that the righteousness of God and the righteousness of humanity are most fundamentally located on the individual level. . . . Let us posit as at least thinkable the alternate hypothesis that for Paul righteousness, either in God or in human beings, might more appropriately be conceived of as having cosmic or social dimensions. Such larger dimensions would not negate the personal character of the righteousness God imputes to those who believe; but by englobing the personal salvation in a fuller reality they would negate the individualism with which we understand such reconciliation.[17]

Yoder argues that justification (being set right with God) is accomplished when Christians are set right with one another. In Paul's ministry, the reconciling of Jews and Gentiles was primary. The "new creation" is a new "race" of humans where the Jewish law no longer forms a barrier between Jew and Gentile, and where gender and economic differences are reconciled as well.

17. Ibid., 215.

> But it is *par excellence* with reference to enmity between peoples, the extension of neighbor love to the enemy, and the renunciation of violence even in the most righteous cause, that this promise takes on flesh in the most original, the most authentic, and most frightening and scandalous, and therefore the most evangelical way. It is the Good News that my enemy and I are united, through no merit or work of our own, in a new humanity that forbids henceforth my ever taking his or her life in my hands.[18]

All of this—a primarily social concept of sin and justification, and a conflict view of atonement suitably politicized—contributes to a complete reinterpretation of the main features of New Testament theology, especially of the Pauline corpus, which, since Luther, has been taken to focus instead on imputed personal righteousness before God on the grounds of faith.

Excursus: Walter Wink on the Domination System

New Testament scholar Walter Wink had expanded on Yoder's claim that the principalities and powers form a system. In its fallen state, Wink calls this the Domination System. Wink's analysis strengthens Yoder's position in several ways.

First, this conceptual move explains the integral relationship between an ethic of nonviolence and an ethic of social and economic justice. That is, Yoder and many others recognize that social justice and nonviolence "go together." Why? Wink provides a sociological-historical explanation.

The Domination System arose in the Middle East sometime between 4000 and 3000 BCE. Before this period, archaeological evidence shows, there were many peaceful civilizations—cities with no walls, no armies, no weapons for battle. After 3000 BCE, warfare proliferates dramatically.[19] By this same date, autocracy was the accepted order of things: the social system was rigidly hierarchical, authoritarian, and patriarchal. Power lost by men through submission to the ruling elite was compensated by power over women, children, hired workers, slaves, and the land.

18. Ibid., 226.
19. Wink, *Engaging the Powers*, 36.

Power inequalities permitted economic inequalities, and the amassing of wealth became necessary for the support of large armies.

The Domination System has its own myth of origins in the *Enuma Elish* (from around 1250 BCE, but based on much older traditions). Here the universe is said to have been created out of the body of a murdered goddess. The gods themselves set the pattern of domination and warfare. The implication is that the very substance of which humans are created is tinged with violence. Furthermore, warfare and domination are necessary to prevent the cosmos from reverting to the chaos from which it was created.

So here is the story that gives meaning to mainline Western culture. It was repeated in Greek and Roman mythology. It continues today in nearly all of the literature and television programming used to socialize children: it is the story of the good guy preserving order by means of violence. It lies behind the social-scientific research programs unmasked by Milbank, whose deep thesis is an "ontology of violence."[20] Unfortunately it has had all too deep an influence on mainstream Christianity, showing up thinly disguised in the "just war" tradition from Augustine to the present.

The contribution that Wink's historical research makes to Yoder's theological program, then, is first to explain historically and sociologically the intrinsic connections between social justice and nonviolence: they are related in virtue of that which they oppose.

Second, it makes all the more plausible Yoder's claim that God's response to evil must be at the social level, not just the level of personal sin. Once a single society falls prey to the mythology of the Domination System, it forces its neighbors to do likewise, and individuals within the societies lose their freedom to object. Consequently, the solution must be to instigate (or re-instigate) a whole new model of sociality (the church); to unmask the idolatrous pretensions of the Domination System (cf. Col 2:15); and to teach individuals that resistance to the system is possible (the example of Jesus).

Finally, Wink's claim that domination is not coeval with civilization provides strong evidence against theological positions that root it

20. See Stanley Hauerwas, "Creation, Contingency, and Truthful Nonviolence: Reflections on John Milbank's *Theology and Social Theory*," in *Faith and Freedom* 4:2 (1995) 12–17.

in a constant human sinfulness extending all the way back to the Fall at the beginning of human history. This, in turn, makes more plausible the claim that there is hope for progressively decreasing the levels of violence, coercion, and economic inequality in contemporary societies.

Excursus: René Girard and Atonement Theory

René Girard has published a study on the relation between violence and religious ritual that can be used to eliminate an anomaly from Yoder's program.[21] Yoder claims that he does not intend to reject the standard account of the work of Christ, but only to place it in a social and cosmic setting. Yet readers are likely to object that he needs to give some positive account of New Testament passages that use the language of temple sacrifice to interpret the atoning work of Christ. Girard's conclusions regarding religious sacrifice allow us to do just that. I argue that, properly interpreted, the sacrificial atonement motifs exactly reinforce Yoder's own interpretation of what Christianity is basically all about.

Girard's thesis is that religious rites of sacrifice, both animal and human, are devices to quell violence among members of a community.

> [I]f left unappeased, violence will accumulate until it overflows its confines and floods the surrounding area. The role of sacrifice is to stem this rising tide of indiscriminate substitutions and redirect violence into "proper" channels.[22]

Thus, the ritual restores the harmony of the community, reinforces its social fabric. The victim used for the sacrifice is a surrogate for members of the community who have excited the animosity of their fellows. The victim, Girard points out, always shares some characteristics identifying it with the community. For example, the Nuer, who sacrifice cattle, describe the "society" of the herd in the same terms that they use for their own human relations. Yet the victims cannot be of the same class as the community itself—human victims are always marginal or distinguished in some way—so that their death does not incur any responsibility for vengeance on the part of community members. Thus, ritual sacrifice allows for the venting of aggression without the "interminable, infinitely repetitive process" of vengeance, which, whenever it turns up

21. René Girard, *Violence and the Sacred*, trans. Patrick Gregory (Baltimore: Johns Hopkins University Press, 1977).

22. Ibid., 10.

in some part of the community, "threatens to involve the whole social body."[23]

Girard notes that sacrifice is generally seen as an act of mediation between a sacrificer and a deity, and argues that the sacrificial process requires a degree of *misunderstanding*. If the celebrants comprehended the true role of the sacrificial act (as Girard describes it) then it would lose its effectiveness. The participants must suppose that it is the god who demands the victim. The reason, Girard speculates, is that "men can dispose of their violence more efficiently if they regard the process not as something emanating from within themselves, but as a necessity imposed from without."[24]

If Girard's anthropology can help us think our way back to a society ordered by a code of vengeance, rather than by a modern legal system,[25] it becomes clear that the sacrificial atonement motif is not an alternative to Yoder's account of Christian theology in terms of non-violence and reconciliation. Now we can see Christ, the lamb of God, as the one victim whose sacrificial death is permanently efficacious for ridding the community of violence (cf. Heb 7:27).

The parallels with Girard's account of ritual sacrifice are startling: The victim must be similar enough to suffer on behalf of community members, yet different enough not to be confused with other, non-sacrificeable members. So Jesus is described as both fully human and as the unique Son of God. The moral ambiguity of the sacrificial victim is found here as well. Jesus is described as the wholly sinless one, yet "reckoned among the transgressors." The symbolism of the Last Supper even maintains a hint of the cannibalism that is so often incorporated in sacrifice.

We even find in cruder versions of this atonement theology the "necessary degree of misunderstanding": the claim that God the Father required the death of his Son as satisfaction for sin.

So if Girard is correct, the point of the interpretation of Christ's death as the once-for-all sacrifice for sin, for communities in which rit-

23. Ibid., 14–15.

24. Ibid., 14.

25. And both Old and New Testament societies were still largely of this type; see Bruce J. Malina, *The New Testament World: Insights from Cultural Anthropology* (Atlanta: John Knox, 1981).

ual sacrifice was still an effective control on the cycle of vengeance and violence, would have been to say that violence and vengeance within the community is henceforth prohibited. And against this background we can see more clearly the importance of Paul's (and Yoder's) emphasis on the new humanity that refuses to count any class of people as outside of the community thus protected from violence by the sacrifice of the Lamb.

What does the sacrificial imagery mean, then, for us who are far removed from cultures where propitiatory sacrifice makes sense? For us, Girard suggests, war and the legal system with its punishments are the primary means of redirecting violence away from protected community members. I would add, as well, that civil religion with its explicit description of loss of life in battle as "sacrifice" maintains the necessary degree of misunderstanding—the illusion that the innocent lives lost on the battlefield are not victims of the citizens' own aggression but are demanded by a righteous god. It may not be pure cynicism when commentators attribute America's small wars to the need to unify the citizens at home for the *domestic* political agenda.

The obvious application of sacrificial atonement imagery to our contemporary situation is to call for a permanent end to violence, both spontaneous and institutionalized. Christ for us, too, is the one victim whose death should be permanently efficacious in ridding our present-day communities of violence. Yoder's image for the work of Christ and of his followers is that of *absorbing evil*; stopping the "eternal, infinitely repetitive process" of violence (Girard) by refusing to retaliate. And, I would add, by refusing as well to find a scapegoat from the margins of our community.

The misunderstanding that it is God who required the death of Jesus as scapegoat for sinners has all too often contributed to the view that God also demands the death of others as payment for sin. Demythologization of atonement imagery requires recognition that it is not God, but our own human principalities and powers that demand the death of criminals, the "sacrifice" of young men on the battlefield. High Christology demands that we recognize God's voice not in the powers demanding sacrificial death, but rather in the one whose life was sacrificed on the cross.

Thus, the addition of Girard's anthropology to this theological program allows for the overcoming of what would be called an anomaly in science—a datum that cannot be reconciled with the theory. The anomaly here is the sacrificial language used in the New Testament to interpret the death of Jesus. This language has led to the development of theories of the work of Christ that are at least different from Yoder's interpretation, and in some cases actually opposed to it. I have used Girard's thesis regarding the social function of ritual sacrifice as an auxiliary hypothesis to interpret the anomalous data in a way that is not only consistent with Yoder's program, but adds additional confirmation.[26]

Church, World, and Eschatology

An important thesis for Yoder, as well as for other theologians in the Anabaptist tradition, is the recognition that "the church is not the world." The sixteenth-century Anabaptists' most distinctive feature was their rejection of the state-church arrangement, which identified the boundaries of the church first with the empire and then with the nation state. The "ana-baptists" (that is, re-baptizers) rejected infant baptism in part because it was the means by which the incorporation of all citizens into the state church was effected.

When Yoder distinguishes the church from the world, he means to say that there is a system—a set of interconnected power structures—that is opposed to the work of Christ. An important question dividing Christian ethicists regards the possibility for moral improvement in social institutions. This question, Yoder would argue, needs to be recast as a set of questions regarding the possibilities for change within both the church and the world, and especially how the church can affect the world.

The church is an alternative social reality in the midst of the world. By its very existence it unmasks the principalities and powers, exposing the illegitimate claims of family, privileged social class, nation. In a variety of ways this unmasking frees church members to lead agapeistic lives. For example, Christians are *freed from* requirements to avenge injuries to family members' honor.

---

26. Yoder commented on an earlier version of this essay. He endorsed the use made here of both Wink and Girard, but cautioned that he would not want to endorse some of the further moves they make.

The church is a laboratory for imagining and practicing new forms of social life. Where it had once been unimaginable that Jews could live in community with pagans, within a generation that "new creature" became a reality. Christians are even now trying to imagine a community in which there is no such thing as male and female (cf. Gal 3:28).

Within the church social practices are, to a degree, healed of their sinfulness. The powers themselves can be redeemed—they can accept their role as servants of God in support of human sociality. For example, leadership becomes a form of service. Economic practices are not primarily for the amassing of wealth, but for the production of something to share. Housekeeping aims at hospitality to the stranger.

In addition, the church has developed unique social practices that aim at maintaining and improving the moral character of the community. One of these is the practice of "binding and loosing" that Jesus is reported to have taught his disciples:

> If your brother does wrong, go and take the matter up with him, strictly between yourselves. If he listens to you, you have won your brother over. But if he will not listen, take one or two others with you, so that every case may be settled on the evidence of two or three witnesses. If he refuses to listen to them, report the matter to the congregation; and if he will not listen even to the congregation, then treat him as you would a pagan or a tax-collector. Truly I tell you: Whatever you forbid on earth shall be forbidden in heaven, and whatever you allow on earth shall be allowed in heaven. (Matt 18:15–18)

This practice has the potential not only for supporting individuals in their faithfulness to the community's teaching, but also offers opportunity both for healing personal grievances and for productive discussions on matters of conduct.[27] When it does involve reevaluation of the community's moral standards it becomes an instance of a second Christian practice, that of communal discernment. Yoder calls this practice the rule of Paul, since its justification in all of the new Protestant movements during the Reformation referred to Paul's first letter to the Corinthians (chap. 14).

---

27. See John Howard Yoder, *Body Politics: Five Practices of the Community before the Watching World* (Nashville: Discipleship Resources, 1992) chap. 1.

The idea behind this practice is that God's Spirit will lead the community in making decisions about doctrine and moral issues through the consensus that arises out of open conversation. The Quakers have worked out most thoroughly and self-consciously an understanding of how the Spirit shapes and guides the church.[28] The practice of discernment can be a powerful tool for cumulative moral development within the Church.

All of these features of the church suggest that conscientious pursuit of the good can and will lead to cumulative moral development, both of Christ-like character among the members and of noncoercive, virtue-enhancing institutions and practices.

However, religious institutions themselves easily become quite powerful and they are especially prone to become idolatrous. So there can be no smug expectation of inevitable moral progress. The prophet will always be needed to call the church to focus critical moral discernment on itself.

The church acts as an agent of change in the world by showing the world alternatives to its coercive practices. While it is simply a fact that the world does not and cannot operate as the church does, there are still vast differences among the powers in terms of the degree to which they approximate the will of God. The church, as an ethical laboratory, can teach the world better ways. For instance, many attribute modern forms of democratic government to skill and lessons learned in free-church polity. The ideas of public education and hospitals came from church institutions.

Yoder's hope for partial realization of God's social will for humankind in history sets him in opposition to Reinhold Niebuhr's "Christian realism." Niebuhr claimed that all human social groups are necessarily less moral than the individuals that comprise them. Yet it would be difficult to say that Yoder's analysis of social institutions is any less *realistic* than Niebuhr's. What accounts for the difference is different views of eschatology (i.e., doctrine of the last things). More specifically, these two theorists have different views of the relation between history and the Kingdom of God.

Niebuhr points out that while all Christians look forward to the *parousia*, the triumphant return of Christ, some interpret this event as a

28. Ibid., chap. 5.

future happening *within* the temporal-historical process; others as necessarily outside of or *beyond* history. Because he sets up the question in terms of the problem of the temporal and the eternal (the claim is that the eternal can never be actualized in the temporal) Niebuhr is forced to side with those whose eschatology transcends history. This, in turn, leads to the conclusion that guilt and moral ambiguity are permanent features of the interim. Christ's overcoming of the world can only mean that Christians know the meaning of history, not that history itself is transformed.[29]

Yoder claims that the New Testament sees our present age, from Pentecost to the *parousia*, as a period of the overlapping of two aeons. These are not distinct periods of time, for they exist simultaneously.

> They differ rather in nature or in direction; one points backwards to human history outside of (before) Christ; the other points forward to the fullness of the kingdom of God, of which it is a foretaste. Each aeon has a social manifestation: the former in the "world," the latter in the church or the body of Christ.[30]

The new aeon was inaugurated by Jesus; Jesus is a mover of history, not merely a teacher of how to understand history's moral ambiguity.[31] The meaning of history is found in the work of the church;[32] the church by its obedience is used by God to bring about the fullness of the Kingdom, of which the church is a foretaste.

The resurrection of Jesus is God's guarantee that the new aeon will ultimately prevail. This entails that the means Jesus chose for participation in history are the right ones: the cross and not the sword, suffering and not brute power determine the meaning of history. One need not choose between *agape* and effectiveness.[33]

So the ultimate effectiveness of self-sacrificing love is guaranteed; but its rightness is not based on effectiveness, but rather on the fact that

---

29. Reinhold Niebuhr, *Moral Man and Immoral Society* (New York: Scribner's, 1932).

30. John Howard Yoder, *The Original Revolution: Essays on Christian Pacifism* (Scottdale, PA: Herald ress, 1971) 55.

31. Yoder, *Politics of Jesus*, 233.

32. Yoder, *Original Revolution*, 61.

33. Yoder, *Politics of Jesus*, 232, 109.

it anticipates the victory of the Lamb.[34] This ethic makes sense only if Jesus's choice not to rule violently is the surfacing of an eternal divine decision; if self-emptying is not only what Jesus did, but is the very nature of God.[35]

> This conception of participation in the character of God's strug-
> gle with a rebellious world, which early Quakerism referred
> to as "the war of the lamb," has the peculiar disadvantage—or
> advantage, depending upon one's point of view—of being mean-
> ingful only if Christ be he who Christians claim him to be, the
> Master. Almost every other kind of ethical approach espoused
> by Christians, pacifist or otherwise, will continue to make sense
> to the non-Christian as well. Whether Jesus be the Christ or not,
> whether Jesus the Christ be Lord or not, whether this kind of
> religious language be meaningful or not, most types of ethical
> approach will keep on functioning just the same. For their true
> foundation is in some reading of the human situation or some
> ethical insight which is claimed to be generally accessible to
> all people of good-will. The same is not true for this vision of
> "completing in our bodies that which was lacking in the suffer-
> ing of Christ" (Col. 1:24). If Jesus Christ was not who historical
> Christianity confesses he was, the revelation in the life of a real
> man of the character of God himself, then this one argument for
> pacifism collapses.[36]

Confirmation

Different theological research programs call for different kinds of data to support them. This is analogous to the different kinds of support that are relevant to, say, different schools of thought in psychology: B. F. Skinner's reinforcement schedules versus Freud's dream analyses and slips of the tongue. Yoder's central thesis is about the proper in-terpretation of the meaning of Jesus, and about what Jesus means for history and ethics.

Since the Scriptures are the only significant source of information about Jesus, it stands to reason that these texts should provide an im-

34. Yoder, *The Original Revolution*, 61.
35. John Howard Yoder, *He Came Preaching Peace* (Scottdale, PA: Herald, 1985) 93.
36. Yoder, *Politics of Jesus*, 237.

portant body of data for Yoder, along with other historical texts and traces that are relevant for assisting in their interpretation. Yoder's more systematic works such as *The Politics of Jesus* contain sophisticated arguments to the effect that his line of interpretation is more faithful to the texts, more fruitful for interpreting obscure passages, than others. Yoder has provided additional scriptural confirmation of his program in published sermons and occasional essays. In this body of literature he has worked through a surprising variety of texts, in each case providing a reading that confirms his interpretation of the life and teaching of Jesus.

However, the other aspect of Yoder's thesis, that Jesus (thus understood) is the ultimate revelation of the character of God and thus of the meaning and purpose of human history, cannot be confirmed merely by Scripture studies without begging the question. The purely theological thesis, the theory about the character of God, can only be fully confirmed eschatologically, although it can acquire some plausibility for Christians from their relations with God in prayer. However, there is a thesis about history embedded in Yoder's theology that may be testable in the interim. Yoder has stated it as follows:

> [I]f *kenosis* [Jesus's renunciation of worldly prerogatives] is the shape of God's own self-sending, then any strategy of Lordship, like that of the kings of this world, is . . . a strategic mistake, likely to backfire.[37]

Yoder pays some attention to the relative effectiveness of nonviolent versus violent means of social and political action. However, his more intriguing contribution here is the suggestion that his version of ethics leads to (what I would call) a new research program in the study of history, part of which is the examination of the effects of violence and nonviolence.

> We now turn to asking . . . whether this "messianic" orientation will have particular implications for history as an intellectual discipline, i.e., for historiography, the recounting of events and the discerning of meanings. Can one gain new light upon the relevance of a Free Church vision of ethics by claiming that it also leads to a new way of interpreting events in the past?

37. John Howard Yoder, *The Priestly Kingdom: Social Ethics as Gospel* (Notre Dame, IN: University of Notre Dame Press, 1984) 145.

Decision in the present is often very much the product of how the past has been recounted to us. If we are then to open up a new future it must be the extension of a rereading of the past. Historiography must be rehabilitated by being taken back from the grasp of the military historians and the chroniclers of battles and dynasties, and informed by other criteria to judge a society's sickness or health.

Instead of reading history as proof of a theory of political science, i.e., the definition *sine qua non* of the state as its monopoly of physical coercion, could we study the story with some openness to the hypothesis that genuine power is always correlated with the consent of the governed or legitimized in some other way? Is there such a thing as a "peace church historiography"?[38]

Yoder mentions a variety of hypotheses that follow from this reorientation of assumptions about history.

1. The sword is not the source of creativity.

   1.1 Theological considerations make a major contribution to the spirit of an age and to political developments.

   1.2 History may be more affected by quiet ministry than by princes.

2. Manhood is not brutality.

   2.1 History and conflict cannot be understood on a simple model of good guys and bad guys.

3. If you wish peace, prepare for it.

   3.1 Preparing for war brings conflict.

   3.2 Practice of constructive methods of conflict resolution will help to undermine unjust institutions and build healthy ones.

4. War is not a way to save a culture.

5. Social creativity is a minority function.

   5.1 The person in power is not always free or strong.

   5.2 Minority groups have more freedom to experiment with new forms of social life.

6. Rulers are not necessarily society's benefactors.[39]

38. Yoder, *Original Revolution*, 160–61.
39. Ibid., 162–76.

In short, Yoder's claim is that "world history," the historiography of "the world" (in the theological sense defined above) produces a distortion of the past, which then provides justification for further coercive practices. Perhaps an equally credible narrative could be constructed, a narrative that is in fact more accurate, which will make it clear that the real historical force is suffering love.

Rebutting Counter-Evidence

Two sorts of possible counter-evidence could be particularly damaging to the theological program sketched here: the complicity of the church in the worst evils of history, and biblical passages that appear to condone or require violence.

The well-known sins not only of individual Christians but especially of the institutional churches themselves rightly raise doubts about Christianity's truth claims, although this is not straightforward falsification, owing to the fact that one of Christianity's central claims has always been its doctrine of sin. The more appropriate approach is to ask whether the observed patterns of goodness and evil are roughly what theological teaching should lead us to expect, and here we have to distinguish among theological traditions. For the Catholic tradition, with its teaching on the non-defectibility of the church, sinful church practices constitute a major anomaly; this is much less the case for the Protestant tradition, according to which the church must be *semper reformanda* (always needing reforming).

Yoder's version of the Anabaptist tradition is even less damaged by the sin of the church: not only can he predict it, he can specify its main cause. The church is a power; all powers are subject to corruption when they seek their own good over that of service to God. When the churches become involved in Constantinian arrangements with the great powers of empire or state, they have much more to protect and will inevitably become corrupted. Thus, the church itself must always be on guard against grasping for power (as the Protestant tradition emphasizes) and *in particular* it must eschew state-church status.

A second advantage of the Anabaptist tradition for answering the problem of corruption in the church is its teaching on church discipline. Much discredit is brought upon Christian teaching by the behavior of individual members of churches (Mafiosi at Mass, for example). However, Anabaptist church discipline was founded on Matthew 18, and when this practice is followed, members' conduct is either brought into accord with church teaching or they are excluded from worship.

So I claim that while evil within and by the churches is indeed a terrible scandal, it presents less of an anomaly for the Anabaptist tradition than for others. Persistently sinful individuals do not count as church members in "believers' churches"; the most heinous institutional sins of Christendom (predictably, according to the Anabaptists) have been committed by churches that have made compromises with the empire or the state.

There are several passages in the New Testament that are regularly used to attempt to rebut pacifist interpretations of Jesus's mission and teaching.

Romans 13:1: "Every person must submit to the authorities in power, for all authority comes from God, and the existing authorities are instituted by him" is often cited as proof that Christians have a responsibility to serve in the military. However, such a reading ignores the context of the text, both the preceding and subsequent verses, and the social setting of the original readers. It is very unlikely that Paul meant to send his Roman readers to join the army, since most Christians then would not have been Roman citizens and thus ineligible for military service. Romans 13 follows a passage calling for peace and nonresistance to evil:

> Never pay back evil for evil. Let your aims be such as all count honourable. If possible, so far as it lies with you, live at peace with all. My dear friends, do not seek revenge, but leave a place for divine retribution; for there is a text which reads, "Vengeance is mine, says the Lord, I will repay." But there is another text: "If your enemy is hungry, feed him; if he is thirsty, give him a drink; by doing this you will heap live coals on his head." Do not let evil conquer you, but use good to conquer evil. (Rom 12:17–21)

We should not be deceived by chapter breaks, added much later, into separating this passage from Rom 13:1, which immediately follows it.

The Revised English Bible's translation of the following verse is: "It follows that anyone who rebels against authority is resisting a divine institution. . . ." All of this makes it much more likely that Paul is cautioning Roman Christians *against* taking up arms; that is, against joining in the armed rebellion against the government!

There is a puzzling passage in Luke's Gospel in which Jesus, on the way to his arrest, tells his disciples to provide swords:

> He said to them, "when I sent you out barefoot without purse or pack, were you ever short of anything?" "No," they answered. "It is different now," he said; "whoever has a purse had better take it with him, and his pack, too; and if he has no sword, let him sell his cloak and buy one. For scripture says, 'And he was reckoned among transgressors,' and this, I tell you, must be fulfilled in me; indeed, all that is written of me is reaching its fulfilment." "Lord," they said, "we have two swords here." "Enough!" he replied. (Luke 22:35–38)

This passage has been used frequently in the pacifism debate: If Jesus had not meant his disciples to kill, why would he have told them now to arm themselves? Is he not preparing them for legitimate self-defense after Pentecost? But, Yoder asks, how could two swords be "enough" for twelve disciples travelling two by two?[40]

One possible reading of Jesus's motives in arming his disciples, of course, is to take him at his word—it is to fulfill the prophecy found in Isa 53:12:

> Therefore I shall allot him a portion with the great, and he will share the spoil with the mighty, because he exposed himself to death and was reckoned among transgressors, for he bore the sins of many and interceded for transgressors.

If Jesus was to be taken as a criminal, to be executed by crucifixion, the punishment for insurrection, the symbols of armed rebellion in the hands of his followers would be appropriate. Two swords might not be enough for defense, but plenty for conviction.

Another passage often used us the Johannine story of Jesus "cleansing the temple" (John 2:13–17). The usefulness of this text for justifying violence depends on a once common but now generally rejected translation. According to the King James Version, Jesus, "when he had made a scourge of small cords, he drove them all [the money changers and those that sold oxen, sheep, and doves] out of the temple, and the

---

40. Yoder, *Politics of Jesus*, 45 n. 44.

sheep and the oxen . . . (v. 15). This act of physical violence by Jesus is then said to set a precedent for his followers.

However, more recent translations make it only the animals that are driven out: "Making a whip of cords, he drove all of them out of the temple, both the sheep and the cattle" (NRSV).[41] Thus, the story is better read as a nonviolent action campaign against the temple authorities.

So these passages, long used as proof texts against pacifists, support contrary readings that are at least as plausible, and perhaps more so.

Conclusion: Theology and Cosmology

Yoder claims that the ministry of Jesus has not only social-ethical and historical significance, but *cosmic* significance:

> Then to follow Jesus does not mean renouncing effectiveness. . . . It means that in Jesus we have a clue to which kinds of causation, which kinds of community-building, which kinds of conflict management, go with the grain of the cosmos, of which we know, as Caesar does not, that Jesus is both the Word (the inner logic of things) and the Lord ("sitting at the right hand"). It is not that we begin with a mechanistic universe and then look for cracks and chinks where a little creative freedom might sneak in (for which we would then give God credit): it is that we confess the deterministic world to be enclosed within, smaller than, the sovereignty of the God of the Resurrection and Ascension.[42]
>
> . . . "cross and resurrection" designates not only a few days' events in first-century Jerusalem but also the shape of the cosmos.[43]

Recall that the core theory of a research program is said to be metaphysical—it tells us about the nature of the reality with which the science is concerned. So here we see the metaphysical claim standing behind Yoder's nonviolent ethic, but also unifying and making sense of the whole of Christian teaching, of Yoder's doctrinal "research program."

41. For a discussion of the problematic aspects of the Greek grammar, see ibid., chap. 10.

42. Ibid., 246.

43. Ibid., 160.

In Yoder's works, then, written over the course of his career as historian, theologian, and ethicist, Christian pacifists find the systematic theological justification for their stance: it is a reflection of the very nature of the cosmos.[44]

44. Much of this article is a slight revision of material excerpted from Nancey Murphy and George F. R. Ellis, *On the Moral Nature of the Universe: Theology, Cosmology, and Ethics* (Minneapolis: Fortress, 1996) chap. 8. I thank the press for permission to publish it here. A much shorter version was published in *Faith and Freedom* (March 1996) 3–11. I also thank James Wm. McClendon Jr. for helpful suggestions for the revision.

4

The War of the Lamb: Postmodernity
and Yoder's Eschatological Genealogy of Morals

P. TRAVIS KROEKER

Postmodernity is an inheritance bequeathed by Nietzsche, who attempted to think through to their nihilistic conclusions the assumptions of
modern Western culture. The foundational assumption of modernity,
Nietzsche asserts, is the death of God[1]—that is, the death of a transcendent suprasensory reality that grounds and measures the visible world
of appearances. The death of God is the cultural deed of the modern
West; it entails the disempowerment of a divinely ordained or sovereign good to bestow life, truth and moral order. The God of Judaism
and Christianity, the transcendent Good of Platonic philosophy no
longer offer hope and consolation, no longer orient modern thought
and action. Nietzsche's prophetic word calls us to take responsibility for
this deed, and to overcome the destructive vestiges of dead traditional
idolatries especially in the realm of morality and cultural creation.

Here lies the agenda of postmodernity. Morality, like truth and
reason, is historically contingent and without final purpose. All moral
meaning is the creative expression of particular, culturally and historically situated human wills. We postmoderns will act in the full recognition that human beings must shape their own meaning by cultural

1. See Friedrich Nietzsche's parable "The Madman," in *The Gay Science*, trans.
Walter Kaufmann (New York: Vintage, 1974) section 125 (cf. 343f.); and cf. Martin
Heidegger's illuminating reflection, "The Word of Nietzsche: 'God is Dead'," in *The
Question Concerning Technology and Other Essays* (New York: Harper & Row, 1977)
53–114.

self-creation without appealing to some higher *hinterweltlich* power for support. Indeed, such appeals are disloyal to the human spirit; they devalue this world and worldly responsibility. The only real question for postmodern culture, in Nietzsche's judgment, is will we become the shrunken-souled "last men" who remain sick with nihilistic despair and *ressentiment* and who seek to inoculate themselves against a harsh chaotic reality by indulging in cheap, homogeneous bourgeois pleasures.[2] Or will it be possible to overcome this modern lassitude of the spirit in order to become culturally creative once again without consoling illusions and false hopes? Will it be possible to reverse the spiritual dissolution of modernity by founding a higher, healthier order of values? Can we give birth to the *Übermensch*? Nietzsche's project is to offer a diagnosis and a cure for the spiritual illness of modernity so that a postmodern culture of spiritual health can be born.

Key to this project is the critique of conventional morality, for at the heart of the human and cultural illness is the spirit of self-deception and revenge, the unwillingness to take full responsibility for who and what we are. Conventional morality not only masks our spiritual illness, it aids and abets it.

Anabaptists may celebrate Nietzsche's (and the Nietzschean) critiques of modern idolatries—especially the pretensions of modern scientific reason to ground and measure all true knowledge of reality and moral order[3]—and welcome his call for a dramatic, historical understanding of morality that overtly recognizes that it is engaged in an agonistic spiritual and cultural struggle. However, they will have to wrestle seriously with Nietzsche's critique of Christianity, for a central

2. See Nietzsche, "Thus Spake Zarathustra," in *The Portable Nietzsche*, ed. and trans. Walter Kaufmann (New York: Penguin, 1968) 129f.

3. Nietzsche comments on the prejudicial "faith" of modern materialistic natural scientists, which assumes reality can be measured objectively by human reason if only the correct methods are applied: "What? Do we really want to permit existence to be degraded for us like this—reduced to a mere exercise for a calculator and an indoor diversion for mathematicians? Above all, one should not wish to divest existence of its *rich ambiguity*: that is a dictate of good taste, gentlemen, the taste of reverence for everything that lies beyond your horizon. That the only justifiable interpretation of the world should be one in which *you* are justified because one can continue to work and do research scientifically in *your* sense (you really mean, mechanistically?)—an interpretation that permits counting, calculating, weighing, seeing, and touching, and nothing more—that is a crudity and naiveté, assuming that it is not a mental illness [*Geisteskrankheit*], an idiocy." *The Gay Science*, section 373.

presumption of his postmodern hypothesis is that the Christian drama and narrative is a major cause of the spiritual sickness, a workshop of idols that stinks of many lies.[4] And while Anabaptists may agree with Nietzsche about many aspects of conventional cultural Christianity, there is no easy way to get around Nietzsche's damning assessment of the perspective expressed in Menno Simons' favorite epigraphical verse from 1 Cor 3:11: "For other foundation can no one lay than is laid . . . Jesus Christ." This foundation is indeed historical and dramatic, but it is also eschatological, and it entails a cosmic authority that judges and measures all reality—with reference to an image that Nietzsche despises—the slain Lamb—and therefore a wisdom that celebrates weakness, foolishness, lowliness, meekness.

Anabaptists proclaim a transcendent and cosmic moral measure, but it is evident only to those who take the faithful path of discipleship, following in the way of the crucified Messiah. Such an eschatological genealogy of morals, engaged in a polemic against the pretensions of modernity—but also of Nietzschean post-modernity—is evident in the work of John Howard Yoder. I wish to offer a few reflections on this battle and the weapons and strategies of each side.

Nietzsche and Yoder on Genealogy: Rome versus Judea

Nietzsche's genealogy of morals is designed as a counter-practice to modern moralism, which pretends a kind of detached objective scholarship (morality "in general") that is nevertheless particular and historical. Conventional moralists remain deliberately blind to the historical evolution of moral ideas as rooted in particular dramatic enactments and embodiments of human agency and valuing. Hence Nietzsche's approach is philological (rather than abstractly conceptual) and physiological (rather than strictly psychological). It is designed to show that morality is always tied to embodied human judgments—ways of seeing and naming what is valued in the world within the changing circumstances and bodily conditions of experience.[5] Nietzsche asks not "what

4. See Nietzsche, *Genealogy of Morals*, trans. W. Kaufmann and R. J. Hollingdale (New York: Vintage, 1967) I, 14. German edition: *Zur Genealogie der Moral, Nietzsche's Werke*, Bd. VII (Stuttgart: Alfred Kroner Verlag, 1921).

5. Nietzsche, *Genealogy of Morals*, Preface; I, 2, 17.

is morality?" but "which morality" are we talking about, where does it come from (*who* invented it, *how* and under what conditions)? In doing so he keeps in view the *polemical* (the subtitle of *On the Genealogy of Morals* is *Eine Streitschrift*) character of the enterprise: doing ethics always entails the enactment and rank ordering of moral judgment; it is never a neutral enterprise.[6] *On the Genealogy of Morals*, then, is Nietzsche's polemical presentation of his ideas on the *origin* (*Herkunft*) of our moral prejudices (*Vorurteile*) in the attempt to understand who we are, under what conditions our moral language and judgments were created, and what life or vitality or "value" they possess.

John Howard Yoder shares this approach to ethics as dramatic, historical, embodied and polemical, and especially on the lookout for taken-for-granted moral assumptions that represent a danger to real life and human, cultural health.[7] Yet the drama Yoder engages is not Nietzsche's "Dionysian drama of 'The Destiny of the Soul,'"[8] the *Untergang* of the heroic soul exploring and doing battle with its own spiritual sickness in order to rise to higher cultural heights. The re-birth Yoder envisions is found in the apocalyptic drama of the war of the Lamb depicted in the words of the seer of Patmos—the author and text most closely identified with spiritual sickness by Nietzsche, who calls it "the most wanton of all literary outbursts that vengefulness has on its conscience."[9] We might note the context of Nietzsche's polemical judgment is his description of the battle between Judea and Rome, a battle in which Yoder would seem to take precisely the opposite side—Judea against Rome. Obviously, then, Yoder does not interpret the battle in the same terms as does Nietzsche, and it is here that Yoder makes an important Anabaptist contribution to understanding healthy Christianity over against its sick moral and cultural forms. The diagnostic criteria

6. In this regard Nietzsche's Calliclean frankness is much to be preferred over the Polus-like pretence of modesty exhibited by certain post-modern followers of Nietzsche, such as Michel Foucault or Jacques Derrida, who appear at times to "stand nowhere."

7. I take Yoder's incisive critique of the typological method employed by H. Richard Niebuhr's *Christ and Culture* to expose precisely this set of issues. See "How H. Richard Niebuhr Reasoned: A Critique of Christ and Culture," in Glen Stassen, D. M. Yeager, John H. Yoder, *Authentic Transformation: A New Vision of Christ and Culture* (Nashville: Abingdon, 1996).

8. Nietzsche, *Genealogy of Morals*, Preface, 7.

9. Ibid., I, 16.

for interpreting sickness and health are developed with reference to different dramas, differing visions of life and its meaning.

Nietzsche understands the spiritual sickness of nihilistic modernity to be rooted in the victory of Judea over ancient Roman virtue—"consider to whom one bows down in Rome itself today."[10] But this representation of the "priestly type" is for Yoder no spiritual victory; indeed such a victor can only be so identified by Roman criteria. The desire of the Christian church to rule the world by the sword of Caesar is an idolatrous temptation. When successfully enacted, it becomes tremendously destructive of the human spirit and of human community and culture. Nietzsche's portrayal of the battle is not historical enough or subtle enough in pursuing the problem "value for what"[11] of the Christian gospel. If we are to understand the battle of postmodernity more objectively—that is, with a greater variety of perspectives in the service of understanding[12]—we will do well to consider Yoder's alternative genealogical account of morals.[13]

Yoder's task can be interpreted as taking a closer look at the evolution of Jewish and Christian moral conceptions in history. Who is the opponent in Yoder's polemical genealogy? Not altogether unlike

10. Ibid.

11. Ibid., I, 17 note.

12. Ibid., III, 12.

13. I realize that to use the term "genealogy" in regard to Yoder's work is potentially misleading, especially in light of the further development of Nietzsche's concept by postmodern "new Nietzscheans" such as Gilles Deleuze and Michel Foucault. See especially Deleuze, *Nietzsche and Philosophy*, trans. H. Tomlinson (London: Athlone, 1983); Foucault, "Nietzsche, Genealogy, History," in Language, *Counter-Memory, Practice: Selected Essays and Interviews*, ed. D. Bouchard (Ithaca: Cornell University Press, 1977). Foucault's work in particular is taken as the genealogical model of moral inquiry by Alasdair MacIntyre in his published version of the Gifford Lectures, *Three Rival Versions of Moral Enquiry: Encyclopedia, Genealogy, and Tradition* (Notre Dame: University of Notre Dame Press, 1990). Of course, Foucault's reading of genealogy is greatly indebted to Nietzsche, but it is possible I think to argue that it is less serious, that its cheerfulness is less a "Dionysian drama" than a Menippean carnival (the parodic and farcical use of history is the primary mark of the genealogist in Foucault's treatment; see 16of. of "Nietzsche, Genealogy, History"). In any case, the meaning of the genealogical approach to morals as I am using it is broader than is suggested in MacIntyre's typology, and need not exclude the marks of tradition or the conditions for "answerability" in speech and action in community. Thus it is possible, I think, to use genealogy also *against* Nietzsche even while affirming aspects of his genealogical strategy.

Nietzsche's opponent—conventional modern moralism, indeed conventional mainstream *Christian* moralism, blind to its own poisonous assumptions; especially its assumptions about power, responsibility, and the origin of good and evil. Like Nietzsche, Yoder will examine this history with new questions and new eyes so as to articulate a new "saving tale" (or at least a novel re-telling and possibly a re-enactment of an old story—not Dionysius, but the crucified Christ) within the modern–postmodern context. And Yoder will do so in a manner that exposes the motives of conventional Christian moralists: pretending to be neutral and pious, they have really stacked the ethics deck by reading their distorted priestly concepts back into the Christian origins of morality.

The sickness here is a desire for worldly power that, in the name of general concepts of "responsibility" and "justice," willfully blinds itself to the true spiritual source of power. Like Nietzsche, then, Yoder seeks a cure for modern (and postmodern) nihilism in which human beings have become mere passive *spectators* of their own inner life, rather than vital and willing *actors* in the multi-valent, polyglot, pluralistic historical drama of existence.[14] Modern moralism, the vision of the mainstream priestly types, is "shrunken"—lacking creative love and imagination, stuck in reactive rancor and the casuistry of retributive justice, focused on false divided worlds rather than attuned to the true power of life itself.

Yes, with all this Yoder could agree. And yet, he takes the opposite side in Nietzsche's "Rome versus Judea" and offers a very different narrative reading of the battle, the illness, and the cure—with reference to a very different representative life, namely (to quote Nietzsche), "This Jesus of Nazareth, the incarnate gospel of love, this 'Redeemer' who brought blessedness and victory to the poor, the sick, and the sinners. . . ."[15] Of course, for Nietzsche this is precisely the sickness itself and can only be understood by him as yet another (deeper) form of *ressentiment* fueled by *divine* retributive justice. Here is an unreal and yet universal moralism that "de-natures" the strong and *inverts* the active, value-pos-

14. See especially Yoder's critical reflections on "establishment" epistemology (rooted in the "Christendom assumption" that there is some "single publicly accessible system of validation and rationality") and his own proposal of what could be called "missionary perspectivism," in "On Not Being Ashamed of the Gospel: Particularity, Pluralism, and Validation," *Faith and Philosophy* 9:3 (1992) 285–300.

15. Nietzsche, *Genealogy of Morals*, I, 8.

iting eye;[16] it is a story that leads to world-weariness, hatred of humanity, *contemptus mundi*. Why? I believe John Milbank is correct when he suggests that it is because Nietzsche ultimately accepts the Roman story of heroic virtue[17] (evident in the aphorism from *Zarathustra* interpreted in Essay III of *Genealogy of Morals*: "Unconcerned, mocking, violent—thus wisdom wants *us*: she is a woman and always loves only a warrior"). Here the *libido dominandi*, the violent will to power constitutes the essence (*wesen*)[18] of healthy human nature. Hence for Nietzsche, vengeful justice that destroys the noble soul and culture can only be self-overcome (*Selbstaufhebung*)[19] by going beyond the dividing, paralyzing demands of the (reactive, moral) law. One must by sheer *willpower* struggle for clearer vision by warring against reactive feelings, training the eye to look outward creatively once again.

For Yoder, the way beyond the Law—by which the Law is fulfilled beyond the divided moralistic knowledge of good and evil, friend and enemy—is the imitation of Christ, the wisdom of God and the power of God. The self-emptying motion of Christ (the *kenosis* of Philippians 2) makes possible the life-enhancing expression of the overflowing fullness of divine love, which seeks not to escape embodied, worldly existence but to redeem it in all its diverse goodness. Hence the transcendent

---

16. Ibid., I, 10–11.

17. See John Milbank, *Theology and Social Theory: Beyond Secular Reason* (Oxford: Blackwell, 1990) chapter 10. While agreeing with Milbank's interpretation of the narrative source of Nietzsche's ethic as heroic virtue, I also agree with David Toole's insightful argument that (*pace* Milbank) Nietzsche is not a nihilist, but rather a philosopher of tragedy who seeks to overcome nihilism. See Toole, *Waiting for Godot in Sarajevo: Theological Reflections on Nihilism, Tragedy, and Apocalypse* (Boulder, CO: Westview, 1998) chapters 3–4. Nevertheless, the kind of tragedy Nietzsche comes to affirm is precisely identified by Deleuze as the *heroic* expression of Dionysius "in which existence *justifies* all that it affirms, including suffering, instead of being itself justified by suffering" (Deleuze, *Nietzsche and Philosophy*, 18), i.e., one heroically and innocently affirms the chaotic, conflictual play of life forces without seeking some cosmic reconciliation or harmony that will redeem the suffering entailed in the violent clash of wills. See Deleuze, *Nietzsche and Philosophy*, chapter 1. This helps clarify the centrality of Nietzsche's statement of opposition—"Dionysius versus the crucified"—which Toole helpfully elaborates in his book as the decision "between the tragic affirmation of chance and the apocalyptic affirmation that what looks like chance is in fact the work of God" (Toole, *Waiting for Godot in Sarajevo*, 206).

18. Nietzsche, *Genealogy of Morals*, II, 12.

19. Ibid., II, 10; III, 27.

power of God does its work "from below" in embodied, particular, self-giving love.

Yoder's Counter-Narrative: Slave-Revolt in Morals?

The importance of apocalyptic symbolism and the slain Lamb in Yoder's work is well known.[20] The particularity of the Church's identity is consistently tied by Yoder to this cosmic vision of God's sovereign rule in creation. The controversial claim that founds Christianity is that this divine cosmic rule made its definitive appearance on earth two millennia ago in the form of a humble servant with a very short public career during which he rejected virtually every available political option, only to be killed nevertheless as a political figure, and to found a new political community—the Church—as the social carrier of that form of cosmic power and authority. For Yoder this means that the form of God's rule is here publicly revealed in the world for all to see, in a form that is neither coercive nor juridical, neither externally imposed nor visibly triumphal—it is visibly characterized by the cross. It is as the slain Lamb that Christ is worshiped as king by the Church in that vivid worship scene of the heavenly court described by John of Patmos, and this symbolism is laden with socio-political meaning and consequence.

The slain Lamb who alone is worthy to receive power is therefore the key to discerning the meaning of history and its ultimate direction. Indeed, this is the "good news" that constitutes the witness and mission of the Christian Church on the earth. I cannot here represent the richness of Yoder's exegetical and historical ruminations in fleshing out his interpretation of this vision. I will focus on two significant foci in his work in order to link them critically to the Nietzschean postmodern problematic as I have sketched it above. The first is his more

20. See, for example, the concluding chapter of Yoder, *The Politics of Jesus: Vicit Agnus Noster*, 2nd ed. (Grand Rapids: Eerdmans, 1994), entitled "The War of the Lamb"; and his 1988 presidential address to the Society of Christian Ethics, "To Serve our God and to Rule the World," in *The Royal Priesthood: Essays Ecclesiological and Ecumenical*, ed. Michael Cartwright (Grand Rapids: Eerdmans, 1994) 127–40. See also Yoder's reflections on apocalypse in "Ethics and Eschatology," *Ex Auditu* 6 (1990) 119–28; and the illuminating discussion by David Toole, *Waiting for Godot in Sarajevo*, chapters 7 and 8, which draw upon Yoder to develop a metaphysics of apocalypse and an apocalyptic politics.

recent reference to the prophetic tradition as depicting what he calls the "Jeremian shift"[21] to show that the political pattern practiced by Jesus was "no new beginning from scratch" but a renewal and extension of a "Hebrew hope" expressed from Moses through the Old Testament prophets.[22] The second is Yoder's critique of Christendom political ethics (whose heir is liberal Christian modernity), the various forms of which he habitually labels "Constantinianism." In these two representative symbols we will be able to trace Yoder's alternative to both modern and postmodern narrative visions.

The messianic Hebrew hope represented by Jesus is the constitution of a shalom community under the rule of God, a hope that by Jeremiah's time had been fatally betrayed by Israel's failed kingship experiment. Yoder clearly advocates the "antiroyal" account of the deuteronomic historian that retells Israel's story from within the paradigm shift to diaspora ethics clearly expressed in the book of Jeremiah—most pithily in Jeremiah's letter to the exiles in Babylon in Jer 29:7, where he says, "seek the peace of the city where I have scattered you . . . for in its peace you will find your peace." In his last book Yoder makes extensive reference to Stephan Zweig's *Jeremias*, a poetic retrieval of the diaspora paradigm of Jewish social life and identity written during World War I. Like diaspora Jews, Christians are called to live out their identity in a condition of "cosmopolitan homelessness."[23] The Jeremian approach that sees the scattering of the people and indeed their exile to Babylon (the paradigm of pagan political idolatry) as "mission" prefigures Christ's attitude to the Gentile world.

The mission of the Church, argues Yoder, is precisely to witness to the flaws in Babel-like unity, rooted in coercive, centralized, sacral authority, the idolatrous politics of Empire that substitutes human for divine kingship and that tries to take charge of human history via external conquest. The rule of divine love and harmony represents a very different pattern of ecumenicity: a pattern of creative diversity, dialogue, a community that welcomes outsiders, and that understands leadership as servanthood. In the Jeremian shift this is represented by cultural lin-

21. See especially Yoder, *For the Nations: Essays Public and Evangelical* (Grand Rapids: Eerdmans, 1997), chapters 2 and 3; and *Royal Priesthood*, 133.

22. Yoder, *For the Nations*, 141f.

23. Yoder, *For the Nations*, 51.

guistic plurality (diaspora culture is polyglot and on the move, not univocal and sovereign), the creation of a synagogue rather than a temple culture (the focus is now on the interpretation of the story in ever new cultural situations, not an altar that stands in cultic support of a sacral regime); it is the building of God's city and God's rule "from below."

This exilic movement takes Israel's exodus from "cosmological empire"[24] into the further recognition that spiritual existence under God can take different socio-political forms, and is not to be identified with a particular spatio-temporal regime. What is at stake here is an understanding of how God's agency is experienced and at work to transform the world. The Jeremian shift represents a movement not only away from pragmatic kingship as the model of how shalom community is built; it is a movement toward the prophetic-eschatological recognition of a new covenant of the heart in which God's rule is universally established.[25] Diaspora ethics signal an end to "compact collectivism" toward a new understanding of participation in God's active rule, and this direction is definitively proclaimed by Christ who is the agent and embodiment of that rule.

And yet, says Yoder, this rule—while focused on the ultimate transformation of all things by divine action (the eschatological completion of history)—is active in embodied community here and now. For Christians the social forms of worship of God as sovereign will take a similar form to diaspora Judaism, but with particular reference to the imitation of the crucified Jesus as Messiah. The key to moral discernment will be to live out of the New Testament vision for community life established by Jesus. The focus here is not a structure of hierarchical authority or institutional establishment or doctrinal creed, but rather the sociological (i.e., visible, embodied) and liturgical (i.e., dramatic, particular, communally focused) "marks" of the community that believes Christ represents the cosmic rule of God.[26] For Christians the

24. I borrow the term from Eric Voegelin, *Order and History*, vol. 4, *The Ecumenic Age* (Baton Rouge: Louisiana State University Press, 1974).

25. Oliver O'Donovan develops this interpretation of the significance of the "Jeremian shift" in his recent *The Desire of the Nations: Rediscovering the Roots of Political Theology* (Cambridge: Cambridge University Press, 1996) 73–81. He states: "From that point on an element of confessional voluntarism enters into Israel's sense of itself" (79). I will return to this point below.

26. The marks of this body politic are spelled out by Yoder most clearly in his

"body of Christ" is the social carrier of the mind of Christ, a *polis* that represents the rule of God for the nations.

Thus understood God's action is decidedly not *hinterweltlich* nor is God's rule ultimately construed in terms of juridical authority. Nor is its agent in the world represented as an "ascetic priest" filled with a reactive desire to rule over the unruly strong or to control history by moving it in the right direction. As Yoder's discussion of causality in the "War of the Lamb" chapter of *The Politics of Jesus* argues, the direction of history is precisely *not* under human control and the eschatological *telos* does not give us a managerial moral measure in a closed causal nexus. The cosmic causality revealed in the slain Lamb does not divide this world from some future or otherworldly ideal, however. Rather it reveals the dramatic nature of causality in all reality to be the drama of divine and human active, not reactive, love. This is the true natural life force that reveals the aristocratic warrior model to be the poison of life, fixated on power and using the gift of life to deny life. The slain Lamb exposes Nietzsche's strong, noble man to be the one engaged in "no-saying," in a "slave revolt" against the dramatic terms of worldly existence.

This becomes evident in Yoder's alternative account of "responsibility," where suffering love is not a strategy for success or an effective technique or tactic for getting one's way in an *essentially* violent or conflictual reality;[27] it is rather a matter of participation in life itself, the character of divine love. This character is embodied in the authority of Christ's *kenosis* and in the kenotic posture and "marks" of the body of Christ, in which differences are not obliterated in some stifling social straitjacket of homogeneous moral conventions. Rather differences can be welcomed and given voice as community is built freely and creatively "from below." The kenotic posture of "condescension" shows divine power taking the form of serving love. Such "slavery" can only

---

little book, *Body Politics: Five Practices of the Christian Community Before the Watching World* (Nashville: Discipleship Resources, 1992). See also *For the Nations*, chapters 2 and 12; and *The Priestly Kingdom: Social Ethics as Gospel* (Notre Dame: University of Notre Dame Press, 1984) chapter 1.

27. This is Nietzsche's claim in *Genealogy of Morals*: "*in itself*, of course, no injury, assault, exploitation, destruction can be 'unjust,' since life operates *essentially* . . . through injury, assault, exploitation, destruction and simply cannot be thought of at all without this character" (II, 11; cf. 12).

be understood as liberation from the compulsive constraints of egoistic power.

Here Yoder's critique of Constantinian Christianity, modern liberalism, and postmodern pluralism begins to come into view.[28] Yoder will refuse the various kinds of metaphysical and moral dualisms that divide up the cosmos into a "visible" pragmatic realm of conventional "responsibility" where the power of violence and external calculi of justice prevail, and an "invisible" spiritual realm where "religious" love and self-denial rule. The spiritual "mind of Christ" and the material "body of Christ" cannot be so divided. The Church cannot be understood as one limited social institution, somehow balanced by the different political and ethical roles of the state and other social institutions. For Yoder, Jesus's life is not only descriptive of how God's ultimate judgment reconciles sinful humanity in a heavenly peace; it is also descriptive of how that ultimate judgment is implemented provisionally in the earthly peace.[29] That is, Jesus's identity as cosmic ruler entails the very worldly enactment of the "Jeremian shift"—a non-sovereign, non-territorial self-definition.[30] Traditional or conventional royal ideology of whatever kind, insofar as it is linked to coercive external rule, has been eschatologically declared a failure even when it appears powerful and successful in the world.

For Yoder, then, the body of Christ is a voluntary community of shared discernment in which all are free to speak and act because all (in all their differences) are gifted and joined together in a new human identity—open in its life to creative divine agency. Such a community that practices forgiveness, love even (indeed especially) of enemies, and servant leadership models what *all* human communities are called to. It can *only* be sustained by the Church's doxological identity, shaped by its worship of the God revealed in Christ;[31] it is not sustained by any established or conventional juridical power. Such a church must therefore by definition be "free" and not authorized or established by any state, since the "responsibility" it practices presupposes voluntary (inner and outer,

28. See Yoder's account and critique of Constantinian and various "neo-Constantinian" positions in *Priestly Kingdom*, chapter 7.

29. See *For the Nations*, 210f.

30. *Royal Priesthood*, 133f.

31. See ibid., 109f., 128f.

visible and invisible) commitment to living out of its vision of divine kenotic, self-giving rule.[32]

It is not difficult to see how this vision stands in critical distinction from Constantinian or Christendom ethics. It should also be clear that this view of human freedom and responsibility in community under the rule of God is quite different from the abstract naked will of modern individualism and the political voluntarism of social contract theory. And yet Yoder's emphasis on voluntareity and the "free church" has recently been criticized in an important book on political theology by Oliver O'Donovan as being "neo-liberal," a freedom purchased at the expense of *belief*.[33] That is, Yoder's voluntareity is rooted in an intellectually flabby liberalism—or perhaps "postmodern liberalism"— that has lost confidence in truth claims and views all social doctrines as inherently coercive. However, for Yoder, the social body politic is precisely not so, and precisely because of its believing vision. It is not in the business of enacting and enforcing judicial authority—it proceeds on a different paradigm of divine rule and justice. It will therefore not alter its processes of and criteria for moral discernment when rulers join the church,[34] nor "employ" instrumentalities of power foreign to its own identity and calling.

And yet, there is something to O'Donovan's charge, though it should be otherwise formulated. Yoder has not adequately attended to or clarified the complex relationships between soul and society, the action of God to transform the will and vision of Christians and the action of God to redeem all of creation. To understand the role of the Church, the embodied mind of Christ, requires such noetic clarification. The great question here concerns how the eternal, spiritual, *invisible* wisdom of God is related to pragmatic political history and particular *visible* social communities (including the Church). In Yoder's insistent and consistent desire to separate "cross" language from personal moral and "psychic" questions,[35] in order to focus on more general social issues (such

32. See ibid., 245f., 265f.; and *Priestly Kingdom*, 22f.

33. See O'Donovan, *Desire of the Nations*, 221–24.

34. See *Priestly Kingdom*, 82f.

35. In his concern to distance himself from forms of unworldly or subjectivist "pietism" that neglect the worldly political claims of the Gospel (*For the Nations*, 143f.; *Royal Priesthood*, 131), Yoder has occasionally resorted to unnecessarily extreme formulations, such as the following: "The challenge to which the proclamation of Christ's

as war and peace) and political forms (the church meeting, patterns of conflict resolution, etc.), I believe he has lost sight of certain aspects of moral discernment that would allow for a better account of idolatrous "Roman" (or Constantinian) politics and how such temptations might be agonistically engaged also in the Church and the academy.[36]

The Platonic Diaspora: Athens and Jerusalem

So far we have been discussing mostly politics and the Church. Yet Yoder spent most of his career in the academy, and it also bears noting that "postmodernity" is largely an academic or at least intellectualist preoccupation. This is relevant because I think the academy, like the Church, is an institution devoted to practices not to be identified with any particular earthly political regime or social or cultural community. It too was the creation of a diaspora movement, an exodus from the

---

rule over the rebellious world speaks a word of grace is not a problem within the self but a split within the cosmos" (*Politics of Jesus*, 161). No less than "pietism" is such a formulation a distortion of the New Testament witness, where the fault line of sin runs through the cosmos, but also through the human self. A more adequate formulation is the following: "Let us posit as at least thinkable the alternate hypothesis that for Paul righteousness, either in God or in human beings, might more appropriately be conceived of as having cosmic or social dimensions. Such larger dimensions would not negate the personal character of the righteousness God imputes to those who believe; but by englobing the personal salvation in a fuller reality they would negate the individualism with which we understand such reconciliation" (*Politics of Jesus*, 215). The problem that remains here, I believe, is Yoder's (ironically liberal individualist) assumption that there is a "fuller reality" than the "personal" one. The point is rather to redefine what is personal in relation to its social and cosmic reality, in which our individual lives receive their fullest meaning and purpose. For my own attempt to do this in the context of Anabaptist theology, see my essay, "Anabaptists and Existential Theology," *Conrad Grebel Review* 17:2 (1999) 69–88.

36. For example, when Yoder says as he does in various places that society exists for the sake of the church—see especially *The Christian Witness to the State* (Newton, KS: Faith & Life Press, 1964) 12f.—he leaves himself open to the most pernicious of Christendom triumphalist ideologies. The church, from my reading of the New Testament, rather exists (as did Christ) for the sake of God's service in the world. How we *formulate* this point is crucial, and a proper formulation will of necessity be more attentive to the tension between visible and invisible church than Yoder is. Otherwise it will fall into a new form of "compact collectivism" that is non-ecumenical and dogmatically closed. *Any* worldly institutional form is limited and partial, not the whole and not the fulfillment of human existence—even the most faithful of churches remains a partial and sinful witness.

compact collectivism of the Greek city-state, prompted by an experience of revelation—a "noetic theophany" (as Eric Voegelin calls it[37]) in the Socratic soul. It is not accidental that Christians, like the Hellenistic Jews of antiquity, have appropriated the diaspora form of the academy—its language, practices, and disciplines. Platonic philosophy can help to clarify the problem of soul and society, the tension between the visible and invisible, in our attempt to formulate an adequate genealogy of Christian morality.

Here the Christian story will more explicitly engage Nietzsche's "Dionysian drama of the soul," but in terms that Nietzsche himself would reject. Plato is an enemy of postmodernism, even as Nietzsche viewed Socrates and Plato as the enemy, and for much the same reason that he so viewed Christ and the Church. That is, Plato too understands the moral drama of soul and society in terms of a theocentric cosmology where the "Good beyond being" orders all reality toward its transcendent, harmonious end. This is for Nietzsche the pernicious creation of the "inner man," the "soul" in which human beings declare war upon their instincts and thus their power—a creative act, says Nietzsche, that required the creation of divine spectators.[38] Such an act of self-violation, when carried too far (as in the case of Plato and Christianity, where the invisible divine world becomes the true reality that orders apparent reality) leads to a paralyzing denial of this-worldly power and reality—hostility to life and "ideals that slander the world"[39] of the sort depicted in John's Apocalypse. One's moral "answerability" (*Verantwortlichkeit*) becomes focused exclusively toward what is invisible and unreal.

What Nietzsche and many postmoderns object to here is the notion that there is a cosmic, all-embracing, reconciling truth beyond rhetorical particularity and worldly perspectivism. In regard to Plato's distinction between sophists (rhetoricians with no commitment to truth, only to the power of persuasion exercised in the power struggle of individual wills) and philosophers (who love divine wisdom and do not claim it as their own possession but seek it through the education of desire, speech, and deed), Nietzschean postmoderns are self-confessed sophists. They reject the intellectual ordering of psyche and polis with

37. See Eric Voegelin, *Ecumenic Age*, chapter 4.
38. Nietzsche, *Genealogy of Morals*, II, 16.
39. Ibid., II, 24.

reference to some transcendent Good known through the contemplative soul. Joyful Dionysian paganism rooted in orgiastic instinct and uninhibited aesthetic play must be recovered from the totalizing *Republic*-an rationality of sober Socrates.

For certain Jewish and Christian intellectuals this postmodern battle against (old, authoritarian, rationalist) Athens has paved the way for a return to liberating Jerusalem as the new philosophical city without foundations. Yoder has in certain ways aided and abetted such thinking, to the detriment of theological ethics. As Gillian Rose has argued, this postmodern move undermines the possibility for a critical, clarifying discussion of the ordered relationships between city, soul, and the sacred.[40] Yoder has tended to lump together the Platonic Christianity of classical theologians such as Augustine with Constantinian political theology in some unfortunate ways.[41] To call Augustine's city of God "otherworldly," representative of a personal pietistic Christianity that is content to leave the earthly city under the rule of empire politics,[42] can only be read as a deliberate distortion. Yoder is, after all, an historian seeking to overcome the historical blindness of moralists to the root causes of our cultural malaise. Is this perhaps an Anabaptist suspicion of intellectual power tied to establishment authorities? If so, I suppose one should be encouraged to see it so evident in an internationally eminent Notre Dame professor, as indeed it was evident also in that great Latin philosopher, Saint Augustine.

Unlike Yoder, however, Augustine did not allow that to prevent him from appropriating what he considered to be the great gifts and treasures of classical philosophy, and employing them in the service of the peace of Christ. Here Augustine remains a powerful resource for a Christian ethics that seeks the whole truth of what it means to worship the cosmic Christ and so to realize peace. Christians, argued Augustine, have much in common with and much to learn from Platonic philoso-

40. See Gillian Rose, *Judaism and Modernity: Philosophical Essays* (Oxford: Blackwell, 1993); and *Mourning Becomes the Law: Philosophy and Representation* (Cambridge University Press, 1996).

41. Note, for example, Yoder's Anabaptist description of the "fall of the church" as located "at the point of that fusion of church and society of which Constantine was the architect, Eusebius the priest, Augustine the apologete, and the Crusades and Inquisition the culmination" (*Royal Priesthood*, 89; cf. 154).

42. *For the Nations*, 82.

phy. Plato coined the term theology (*Republic*, Book II) and he transformed philosophy from a science of physical causality to the study of moral wisdom through the revelation of an invisible spiritual causality.[43] Of course Augustine also points out what he thinks is missing in the Platonists, a revelation of the perfect image of the invisible God, an image that would have surprised them by the form it took—a humble servant. Insofar as Christians worship God through the image of the suffering servant, their moral logic will reflect this. The "royal road" of spiritual liberation in the world is humble service, and this road is given to all peoples as a mystery not conceived in any human soul or culture.[44] Augustine is helpful in clarifying the relations between the Jewish and Greek diasporas with reference to Christ.

Rather than pursue that discussion here, however, I will turn to a New Testament writer whose letters were foundational for Augustine, Menno Simons, and Yoder—Paul the Apostle.[45] In 1 Corinthians the Hellenistically educated rabbi Paul ties the noetic concerns of the Greeks and the messianic hopes of the Jews to the eschatological revelation of the wisdom and power of God in the crucified Jesus.

It is clear from reading Paul's letters that he does not consider himself to be a systematic theologian, the custodian of a timeless deposit of doctrine, nor is he a systematic philosopher. Rather he is called to bear witness to a dramatic historical event: the incursion of divine wisdom and power into the world in order to cure it and restore it to health. This is what all Christians are called to be and do; Paul's first letter to the Corinthians is occasioned by their confusion over what this calling entails. They have been swayed by the eloquent and persuasive rhetoric of gnostic teachers, and this has divided them into ideological or intellectual camps headed by particular teachers. The quarrel concerns, precisely, who is the greatest *sophos*? Paul's message in 1 Corinthians

43. Augustine *City of God* 8.3; for the Socratic account of his experience in the search for a genealogy of morals, a more adequate account of spiritual causality and motivation, see the *Phaedo*, 95–102.

44. Augustine *City of God* 10.32.

45. Let us not forget what Nietzsche said of him: "Paul was the greatest of all apostles of vengeance," the "dysangelist" whose lying invention of God and spiritual causality is rooted in resentful rebellion against reality, and masks Paul's real desire which is to rule the world. See "The Antichrist," 42f. in *The Portable Nietzsche*, 616–56. Such a view of Paul is *au courant* in the fashionable Pauline scholarship of the postmodern liberal academy.

is to deflate human pretensions with reference to the cross, the hidden wisdom and power "of God" that is contrasted to the human possession of wisdom and noetic power throughout chapter 1. God is the subject, not the object of Paul's teaching, and the cross of Christ as the visible embodiment of God's wisdom makes a fool of worldly human wisdom. When it is turned into but another form of worldly wisdom, then it makes God and God's wisdom into but another human ideology, a self-justifying image, an idol—"*I* belong to Paul," or "*I* belong to Augustine," or "*I* belong to Yoder," or "*I* belong to Christ." At this point the worship of God has become the worship of a creature, a blinding and destructive form of life.

This is not, however (says Paul in chapter 2), to disparage wisdom. It is rather to suggest that divine wisdom is hidden, and not to be found in rhetorical eloquence or persuasive speech. Among the mature (*hoi teleioi*) we can speak of this eschatological wisdom beyond visible human sight. The agent of this hidden power that reveals the hidden meaning of the cross is the divine Spirit "of God" and "from God." And it is here that Paul delineates and "rank orders" various types of human being, spiritually discerned. The created human being is a *psychikos*, a living, willing, feeling, thinking being who is nevertheless fallen into the divided state of the knowledge of good and evil, a self-sufficient and thoroughly blind egoist. Unredeemed *psychikoi* then are really better described as *sarkikoi*, people of flesh, insofar as they are pulled toward the immediate, mortal, transitory realm of visible creation, the realm over which the human self has a measure of god-like knowledge, control and power. Such human beings live according to the flesh by trying to construct their own meaning in the world, make their own mark, take their own measure independent of the divine and invisible source of life. Such a life is sinful not because it is embodied but because it cannot see and embrace the spiritual meaning of bodily life—it ends up in strife (political, intellectual, ecclesial, and indeed with itself, as Romans 7 shows), a strife that by its very nature *negates* what is good, the power to affirm and celebrate life. No innocence is possible here without complete self-deception.

By contrast Paul identifies the *pneumatikos*, the spiritually mature person who is oriented by the divine Spirit toward the invisible (hidden and mysterious) divine wisdom. Indeed the Spirit not only enables the inner apprehension of divine truth but provides the very language that makes conversation about it possible (2:13). Once again, this spiritual condition is not disembodied, just as the life of the flesh is not non-spiritual. But there is present a different kind of discernment about the meaning of bodily life, a different mind (*nous*), the *nous* of Christ. This inner mind makes judgments about the whole range of bodily life; the hidden wisdom of the cross of Christ relates as much to personal intimate questions of sexuality as to the questions about law courts and civil religion. Without the inner purification of the heart and mind, without proper spiritual orientation of mature *pneumatikoi*, the rule of Christ or the rule of Paul (as Yoder calls "binding and loosing" and the "open meeting" respectively) are subject to the same distortions as any other earthly, fleshly forms of rule. No visible form of any kind can guarantee the proper bodily enactment of the mind of Christ, since God's wisdom remains precisely hidden.

Furthermore, as Paul also argues in 1 Corinthians, no single person or group or perspective or charism can claim to *possess* knowledge of God's wisdom—it always remains a complete gift (8:2–3). In contrast to the "puffing up" of noetic insight, divine love "builds up" by taking the focus away from doctrine and rhetorical brilliance or dialectical ability and placing it on real other human beings. Love, which is the freedom to serve God and neighbor "from below," brings the other into my field of vision not as economic or intellectual competitor, not as ethnic or cultural or gendered "other," but as my sister or brother who represents Christ (8:12). To participate in this renewed field of vision requires a spiritual death, death to the idolatrous, falsely externalized symbols, creeds and authorities that *prevent* communication and block the transforming work of the divine Spirit. This is the way out of the illness of *ressentiment*, petty quarreling, the paralysis of self-obsessed *gnosis*, the juridical model of righteousness. It is the way of serving love rooted in the gift of life itself, the power of cosmic love. This also represents the re-birth of dialogical community where consciousness or soul, the *inner* or *hidden* life of human beings, is not hermetically sealed within the individual skull of a "subject" but is found above all in the shared "mind of Christ." Here all perspectives are nurtured to build up the conscience of each and of all in *mutual* responsibility and service. This process is also abundantly *personal*—as one should expect in a cosmos created and sustained by a personal God whose rule is embodied in person: the slain servant.

With this, I trust, Yoder could finally agree. We do not need a rhetorically brilliant postmodern theology or postmodern Christianity that "out-narrates" all rivals, which is, after all, another form of the Constantinian temptation. What we need are disciples of the slain Lamb who are prepared to follow in obedience in their daily lives—in their thoughts, speech, and deeds, without pretension, without boasting, without rancor. Such an ethic of conscience walks, not by the external juridical sight of guilt and punishment, but by faith, a faith that all created reality will be drawn up through death into eschatological completion, the "all in all" of divine love.

5

Foucault, Genealogy, Anabaptism:
Confessions of an Errant Postmodernist

PETER C. BLUM

Whoever fights monsters should see to it that in the process he does not
become a monster.

   —Nietzsche[1]

I

My purpose in this essay is to share with you my experience, as a self-
identified Anabaptist Christian, of reading some so-called postmodern
social thought, especially that of Michel Foucault. I would like to begin,
however, with some comments on the problematic terms of my title.

    I have very little interest in clarifying exactly what postmodernism
is, partly because I simply find that project uninteresting, and partly
because I don't believe postmodernism *is* anything, exactly. It seems
fair, nonetheless, that we allow that there are postmodernists, inasmuch
as there are a bunch of scholarly folk nowadays who refer to themselves
as such. The situation here seems to me analogous, in fact, to that of the
term "Christianity." I'm often inclined to think that there isn't anything
that Christianity *is* exactly, yet there are and have been numerous folk
who refer to themselves as Christians, including myself. Indeed, many

1. Friedrich Nietzsche, *Beyond Good and Evil: Prelude to a Philosophy of the Future,*
trans. Walter Kaufmann (New York: Vintage, 1966) 89.

people who are not focally concerned about whether or not they are Christian are routinely categorized as such, because of the places they go, the books they read, the habits they exhibit, or the people they sup with. It is in this manner, roughly, that I sometimes find myself being thought of, or even thinking of myself, as a postmodernist.

The sense in which I am an *errant* postmodernist is a bit more complicated. I am errant theoretically, inasmuch as I am inclined *not* to commit to postmodernism precisely as "ism." The thinkers who inspire me, who are often called postmodernist, seem to me consistently to question the very possibility of a full-fledged "ism." Nietzsche wrote that "the will to a system is a lack of integrity,"[2] and I strongly suspect that he was right about this (among other things). When I look at various attempts to articulate postmodernism as an "ism," as the systematic avoidance of system, as a theory that undermines all theories, I suspect that there is a joke being circulated. Nietzsche gets the joke, and so do Derrida and Foucault, as far as I can tell. The funny thing is that many who try to tell the joke do not seem to get it. If I treat my postmodernism as an "ism," then I have not gotten the joke either.[3]

Now, one might suggest that my anti-"ism"-ism is exactly what makes me a real, genuine, certified postmodernist. Rather than pursue the laughter that lies in that direction, I will simply move on for now. I will note, in passing, that there are other senses in which I am errant. I believe that there are no absolute foundations, yet I constantly fight the temptation to make of this very insight an absolute foundation. I am aware of the circularity of human understanding, yet I tirelessly seek noncircular ways to enlighten others of this very idea. I know that the Enlightenment has run off its road—into a different ditch, perhaps, than that of which Lessing wrote. Still, the old Enlightenment clearly remains as one of the armies at war within my intellectual members.

I should also note that my semantic puzzlement does not subside when we turn to the word "Anabaptist." With the increasing credence

2. Friedrich Nietzsche, *The Portable Nietzsche*, trans. and ed. Walter Kaufmann (New York: Viking Penguin, 1954) 470.

3. I have been pushed in the direction of appreciating inconsistency as a virtue not only by Foucault and Nietzsche, but also by Kierkegaard, and more particularly by Leszek Kolakowski. Cf. Kolakowski, "In Praise of Inconsistency," in *Toward a Marxist Humanism: Essays on the Left Today*, trans. Jane Zielonko Peel (New York: Grove Press, 1968) 211–20.

that is apparently given to so-called "polygenesis" by historians of Anabaptism, along with increasing recognition of the "theology-ladenness" of various attempts to define Anabaptism,[4] it seems we may at least consider the possibility that there is not anything in particular that Anabaptism *is*. Being neither an historian nor a theologian, but only a social theorist, I have the luxury of leaving this matter aside as outside the realm of my expertise. This implies, of course, that I otherwise speak within my expertise, and I hope you will not take that implication too seriously.

One more problematic term: "confessions." It is a term that I am probably misusing rather badly. What I intend to convey is not that my comments here carry some special sort of intellectual or spiritual weight (like Rousseau's or Augustine's), nor that you can expect anything embarrassingly steamy or aberrant (as in "Confessions of an Amish Cocaine Dealer"). Rather, I intend to convey that my remarks about Foucault and Anabaptism arise from very personal ruminations, and I have chosen to present them as such, rather than placing myself at some rhetorical remove from the matters at hand. Whether this approach is premodern, modern, postmodern, hypermodern, or whatever else, I will leave for you to decide (if you care). As Foucault writes: "Do not ask who I am and do not ask me to remain the same: leave it to our bureaucrats and our police to see that our papers are in order. At least spare us their morality when we write."[5]

Whether my comments are in any sense "Anabaptist," in the end, is probably the issue of greater concern to me. "Confession" here carries this sense as well: I may adopt a playful postmodern tone herein, but I do not wish thereby simply to distance myself from accountability.

4. The seminal article for "polygenesis" discussions of Anabaptist origins is James M. Stayer, Werner O. Packull, and Klaus Deppermann, "From Monogenesis to Polygenesis: The Historical Discussion of Anabaptist Origins," *Mennonite Quarterly Review* 49 (1975) 83–122. For some particularly interesting examples of subsequent reflection on theological "uses" of Anabaptist history, see J. Denny Weaver, "The Anabaptist Vision: A Historical or a Theological Future?" *Conrad Grebel Review* 13 (1995) 69–86, and the essays in John D. Roth, ed., *Refocusing a Vision: Shaping Anabaptist Character in the 21st Century* (Goshen, IN: Mennonite Historical Society, 1995).

5. Michel Foucault, *The Archaeology of Knowledge*, trans. A. M. Sheridan Smith (New York: Pantheon, 1972) 17.

II

What has drawn me to the work of Michel Foucault, more than any-thing else, is his stubborn refusal to be a theorist. The initial capital letter is important here. I do not advance the wildly implausible claim that there is no theory in Foucault's writings in any sense. In stating that Foucault is not a theorist, I am drawing attention to his obstinate avoidance of overarching or all-encompassing theoretical consistency, and especially to his evasion of the role of intellectual guru or "ex-pert." Among the more putatively vicious elements of Foucault's sup-posed "relativism" is his unwillingness (or inability) to outline positive alternatives to the discursive and institutional frameworks that are undermined by his historical critiques. To many readers, the dark, un-remittingly deconstructive tone of Foucault's thought appears inimical to any Christian outlook, including an Anabaptist outlook. My own reading of Foucault, however, has led me to conclude that this appear-ance is only superficial.

As I have been reading and teaching Foucault[6] for the last several years, I have been struck by how the idea of *particularity* provides a good pedagogical fulcrum for beginning to understand him. I choose this word, "particularity," rather than "relativism" or "contextual-ism," because I think it more effectively conveys some of the central Nietzschean motivations behind Foucault's avoidance of Theory. It will also help me to articulate for you how I have come upon Foucault and at least some Anabaptist thinkers, apparently making camp at the same site.

Lest I sound as if I am trying to make some kind of deep theoreti-cal comparison (or even worse, a *synthesis*) of "Foucault's Thought" and "Anabaptist Thought," I want to be clear that I am focusing on particular texts. For Foucault's most explicit ruminations regarding genealogy as an enterprise, and more specifically its insistence on the primacy of par-

---

6. I.e., especially the "middle" Foucault, whose "methodology" is most clearly (and deliberately) Nietzschean genealogy. The major books of this period are *Discipline and Punish: The Birth of the Prison* trans. Alan Sheridan (New York: Pantheon, 1977), and *The History of Sexuality*, vol. 1, trans. Robert Hurley (New York: Vintage, 1980). While I believe that the theme of particularity is present throughout Foucault's writings, I find that it is most explicit when he is most consciously drawing from Nietzsche.

ticularity, I will rely mainly on two essays: "What is Enlightenment?"[7] and "Nietzsche, Genealogy, History."[8] I will begin with Foucault, and will identify my Anabaptist texts of choice presently.[9]

Foucault is clear in his insistence that genealogy does not amount to a theoretical outlook, or to a methodological doctrine in any standard sense. Yet he is also clear that a genealogical approach to inquiry involves adopting a certain stance—a stance which, he argues, is in continuity with the central Enlightenment theme of freedom and maturity, of liberation from authority:

> The critical ontology of ourselves has to be considered not, certainly, as a theory, a doctrine, nor even as a permanent body of knowledge that is accumulating; it has to be conceived as an attitude, an ethos, a philosophical life in which the critique of what we are is at one and the same time the historical analysis of the limits that are imposed on us and an experiment with the possibility of going beyond them.[10]

Foucault is also clear in his insistence that genealogy must eschew the universal in favor of the particular. It is "gray, meticulous, and patiently documentary,"[11] seeking the disjunctive irregularities of emergence (*Entstehung*) and descent (*Herkunft*), rather than the monolithic ultimacy of origin (*Ursprung*).[12] Rather than seeking a grand historical

---

7. Michel Foucault, *The Foucault Reader*, ed. Paul Rabinow (New York: Pantheon, 1984) 32–50.

8. *Foucault Reader*, 76–100.

9. The secondary literature on Foucault is immense and labyrinthine, and I would not be able to trace the ways in which it has influenced my reading of his work, both positively and negatively. It might be helpful to some readers, however, to know that I have been influenced most clearly by C. G. Prado, *Beginning With Foucault: An Introduction to Genealogy* (Boulder, CO: Westview, 1995) and Gary Gutting, ed., *The Cambridge Companion to Foucault* (Cambridge and New York: Cambridge University Press, 1994). I am also deeply indebted to students at Hillsdale College in seminars that I have taught on the sociology of knowledge and on Anabaptist Christianity, where some of the thoughts presented here were first tentatively formulated and criticized.

10. *Foucault Reader*, 50.

11. Ibid., 76. Foucault's reference to the color gray follows Nietzsche's explicit preference for laborious engagement (which he identifies with the color gray) with the actual historical development of morality, over "gazing around haphazardly in the blue . . . " Friedrich Nietzsche, *On the Genealogy of Morals*, trans. Walter Kaufmann and R. J. Hollingdale [New York: Vintage, 1989] 21).

12. *Foucault Reader*, 77–86.

narrative that frames the present as an unavoidable *telos*, genealogy "maintain[s] passing events in their proper dispersion."[13] Indeed, as so often becomes a central issue in discussions of Foucault, genealogy refuses to accept the Platonic finality of Truth:

> Truth is undoubtedly the sort of error that cannot be refuted because it has hardened into an unalterable form in the long baking process of history. Moreover, the very question of truth, the right it appropriates to refute error and oppose itself to appearance, the manner in which it developed (initially made available to the wise, then withdrawn by men of piety to an unattainable world where it was given the double role of consolation and imperative, finally rejected as a useless notion, superfluous and contradicted on all sides)—does this not form a history, the history of an error we call truth?[14]

Now, both Nietzsche and Foucault are frequently read as advancing a truth claim to the effect that there is no truth, to the endless delight of self-referential incoherence detectives. I take for granted here that neither of them may be dismissed as making simplistically self-refuting claims. As is becoming increasingly appreciated in the secondary literature, Foucault joins Nietzsche not in arguing that there is no truth of any sort, but in asking why we are so insistent on the primacy of Truth, why it is of such momentous import.[15] Consider the following possible reply to this Nietzschean question:

> We want what we say not only to be understandable, credible, meaningful. . . . We hanker for patterns of argument which will not be subject to reasonable doubt. . . . To say it another way, *the*

13. Ibid., 81.

14. Ibid., 79–80.

15. I capitalize the first letter of the word "Truth," in order to emphasize this Nietzschean question. One might imagine hearing an ominous Wagnerian *Leitmotiv* whenever it is used here. This is not to suggest (as was understood by one person responding to my original presentation) that it is straightforwardly possible to distinguish the sense of "Truth" being developed here from other senses which are not as problematic. While Nietzsche and Foucault both clearly use the word "truth" in more than one way, and further assume that there *are* truths in some sense(s), I find no clear warrant for concluding that there is any usage in any context which they would not consider susceptible to the question. For a helpful discussion of the multivocity of the word "truth" in Foucault, see Prado, *Beginning With Foucault*, 119–50.

> *hunger for validation is a hunger for power*. We want people to
> *have* to believe what we say.

The writer of this passage is neither Foucault nor Nietzsche, but
John Howard Yoder. It is from Yoder's pen that my primary Anabaptist
texts of choice issue. Yoder wrote two essays in his later years that explicitly address particularity as a problem in relation to the gospel of Jesus
Christ, "'But We Do See Jesus': The Particularity of Incarnation and the
Universality of Truth,"[16] and "On Not Being Ashamed of the Gospel:
Particularity, Pluralism, and Validation,"[17] from which the above quote
is drawn.[18] In both essays, Yoder's strategy is interestingly similar to that
of Foucault, in that he responds to questions not by answering them in
their own terms, but by inquiring into where the questions come from,
by showing that the frame of reference within which they are raised is
not as monolithically self-evident as we might have assumed.

My claim, in fact, is that Yoder may be read as providing us with
at least the beginnings of a genealogy of the problem of particularity. Particularity is a problem for us, as would-be heralds of the gospel, in light of what Yoder often refers to as "the wider world." Yoder
sketches a phenomenology of the individual experience of passing from
narrow particularity into a wider world, cast in terms that are strikingly similar to the terms that Foucault identifies with the core of the
Enlightenment:

> The psychological and sociological momentum which makes
> the respectively "wider world" more convincing is not derived
> from rational demonstrations (where would one stand to deliver
> them?) but from the social experience of growth and migration
> from the world of one's past toward a wider, or more accept-
> ing, or more complex, or more tolerant, or more decisive, or
> wealthier world into which one has moved. Narrowness is as-

16. John Howard Yoder, *The Priestly Kingdom: Social Ethics as Gospel* (Notre Dame,
IN: University of Notre Dame Press, 1984) 46–62.

17. John Howard Yoder, "On Not Being Ashamed of the Gospel: Particularity,
Pluralism, and Validation," *Faith and Philosophy* 9 (1992) 285–300.

18. Yoder, "On Not Being Ashamed of the Gospel," 287; my emphasis. Particularity
is also a central concern in John Howard Yoder, "Theological Revision and the Burden
of Particular Identity," in *James M. Gustafson's Theocentric Ethics: Interpretations and
Assessments*, ed. Harlan R. Beckley and Charles M. Swezey (Macon, GA: Mercer
University Press, 1988) 63–94, the content of which overlaps significantly with the
other two essays cited.

sociated with parental authority; breadth with the teacher who
has liberated one therefrom.[19]

The experience of achieving greater maturity, of gaining independence
from prior authority figures, of getting a view from what naturally seems
a greater height, leads one to shift one's epistemological allegiances to
the regime of the wider world. This is not an Origin (*Ursprung*) of the
problem of particularity, but a site of its "emergence" (*Entstehung*). The
liberation experienced is generally assumed to bear a sort of finality, because it is so often intellectually and emotionally traumatic, but according to Yoder, it is of great importance that we grasp how "perennial"
the form (not the content) of the experience really is. "There is always a
wider world claiming that its truths are self-evident. . . . [T]hat was the
case in the first century. It is not a new contribution of 'modernity.'"[20]
A tendency to push for Truth that coerces belief has its genesis in the
shock of having been so parochial. That is, we can trace its genealogy to
our abhorrence of prior errors:

> The search for foundations, the urge to find some argument,
> some mental move, some court of appeal beyond appeal, is
> thus a learned personal psychic defense against the constantly
> repeated experience of being overpowered by a wider world. It
> is psychologically natural, but by the nature of things it is insa-
> tiable and logically unrealistic.[21]

To restate Yoder's point, particularity is a problem only by the lights of a
"wider world," and we need not simply assume the Truth of the particular "wider world" that raises the question. Yoder has obviously provided
no decisive inductive disproof of a "widest" world, whose perspective
would indeed be equivalent to Truth. But what would it be like to have
a reason for thinking that *this* is *it*? My suspicion is that we cannot even
make sense of the possibility.[22]

19. Yoder, "On Not Being Ashamed of the Gospel," 286–87.

20. Ibid.

21. Ibid.

22. To explicitly state what should be understood here: There is clearly no way to
show that we will NEVER be in a position to have such a reason. My suggestion is
only that we cannot *now* make sense of what this would even be like (to say nothing
of estimating its likelihood), and that this gives us at least some warrant for supposing
that the possibility is extremely unlikely in the future. See MacIntyre's discussion of
the force of his arguments in comparison with that of Wittgenstein's "private language

Of course, none of this is to say that "the desire for some kind of transtribal validation"[23] is simply a mistake. As Yoder notes, this desire implies respect for interlocutors, inasmuch as we refuse simply to reduce persuasion to brute force. It also implies that our convictions are genuinely held, and not diluted to meek and meaningless "matters of opinion." Yoder is clear in his rejection of the modern ideal of coercive truth, but he is also clear in his refusal of the equally modern truth-claim that there is no truth:

> We must abandon the chimerical vision of a set of semantic or definitional moves which would transcend the limits of one's own identity, rationally coercing assent, without taking account of a particular interlocutor or a specific dialogical setting. . . . Yet we must not abandon the claim that the validity of what we believe is founded on grounds more solid than whim, flipping a coin, accident, or provincial bias. Instead of seeking to escape particular identity, what we need, then, is a better way to restate the meaning of a truth claim from within particular identity.[24]

III

So far, Yoder's resonance with Foucault seems, to me, significant. Foucault insists that he, as an intellectual, is never in a position to offer either Truth or solutions to problems in any strong sense. Yet he is equally insistent that genealogy is an ethically significant pursuit. He seeks not to give historical accounts that are True, but to allow people in particular local contexts the freedom to think beyond the categories that have hardened into Truth, to liberate themselves from thought that has become oppressive. Liberate themselves into what? Foucault seems to assume that only they (the people being liberated) can decide that. If Foucault makes a recommendation, and we mistake him for a Theorist, then Foucault believes his recommendation will only become a new form of oppression. Indeed, the ascendance of further oppression is apparently assumed as inevitable:

---

argument." Alasdair MacIntyre, *After Virtue: A Study in Moral Theory*, 2nd ed. (Notre Dame, IN: University of Notre Dame Press, 1984) 101–2.

23. Yoder, "On Not Being Ashamed of the Gospel," 289.

24. Ibid., 290.

> Humanity does not gradually progress from combat to combat
> until it arrives at universal reciprocity, where the rule of law
> finally replaces warfare; humanity installs each of its violences
> in a system of rules and thus proceeds from domination to
> domination.[25]

Herein lies an aspect of Foucault's thought which many find hardest to swallow. If we are doomed to some sort of domination or other, are we not also doomed to apathy? Does not such pessimism lead to quietistic acquiescence to the status quo? Are we not deprived of our ability to distinguish better or worse social arrangements? Foucault responds negatively. In one of his more famous and often-anthologized interviews, he says:

> My point is not that everything is bad, but that everything is
> dangerous, which is not exactly the same as bad. If everything is
> dangerous, then we always have something to do. So my position
> leads not to apathy but to a hyper- and pessimistic activism.[26]

It is not change *per se* that is portrayed as a villain in Foucault's view, but Theories that promise radical or global change. "In fact we know from experience," he writes, that "programs for a new man that the worst political systems have repeated throughout the twentieth century" have "led only to the return of the most dangerous traditions." Foucault's preference is for "specific transformations."[27]

It is worth noting that the general orientation sketched here is not unique to Foucault, nor to thinkers known as postmodern. Returning to the more confessional mode, I have been impressed by the resonance here with elements of what is often called the conservative intellectual tradition (whose luminaries include Edmund Burke, Alexis de Tocqueville, Michael Oakeshott, and Russell Kirk[28]), and with the "classical" liberalism of "Austrian" economists such as Ludwig von Mises

25. *Foucault Reader*, 85.

26. Ibid., 343.

27. Ibid., 46–47.

28. Cf. Russell Kirk on the "principle of prudence:" "Liberals and radicals, the conservative holds, are imprudent: for they dash at their objectives without giving much heed to the risk of new abuses worse than the evils they hope to sweep away. . . . Sudden and slashing reforms are perilous as sudden and slashing surgery. The march of providence is slow; it is the devil who always hurries." Russell Kirk, ed., *The Portable Conservative Reader* (New York: Penguin, 1982) xvii.

and Friedrich Hayek,[29] and with the thought of at least some "neocon-servatives" such as Peter L. Berger[30] and Thomas Sowell.[31] These, among others, have argued in various ways (which I find compelling) against the notion that human beings can ever be in a position to formulate a definitive blueprint for human society and culture.[32] A consistent theme that runs through all of these thinkers, though it is emphasized to vary-ing degrees, is a deep awareness of the corruption that accompanies power.

What is often portrayed as unique to Foucault's perspective is his conceptualization of power, not as a resource that is possessed disproportionately by various persons or groupings in society, but as an inescapable medium within which we live and interact with each other, as deeply intertwined with—and in fact conceptually inseparable from—knowledge. Part of the key to Foucault's "pessimistic activism" is his refusal to conclude from the ubiquity of power relations either to the futility of action, or to the loss of any real significance for the term "knowledge":

> Perhaps . . . we should abandon a whole tradition that allows us to imagine that knowledge can exist only where the power relations are suspended and that knowledge can develop only outside its injunctions, its demands and its interests. Perhaps we should abandon the notion that . . . the renunciation of power is one of the conditions of knowledge. We should admit that power produces knowledge . . . that power and knowledge di-rectly imply one another; that there is no power relation with-out the correlative constitution of a field of knowledge, nor any

29. James Miller notes that Foucault was familiar with the "Austrian School" econ-omists, and recommended their writings to his students. Cf. James Miller, *The Passion of Michel Foucault* (New York: Simon & Schuster, 1993) 310. Miller's assumption is apparently that this association casts a negative light on Foucault, an assumption that I do not share.

30. Cf. Peter L. Berger and Richard J. Neuhaus, *Movement and Revolution* (Garden City, NY: Anchor, 1970) 20–30.

31. Cf. Thomas Sowell, *A Conflict of Visions* (New York: Morrow, 1987).

32. I would also suggest that there is very significant conceptual overlap here with the interest in anarchism displayed by Jacques Ellul, *Anarchy and Christianity*, trans. Geoffrey W. Bromiley (Grand Rapids: Eerdmans, 1991), and Vernard Eller, *Christian Anarchy: Jesus' Primacy Over the Powers* (Grand Rapids: Eerdmans, 1987).

knowledge that does not presuppose and constitute at the same
time power relations.[33]

It would take us much too far afield to revisit Foucault's conception of
power here in any detail. What I wish to emphasize, again, is how interesting it is to compare his perspective with that of Yoder.[34] In the case of
power, some striking similarities in themes are still discernible. For example, Yoder has alluded approvingly to an emphasis in the Reformed
tradition on the epistemological dimensions of sin:

> What Protestants call "the noetic effect of sin" poisons not only
> the ability to will and to do the good, but even the ability to
> know what it is. What we know does not all become false. Yet
> what we know naturally is warped, blurred, inadequate. That is
> one aspect of the need for revelation.[35]

Though the terms are vastly different, the upshot here is arguably not
significantly different from Foucault's words above. Perhaps, we could
say, we should admit that any and all of our knowledge is clouded by
human fallenness. Perhaps we should give up on the ideal of knowledge
that is not touched by sin.

Yet there are striking divergences that emerge here as well. Central
to Yoder's reputation as a "sectarian" theologian is his frequent insistence that Christians are not called to make history come out right, but
to be faithful.[36] Discipleship involves a renunciation of resistance to the
powers of this world which is not simply fatalistic, though it may appear
so by the world's standards. Jesus' politics are the politics of the cross.

33. Foucault, *Discipline and Punish*, 27.

34. In what follows, I am deeply indebted to Eric Ortlund, with whom I engaged
in several stimulating discussions of Foucault and Yoder in the course of preparing his
senior honors thesis at Hillsdale College in the Spring of 1998.

35. Yoder, "Theological Revision and the Burden of Particular Identity," 81. The
discussion from which this is drawn is in Yoder's contribution to the Gustafson volume
mentioned in note 18, but it is explicitly cited by Yoder in "On Not Being Ashamed
of the Gospel," 299 n. 18. Yoder recommends a very helpful and incisive discussion
of this idea by Merold Westphal, "Taking Paul Seriously: Sin as an Epistemological
Category," in *Christian Philosophy*, ed. Thomas Flint (Notre Dame, IN: University of
Notre Dame Press, 1990) 200–226.

36. Cf. John Howard Yoder, *The Politics of Jesus*, 2nd ed. (Grand Rapids: Eerdmans,
1994) 237–41. (Equivalent pagination in the 1st ed. [Grand Rapids: Eerdmans, 1972]
is 244–48.)

Such a political stance assumes, I would argue, the sort of picture of power that is painted by Foucault, yet places hope in a radically different sort of power which derives its force from voluntary powerlessness that points toward the Wholly Other. Yoder further argues that the political vicissitudes of the life of the church place a certain epistemic "spin" on its decisions and confessions: "The community pulls back . . . from any claim to catholic generalizability and infallibility, yet it is believingly, modestly ready to say of consensus reached today, 'It seemed good to the Holy Spirit and to us.'"[37]

The difference between this Spirit-led consensus of the gathered community at a given time and the local and limited projects for liberation envisioned by Foucault is apparently quite difficult to flesh out by any straightforward example. This is precisely because, for both Yoder and Foucault, the discernment must ultimately be local. Yet Foucault is much more unwilling than Yoder to speak in generalities. Yoder, after all, remains committed to the ability of the gospel to travel between cultures, to remain the same in some important sense, while being carried by widely varying discursive formations, as Foucault might say. Consider Yoder's treatment of "pluralism/relativism" as more of a language to speak than a substantive outlook:

> What we need to find is the interworld transformational grammar to help us to discern what will need to happen if the collision of the message of Jesus within our pluralistic/relativist world is to lead to a reconception of the shape of the world, instead of to rendering Jesus optional or innocuous. To ask, "Shall we talk in pluralistic/relativist terms?" would be as silly as to ask in Greece, "Shall we talk Greek?" The question is what we shall say. We shall say, "Jesus is Messiah and Lord"; but how do you say that in pluralist/relativist language?[38]

The primacy of particularity and the ubiquity of power, for Foucault, mean that the only possible *general* project is the *via negativa* of genealogy. The crucial difference in Yoder, I believe, is the conviction that the gospel is not a theory or a doctrine, but a particular *person* who adopts an exemplary (and in fact, theoretically scandalous) stance toward power. It is the *confession* (which is importantly different from a

37. Yoder, *Priestly Kingdom*, 35.
38. Ibid., 56.

theory or doctrine, I suspect) that "the particularity of the incarnation *is* the universality of the good."[39] Yoder argues that the power of the gospel lies precisely in its being emphatically particular and unashamedly noncoercive. "If we cannot transcend the vulnerability of belief by positing as accessible a nonparticular 'natural,' might we then celebrate confessionally that light and truth have *taken on the vulnerability of the particular?*"[40]

This brings us, of course, into the purview not only of Yoder's essays on particularity, but of the whole argument of his *Politics of Jesus*. My intent is not to review Yoder's arguments in general, but to call attention to the possibility of revelation that he endeavors to articulate—revelation which is historically and culturally particular, but which derives its universality precisely therefrom. Jesus' particularity is exactly what makes it possible for us, who would continue to spread his good news, to

> use any language . . . to enter any world in which people eat bread and pursue debtors, hope for power and execute subversives. The ordinariness of the humanness of Jesus is the warrant for the generalizability of his reconciliation. The nonterritorial particularity of his Jewishness defends us against selling out to any wider world's claim to be really wider, or to be self-validating.[41]

To wax a bit overly dramatic, perhaps, we might think that this move on Yoder's part is exactly contrary to any sort of rejoinder that Foucault would expect. I suspect that this is overly dramatic because Foucault, just like any other hearer of the gospel, is not pinned to any intellectual mat, is not forced into admitting that Yoder's confession is Truth. Foucault might rightly remind us that Yoder's move of emphasizing a person rather than discourse does not itself escape discourse, and the dance would then continue.

39. Ibid., 62.

40. Ibid., 44; emphasis added.

41. Ibid., 62. See also Yoder's explicit discussion of the problem of relativism in "Meaning After Babble: With Jeffrey Stout Beyond Relativism," *Journal of Religious Ethics* 24 (1996) 125–39.

IV

So if there is no happy ending, wherein Yoder produces the magic Anabaptist incantation that reverberates in Foucault's soul and forces him to faith, then what may we take from this comparison? Of what significance are my confessions that arise from reading Yoder and Foucault together? At the risk of being rather more linear than a postmodernist should be, allow me to suggest three lines of questioning that I think we should pursue. These suggestions are as "confessional" as the rest of my reflections; they arise not of themselves from the texts I've been citing, but from my own thoroughly particular reading of them.

First, I suggest that we question our allergic reactions to the so-called pluralist/relativist flavor of putatively postmodern thinkers. Here I believe that I am only echoing Yoder: "We may be tactical allies of the pluralist/relativist deconstruction of deceptive orthodox claims to logically coercive certainty, without making of relativism itself a new monism."[42] At least in this sense, I suppose it is apt that my paper is categorized among those "*for*" postmodernity.[43] Just don't ask me to remain the same.

Second, I suggest that we question our current institutional tendencies away from the primacy of the local gathered community. The sort of Anabaptism that I continue to find worth identifying myself with is the sort that understands its position among other major alternatives on the ecclesiological map. I am still here among Anabaptists, and not in some other fold, partly because we are neither told how we must read scripture by a denomination or conference, nor left alone to puzzle it out as individuals. We struggle prayerfully together in discernment as

42. Yoder, *Priestly Kingdom*, 61. Nietzsche himself is as clear in his rejection of leveling or paralyzing relativism as he is in his embracing of "perspectivism:" "There is *only* a perspective seeing, *only* a perspective "knowing": and the *more* affects we allow to speak about one thing, the *more* eyes, different eyes, we can use to observe one thing, the more complete will our "concept" of this thing, our "objectivity," be. But to eliminate the will altogether, to suspend each and every affect, supposing we were capable of this—what would that mean but to *castrate* the intellect?" Nietzsche, *On the Genealogy of Morals*, 119.

43. The paper was originally presented in a conference session entitled "Anabaptism For Postmodernity," which was balanced by another session, "Anabaptism Against Postmodernity." The irony of the (modern) "either/or" categorization was not lost on the participants in either session.

gathered local communities, where we know and care for one another. Our commitment to this approach is undergoing serious test, as there are those who seek to have congregations removed from conferences when their discernment is not acceptable, who make such decisions by vote from a distance, knowing few, if any, of the persons whose lives the decision effects. It is such disturbing political moves among contemporary Mennonites which, in part at least, deepen my inclination to listen to Foucault.[44]

My final suggestion is that we persistently question any and every alliance, intellectual or political, not primarily in light of some body of doctrine that we take to be Anabaptist, but in light of the crucified and resurrected Lord that the sixteenth-century Anabaptists wished both to know and to follow in life. Do not mistake my suggestion: I do not say make no alliances, for I have no indication that such a course is possible or desirable. But when alliances become allegiances, we are confronted with the old problem of idolatry, and some postmodern prophecy might be called for.

In place of any synthetic conclusion, I cannot do better than to recall Foucault's words, quoted above: "My point is not that everything is *bad*, but that everything is *dangerous* . . . ."[45]

---

44. My allusion here is to several disciplinary actions taken by Mennonite conferences in the United States toward congregations that have explicitly chosen to accept, as members, non-celibate homosexual individuals. Unfortunately, because of the volatility of this issue in current Mennonite discussions, I fear that my concern might easily be misunderstood. My point here is not simply that I endorse these congregations' understanding of homosexuality and the church. Rather, my point is that congregations have apparently engaged in prayerful and often painful discernment on the local level, usually over the course of several years, only to have this process summarily negated at the conference level via questionable exercise of organizational power. See Susan Biesecker-Mast, "A Genealogy of the Confession of Faith in a Mennonite Perspective," *Mennonite Quarterly Review* 81 (2007) 371–97.

45. *Foucault Reader*, 343; emphasis added.

6

Yoder's Patience and/with Derrida's *Différance*

PETER C. BLUM

"Have patience; have patience; don't be in such a hurry.
When you are impatient, you only start to worry.
Remember, remember, that God is patient too, and
Think of all the times that others have to wait for you!"

   —Music Machine, "Patience (Herbert the Snail)"[1]

Is this a test?
It has to be. Otherwise I can't go on.
Draining patience. drain vitality . . .

But I'm still right here, giving blood and keeping faith.
I'm gonna wait it out . . .

If there were no desire to heal
The damaged and broken met along this tedious
        path I've chosen here,
I certainly would've walked away by now . . .

And I still may.
Be patient.

   —Tool, "The Patient"[2]

1. This song is from an album originally released in 1977 entitled *Music Machine: The Fruit of the Spirit* (sound recording) (Original record label: Candle; Compact Disc released in 1998 by BCI).

2. Tool, "The Patient," on *Lateralus* (sound recording) (BMG / Volcano / Pavement

I

The two sets of song lyrics with which I open these ruminations are separated in time by about a quarter of a century. They are separated in mood—or perhaps we should say "attitude"—by a distance not so easily measurable. One is a children's song that has been sung in countless Bible School sessions since the late 1970s. The other is a recent song by a so-called "alternative" rock band, the sort of band whose compact discs are often decorated with stickers warning parents of "explicit" content, or in some cases have had alternate packaging in plain white in order to qualify morally for the bins at Wal-Mart. Both songs are about patience, and I call attention to them here because my central theme is patience.

Patience means waiting; being good and waiting your turn. Being patient means lacking, sitting uneasily in some "not-yet." Being patient means being like God. Being patient means waiting for God.

Being a patient means healing, being cared-for, being cured. Being a patient means hurting, waiting for treatment, waiting for the antibiotics to kick in, waiting for morning when we can call the doctor again. Being a patient means—to reverse T. S. Eliot's simile—being "etherized upon a table" like the "evening . . . spread out against the sky."[3]

I want to talk about patience, but I am impatient to do so. I am impatient with patience. This is a tension that I would like to focus on. I don't want us to feel it in order to make it go away. I want us to focus on it precisely so that we can feel it more clearly, more acutely.

That I wish to explore patience with simultaneous reference to John Howard Yoder and to Jacques Derrida could be considered comparable to playing a compact disc on which there are both lighthearted Bible School songs and angry electric thrashing. Even well beyond the boundaries of his own confessional community, Yoder was (and remains, via his work) a respected Christian theologian, known for his life-long insistence that following Jesus Christ in life is a real possibility. Jacques Derrida, though he is probably the most famous living philosopher, is vilified at least as often as he is lauded. One might say that he is

/ CZ, 2001). The notes credit all songwriting collectively to Tool (Danny Carey, Justin Chancellor, Adam Jones, and Maynard James Keenan).

3. T. S. Eliot, "The Love Song of J. Alfred Prufrock," *Collected Poems 1909–1962* (New York: Harcourt Brace, 1963) 3.

the Marilyn Manson of contemporary Western intellectual life. Yoder and Derrida may not seem to have much in common at first glace. But I would suggest that it is important for us to trace the way in which the apparent tension between them might give way to tension *within* the thought of each, and that this same tension might serve rather than hinder us if we allow it into our own thinking.

Consider some similarities between Yoder and Derrida. Both make claims that seem wildly incredible from the perspective of the academic orthodoxies that they challenge. As if Yoder's being a *pacifist* is not sufficient to brand him as an unreasonable extremist, he audaciously claims more generally that Jesus not only *should* be, but in fact *can* be normative for Christian ethics—*pace* academic assumptions about how contemporary biblical scholarship makes this difficult or even impossible.[4] His advocacy for a church that visibly embodies a radical social alternative, when not rejected as morally and politically problematic, seems downright utopian. Derrida similarly irritates his academic colleagues with apparently ludicrous claims that speaking derives from writing rather than vice-versa, or that the meaning of words is "undecidable," and even that there is nothing "outside texts." Because of the apparent extremity of their claims, both Yoder and Derrida have widely elicited academic responses which amount to summary dismissal. Yoder's "sectarian" ethic seems at best irresponsible, and at worst separatist and quietist. Derrida's "deconstructionism" apparently undermines meaning in general, hence undermining our ability to say anything meaningful about morality (among other things), but also (thank goodness!!) undermining itself. We may concede that they are brilliant rhetoricians, but inasmuch as they make any specific claims, they need not be taken very seriously.

There is a clear sense, of course, in which these sorts of reactions both to Yoder and to Derrida are waning recently, and they are both treated with increasing seriousness—not only by such inbred groups as Mennonites and deconstructionists, but by the scholarly mainstream. To those of us who are more favorably disposed to either or both, this is surely a welcome development. Or is it? Both Yoder and Derrida, despite their own deep distrust of and warnings about systematizing, are

4. This is presented by Yoder as one of the central theses of *The Politics of Jesus* (1st ed.: Grand Rapids: Eerdmans, 1972; 2nd ed.: Grand Rapids: Eerdmans, 1994).

increasingly the subjects of scholarly commentary geared toward exposing the implicit systems that presumably bind together their various writings, just waiting for the careful expositor to render them as series of explicit propositions. Nancey Murphy provides a succinct statement of the tendency that I have in mind here:

> Yoder disclaimed being a systematic theologian. He believed (rightly, I think) that theology should be written in the service of the church, addressing issues as they arise, and not driven by any philosophical or systematic motivations. However, this perspective on the nature of theology does not prevent others from looking at Yoder's many writings and perceiving the organization and coherence of the whole.[5]

Murphy's observation here is clearly correct in a broad sense. "Anti-system" thinkers such as Kierkegaard and Nietzsche have been endlessly summarized and presented in very systematic ways. This seems not only natural, but in fact unavoidable. Murphy's own discussion of Yoder using the Lakatosian notion of a "research program" is in fact quite suggestive and useful. I have no doubt that the same heuristic would prove fruitful if applied to Derrida's writings.

I will not argue that systematizing either Yoder or Derrida is simply an *error*. Indeed, insofar as my discussion here involves an attempt somehow to think Yoder and Derrida together, I am quite sure that it will not escape being systematic in some relevant sense. Assuming, however (following Foucault) that "everything is dangerous,"[6] my impulse is to look for the *danger* in systematizing them, which is not the same thing as looking for an *error*. Yoder himself has told us: "[O]nce we have learned how the word-spinners mislead us, we must also recognize that their skills are the only ones we have with which to defend ourselves against their temptations."[7] I will employ a bit of system in

5. Nancey Murphy, "John Howard Yoder's Systematic Defense of Christian Pacifism," 45–68 in Stanley Hauerwas, Chris K. Huebner, Harry J. Huebner, and Mark Thiessen Nation, eds., *The Wisdom of the Cross: Essays in Honor of John Howard Yoder* (Grand Rapids: Eerdmans, 1999). Reprinted as chapter 3 in this volume.

6. Paul Rabinow, ed., *The Foucault Reader* (New York: Pantheon, 1984) 343. See my discussion of this in connection with Yoder in Peter C. Blum, "Foucault, Genealogy, Anabaptism: Confessions of an Errant Postmodernist." Reprinted as chapter 5 in this volume.

7. John Howard Yoder, "Walk and Word: The Alternatives to Methodologism,"

order to suggest that we should remain deeply suspicious of system. The bit of system that I plan to use is the one with which I began: *patience*. I would like to take up the idea of patience, as it figures in the posthumous essay by Yoder included in his *Festschrift*,[8] and treat it temporarily as if it were a key with which I can systematically unlock some doors into Yoder's distrust of system.

In Derrida's terms, I intend to use the notion of patience *strategically*. Derrida himself characterizes *différance* "as the *strategic* note or connection—relatively or provisionally *privileged*—which indicates the closure of presence. . . ."[9] Strategic use of a "word" or a "concept" (*différance* is neither, for Derrida) does not imply that it is some sort of Archimedean point, either ontologically or epistemologically. It is privileged *provisionally* for the purposes of a specific inquiry.

II

If we follow Derrida's lead and recall that his own use of "*différance*" in the essay so titled is strategic, it will provide us with something of a point of reference from which to consider patience as strategic as well.[10] Derrida's early work focused on a general critique of what he called (following Heidegger) "the metaphysics of presence." This was carried out, first of all, in a careful analysis of Edmund Husserl's phenomenological theory of meaning. "Presence" in that context may be understood roughly as the sort of presence before consciousness that had already been Descartes' ideal, an indubitable clarity and distinctness that could

---

in Stanley Hauerwas, Nancey Murphy, and Mark Nation, eds., *Theology Without Foundations: Religious Practice and the Future of Theological Truth* (Nashville: Abingdon Press, 1994) 77–90, at 85.

8. John Howard Yoder, "'Patience' as Method in Moral Reasoning: Is an Ethic of Discipleship 'Absolute'?" in Hauerwas et al., *Wisdom of the Cross*, 24–42

9. Jacques Derrida, "*Différance*," in Richard Kearney and Mara Rainwater, eds., *The Continental Philosophy Reader* (London: Routledge, 1996) 441–49, at 441; Derrida's emphasis.

10. It is worth noting how difficult it is for us to do so now. Derrida's fame has given rise to what can only be considered an industry in secondary literature, and various terms in Derrida's strategic lexicon have been transformed into static keys for systematic locks, "*différance*" being one of the most commonly discussed. It may require a considerable effort to think of the use of a term as *provisional* when it has solidified into an established chunk of academic jargon.

serve as a sure epistemic foundation. Derrida attacked this notion by juxtaposing it with the general understanding of signs that emerged from the work of Ferdinand de Saussure. Regardless of what details of Saussure's views have or have not been taken up by subsequent linguistics or semiotics, Derrida rightly emphasizes the broad-based acceptance of his two central insights, namely, (i) the *arbitrariness* of signs, and (ii) the *differential* character of signs. Both insights are nicely captured in Derrida's phrasing: "The elements of signification function not by virtue of the compact force of their cores but by the network of oppositions that distinguish them and relate them to one another."[11] An individual sign does not have meaning all by itself, in isolation from other signs; meaning is in the differences between signs, and the differences between signs in one sign system need not map directly onto those of another sign system.

That signs do not mean by themselves individually entails that the meanings of signs are never simply "present" in the Cartesian/Husserlian sense. "[T]he movement of signs defers the moment of encountering the thing itself, the moment at which we could lay hold of it, consume it or expend it, touch it, see it, have a present intuition of it."[12] This is precisely what leads Derrida to deploy the term *différance*:

> [T]he signified concept is never present in itself, in an adequate presence that would refer only to itself. Every concept is necessarily and essentially inscribed in a chain or a system, within which it refers to another and to other concepts, by the systematic play of differences. Such a play, then—*différance*—is no longer simply a concept, but the possibility of conceptuality, of the conceptual system and process in general.[13]

The differences that constitute meaning in a language, though they are clearly arbitrary, have not simply "fallen from the sky," as Derrida says.[14] They must have a cause, we would assume; they must have come from "somewhere." The problem is that there is no "somewhere" that we can point to from which they might have come but which itself lies beyond or outside of the play of differences. If a meaning could be in-

11. Derrida, "*Différance*," 448.
12. Ibid., 447.
13. Ibid., 449.
14. Ibid.

tuited clearly and distinctly in the way that Descartes or Husserl would like, then according to Saussure's view, *it could not in fact be a meaning*! An "intuition" of meaning would always already have entered into the play of differences. If presence were required in order to make sense of a cause, "we would therefore have to talk about an effect without a cause, something that would very quickly lead to no longer talking about effects."[15] Derrida's approach here is, by his own admission, a discursive move akin to negative theology.[16] He "defines" *différance* as "the movement by which language, or any code, any system of reference in general, becomes 'historically' constituted as a fabric of differences."[17] *Différance* is emphatically not God, but the non-word "*différance*" does not denote in basically the same way that "God" does not denote according to the apophatic tradition. The terms of his "definition" are used not in their traditional metaphysical senses, he tells us, but "out of strategic convenience."

The sense in which all of this remains *provisional* is precisely the sense in which it all remains wedded to a particular beginning. The beginning, stated much too simplistically, is still his juxtaposition of principles drawn from phenomenology and structuralist semiotics. The point is not that Derrida has somehow created a *new* beginning; even less that he has somehow either surpassed all beginnings, or found THE beginning. Derrida's project, rather, is to grab hold of some of the main resources of the scaffolding on which we have arranged our thinking, and to shake them vigorously, to make them rattle. This is my reading of what Derrida generally calls "deconstruction" (though that word has been so thoroughly "terminologized" that it is even less capable of serving as a disruptive "non-word" than "*différance*").

Derrida's general approach here (especially under that notorious name) has often been understood as leading directly to some sort of "nihilism," i.e., as undermining our ability successfully to mean anything that we say, or to say anything that we mean, or something equally hideous.[18] Recent work both by and about Derrida has fortunately miti-

15. Ibid.
16. Ibid., 444.
17. Derrida, "*Différance*," 450.
18. Dismissal of Derrida as a nihilist is most often based, I would argue, on superficial (if any) reading of his work. It must be stated, however, that some careful and

gated such worries to some extent. Unlike some of his more excitable readers, Derrida has never assumed that deconstruction constitutes some sort of straightforward *refutation* of any particular point of view. His concern is apparently that our general way of embracing *any* point of view is problematic, at least insofar as it is haunted by the expectation of *presence*. As long as we expect presence, presence will be deferred; as long as we expect sameness, there will be difference. This is *différance*. To reach for another gross oversimplification, deconstruction is provisional because what is being deconstructed is provisional to begin with.

This is, in fact, one of the main reasons why "deconstruction" is so *deeply* disconcerting to many of us. We simply do not want provisional views. We want *Truth*, in the sense that so exercised Nietzsche. Derrida does *violence* to the very idea of truth, we often think. Consider, however, that from Derrida's perspective the very idea of truth is, in an important sense, already violence. The longing for truth as presence is one way of trying, in terms that Derrida has learned from Emmanuel Levinas, to reduce the Other to the Same.[19] Derrida's first extended reflection on Levinas[20] clearly identified this "reduction" as a form of violence—ultimately a *discursive* form of violence. "Predication is the first violence," he tells us.[21] Indeed, Derrida makes it sound as if violence is *unavoidable*:

> A Being without violence would be a Being which would oc-
> cur outside the existent: nothing; nonhistory; nonoccurrence;
> nonphenomenality. A speech produced without the least vio-
> lence would determine nothing, would say nothing, would offer

---

even somewhat sympathetic readers of Derrida conclude that a vicious nihilism of some sort lurks in his thought. The most prominent current examples are Catherine Pickstock and John Milbank. I am not persuaded that they are correct, but detailed engagement with their arguments is far beyond my present scope. For some orientation to the issues involved, see Guy Collins, "Defending Derrida: A Response to Milbank and Pickstock," *Scottish Journal of Theology* 54 (2001) 344–65.

19. Levinas's term is *meme* (contrasted with *l'autre*).

20. Jacques Derrida, "Violence and Metaphysics: An Essay on the Thought of Emmanuel Levinas," in *Writing and Difference*, trans. Alan Bass (Chicago: University of Chicago Press, 1978) 79–153.

21. Ibid., 147.

> nothing to the other; it would not be *history*, and it would *show* nothing . . . .[22]

I already do a sort of violence when I speak to the other. If it were not so, I would not be speaking *about* anything; I would not really be *saying* anything. If there were such a thing as a nonviolent language, it "would be a language which would do without the verb *to be*. . . ."[23]

III

How tempting it would be at this point to expect relief when we turn from Derrida back to Yoder. Being a believing Christian, Yoder surely insists on *truth* more clearly than Derrida does. Being a much "clearer" thinker and writer than Derrida, Yoder surely has a more clearly discernable project, one which we can thematize or systematize. Being a pacifist, Yoder surely would reject Derrida's suggestion that violence is unavoidable, that we are already being violent when we *speak*. Rest assured that I am not about to claim that Yoder and Derrida are simply up to the same thing, that Yoder is Derrida in Mennonite clothing. I do want to suggest, however, that there is a reading of Yoder that drastically reduces the apparent distance between them, and that this reading should not be lost amidst the proliferation of Yoderian systems. I have already indicated that "patience" will occupy a central strategic place. Let me be more clear now as to my strategy: By attending to Yoder's reflections on patience, and placing them in the context of (i) his critical stance toward what he called "Constantinianism," and (ii) the "epistemological" preoccupations of some of his late essays, I want to suggest that there is at least a deep kinship between Yoder and Derrida in terms of their avoidance of system. A central claim that I wish to advance is that this avoidance has everything to do with violence.

Yoder's "essay" on patience is not really an essay, of course. It originated as a memo in 1982, and has since been distributed in various forms, often under the more apt title, "Methodological Miscellany."[24] It retains something of the feel of a document in process. Nonetheless,

---

22. Ibid.
23. Ibid.
24. Yoder, "Patience," 24 n. 1.

its overall tone is one of a general response by Yoder to the charge that his views are, in some undesirable sense, "absolutist." Yoder rejects either "absolutist" or "relativist" as a way of describing his approach, and uses the word "patience" to convey the sense in which he wishes to steer between these two standard options. The clearest indication of how Yoder defines "patience" is in his equation of "reasons for 'patience'" and "considerations which call for purported 'absolutes' to be mitigated, yet without justifying the dominant constructions [such as "relativism"]."[25] That he writes here of *purported* absolutes is more significant than it may seem at first. Yoder claims that none of the various kinds of patience he discusses is anything but what should be expected of "any kind of decent person taking a position on the grounds of moral conviction on any important subject."[26] But just as Murphy finds system behind Yoder's protests that he is not being systematic, I would suggest that what we find here may be rather less pedestrian than Yoder himself implies.[27]

I have already discussed in another context,[28] in connection with Foucault, how some of Yoder's other "late"[29] essays may be understood as fully consistent with a broadly Nietzschean hesitation regarding claims to possess *Truth*, a hesitation shared by Derrida as well as by Foucault. Here I want to call attention to the light that this might cast on Yoder's understanding of patience. Patience regarding purported absolutes is, I submit, an integral part of Yoder's more general convic-

---

25. Ibid., 25.

26. Ibid., 35.

27. Though I emphatically *do not* wish to soften the most important ingredient in his disclaimers: *viz.*, that his considerations are "radically ecumenical" and not "sectarian" (ibid.).

28. Blum, "Foucault, Genealogy, Anabaptism." The Yoder essays in question include "'But We Do See Jesus': The Particularity of Incarnation and the Universality of Truth," 46–62 in *The Priestly Kingdom: Social Ethics as Gospel* (Notre Dame, IN: University of Notre Dame Press, 1984); "On Not Being Ashamed of the Gospel: Particularity, Pluralism, and Validation," *Faith and Philosophy* 9 (1992) 285–300; "Walk and Word" (op. cit.), and "Meaning After Babble: With Jeffrey Stout Beyond Relativism," *Journal of Religious Ethics* 24 (1996) 125–39.

29. I keep injecting the qualifier "late" because I suspect, based on both his writings and my personal conversations with him, that Yoder's actual *interest* in what I am calling "epistemological" issues (as opposed to the occasional need to discuss them regardless of interest) grew significantly during the last decade and a half of his life.

tion that the sharing of good news—of gospel—must be non-coercive. Note his comments in connection with patience type 6: "My meeting the interlocutor on his own terms is not merely a matter of accepting the minority's conversational handicap although it is that. It is also a spirituality and a lifestyle."[30] He expands on this with a footnote: ". . . [N]onviolence is not only an ethic about power but also an epistemology about how to let truth speak for itself."[31]

Patience is by no means incompatible with the strong conviction that one's views are in fact true, a point that comes across clearly in Yoder's essay. It may seem that my attempt to identify patience in Yoder's thought with some sort of Nietzschean suspicion is at least overwrought, if not completely misguided. Being patient with others who disagree is quite different, we might think, from adopting an attitude of suspicion that makes us unable ever to say "this is true" without a set of unpleasant qualifiers about the perspective from which it *seems* so to us. Being patient in a discursive situation where one is in the minority—and thus where one is especially aware of the violent potential of discourse—is quite different, we might think, from pronouncing that discourse just *is* violent. Insofar as it is one of my intentions here to be a sort of champion of difference, I will certainly not deny the validity of this line of thinking. It is especially clear that Yoder stresses the possibility of nonviolent discourse in a way that Derrida apparently disallows. I believe that there is still more to be said, however. The question of the *differences* between the two is not the same as the question of the *distance* between the two. A bit of further examination of the "Patience" essay, though it does not reduce the differences, may reduce the distance.

It is most clear in patience type 13 ("the 'modest' patience of sobriety in finitude") that patience is not simply a communicative attitude adopted on the near side of an epistemic certitude, and hence added onto the certitude externally as a supplement. This patience amounts to more than simply a polite fallibilist admission that the probability of my being wrong never reaches zero. Yoder spells it out precisely in terms of the need for ones fallibility to be embodied in discourse:

> [T]he certainty in which we have to act one day at a time must never claim *finality*. Our recognition that we may be wrong

30. Yoder, "Patience," 28.
31. Ibid., 28 n. 9.

> must always be *visible*. One way to say this would be to begin
> every statement one ever makes with "as far as I know" or "until
> further notice." That I do not begin every paragraph this way
> does not mean that I do not mean it.[32]

This is not so far, after all, from the suspicion alluded to above.
Citing Hubmaier and Denck's openness to correction from their per-
secutors, Yoder's footnote[33] notably ties this patience to the context in
which violence might be done to the one making the truth-claim. Type
12 ("the 'contrite' patience of repentance") alludes to the possibility of
the claimant's own complicity in violence toward others. One crucial
implication here is not only that I may be wrong, but that my conviction that I am right may be the occasion for violence, quite apart from
its truth or falsity. The primary import of truth and falsity is not *in-
tra*personal (the *presence* of truth within the Same), but *inter*personal
(truthfulness toward the Other).

When Yoder pursues what he calls a "phenomenology of the moral
life," truthfulness (as opposed to Truth) emerges as a primordial requisite for human association:

> There is, as a matter of empirically undeniable fact, a human
> social fabric characterized by communication. . . . For society to
> be viable, most of this communication has to be "true" most of
> the time; i.e., it has to provide a reliable basis for structuring our
> common life, counting on each other and not being routinely
> disappointed.[34]

It is in this context that proscriptions against lying develop, with
practice pushing them toward solidification as norms. Because they
are applied in everyday contexts, they are "probably concretized as sin-
ning against some simple notion of 'correspondence' between words
and reality."[35] This process is proceeding apace long before the ethical
theorist arrives and tries to decide between utilitarianism, deontology,
virtue theory, or other accounts of what makes it True that one should

32. Ibid., 31.
33. Ibid., 31 n. 15.
34. Yoder, "Walk and Word," 80.
35. Ibid.

not lie. "The life of the community is prior to all possible methodological distillations."[36]

The point at which I would like to suggest that the distance between Yoder and Derrida is especially narrow is at the point of their concern for the violence that we would do to the Other. Our impulse is to reduce the Other to the Same, to make the Other an object that fits into the world of which I am the center, to reduce the other to a concept that is intelligible primarily with reference to *me*. Patience is about the primacy of the Other *vis a vis* "the Truth."

This is where patience also shades into the disavowal of Constantine. The reversal of priorities for the church that Constantine represents, for Yoder, is at bottom a trading of noncoercive witness to the Other for a coercive encompassing that we mistake for redemption. Gerald Schlabach has rightly pointed out that Constantinianism in a sociopolitical sense is but one manifestation of a broader phenomenon. He writes: "The Deuteronomic problem is the problem of how to receive and celebrate the blessing, the shalom, the good, or 'the land' that God desires to give, yet to do so without defensively and violently hoarding God's blessing."[37]

So what about the difference that still glares across this divide, even though it may be more narrow than we thought at first? We noted that Derrida seems to envision violence as unavoidable, as endemic to any discourse, to any "saying that . . . ." Yoder, on the other hand, seems confident that there can be nonviolent discourse. The question of who is correct is beyond my present scope, yet I wish to suggest in passing that, in this case too, the difference may not be a matter of great distance. There are hints throughout Yoder's writings that a commitment to nonviolence, though never *less* than a commitment not to kill, is perhaps never *simply* that, is never a commitment that pretends that killing or not killing is the *only* choice. In response to the allegation that his view would imply that he is more "pure" than others, he responds: "The Niebuhrian or the Sartrian has no corner on dirty hands. The question

---

36. Ibid., 82.

37. Gerald W. Schlabach, "Deuteronomic or Constantinian: What is the Most Basic Problem for Christian Social Ethics?" in Hauerwas et al., *Wisdom of the Cross*, 449–71.

is not whether one can have clean hands but which kind of complicity in which kind of inevitable evil is preferable."[38]

IV

If I have been even moderately successful in my strategic deployment of Yoder's notion of "patience," we should now be able better to feel the tension with which I began, between the lighthearted patience that is certain of God's rule (the patience of Herbert the Snail) and the patience that asks "Is this a test?" and that may still walk away rather than waiting (the patient of Tool). Patience itself is something with which we are less than patient. "Lord, grant me patience. And Lord, please grant it to me *now!*"

What if Yoder's patience is supposed to be patience with Derrida's *différance*? What if that for which we patiently wait, though it is "to come," will never be *present*? Patience is all well and good, as long as I am certain that my patience will "pay off." Images of sudden rapture and of the confusion of those "left behind" appeal as widely as they do because they are visions of vindication not only for God, but *for us*. The more certain I am that I am going to win, the more patient I can be. The more probable it becomes that everything will turn out "right" (by my own lights), the less I will be prone to losing my patience.

Here is where we may note what at the outset I referred to as the tension *within* each of the two thinkers we are attending to. Derrida has emphasized that the difference/deferral of *différance* will not go away; we don't get the presence that we long for. But more recently, he has increasingly written in an eschatological vein, of what he calls "the messianic," which is emphatically "to come," even though it will not be present.[39] Yoder has emphasized the unfaithfulness of the Constantinian settlement, the importance of witnessing by letting the church be the church, and by letting God be God. But letting the church be the church is letting the church be *visible*, and how does one do that both faithfully

38. Yoder, "Patience," 40.

39. Cf. Derrida, *Specters of Marx* (London: Routledge, 1994), and *The Politics of Friendship*, trans. George Collins (London: Verso, 1997).

and patiently? How might we find the level of patience that lets God be God by not trying too hard the MAKE the church be the church?[40]

Patience is waiting. It is sitting uneasily in a "not-yet," without control of its own fulfillment. Patience knows not the times or the seasons. Patience knows that it waits for what is to come, but it does not know if what is to come will ever be present. If it were not so, it would not be patience. Patience is something that we may not truly have until we are impatient with it. Hence, I cannot conclude by assuring you that your patience—our patience—will be rewarded in the way that we would like it to be. We know that it will be rewarded insofar as we have been promised this by the one in whom we trust. But in the way that we would like it to be? That is left unanswered, and it remains the more disconcerting question; it remains *unheimlich*; it makes us tremble. As we pray for patience now, perhaps we will tremble. Indeed, we should do both. We should pray, and we should tremble.

40. The latter problem is a main theme of Peter C. Blum, "Totality, Alterity, and Hospitality: The Openness of Anabaptist Community," *Brethren Life and Thought* 48 (2003) 159–75.

7

Patience, Witness, and the Scattered Body of Christ:
Yoder and Virilio on Knowledge, Politics, and Speed

CHRIS K. HUEBNER

The war-machine is not only explosives, it's also communications, vectorization. It's essentially the speed of delivery. . . . Pure War, not the kind which is declared.

—Paul Virilio

Exploding Peace

Among the many strange twists and turns that John Howard Yoder takes in his wild and wide-ranging reflections on theological nonviolence, two crucial and closely related moments are his understanding of patience as method and his interpretation of the scattered, diasporic body of Christ. This essay explores the connection between these two key aspects of Yoder's work. It does so by bringing Yoder into conversation with the contemporary French war theorist Paul Virilio. Virilio is best know for his penetrating analyses of the proliferation of violence in the contemporary cultures of "advanced" Western capitalism, and in particular for his interpretation of violence as speed. Among other things, Virilio helps us see that to understand violence and war we must look beyond mere conflict. More important than explosions, bunkers, troop deployments, and other instances of overt conflict, Virilio claims that violence involves a way of organizing political space and its characteristic modes of knowledge. We must move beyond war to an examination of what he calls the "war-machine," beyond a focus on violent activities in and of themselves to an understanding of the conditions that make violent activity possible, and the changing conditions that have made it extreme, total, and ubiquitous. It is at this point that Virilio highlights the epistemological and political prioritization of speed. He develops this claim through a reading that stresses the connection between technological developments involving the commodification of knowledge as information and the rapid and wide-ranging developments in the techniques of surveillance. Because of the largely unquestioned triumph of these forms of power, Virilio argues that violence has come to organize the very way we think, including the way we have come to think about peace.

While Virilio's analysis of the contemporary war-machine is valuable in its own right, I am particularly interested in exploring his interpretation of violence as speed in terms of the bearing it has on contemporary peace theology. Virilio explodes our limited understanding of peace, demonstrating that it is much more complicated and multifaceted than is often assumed. Peace is not simply the contrary of violence in some straightforward way, as if they can be located on the same plane or placed on opposite ends of the same spectrum. Moreover, our understanding of peace and violence is limited if we think of them as political implications that are drawn from theoretical claims to knowledge in a secondary sort of way. Rather, Virilio's readings of the war machine show that political matters are intimately bound up with questions of knowledge themselves. He demonstrates, in other words, that knowledge is always already political.

Since violence is reflected in the very way we think about thinking, it follows that peace must name a simultaneous counter-politics and counter-epistemology that radically shifts the terms of the debate. To return to the metaphors above, it occupies a different plane and inaugurates an entirely new spectrum of possibilities. This is hinted at in Virilio's examination of situations in which there is an absence of overt violence, such as the state of mutual deterrence between nation-states or technologies that are able to minimize destruction and human casualties. The crux of Virilio's position is that these are *not* to be understood as advances toward peace. Rather, they are developments in the shifting reality of war. In a similar vein, he suggests that the discourse of peace must refrain from humanitarian abstractions such as development or the common assumption that violence grows out of limits imposed on free access to information—that violence is the result of miscommunication. In short, Virilio maintains that these "liberal" interpretations of peace fail to break sufficiently with the kinds of militaristic epistemological and political categories that breed and sustain violence.

The most general lesson of Virilio's work is thus that the idea of a peaceable alternative to violence requires a radical reconfiguration of what might be called the knowledge-politics complex. It is at this point that Virilio is helpful for understanding the meaning of peace in Yoder's theology. In particular, I shall argue that Yoder is best understood as identifying many of the same conditions of violence and attempting to provide the same kind of double-sensed reconfiguration of knowledge and politics that Virilio calls for. Most importantly, reading Yoder's work against the background of Virilio highlights the significance of Yoder's appeal to the practice of patience as a way of resisting the violent logic of speed. It also helps explain how his conception of epistemological patience is related to his notion of the body of Christ as a scattered, diasporic body.

Such an approach to Yoder stresses that his interest in questions of peace and violence goes all the way down. They do not rest on some neutral methodological ground. This emphasis is necessary because too many interpretations of his work continue to distort his account of the gospel message of peace by forcing it into political and epistemological categories whose status he calls into question as instances of violence. To take one example, Yoder's understanding of peace is often obscured by those who read him with the assumption that we already know what peace is. This is particularly problematic when peace is taken to name some identifiable state of affairs or some kind of ideal that it is up to us to bring about. Many continue to enlist Yoder's name in support of an apologetic strategy designed to defend Christian pacifism against those who doubt its capacity to be effective. In doing so, undue stress is placed on the potential of the church to *transform* society.[1] It is suggested that the church can be a "potent force" which has the "power to shape his-

1. See, e.g., Duane K. Friesen, *Artists, Citizens, Philosophers: Seeking the Peace of the City* (Scottdale, PA: Herald, 2000) 33.

tory," claiming that a better future can thus be *secured*, albeit nonviolently.[2] Among other things, I am suggesting that reading Yoder as a
conversation partner with Virilio is valuable precisely in that it helps to
avoid this kind of ongoing preoccupation with effectiveness.

By way of situating and anticipating the discussion that follows,
I offer three claims that guide my interpretation of Yoder's work more
generally: First, like Barth, Yoder refused to let the doubters set the
agenda for Christian theology. Second, Yoder consistently rejected the
kind of instrumentalist thinking that such an apologetic approach exemplifies as contributing to just the kind of violent operation of power
to which the church is called to witness an alternative. Yoder did not
seek a new nonviolent way of transforming society or securing the future. Rather, he claimed that the peace of Christ involves a rejection of
the possessive logic of security and social control. A key part of Yoder's
theology is his critique of the Constantinian project of outfitting history
with handles designed to move it in the right direction. The pacifism of
Christian discipleship thus crucially involves giving up the assumption
that it is up to us to make history come out right.[3]

Third, and perhaps most important for the purposes of the present
discussion, it is important to recognize that Yoder never assumed that
he finally knew what peace was. This is perhaps most clearly exemplified in what might be called the negative orientation of his theology—
the sense in which his work consists in a series of exercises dedicated
to unthinking the necessity of violence. Many of his writings can be
described as an attempt to delegitimate theological strategies designed
to guarantee the securing of power. His is thus a profoundly critical theology that functions as an ongoing critique of the will to seize
power, and in particular those expressions of power that turn on what
he described as "seizing godlikeness."[4] To the extent that he worked
in a more positive fashion, it is important to recognize that Yoder did

2. Ibid., 127, 217, 237.

3. See, e.g., John Howard Yoder, *The Politics of Jesus*, 2nd ed. (Grand Rapids:
Eerdmans, 1994) 228, 232.

4. John Howard Yoder, *The Priestly Kingdom: Social Ethics as Gospel* (Notre
Dame, IN: University of Notre Dame Press, 1984) 145. For a fascinating discussion
of Yoder's critique of desire to seize God's will, see J. Alexander Sider, *"To See History
Doxologically": History and Holiness in John Howard Yoder's Ecclesiology* (PhD diss.,
Duke University, 2004) especially ch. 2.

not write a systematic treatise on the nature of Christian pacifism, but rather engaged in an ongoing series of experiments in understanding the peace of Christ. His work is thus necessarily fragmentary and ad hoc. It is episodic, exploratory, and experimental. He offered a collage, a series of sketches designed to reveal certain tendencies, not a final or total perspective on the very nature of peace as such. My attempt to bring Yoder into contact with Virilio is offered in this same spirit, as an experimental sketch that Yoder did not himself provide. It is not an attempt to bring us one step closer to the final word on peace, but at attempt to reveal further tendencies that too often go unnoticed by those readers of Yoder's work who continue to filter his understanding of peace through existing political and epistemological categories.

Violence and Technical Knowledge: Speed as the Essence of War

As noted above, the basic tendency that Virilio identifies is the close relationship between violence and speed. As Virilio himself puts it, "The war-machine is not only explosives, it's also communications, vectorization. It's essentially the speed of delivery. . . . Pure War, not the kind which is declared."[5] Building upon and at the same time calling into question Marxist interpretations of the politicization of wealth, Virilio calls for a more thoroughgoing recognition of the political character of speed.[6] Indeed, he suggests that it is possible to see violence as primarily a function of speed and as only secondarily connected with wealth. That is because wealth is itself the product of the kind of power and mobility speed engenders. More specifically, Virilio claims that the logic of violence as speed is best understood in terms of the shift from geo-politics into chrono-politics. Violence unfolds and develops in a transformation from a geographical analysis of space to the merging of space-time.[7] This is reflected in the increasing technologization of the war-machine. By way of example, Virilio identifies three stages in the expanding power of weapons systems.[8] The first instruments of war

5. Paul Virilio and Sylvère Lotringer, *Pure War*, 2nd ed., trans. Mark Polizzotti (New York: Semiotext(e), 1997) 27.

6. Ibid., 35, 49.

7. Ibid., 13.

8. Ibid., 175.

were those of obstruction: "ramparts, shields, the size of the elephant." The war machine originally hinged on the deployment of bunkers, walls, and other physical fortifications designed to define and manage space and thereby to inhibit the movement of one's enemies. The next stage arrives with instruments of destruction, from the development of artillery to the invention of the nuclear bomb and reaches its apex in the "false peace" of nuclear deterrence. Finally, Virilio claims that war reaches still a different stage with the deployment of weapons of communication.

Contemporary war is thus best characterized as a kind of virtual "infowar" or "cyberwar," whose primary mechanism is the "information bomb." Infowar involves the widespread participation of the media and the deployment of technologies of mass communication of the kind that make the phenomenon of terrorism possible.[9] Virilio writes, "yesterday's war was a *totalitarian* war, in which the dominant elements were quantity, mass, and the power of the atomic bomb. Tomorrow's war will be *globalitarian*, in which, by virtue of the information bomb, the qualitative will be of greater importance than geophysical scale or population size. . . . Not 'clean war' *with zero deaths*, but 'pure war' *with zero births* for certain species which have disappeared from the biodiversity of living matter."[10]

As the logic of violence unfolds and intensifies, war is becoming less and less about territory and more about the management of information. In its earlier stages, war was about the defence and takeover of geographical space. Now the army only moves in once the battle is already over. In each new stage of weapons development, space is compressed by a newfound capacity for speed. This gives rise to what Virilio calls the "aesthetics of disappearance." The merging of technology and violence gives rise to a new gnostic "mortification of the flesh."[11] As violence grows and intensifies, the city and other local forms of geographical and physical space, not to mention the body, are literally dis-

9. See Paul Virilio, *Ground Zero*, trans. Chris Turner (New York: Verso, 2002).

10. Paul Virilio, *The Information Bomb*, trans. Chris Turner (New York: Verso, 2000) 144–45.

11. Virilio, *Ground Zero*, 12. Among other things, this recent work is an attempt to links the question of violence to the contemporary fascination with the "neo-eugenic" project of the technological self-perfection of human life.

appearing. As Virilio himself puts it, "the world disappears in war, and war as a phenomenon disappears from the eyes of the world."[12]

In a related point of emphasis, Virilio maintains that our visual capacities are themselves transformed by the war-machine insofar as the "visual field" is reduced to the "technical sightline" of a military device.[13] As perception is mediated by the logic of violence as speed, a new vision of the world emerges. With the perfection of near-instantaneous real-time speed of delivery, television is transformed into a "planetary grand-scale optics" or "tele-surveillance," which fosters a preoccupation with security and a kind of universal voyeurism.[14] Local space and time disappear and are replaced by a single, global and virtual "real-time." With the triumph of this sort of "sightless vision" and the arrival of an "age of intensiveness," space is further compressed and power becomes even more total. Unlike Jean Baudrillard, who welcomes the disappearance of politics into a trans-political age of the "intensity of the instant," Virilio is harshly critical of this development as signalling a totalizing proliferation of violence.[15]

Because of the rise of technology in its relation to the military-industrial complex, Virilio argues that the logic of violence increasingly comes to dominate the very way we understand knowledge. This claim is further developed by means of the identification of a shift from strategy to logistics. By logistics, Virilio means the triumph of means over intelligence, where "rationality is considered only in terms of its efficiency, whatever the horizon."[16] Whereas violence begins with a strategic conception of quantitative, calculative rationality designed to manoeuvre and prepare for attacks in geographical space, it is transformed by means of the logic of speed into a logistical conception of technological, instrumental rationality dedicated to management and

---

12. Paul Virilio, *War and Cinema: The Logistics of Perception*, trans. Patrick Camiller (New York: Verso, 1984) 66, as quoted in John Armitage, "Beyond Postmodernism? Paul Virilio's Hypermodern Cultural Theory," *Ctheory* 23:3 (2000). Online: http://www.ctheory.net/articles.aspx?id=133.

13. Virilio, *War and Cinema*, 13, as quoted by Armitage, "Beyond Postmodernism?"

14. Virilio, *Information Bomb*, 12–13.

15. See, e.g., Virilio, *Pure War*, 34.

16. Ibid., 26.

hyper-centralization.[17] With the triumph of effectiveness, Virilio again claims that war and violence become increasingly total and omnipres-ent. The logic of violence tends towards what he calls "Pure War." From the standpoint of logistical rationality, violence is no longer "acted out in repetition," but involves an ongoing state of "infinite preparation."[18] In such a situation of pure war, "all of us are already civilian soldiers" participating in "acts of war without war."[19]

Virilio suggests that this totalizing logic of war and violence is ex-emplified in the way states tend no longer to be interested merely in the outward colonization of other peoples—what he calls "exo-colonization." Rather, Virilio claims that nations are increasingly engaged in projects of endo-colonization—the "inward" colonization of one's own popula-tion by means of systematic underdevelopment and "pauperization" in the name of a more complete investment in the economy of war: "In the society of national security . . . the armed forces turn against their own population: on the one hand to exact the funds necessary for Pure War, the infinite development of weaponry . . .; and on the other to control society."[20] Echoing Michel Foucault's account of "surveillance societies" and Gilles Deleuze's discussion of "control societies," Virilio claims that logistical rationality justifies a strategy of policing and managerial con-trol designed to condition people for more effective participation in the ever-expanding war-machine.

A Violent "Peace"?

The strength of Virilio's work consists in its incisive and penetrating analysis of the logic of contemporary war and the proliferation of vio-lence even in what is claimed to be a state of peace. Most importantly, Virilio's readings of contemporary culture help one to appreciate the sense in which much discourse about peace is dangerously misguided because it is blinded by its own complicity in the logic of violence and the war-machine. This is precisely the same danger that lurks in the work of those who enlist Yoder in support of the kind of transforma-

17. Ibid., 99.
18. Ibid., 92.
19. Ibid., 26, 32.
20. Ibid., 94.

tive social strategy mentioned above. In Virilio's terminology, this is to defend a logistical conception of peace that is bound to fail because it is thoroughly embedded in the very logic of violence. My attempt to read Yoder by way of Virilio in this manner is meant to suggest that Yoder's theology involves many of the same resources and interpretive moves that Virilio deploys in revealing the totalizing logic of Pure War and the war-machine. Among other things, I am suggesting that Virilio's analysis of the war-machine can be read as an updated and more militarily sophisticated version of what Yoder calls Constantinianism. In other words, the tendencies Virilio identifies can be added to the list of the many neo-Constantinianisms that Yoder insisted on identifying as an unsettling reminder to those who like to claim that we have reached something called post-Christendom that allegedly provides a newfound opportunity for the nonviolent church to articulate its theology on equal ground with the now disestablished established church.[21] In short, Virilio articulates various tendencies of the logic of violence with which I think Yoder would be largely in agreement. Yoder's resistance to the triumph of effectiveness, his refusal to read the peace of Christ in terms of the instrumentalist project of "putting handles on history in an attempt to move it in the right direction," is an attempt to call into question just the kind of policing of time Virilio identifies as characteristic of the rise of logistics. Indeed, Virilio's claim that "the will to organize time is a questioning of God" would serve nicely as a guiding hermeneutical principle for the interpretation of Yoder's theology as a whole.[22] At the same time, Yoder's interpretation of Constantinian violence also echoes Virilio's account of the aesthetics of disappearance, as he narrates the slide of the visible, embodied church into a preoccupation with the doctrine of the church's invisibility. On Yoder's reading, the church's complicity with violence is intimately linked to the disappearance of the visible church as an embodied politics of resistance. More recently, Yoder's interest in patience as an attempt to imagine a counter-epistemology of peace can be read against the background of

21. This tendency is perhaps best represented by J. Denny Weaver, *Anabaptist Theology in the Face of Postmodernity: A Proposal for the New Millennium* (Telford, PA: Pandora, 2000).

22. Virilio, *Pure War*, 128.

an appreciation of the logic of violence as speed that Virilio so helpfully articulates.

But not only are these important features of Yoder's work illuminated and enhanced by this kind of positive engagement with Virilio. What is even more important for the purposes of understanding Yoder's theology is the sense in which he is able to avoid certain weaknesses that have been associated with Virilio's work. While Virilio is helpful in diagnosing contemporary escalation of violence even in the absence of acts of war, he is noticeably less instructive in articulating the possible forms that resistance might take. When he is pushed on the question of what it would mean to resist the kind of totalizing violence he outlines, he tends to fall back on typically banal liberal clichés that appeal to education and better understanding. When asked "What strategies can we adopt to fight this exponential growth of destructive power?" Virilio answers: "Today, the target is to try to have an understanding of speed. Understand what's been happening for twenty-five years."[23] There is, of course, some truth to such an appeal for increased understanding, insofar as it can make us aware of our unacknowledged complicity with the war-machine. But if that is all there is to say on the matter, it remains a rather thin account of resistance. The significance of Yoder's work in this context is that it provides the kind of thick descriptions of counter-political and counter-epistemological practices that Virilio calls for but does not finally deliver.

The Territorial Lure of the Slow?
A Critique of Virilio and a Yoderian Rejoinder

At the same time, I want to suggest that Yoder's theology is better suited to respond to criticisms that have been directed at Virilio's account of the contemporary merging of violence and technology. In particular, William Connolly has argued that Virilio's work is limited by its near single-minded preoccupation with speed and the crisis of the physical dimension. Connolly claims that Virilio's interpretation of the logic of speed is overdetermined by the "military paradigm," such that he fails to appreciate the possibility of other, less threatening "modali-

23. Ibid., 62.

ties and experiences of speed."[24] In particular, he suggests that Virilio undervalues the "positive" contribution speed might make in "desanctifying" closed and exclusionary identities.[25] Connolly also maintains that Virilio's critical analysis of the transition from geo-political space to the chrono-political merging of space-time reveals an underlying commitment to the centred, territorial "memory of the nation" as the place where political deliberation should occur. In other words, Virilio remains committed to a concentric model of identity as a closed and bounded site of power from which identity emerges as a possession to be secured and protected against external threats. Connolly argues that such a spatial orientation is equally part of the logic of violence. And yet it is important to be clear that Connolly does not offer these objections as a complete refutation of Virilio's analysis of the relationship between speed and violence. Rather, he calls for a more ambiguous appreciation of the logic of speed. Connolly writes,

> Speed can be dangerous. At a certain point of acceleration, it jeopardizes freedom and shortens the time in which to engage ecological issues. But the crawl of slow time contains injuries, dangers, and repressive tendencies too. It may be wise therefore to explore speed as an ambiguous medium that contains some positive possibilities. The positive possibilities are lost to those who experience its effects only through nostalgia for a pristine time governed by the compass of the centered nation, the security of stable truth, the idea of nature as a purposive organism or a set of timeless laws, and the stolidity of thick universals.[26]

Whether or not Connolly's criticisms of Virilio are entirely on the mark is a question that merits further attention. Though I think it is misleading to interpret Virilio as if he were recommending a return to concentric and exclusionary identities of possession and control in which there is no room for any recognition of the positive value of speed, it would be easier to avoid such a misreading if he were more articulate about the possibilities of resistance. But that is a discussion that must be reserved for another context. What is more important for the purposes

24. William Connolly, "Speed, Concentric Cultures, and Cosmopolitanism," *Political Theory* 28 (2000) 596.

25. Ibid., 597.

26. Ibid., 598.

of the present discussion is to recognize that Yoder's theology provides just the kind of ambiguous analysis of the relationship between violence and speed that Connolly calls for Virilio to acknowledge. In short, I want to argue that the value of Yoder's nonviolent theology is that it provides both an appreciation of the logic of violence as speed that Virilio identifies, but also an appreciation of the violence of territoriality that Connolly points to in order to justify his more positive appreciation of the value of speed. In doing so, Yoder is simultaneously critical of both the logic of violence as speed and the aesthetics of disappearance that Virilio identifies, on the one hand, and the equally violent logic of the bounded, territorial space of possessive identity that Connolly worries about, on the other.

For the remainder of this essay, I will briefly outline some of the key resources that I take to support such a reading of Yoder's work. Against the background of Connolly's critique of Virilio, I begin with Yoder's discussion of the counter-political nature of the church as the diasporic, scattered body of Christ. From there, I will work backwards to the question of violence and speed I began with, but this will now be approached from the standpoint of Yoder's counter-epistemological notion of "patience as method." Finally, it will be instructive to note how these two closely interrelated moments in Yoder's nonviolent theology come together in his understanding of the practice of witness.

The Scattered Body of Christ

Like Virilio, Yoder's theology implies that the logic of violence manifests itself in an aesthetics of disappearance. It is for this reason that his work highlights the importance of the visible otherness of church as the body of Christ. But this is not to recommend a static, concentric conception of space of the kind that Connolly foists onto Virilio. Rather, Yoder's ecclesiology is best read as an ongoing experiment in the possibility of a nonviolent and non-concentric organization of political space. One of the most important aspects of Yoder's ecclesiology in this regard is his account of the diasporic, non-territorial existence of the church. This is in turn best understood against the background of Yoder's claim that the church must cultivate a readiness for radical reformation that consistently rejects the essentially violent temptations towards closure, finality, and purity that haunt so much contemporary theology—including much theology that claims to be oriented towards peace. In other words, Yoder's reading of the scattered body of Christ is most importantly an attempt to articulate an ecclesiology that resists the Constantinian temptation to self-absolutization.

Yoder's commitment to a non-concentric model of identity is reflected in his appreciation of the significance Jewish diaspora existence. "Dispersion is mission."[27] Scattering is the grace of God. It is possible to remain Jewish in exile, not because Jewish identity is strong, unbending, and self-sustaining. Rather, because it understands its peoplehood as a gift over which it is not finally "in charge," Jewish identity is fluid in a way that allows it to flourish in many different social settings.[28] Because its life is gift, God is able to "renew the life of faith anywhere."[29] It is significant that Yoder uses the terminology of renewing. The continued survival of the people of God is crucially not understood in terms of the category of preservation, but rather in terms of its receptivity to God's ongoing generosity. Jewish identity in exile is not to be secured by reproducing and protecting what has been left behind at "home." Rather, it is continuously refashioned as it enters into and interacts with different social contexts. In doing so, Jewish identity itself undergoes significant and unpredictable changes, even while it remains in some ways "the same."

On such a reading, the Jeremian call to "seek the peace of the city" names a way of engaging the world that simultaneously refuses both the universalist (chrono-political) temptation to privilege the language of the wider culture and the isolationist (geo-political) temptation to preserve and maintain the language of "home" in a kind of sectarian withdrawal. Diaspora Judaism neither fully renounces its past identity for unqualified citizenship in the new world, nor does it seek merely to preserve and maintain itself as a kind of static given. Both options presume a territorial conception of self-identity that defines itself over against otherness. The significance of the diasporic scattering of the body is

27. John Howard Yoder, *For the Nations: Essays Public and Evangelical* (Grand Rapids: Eerdmans, 1997) 52.

28. See ibid., 61, 66–70, for a discussion of the "Jewishness of the case against 'taking charge' of the course of history" (68).

29. Ibid., 53.

that it allows identity to be understood as an ongoing negotiation with the other. Accordingly, Yoder suggests that in becoming resident aliens, Jewish diaspora existence represents a third alternative to the standard options of universalist denial of the body and its existence in space and the isolationist preservation of it through policed boundaries.

Yoder's depiction of Jewish identity—and by extension his understanding of the church as the body of Christ—is thus similar to the "non-concentric" model of identity and social existence that Connolly calls for.[30] The diasporic notion of a scattered body rejects the idea of a closed and bounded space existing within a series of outwardly expanding circles. Identity is, rather, viewed as a negotiation of exchange, sometimes affirming, sometimes critical. It involves multiple networks of overlap and engagement with other cultural identities, each of which is itself interpreted as a potential gift in the hope that it participates somehow in the unpredictable and excessive economy of God. Because it renounces the temptation to understand its identity as a stable entity to be protected and preserved, one's social existence in space is thus "complicated and compromised by numerous crosscutting allegiances, connections, and modes of collaboration."[31]

Patience as Method

In addition to his nonviolent reconfiguration of political space, Yoder's theology equally involves the development of a nonviolent counter-epistemology. This is at least part of the meaning behind his oft-repeated declaration of the epistemological priority of the church to the world. In other words, the world names a series of violent habits of thought that are dedicated to security and insulation against risk. By contrast, Yoder's nonviolent epistemology does not attempt to secure or defend the truth of its distinctive claims against all comers. It is not an attempt to make Christianity necessary by developing arguments designed to make others "have to believe."[32] Rather, it assumes that truthfulness is an utterly contingent gift that can only be given and received and

30. Connolly, "Speed, Concentric Cultures, and Cosmopolitanism," 603.

31. Ibid.

32. See John Howard Yoder, "On Not Being Ashamed of the Gospel: Particularity, Pluralism, and Validation," *Faith and Philosophy* 9 (1992) 287.

that it emerges at the site of vulnerable interchange with the other. Accordingly, it is fundamentally open-ended and radically concrete, refusing any self-legitimating appeal to theoretical abstraction. Among the most important aspects of such a nonviolent epistemology is Yoder's understanding of "patience as method."

Much contemporary critical theory locates the problem of epistemological violence in the existence of totalizing metanarratives. The possibility of a nonviolent epistemology is then said to involve an appreciation of micronarrative particularity in which knowledges are given more fragmentary and ambiguous forms of expression. While Yoder is critical of the kind of violence associated with epistemolgies of totalizing metanarrative singularity, his reconfiguration of knowledge moves beyond the tendency to focus on metanarrativity as such to emphasize the significance of speed of delivery. Epistemological violence is associated not only with the scope of narrative, but it is also located in the speed with which such narratives, whether macro or micro, unfold.

In other words, epistemological non-Constantinianism is not merely opposed to metanarrative but also to hypernarrative. The problem with much contemporary theology is that it features a preoccupation with the epistemological and rhetorical movement of speed. This can be seen in the current preference for developing sweeping historical narratives that are not continuously problematized the way Yoder's reading of non-Constantinianism is. In short, theology operates according to a violent logic of speed whenever it is unwilling to risk the possibility that truthfulness is the outcome of ongoing, timeful "open conversation."

The value of Yoder's work is that it lingers. Not only is it important to appreciate his account of patience as an epistemological virtue in which the church cultivates a readiness for radical reformation as an alternative to manipulative and possessive modes of enquiry. Perhaps even more important that what he actually says about patience is the sense in which Yoder's work practices patience. Yoder's theology proceeds patiently, entering vulnerably into the world of another, rather than employing an accelerated and possessive or logistical hermeneutics of mastery and control. This is also exemplified in the way he keeps coming back to and complicating his understanding of non-Constantinianism with various versions of neo-Constantinianism, as noted above. In addition to the vision of a non-Constantinian epistemology of peace Yoder offers, patience is instructively exemplified in Yoder's own rhetorical practice in a way that distinguishes it from much contemporary theology and ethics. Yoder patiently enters into the messy world of concrete social reality, refusing to outfit history with handles for easier, more efficient negotiation, while others remain captured by the temptation to master contingency in their deployment of fast-moving hypernarrative strategies. He refuses to short-circuit debate and genuine engagement by moving on too quickly. And it is because he appreciates the connection between violence and speed in this way that Yoder helps to envision the possibility of the church as counter-political and counter-epistemological interruption of the logic of violence. The Constantinian logic of violence deploys speed as an evasion of risk, as an attempt to make theology necessary and secure. But Yoder argues that Christian theology fails when it tries to escape vulnerability because the gospel message of peace is a gift given in Jesus Christ.

One can see such an attempt to practice patience exemplified in Yoder's life-long engagement with the just war tradition. For the standpoint of the present discussion, what is particularly noteworthy about Yoder's numerous encounters with the just war tradition is the sense in which they embody a spirit of charitable receptivity to the voice of the other. He takes the possibility of a just war more seriously than many of his fellow pacifists. In fact, there is a sense in which he takes the just war tradition more seriously than many defenders of just war themselves. Yoder argues that christological pacifists have a stake in defending "the integrity of just-war thought" as a tradition "with teeth," and proceeds to do so by calling it to be more "honest" than it characteristically has been in articulating and observing the criteria for the discrimination of just and unjust wars.[33] In particular, he calls contemporary defenders of just war to be more honest in recognizing the stringent limits and

33. John Howard Yoder, *When War is Unjust: Being Honest in Just-War Thinking*, 2d ed. (Maryknoll, N.Y.: Orbis Books, 1996), 5. For a further discussion of Yoder's stake in defending the integrity of the just war tradition, see Reinhardt Hütter, "Be Honest in Just War Thinking! Lutherans, the Just War Tradition, and Selective Conscientious Objection," in *The Wisdom of the Cross: Essays in Honor of John Howard Yoder*, ed. Stanley Hauerwas, Chris K. Huebner, Harry J. Huebner, and Mark Thiessen Nation (Grand Rapids: Eerdmans, 1999) 69–83; and Tobias Winwright, "From Police Officers to Peace Officers," in *The Wisdom of the Cross*, 84–114.

restraints the tradition imposes on warfare.[34] Instead of suggesting that the just war tradition is essentially violent, and that it therefore must be rejected *as such*, Yoder seeks charitably to engage the just war tradition on its own terms and calls it to be clearer in articulating its general presumption against violence. In doing so, Yoder sets out to challenge two common and interrelated assumptions that inhibit debate about violence and nonviolence in the Christian tradition. First, he calls into question the assumption that the just war tradition is the majority view in the Christian tradition. Second, he challenges the idea that pacifism and just war are "diametrically opposed" stances.[35] Rather, he argues that the consistent embodiment of the just war tradition is an historical rarity, and that the majority stance involves a "realistic" or "blank check" endorsement of war in the name of national self-interest. When just war is thus properly situated alongside pacifism as a minority view, Yoder suggests that both pacifists and the defenders of the just war tradition have much to learn from a more serious engagement with one another.

To say that Yoder's engagement with the just war tradition exemplifies a stance of charitable receptivity to his dialogue partners is not to suggest that he is uncritical of the just war position. Indeed, there is a sense in which he is far more critical than many other pacifist approaches because his criticisms are more direct than the more common "theoretical" objections to the idea of just war in general. The value of Yoder's engagement with the just war tradition is that he strives to move beyond the general question of the rightness or wrongness of war as such and proceeds more deeply into the particularities of the debate, such as a discussion of the kinds of christological commitments involved in their various conceptions of charity or an examination of the kind of social formation the rival stances presume. It is also noteworthy that he often preferred to redirect the discussion to more specific questions such as the possibility of Christian participation in police work.[36] Instead of claiming to produce a final adjudication of the debate between pacifists and just warriors, much of Yoder's work is dedicated to making that discussion more complicated by elaborating the subtle differences

34. Yoder, *When War is Unjust*, 50.
35. Yoder, *When War is Unjust*, 6, 63.
36. See Winwright, "From Police Officers to Peace Officers," 108-114.

and varieties these stances have taken.[37] In all of these ways, he seeks to resist a logistical, totalizing, and concentric model of dialogue between pacifists and just warriors that is rooted in a logic of speed.

In Yoder's hands, pacifism and the just war tradition are not presented as two entirely distinct or concentric wholes. Rather, there are numerous strands of overlap and willingness to entertain the possibility of ongoing development and reformation in a way that cannot be predicted in advance. As Yoder himself puts it, "The exposition I have chosen is to let the panorama of diverse theories unfold progressively, from the dialogue already in progress, rather than proceeding 'foundationally' on the ground of what someone might claim as 'first principles.'"[38] Yoder's interest in defending the integrity of the just war tradition is part of a larger attempt to create conditions for productive dialogue and disagreement to take place. He worries that contemporary discussions too often short-circuit the possibility of genuine debate by oversimplifying and failing to engage the detailed complexity of rival stances. But what is important to recognize for the purposes of the present discussion is that this way of understanding dialogical engagement grows out of his attempt to articulate a nonviolent reconfiguration of knowledge. While he aims to make the just war tradition vulnerable to a pacifist interpretation of the Christian tradition, Yoder's work is equally an attempt to make Christian pacifism vulnerable to a just war understanding. This does not occur at the cost of critical engagement. Rather, Yoder seeks to show that such a discussion need not be an all-or-nothing affair. He denies the temptation to throw out the just war tradition as such in the way that pacifists too often do. Yoder's engagement with the just war tradition differs strikingly from other pacifist critics of just war who, in making their criticism too complete and thorough, embody the violence I have called methodological Constantinianism. Accordingly,

---

37. See, e.g., Yoder, *When War Is Unjust*, 71, where he argues that "the just-war tradition is not a simple formula ready to be applied in a self-evident and univocal way. It is rather a set of very broad assumptions whose implications demand–if they are to be respected as morally honest–that they be spelled out in some detail and then tested for their ability to throw serious light on real situations and on the decisions of persons and institutions regarding those situations." See also the examination of the many different varieties of religious pacifism in Yoder, *Nevertheless*.

38. John Howard Yoder, "How Many Ways Are There to Think Morally About War?" *Journal of Law and Religion* 11:1 (1994) 84.

one of Yoder's main contributions is his attempt to cultivate the kind of patience required to keep the debate alive. He does this from a standpoint that unapologetically defends a particular strand of the Christian pacifist tradition. But he also does so in a way that attempts to take seriously the alternative of just war as a genuine option in the Christian tradition. Whether defenders of the just war tradition respond in kind by treating such an understanding of Christian pacifism as a genuine option is something he cannot guarantee. It can only be hoped that a gift offered in a spirit of vulnerably is received and exchanged as a counter-gift in return.

The Practice of Witness

It is instructive to note that Yoder's joint emphasis on the diasporic, scattered body of Christ and his understanding of patience as method are brought together in his account of the missionary character of the church, and in particular the practice of witness. In short, the category of witness captures both the assumption that the church is called to be *for* the nations, and the recognition that it must remain nonviolent in being so oriented. Witness is rooted in the confession of the lordship of Christ, and the conviction that the model of lordship Christ embodies is the rule of the lamb. Yoder claims that "to confess that Jesus Christ is Lord makes it inconceivable that there should be any realm where his writ would not run. That authority, however, is not coercive but nonviolent; it cannot be imposed, only offered."[39] Because Christians confess that Jesus is lord of the whole cosmos, the church is called to share the gospel message as good news for the world. But because this good news involves a breaking of the cycle of violence that includes the renunciation of logistical effectiveness and possessive sovereignty, it can only be offered as a gift whose reception cannot be guaranteed or enforced. A non-Constantinian understanding of witness does not begin with a theory of universal validation through which the truth of the gospel message can *then* be justified to all people. Yoder maintains that this is just another manifestation of the Constantinian preoccupation with effectiveness in attempting to make history come out right. He is thus calling into question the sense in which the category of wit-

39. Yoder, *For the Nations*, 25.

ness itself tends to be understood in terms of the violent logic of speed. Yoder's genealogical analysis of Constantinianism suggests that such an "apologetic" conception of witness is only intelligible against the background of the presumption that humans are responsible for controlling the world. However, witness looks different from the standpoint of the non-Constantinian church's *hope* that God is in control of history.

To say that witness is gift is to say that the gospel message is offered in the absence of any additional handles designed to make it better stick. The "test" of witness is not simply whether or not it is received "in fact," but whether it is received *as gift*. The gift of good news is to be received "as it is" or "in its own right" and not by means of an additional vehicle or medium that might guarantee its successful passage. Because the gospel message is that of a peace that rejects the primacy of effectiveness, the message itself is the only available medium. Accordingly, Yoder claims that "the challenge to the faith community should not be to dilute or filter or translate its witness, so that the 'public' community can handle it without believing, but to so purify and clarify and exemplify it that the world can perceive it to be good news without having to learn a foreign language."[40] While Yoder emphasizes that the good news turns on its being received by the listener, this is not to suggest that it is preoccupied with what people want to hear.[41] Such an assumption would suggest that there is a sense in which the gift is "known" prior to its being received in such a way that it equally ceases to be a genuine gift.[42] Rather than identifying underlying conditions or developing new strategies for the effective deliverance of the "truth," the church is called to embody its otherness in such a way that makes intelligible the truth of Christ for the world. To emphasize the missionary existence of the peace church is to suggest that it lives not as instrument, but as example. The task of the church is thus not to "Christianize" the world, but to *be* the church. As Yoder himself puts it, the primary meaning of witness is "the functional necessity of just being there with a particular identity."[43] Witness thus

---

40. Yoder, *For the Nations*, 24.

41. Yoder, "A People in the World," in *The Royal Priesthood: Essays Ecclesiological and Ecumenical*, ed. Michael G. Cartwright (Grand Rapids: Eerdmans, 1994) 86.

42. See Yoder, *For the Nations*, 24, n. 22: "'Good news' is a kind of knowledge which is not known until one receives it, but then is received as good."

43. Yoder, *For the Nations*, 42.

names a way of life characteristic of the body of Christ, a scattered body whose existence is non-territorial and non-concentric. In so being, the church is called to provide a concrete example of good news to and for the world. The good news is that of an alternative way of life that is not rooted in the violent impulse towards self-preservation, but rather the nonviolent and vulnerable receptivity of the other as gift.

In conclusion, let me renarrate this interpretation of Yoder's political and epistemological reconfigurations of peace in terms of the logic of violence as Virilio articulates it. Like Virilio, Yoder rejects an outlook of split-second responsiveness and technical effectiveness that ultimately turns on the desire to secure power. But at the same time, this is not a complete refusal of movement that might justify an attitude of territorial enclosure. Yoder's account of the church and its characteristic modes of knowledge are an attempt to develop a conception of timefulness that resists both the absolute prioritization of speed and its ultimate overcoming. A pacifist outlook is constantly moving, sometimes radically, but only because it involves the patience to hear all the relevant sides of the conversation. This is a crucial lesson to learn not least because it recognizes that the standard alternatives of a static exclusivism that silences the voice of the other and a hyper-accelerated tolerance that allows a space for the other to talk without hearing what it has to say are equally implicated in a totalizing knowledge-politics complex that is finally violent precisely because it is primarily motivated by an attempt to insulate against risk. The great significance of Yoder's work lies in its ability to demonstrate that no such approach is capable of receiving the gracious gift of God in Jesus Christ that is peace itself.

8

On Exile: Yoder, Said, and a Politics of Land and Return

ALAIN EPP WEAVER

We travel like other people, but we return to nowhere. As if traveling
is the way of the clouds. We have buried our loved ones in the
    darkness of the clouds, between the roots of the trees.
And we said to our wives: go on giving birth to people like us
    for hundreds of years so we can complete this journey
To the hour of a country, to a meter of the impossible. . . .

We have a country of words. Speak speak so we may know the end of
    this travel.

   —**Mahmoud Darwish**

The Palestinian poet Mahmoud Darwish quoted in the epigraph
captures well the ambiguities of exile: travel without end; the pain of
disconnection and the nostalgia of memory; the realization, encoded
in the closing demand to "Speak speak," that for a people who have
"a country of words," return from exile, the end of travel, will more
likely than not be textual rather than physical.[1] Darwish thus shows the
reality of millions of Palestinians exiled from their land, living without
fixed destination, and sustained by the tenuous hope of return.

1. Mahmoud Darwish, "We Travel Like Other People," Larry Towell, *Then Palestine*
(New York: Aperture, 1998) 32.

How should Palestinian exile, and exile more generally, be understood theologically? How should Christians understand the dreams of many exiles, dreams that often appear hopeless, of return to their homes? John Howard Yoder would probably have objected to starting with such general questions—they might have struck him as too "methodologistic," beginning theological reflection with abstract questions rather than with God's story in Scripture and the church.[2] Nevertheless, the drama of exile, especially as displayed in Jeremiah's call to the exiles to seek the peace of the city in which they find themselves (Jer 29:7), played a key role in shaping Yoder's reading of Scripture, his ecclesiology, and his missiology. As early as 1973 Yoder was probing the fruitfulness of the theme of exile for theology, considering exile and exodus as two faces of liberation.[3] Exile, while painful, opens up a new chapter in the history of the radical reliance of the people of God on God alone. God's people, for Yoder, are called to a nonviolent dependence on God that eschews the sovereignty of the sword in favor of embodying an alternative politics amidst the Babylons of the world.

Yoder tentatively wondered about the relevance of this exilic, Jeremian vision for displaced peoples. Was there "something about this Jewish vision of the dignity and ministry of the scattered people of God which might be echoed or replicated by other migrant peoples?" he asked. "Might there even be something helpful in this memory which would speak by a more distant analogy to the condition of peoples overwhelmed by imperial immigration, like the original Americans or Australians, or the Ainu or the Maori?"[4] Yoder recognized the potential affront of his question, I believe, and thus phrased it carefully. Nevertheless, the provocation remains: can those who have been violently uprooted from their lands embrace as good news the prophetic admonition to build houses and plant gardens in exile?

---

2. For Yoder on "methodologism," see his article, "Walk and Word: The Alternatives to Methodologism," in *Theology without Foundations: Religious Practice and the Future of Theological Truth*, ed. Stanley Hauerwas, Nancey Murphy, and Mark Nation (Nashville: Abingdon, 1994) 77–90.

3. John Howard Yoder, "Exodus and Exile: Two Faces of Liberation," *CrossCurrents* 23 (1973) 279–309.

4. Yoder, *For the Nations: Essays Public and Evangelical* (Grand Rapids: Eerdmans, 1997) 82.

Yoder's appropriation of Jeremiah's call to the exiles holds significant promise for a hermeneutics of Scripture, for an interpretation of
church history, and for the articulation of a nonviolent ecclesiological politics. However, can the call to seek the peace of the city of one's
exile also be heard as good news, even if only by distant analogy, by
the millions upon millions of people in the modern period who have
been violently uprooted by imperial and colonial practice? What does
Jeremiah's call mean for a return to one's land, for justice for the exiled
refugee? Are justice and return endlessly deferred, postponed until the
eschaton?

I propose to tackle these questions through an examination of the
way the motif of exile functions in the thought and politics of the prolific and provocative Palestinian-American critic Edward Said, whose
writings display the agonies and the promise of exile. Said offered a
multifaceted appraisal of exile: while insisting on its harrowing character, he also expounded at length on the critical epistemological and
moral possibilities opened up by exile. I contend that an exilic consciousness of not being fully at home in one's home so long as injustice
endures can contribute to a theology of living rightly and justly in the
land. This view from exile, Said's work teaches us, poses a challenge to
exclusionary politics that would deny a just place in the land for both
Palestinian and Israeli.[5]

An initial caveat: Said, given his relentless critique of religion, his
stark opposition between religious (bad) and secular (good) criticism,
and his desire to keep religion in proper bounds, might appear an odd
thinker to bring into conversation with Yoder, someone who operated
within an explicitly theological horizon, who lived under the authority
of God's Word and the church, and who resisted liberalism's attempts
to confine the church's witness.[6] Apart from noting the similarities in

5. The difference that the exilic perspective makes for an assessment of the
Palestinian-Israeli conflict is developed briefly at the end of this chapter. I address this
topic more thoroughly in my *States of Exile: Visions of Diaspora, Witness, and Return*
(Scottdale, PA: Herald, 2008).

6. The religious-secular opposition will surface several times in the following
section. Rather than attempting to parse the different, and to my mind ultimately
incoherent, ways in which Said uses this opposition, I will only note that I find the
opposition to lack critical persuasiveness. For a helpful critique of Said on "religious"
and "secular" criticism, see William D. Hart, *Edward Said and the Religious Effects of
Culture* (Cambridge: Cambridge University Press, 2000).

the wide-ranging, amateur character of their intellects, what theologically useful observations can possibly come of bringing Yoder into conversation with such an aggressive, even dogmatic, secularist?[7] Clearly, Said's treatment of religion is problematic at many levels. Nevertheless, I maintain that in Said's appropriation of exile we find a distant analogy to Jeremiah's vision for the people of God in exile and that exploring these distant analogies, what Karl Barth called "secular parables of the kingdom," provides provocative material for reflection as Christians seek to articulate theologies of exile, land, and return.[8]

John Howard Yoder on the Theological Politics of Exile

Just as "Constantinianism" named for Yoder the perennial threat and temptation for the people of God, so did the Jeremian vision of the people of God living faithfully in exile form Yoder's positive vision for the church.[9] Grasping the importance of Jeremiah's call to the exiles for Yoder sheds light on his reading of Scripture, his understanding of church history, and his theology of Judaism.[10]

7. Said's defense of "amateurism" as an intellectual stance that revels "in making connections across lines and barriers, in refusing to be tied down to a specialty, in caring for ideas and values despite the restrictions of a profession" brings to mind Yoder's wide-ranging intellect and his fruitful bringing together of scholarship in biblical studies, church history, ethics, theology, and beyond. See Said, *Representations of the Intellectual* (London: Vintage, 1994) 57.

8. For a discussion of Barth's treatment of "secular parables of the Kingdom," see chapter 6 of Alain Epp Weaver, *States of Exile*.

9. For Yoder, "Constantinianism" did not simply name the church's alliance with and dissolution into the violent politics of empire, but also designated the perennial temptation for the church to abandon discipleship to its nonviolent Lord in favor of alignment with other, allegedly wider, social movements. For a nuanced treatment of Yoder on "Constantinianism," see Michael G. Cartwright, "Radical Reform, Radical Catholicity: John Howard Yoder's Vision of the Faithful Church," in John Howard Yoder, *The Royal Priesthood: Essays Ecclesiological and Ecumenical* (Grand Rapids: Eerdmans, 1994) esp. 5–14. See also Craig A. Carter, *The Politics of the Cross: The Theology and Social Ethics of John Howard Yoder* (Grand Rapids: Brazos, 2001) 155–78, and Alain Epp Weaver, "After Politics: John Howard Yoder, Body Politics, and the Witnessing Church," *Review of Politics* 61 (1999) 649–52.

10. Yoder's unpublished writings on Judaism, mostly consisting of lectures delivered at Bethel College in Kansas, Earlham College in Indiana, and the Tantur Ecumenical Institute in Jerusalem, were collected by Yoder as *The Jewish-Christian Schism Revisited: A Bundle of Old Essays* (Elkhart, IN: Shalom Desktop Publication,

Let us begin with Scripture. Any Christian reading of the Old Testament must inevitably grapple with the plurality of voices and genres presented therein, interpreting its multiple strands and perspectives from God's definitive revelation in Jesus Christ. The pacifist Christian, in particular, must struggle to understand the continuity of the two Testaments without resorting to a Marcionite dismissal of the God of the Old Testament and its wars of conquest as different from the God of love incarnated in Jesus Christ; rather, we must insist that the Triune God who reveals the nonviolent "grain of the universe" in Jesus's life, death and resurrection is the God of Israel.[11]

The theological vision from exile, Yoder argued, is one of "not being in charge." The exiles in Babylon do not rule the empire, or even a little corner of it, but instead live without sovereignty in the midst of empire. Because "God is sovereign over history, there is no need to seize (or subvert) sovereignty in order for God's will to be done." Living outside of the land, the community in Babylon relies solely on God for the sustaining of its life and becomes nonviolent in style and substance.[12] The continuity of this exilic vision with Yoder's ecclesiology should be clear: the church is the community called to go out into the world, into diaspora (Matthew 25), a community that refuses to wield violent force, pointing instead to God's sovereignty and the conviction that Jesus has

---

1996). These essays were then published posthumously as *The Jewish-Christian Schism Revisited*, ed. Michael Cartwright and Peter Ochs (Grand Rapids: Eerdmans, 2003); the volume includes introductions and an afterword by editors Cartwright and Ochs and responses to each chapter by Ochs. All citations are from the posthumously published edition.

11. The phrase, "with the grain of the universe," is Yoder's. See his article, "Armaments and Eschatology," *Studies in Christian Ethics* 1 (1988) 43–61. Stanley Hauerwas appropriated it as the title of his Gifford lectures; see Hauerwas, *With the Grain of the Universe: The Church's Witness and Natural Theology* (Grand Rapids: Brazos, 2001). Both Yoder and Hauerwas assume in their writings that it is the same Triune God to whom both Testaments witness and whose nonviolent, self-giving love embodies the true "grain of the universe." For seminal studies that emphasize the identity of the Triune God with YHWH, the God of Israel, see R. Kendall Soulen, *The God of Israel and Christian Theology* (Minneapolis: Fortress, 1996) and Scott Bader-Saye, *Church and Israel after Christendom: The Politics of Election* (Boulder: Westview, 1996).

12. John Howard Yoder, *Jewish-Christian Schism*, 191.

already triumphed over the powers of death, a triumph which will ulti-mately be revealed to all.[13]

If the continuity between Jeremiah's vision for the exiles and New Testament ecclesiology (as interpreted by Yoder) should be clear, the relationship between the call to exile and other parts of the Old Testament, such as the embrace of sovereign kingship in the land or the violent conquest of the land, might well appear to be one of tension, even conflict.[14] Yoder resolved this tension by focusing his attention on one thematic strand in the Old Testament, namely, Israel's radical de-pendence on God alone. Yoder did not deny and need not have denied that Scripture contains multiple strands, some of them in tension with one another; he did believe, however, that by identifying a strand within Scripture that repeatedly insists on God's absolute sovereignty and the people's concomitant dependence on God alone, one could highlight the continuity between YHWH the God of Israel and the Triune God incarnate in the non-violent Messiah.[15]

Exile, Yoder suggested, did not simply equal punishment in Israel's history, but represented a new opportunity for mission in the world and stood in continuity with God's previous gracious acts of dispersal, dispersal which highlighted the people of God's absolute dependence on God. Interpreting the Babel story in Genesis 11, Yoder wrote that

13. Consider, for example, the following: "That Christian pacifism which has a theological basis in the character of God and the work of Jesus Christ is one in which the calculating link between our obedience and ultimate efficacy has been broken, since the triumph of God comes through resurrection and not through effective sov-ereignty or assured survival" (Yoder, *The Politics of Jesus: Vicit Agnus Noster*, 2nd ed. [Grand Rapids: Eerdmans, 1994] 239).

14. For a treatment of the theme of exile in Scripture, see the work of one of Yoder's students, Daniel Smith-Christopher, *A Biblical Theology of Exile: Overtures to Biblical Theology* (Minneapolis: Fortress, 2002).

15. Some might accuse Yoder of random selectivity in highlighting this particular strand in his attempt to provide a unified reading of the Old Testament that stands in continuity with the New. The selectivity was certainly not random, in that Yoder read Scripture, as should all Christians, through the lens of God incarnate in Jesus of Nazareth. To those who would reject the attempt to provide a coherent reading of Scripture, championing instead a "postmodernist" interplay of competing, conflicting voices within Scripture, it can only be answered that the postmodern valorization of a plurality of voices, none with more interpretive weight than the others, is itself a particular way of unifying the texts, one with its own implicit ethical and theological agenda, an agenda, one might add, which does not make the rejection of violence central to God's purposes in the world.

"Diversity was the original divine intent; if God is good and diversity is good, then each of the many diverse identities which resulted from the multiplying of languages and the resultant scattering is also good."[16] The exile to Babylon then becomes on this reading another act of gracious dispersal: while the false prophets preach a premature return to the land, Jeremiah calls on the exiles to "seek the peace/salvation (*shalom*) of the city" (29:7).

Just as the exiles in Babylon live dependent on God and without reliance on their own sovereignty, so do the narratives of Exodus and the conquest of the land in the wars of YHWH exhibit a radical, completely dependent trust in God. "'Trust in JHWH/Adonai' is what opens the door to His saving intervention," claimed Yoder. "It is the opposite of making one's own political/military arrangements."[17] When addressing the question of Israelite monarchy with its violent exercise of sovereignty, Yoder turned to such texts as Judges 9, 1 Samuel 8, and Deut 17:14ff., texts that exhibit "the antiroyal strand of the earlier history" of Israel that rejected any sovereign other than God. Exile, for Yoder, was not a brief hiatus between monarchy and the return to the land; rather, monarchy formed a problematic interruption in a history

---

16. Yoder, *For the Nations*, 64. For a more extended engagement with Genesis 11, see Yoder, "Meaning after Babble: With Jeffrey Stout beyond Relativism," *Journal of Religious Ethics* 24 (1996) 125–39.

17. Yoder, *Jewish-Christian Schism*, 71. Yoder did not address, to my knowledge, the question most pressing to Palestinian Christians when reading the narratives of the Exodus and the entry into the Land, namely, the genocide of the native inhabitants. Yoder's appropriation of YHWH war is helpful and impressive; what one misses in Yoder is any appreciation for how these narratives leave the Canaanites and others outside of the sphere of moral concern. One can, of course, follow historical criticism and question the historicity of the Exodus or the conquest, but one cannot escape the fact that the voice of the Canaanite is simply silent in the texts. Instead, their cities and lands are taken over—a vision of landlessness that stands in haunting analogy to the destruction of over 400 Palestinian villages in 1948. One can observe, of course, that other parts of Scripture clearly bring the nations, the Gentiles, within the orbit of God's redemptive action: what Yoder did not do (but, I would contend, should have done) was to argue that other parts of the Scriptural witness correct for the partially defective understanding of God present in the narratives of YHWH war. For a classic polemic noting the erasure of Canaanites and Palestinians from the sphere of moral concern, together with a critique of the attempt of a contemporary Jewish political theorist to appropriate Exodus as a model for radical politics, see Edward Said, "Michael Walzer's Exodus and Revolution: A Canaanite Reading," in *Blaming the Victims: Spurious Scholarship and the Palestinian Question* (London: Verso, 1988) 161–78.

of dispersal as mission. "The move to Babylon," Yoder argued, "was not a two-generation parenthesis after which the Davidic or Solomonic project was supposed to take up again where it had left off. It was rather the beginning, under a firm, fresh prophetic mandate, of a new phase of the Mosaic project."[18] "Jeremiah's abandoning statehood for the future," Yoder continued, "is thus not so much forsaking an earlier hope as it is returning to the original trust in JHWH."[19]

Yoder thus identified a strand within the multiplicity of texts in the Old Testament that insists on complete dependence on God alone. Reading back from the Resurrection, we can not only observe that this strand stands in continuity with Jesus's nonviolent trust in God unto death, but can identify certain aspects of that strand, such as Jeremiah's counsel to the exiles, as very close to the nonviolent coming of God in Jesus.[20] Jesus "rounds out" the mitigation of violence within the prophetic portions of the Old Testament, "and says that what it meant for Abraham to let God's future be in God's hands, and what it meant for Moses and Joshua to let the survival of the people be a miracle, means that now we don't have to kill anybody." This view is not "evolutionary" in that it does not assume some "survival of the fittest" in a contest of ideas, but Yoder concedes that its assumption of "organic growth under guidance" is in some ways similar to models that see evolutionary development within Scripture.[21]

"How can we sing the Lord's songs in a foreign land?" the Psalmist asks. "Painful as the question is," Yoder responded, "that is what the Jews learned to do, and do well."[22] Exile marked a new beginning in the history of God's people, one that would continue in the history of the early church and in the life of the Jewish people in diaspora. While the church would lose sight of its calling to live as an embodied alternative to the violent politics of empire, becoming entangled in various forms of Constantinian compromise, Jewish communities in exile more successfully stayed true to the Jeremian call. "Occasionally privileged after

18. Yoder, *For the Nations*, 53.

19. Yoder, *Jewish-Christian Schism*, 71.

20. Yoder, *For the Nations*, 74–75.

21. Yoder, *Christian Attitudes to War, Peace, and Revolution*, ed. Theodore J. Koontz and Andy Alexis-Baker (Grand Rapids: Brazos, 2009) 327.

22. Yoder, *For the Nations*, 56.

the model of Joseph," Yoder noted, "more often emigrating, frequently suffering martyrdom nonviolently, [Jews] were able to maintain identity without turf or sword, community without sovereignty. They thereby demonstrated pragmatically the viability of the ethic of Jeremiah and Jesus. In sum: the Jews of the Diaspora were for over a millennium the closest thing to the ethic of Jesus existing on any significant scale anywhere in Christendom."[23] Jewish communities in Diaspora thus lived as embodied critiques of Constantinian Christendom. Zionism, in contrast, as a late nineteenth-century form of European nationalism, represents a sharp departure from Jeremiah's exilic vision.[24] An analysis of the ways in which Zionist discourse negates the diaspora and an assessment of the possibilities of retrieving an exilic politics after Zionism will be my concern in the final part of this essay.

The Moral Task of the Exilic Intellectual

How can Yoder's theological politics of exile speak to the Palestinian experience of dispossession? Palestinian existence is at root one of exile. Dispersed geographically and separated by borders, Palestinians nevertheless form "a community, if at heart a community built on suffering and exile."[25] In the Arab-Israeli war of 1948, in what Palestinians call the *Nakba* (Arabic for "catastrophe"), well over 700,000 Palestinians fled in fear from the fighting or were driven from their homes by the Israeli military forces that proceeded to destroy more than 500 villages. Many of these refugees and their descendants now live in United Nations–administered camps throughout the Middle East, denied the

23. Yoder, *Jewish-Christian Schism*, 81–82.

24. Zionism, for Yoder, represents Judaism's full assimilation into the Christendom of the West: "The culmination of the Christianization of Judaism, then, is the development of Zionism. Zionism creates a secular democratic nation state after the model of the nation states of the West. It defines Jews, for the purpose of building the state, in such a way that it makes no difference if most of them are unbelieving or unobservant. In America the Jews are 'like a church' with a belief structure, lifestyle commitments, and community meetings; in Israel Judaism is a nation and the belief dimension no longer matters. To be born in the state of Israel makes one less of a Jew, in the deep historical sense of the term, than to be born in a ghetto" (Yoder, *Jewish-Christian Schism*, 154).

25. Edward Said, *After the Last Sky: Palestinian Lives* (London: Vintage, 1986) 5.

possibility of returning to their homes and properties.[26] Some of these uprooted Palestinians remained in what became the State of Israel, classified as "present absentees" under the Absentee Property Law of 1951 and prevented from returning to their land.[27] Tens of thousands more Palestinians, many of them already refugees, became refugees once more in 1967, driven out of Mandate Palestine across the Jordan River by Israeli forces.

Since 1967, for Palestinians in the occupied territories of the West Bank, East Jerusalem, and the Gaza Strip, dispossession has taken a variety of forms. The Israeli civil administration confiscates land from Palestinians for the construction of colonies that are illegal under international law. Israeli bulldozers destroy Palestinian homes and rip up Palestinian orchards and vineyards. The Israeli Interior Ministry uses a variety of pretexts to strip Palestinians of identity cards that allow them to live in their Jerusalem homes, while thousands of Palestinians born in the Occupied Territories who went abroad for work, study, or family reasons are barred from re-entry. Roadblocks and walls separate Palestinian from Palestinian, making travel between the West Bank and the Gaza Strip impossible, while travel within the north and south of the West Bank is strictly regulated through a complex permit system and network of checkpoints.[28]

26. A comprehensive source of information on Palestinian refugee history, their legal status, and their present living conditions is *A Survey of Palestinian Refugees and Internally Displaced Persons, 2004–2005* (Bethlehem: BADIL Resource Center, 2006). For treatments of the war of 1948 and the Palestinian Nakba, see *The War for Palestine: Rewriting the History of 1948*, ed. Eugene L. Rogan and Avi Shlaim (Cambridge: Cambridge University Press, 2001); Ilan Pappé, *The Making of the Arab-Israeli Conflict, 1947–1951* (London: I. B. Tauris, 1992); Benny Morris, *The Birth of the Palestinian Refugee Problem, 1947–1949* (Cambridge: Cambridge University Press, 1987); Avi Shlaim, *Collusion Across the Jordan: King Abdullah, the Zionist Movement, and the Partition of Palestine* (Oxford: Clarendon, 1988); Nur Masalha, *Expulsion of the Palestinians: The Concept of "Transfer" in Zionist Political Thought, 1882–1948* (Washington, DC: Institute for Palestine Studies, 1992); Walid Khalidi, ed., *All That Remains: The Palestinian Villages Occupied and Depopulated by Israel in 1948* (Washington, DC: Institute for Palestine Studies, 1992); and Meron Benvenisti, *Sacred Landscape: The Buried History of the Holy Land since 1948* (Berkeley: University of California Press, 2000).

27. For more on internally displaced Palestinians inside Israel, see *Catastrophe Remembered: Palestine, Israel, and the Internal Refugees*, ed. Nur Masalha (London: Zed, 2005).

28. Critical descriptions of the Israeli matrix of control in the Occupied Territories

Palestinians are thus continually ripped out of their contexts and find themselves travelers in a strange world. "The Palestinian is very much a person in transit," Said noted. "Suitcase or bundle of possessions in hand, each family vacates territory left behind for others, even as new boundaries are traversed, new opportunities created, new realities set up."[29] If exile creates "new opportunities," it also is profoundly alienating. "Exile is a series of portraits without names, without contexts. Images that are largely unexplained, nameless, mute."[30] Without continuity of place, Palestinians experience no continuity of identity. "Palestinian life is scattered, discontinuous, marked by the artificial and imposed arrangements of interrupted or confined space, by the dislocations and unsynchronized rhythms of disturbed time," Said explained, "where no straight line leads from home to birthplace to school to maturity, all events are accidents, all progress is a digression, all residence is exile."[31]

De-centered, out of place, Palestinian life becomes one of travel without fixed destination: "Our truest reality is expressed in the way we cross over from one place to another," Said insisted. "We are migrants and perhaps hybrids in, but not of, any situation in which we find ourselves. This is the deepest continuity of our lives as a nation in exile and constantly on the move."[32] Rupture of continuity is the fate of the defeated, while the victors, the powerful, remain in place. "Continuity for *them*, the dominant population," Said noted, as opposed to "discontinuity for us, the dispossessed and dispersed."[33] Said's emphasis on the Palestinians' "privilege of obduracy," their steadfastness (*sumud*), the declaration that "here we are, unmoved by your power, proceeding with our lives and with future generations," is a way of desperately trying to hold on, amidst the transit of exile, so that the de-centeredness of exile does not become dissolution.[34]

---

include Eyal Weizman, *Hollow Land: Israel's Architecture of Occupation* (London: Verso, 2007) and Jeff Halper, *Obstacles to Peace: A Re-Framing of the Palestinian-Israeli Conflict* (Jerusalem: The Israeli Committee against House Demolitions, 2004).

29. Said, *After the Last Sky*, 130.

30. Ibid., 12.

31. Ibid., 20–21.

32. Ibid., 164.

33. Ibid., 20–21.

34. Ibid., 68.

Said strenuously objected to any attempts to romanticize exile. "Exile is one of the saddest fates," he wrote. "There has always been an association between the idea of exile and the terrors of being a leper, a social and moral untouchable."[35] For Palestinians, the experience of exile has not only been physically and emotionally painful, but it has had negative effects on individual exiles and on the exiled community as a whole. "Our collective history *fil-kharij* ('in the exterior') or in the *manfa* and *ghurba* ('exile' and 'estrangement') has been singularly unsuccessful," Said judged, "progressively graceless, unblessed, more and more eccentric, de-centered, and alienated."[36] Exile can turn people inward, generating a form of sectarian withdrawal that shuns those outside the community. Exile is a "jealous state" that can create "an exaggerated sense of group solidarity, and a passionate hostility to outsiders, even those who may in fact be in the same predicament as you."[37] Ripped out of place, the exile often seeks solace in uncritical commitment to political parties and institutions, a tendency that Said, as a perpetual critic of the Palestine Liberation Organization, carefully resisted.

Meanwhile, those who resist the temptation to subscribe blindly to political programs face the temptation of individualistic withdrawal away from all communities. Exile is marked by "the sheer fact of isolation and displacement, which produces the kind of narcissistic masochism that resists all efforts at amelioration, acculturation, and community. At this extreme," Said warned, "the exile can make a fetish of exile, a practice that distances him or her from all connections and commitments."[38]

Critiquing attempts to find a moral within exile, Said demanded that the brute reality of life in the refugee camp be given priority over literary treatments of exile in any critical evaluation of forced displacement. "Exiled poets and writers lend dignity to a condition legislated to deny dignity—to deny an identity to people," Said maintained. "To concentrate on exile as a contemporary political punishment, you must therefore map territories of experience beyond those mapped by the

35. Said, *Representations of the Intellectual*, 35.

36. Said, *After the Last Sky*, 51.

37. Said, *Reflections on Exile and Other Essays* (Cambridge: Harvard University Press, 2000) 178.

38. Ibid., 183.

literature of exile itself. You must first set aside Joyce and Nabokov and think instead of the uncountable masses for whom UN agencies have been created."[39] Literature and religion run the risk of downplaying the horrors of exile in the interests of extracting new insights from exile itself. In contrast, Said countered:

> On the twentieth-century scale, exile is neither aesthetically nor humanistically comprehensible: at most the literature about exile objectifies an anguish and a predicament most people rarely experience first hand; but to think of the exile informing this literature as beneficially humanistic is to banalize its mutilations, the losses it inflicts on those who suffer them, the muteness with which it responds to any attempt to understand it as "good for us." Is it not true that the views of exile in literature and, moreover, in religion obscure what is truly horrendous: that exile is irremediably secular and unbearably historical?[40]

Here Said's critical evaluation of exile would appear to run directly counter to Yoder's exilic theological appropriation of exile. Said's caution about an aesthetic or religious amelioration of exile's pains serves as a needed reminder that we must not lose sight of the fact that exile does not simply name a concept but designates a condition in which millions of people live. Romanticized treatments of exile are neither theologically nor politically persuasive.

Can nothing, then, be learned from exile? Said's own writings suggest otherwise. Just as Yoder articulated a missiological vocation for the people of God in exile, so Said argued that exile opens up an intellectual and moral space that provides for the intellectual a place from which to resist co-optation into becoming an apologist for power and creates a discomfort with being settled in one's home so long as injustice forces homelessness on others.

For Said, exile is the proper *place* for the critic, the intellectual. "If you think about exile as a permanent state, both in the literal and in the intellectual sense, then it's a much more promising, if difficult, thing. Then you're really talking about movement, about homelessness

39. Ibid., 175.

40. Ibid., 174. "Secular" in this context appears to mean for Said that exile cannot be placed into a larger transcendental, theological context of meaning. It is an agonizingly concrete situation with no hope for amelioration (other than what the exile herself can produce).

in the sense in which [Georg] Lukàcs talks about it in *The Theory of the Novel*—'transcendental homelessness'—which can acquire a particular intellectual mission that I associate with criticism."[41] While exile "is an *actual* condition," it also functions in Said's thought as "a *metaphorical* condition." Developing a distinction between insider and outsider intellectuals reminiscent of Yoder's contrast between the Constantinian and free churches, Said differentiated between those on the one hand who belong fully to the society as it is, who flourish in it without an overwhelming sense of dissonance or dissent, those who can be called yea-sayers; and on the other hand, the nay-sayers, the individuals at odds with their society and therefore outsiders and exiles so far as privileges, power, and honors are concerned.[42]

The responsibility of the intellectual is to offer a critique from exile. "Exile for the intellectual in this meta-physical sense," according to Said, "is restlessness, movement, constantly being unsettled, and unsettling others. You cannot go back to some earlier and perhaps more stable condition of being at home; and, alas, you can never fully arrive, be at one with your new home or situation."[43] Even those who have not experienced the pain of being physically uprooted from their homes can be marginal to the powers (of the academy, government, the news media, etc.) that reward uncritical support for policies that oppress, exclude, and dispossess. "Exile means that you are always going to be marginal. Exile is a model for the intellectual who is tempted, and even beset and overwhelmed, by the rewards of accommodation, yea-saying, settling in."[44] Furthermore, the exilic intellectual should not succumb to

41. Said, *Power, Politics, and Culture: Interviews with Edward Said*, ed. Gauri Viswanathan (New York: Pantheon, 2001) 56.

42. Said, *Representations of the Intellectual*, 39. Said insisted that intellectuals should not become yea-sayers for their communities, and he served as a vociferous critic of the PLO and its often misguided handling of the Palestinian struggle. Yoder, too, was no "yea-sayer," or apologist, for the Mennonite community, but rather reserved his most polemical barbs for critiques of the Mennonite churches. See, e.g., "Anabaptist Vision and Mennonite Reality," in *Consultation on Anabaptist-Mennonite Theology: Papers Read at the 1969 Aspen Conference*, ed. A. J. Klassen (Fresno: Council of Mennonite Seminaries, 1970) 1–46.

43. Said, *Representations of the Intellectual*, 39.

44. Ibid., 46.

a morose despair. "The intellectual in exile is," according to Said, "necessarily ironic, skeptical, even playful—but not cynical."[45]

Even more than to Georg Lukàcs's notion of "transcendental homelessness," Said's positive appropriation of exile for his construal of the intellectual vocation owed a debt to the reflections of the German Jewish theorist Theodor Adorno on "dwelling." In his autobiographical reflections, *Minima Moralia*, Adorno asserted:

> Dwelling, in the proper sense, is now impossible. The traditional residences we grew up in have grown intolerable: each trait of comfort in them is paid for with a betrayal of knowledge, each vestige of shelter with the musty pact of family interests. . . . The house is past . . . it is part of morality not to be at home in one's home.[46]

Adorno's insight, amplified by Said, is that particular economic and political configurations make the condition of having a home, of landedness, possible. It is "part of morality," then, to recognize how these economic and political systems also exclude others from the condition of landedness. In the case of Palestine-Israel, this insight can be employed to suggest that no one, neither Palestinian nor Israeli, can truly be at home in the land so long as the structures that generate homelessness are perpetuated.

Adorno, having grasped the impossibility of dwelling securely, given the knowledge of the conditions that make such dwelling possible, looked to the text, to literary production, for new dwelling. "In his text, the writer sets up house. For a man who no longer has a homeland, writing becomes a place to live." However, text provides only elusive comfort, for "in the end, the writer is not even allowed to live in his writing."[47] Said developed Adorno's argument, claiming that the intellectual, in her writing, "achieves at most a provisional satisfaction, which is quickly ambushed by doubt, and a need to rewrite and redo that renders the text uninhabitable."[48] A comparison to Yoder proves useful at this point: while doubt and existential agony drive Said's exilic

45. Ibid., 45.

46. Theodor Adorno, *Minima Moralia: Reflections from Damaged Life* (London: New Left, 1951) 38–39. Quoted in Said, *Reflections on Exile*, 564–65.

47. Adorno, *Minima Moralia*, 87. Quoted in Said, *Reflections on Exile*, 568.

48. Said, *Reflections on Exile*, 568.

intellectual to rewrite her text again and again, for Yoder the exilic community—the church—is driven not by doubt but by the workings of the Holy Spirit to engage continually in the theological, missionary task of bringing the gospel into new thought worlds. Lacking any theological horizon, Said could only view the *poeisis* of the text as production and construction, whereas for the church the textual task of revising and renewing its proclamation of the gospel occurs within the framework of *pathos,* of a suffering receptivity to the word of the triune God.[49]

Said did, it turns out, "redeem" exile by stressing its moral possibilities. The exile, because she is not at home in her home, can resist accommodation to the powers, intellectual and political, that exclude and dispossess. Is this critically laudable aspect of exile, however, compatible with a struggle to end the physical condition of exile? Specifically, in the case of Palestinian refugees and other Palestinians who have lost their lands, can one work for *al-awdah* (return) and not lose the moral perspective granted by exile? We are thus returned to our earlier question of whether or not Yoder's exilic politics can speak to a theology of landedness, of justice in the land. To help us answer these questions, I now examine how Said discussed the matter of return.

On the one hand, return was clearly not *only* a metaphorical concept for Said. In a volume of essays examining Palestinian refugee rights and ways to press for return and compensation, Said expressed dismay with what he viewed as the current Palestinian leadership's historical amnesia and willingness to forgo the demand for return. What Palestinians must do, Said urged, is to "press the claims for return and compensation in earnest with new leaders." Said cited as exemplary the work of the Badil Resource Center and the Palestinian researcher Salman Abu Sitta, praising their efforts to develop concrete plans and campaigns for the actual return of refugees.[50]

On the other hand, Said also discussed return in a more metaphorical fashion and warned against establishing an easy symmetry between exile and return that would threaten to undermine the moral insights cultivated in exile. "All of us speak of *awdah*, 'return,'" Said re-

49. For a persuasive discussion of *pathos* in theology and the role of *poeisis* within that *pathos,* see Reinhard Hütter, *Suffering Divine Things: Theology as Church Practice* (Grand Rapids: Eerdmans, 2000).

50. Said, "Introduction: The Right of Return at Last," in *Palestinian Refugees: The Right of Return,* ed. Naseer Aruri (London: Pluto, 2001) 6.

flected, "but do we mean that literally, or do we mean 'we must restore ourselves to ourselves'? The latter is the real point, I think, although I know of many Palestinians who want their houses and their way of life back, exactly. But is there any place that fits us, together with our accumulated memories and experiences?"[51] Exile, by separating people from place, threatens to tear people from their history, de-centering and disorienting them to the point of threatening their identity. What return would then mean is a "return to oneself, that is to say, a return to history, so that we understand what exactly happened, why it happened, and who we are. That we are a people from that land, maybe not living there, but with important historical claims and roots."[52]

The greatness of Palestinian poet Mahmoud Darwish, according to Said, consists in his refusal in his poems to provide the reader with an easy return, with simple closure. Darwish's work "amounts to an epic effort to transform the lyrics of loss into the indefinitely postponed drama of return. . . . The pathos of exile is in the loss of contact with the solidity and the satisfaction of earth: homecoming is out of the question."[53] A return that forsakes the moral insights of exile, a return that reaches back to retrieve a pristine past without concern for the human cost, must be avoided. The Zionist project of a return to bring closure to Jewish exile stands for Said in marked contrast to the positive dimensions of Palestinian exile. Darwish, Said contended, captures the key dimensions of the exilic experience, dimensions vital to the critical intellectual's task: "Fragments over wholes. Restless nomadic activity over the settlements of held territory. Criticism over resignation. . . . Attention, alertness, focus. To do as others do, but somehow to stand apart. To tell your story in pieces, *as it is*."[54] The openness of exile presents more powerful political and moral possibilities for the intellectual than the closed symmetry of Zionist return. The broken story of Palestinian exile occurs "alongside and intervening in a closed orbit of Jewish exile and a recuperated, much-celebrated patriotism of which Israel is the emblem. Better our wanderings," Said went on to suggest,

51. Said, *After the Last Sky*, 33.
52. Said, *Power, Politics, and Culture*, 429.
53. Said, *Reflections on Exile*, 179.
54. Said, *After the Last Sky*, 150.

"than the horrid, clanging shutters of their return. The open secular element, and not the symmetry of redemption."[55]

An Exilic Politics of Land and Return?

Said's positive appropriation of exile as a critical posture provides, I believe, a positive answer to Yoder's question about whether or not Jeremiah's vision for the exilic community might speak by distant analogy to other dispossessed peoples. Pressing questions remain, however. Can Yoder's exilic politics of the church as the nonviolent body of Christ in diaspora speak to the call for justice and right living in the land, to the desire, indeed the justice, of people returning to their homes? Gerald Schlabach, in a friendly challenge to Yoder's Jeremian reading of Scripture and church history, provides a helpful reminder of the Deuternomic admonition to live rightly in the land (cf. Deuteronomy 6–9). European-American Christians, particularly those in urban and suburban settings whose livelihoods are not dependent on the cultivation of the land, could be tempted to confuse Jeremiah's vision for life in exile with the rootless virtual reality of much postmodernist thought. Such confusion would be self-deceptive in that it would obscure the ways in which general North American prosperity has been built at the expense and on the land of its original inhabitants, and it would further avoid the desire of many exiled peoples to return to live justly in the land. Schlabach sharply observes that "we do no favor to any dispossessed people if we think of land only in a figurative rather than an earthy sense."[56]

If, however, we do not avoid the challenges of return and justice, can we envision a politics of return, a politics of living rightly in the land, that does not simply replicate injustice and create new exiles in the wake of return? Traditional Zionist discourse about a Jewish return from exile not only depends on a binary opposition between exile and

55. Ibid. Note once more Said's rather wooden use of the religious-secular opposition. What Said cannot imagine is a religious criticism that prizes the "open" character of exile precisely because it confesses God's redeeming defeat of the powers of sin.

56. Gerald Schlabach, "Deuteronomic or Constantinian: What Is the Most Basic Problem for Christian Social Ethics?" in *The Wisdom of the Cross: Essays in Honor of John Howard Yoder*, ed. Stanley Hauerwas, Chris K. Huebner, Harry Huebner, and Mark Thiessen Nation (Grand Rapids: Eerdmans, 2002) 463.

return but also involves the erasure of the indigenous Arab Palestinian presence and the positing of an "empty land" in which the drama of the return from exile might unfold.[57] In practice, this discourse translated into the expulsion of hundreds of thousands of Palestinians from their homes and continues to underwrite Palestinian dispossession today. After surveying the polemic against diaspora in mainstream Zionist thought, I will argue that striving for a future in Palestine-Israel not bound up with the violent uprooting of others paradoxically entails the articulation of *an exilic politics of land and return*. "Christians can live rightly in the 'land' that God gives," Schlabach suggests, "only if they sustain a tension with landedness itself."[58] Part of this tension is not being fully at home in the land so long as others are excluded from the benefits of landedness, with exile allowed to shape understandings of home.

"The binarism of homeland/exile is central to Zionism," according to Laurence Silberstein, who delineates a series of binary oppositions issuing from the root opposition of exile to homeland:

> homeland as a source of security, stability, refuge, nurturing, safety/exile as site of danger, insecurity, instability, threat, anxiety; *heimlich/unheimlich*; homeland is good/exile is bad; homeland is productive/exile is parasitic; homeland is conducive/exile is not conducive to redemption through labor; homeland is welcoming/exile is hostile; homeland is life-giving/exile is

57. See, for example, Amnon Raz-Krakotzkin, "Peace without Arabs: The Discourse of Peace and the Limits of Israeli Consciousness," in *After Oslo: New Realities, Old Problems*, ed. George Giacaman and D. J. Lønning (London: Pluto, 1998) 59–76, and, by the same author, "A National Colonial Theology: Religion, Orientalism and the Construction of the Secular in Zionist Discourse," *Tel Aviver Jahrbuch für deutsche Geschichte* 30 (2002) 312–26, and "Exile, History and the Nationalization of Jewish Memory: Some Reflections on the Zionist Notion of History and Return," Annual Meyerhoff Lecture at the University of Pennsylvania, February 1, 2006. I do not mean, through this analysis of the ways in which Zionist discourse and practice have worked historically to dispossess Palestinians, to deny the possibility that other forms of Zionism—Zionisms not dependent on the dispossession of others—might be possible. The "cultural Zionism," for example, of an Ahad Haam or a Judah Magnes, would be cases in point. In his interview with Ari Shavit, Said rejects any talk of de-Zionization or a simple dismissal of Zionism as a valid term. Jews should be able to be Zionists, Said believes, and "assert their Jewish identity and their connection to the land, so long as it doesn't keep the others out so manifestly." See Said, *Power, Politics, and Culture*, 451.

58. Schlabach, "Deuteronomic or Constantinian," 470.

life-threatening; homeland is creative/exile is stultifying; homeland is nurturing to Jewish national culture/exile is destructive;
homeland is unifying/exile is fragmenting.[59]

These binary oppositions present life in exile as an intolerable condition whose only cure can be found in immigration to the homeland.
The Hebrew word for immigration to Israel, *aliyah*, or "ascent," encodes
the negative valuation that Zionism accords life in diaspora. Those who
grow disenchanted with life in Israel, meanwhile, are classified as *yori-
dim*, or "those who descend."

Zionism, in most of its traditional forms, thus meant the "negation
of the diaspora" (*shelilat ha-galuth*).[60] "The fulfillment of the Zionist
dream," Silberstein explains, "depends upon acts of deterritorialization
and reterritorialization. . . . Jews and Jewish culture must be deterritorialized from diaspora spaces and reterritorialized in the spaces of
the homeland." Silberstein also perceptively notes that the "reterritorialization" of Jewish immigrants into Mandate Palestine eventually
involved the "deterritorializing and reterritorializing of large numbers
of Palestinian Arabs, particularly during the 1948 War."[61] Israeli political theorist Amnon Raz-Krakotzkin argues persuasively that the
traditional Zionist negation of the diaspora went hand in hand with
a negation of a prior Palestinian presence in the land. "The definition
of Zionist settlement as an expression of 'shelilat hagalut' [negation of
diaspora] and 'shivat haam' [the return of the nation] to its homeland,"
Raz-Krakotzkin contends, "prevented relating to the collective yearn-
ings of the local Arab population and its perspective. It [also] undoubtedly made it impossible to turn the fact of this collective's existence
into an essential foundation for establishing a new Jewish identity."[62]

59. Laurence Silberstein, *The Postzionism Debates: Knowledge and Power in Israeli
Culture* (New York: Routledge, 1999) 20, 22–23.

60. For discussions of the Zionist negation of the diaspora beyond those of
Silberstein and Raz-Krakotzkin, see Shalom Ratzaby, "The Polemic about the Negation
of the Diaspora in the 1930s and Its Roots," *Journal of Israeli History* 16 (1995) 19–38,
and Eliezer Don-Yehiya, "The Negation of Galut in Religious Zionism," *Modern
Judaism* 12 (1992) 129–55.

61. Silberstein, *Postzionism Debates*, 20.

62. Quoted and translated in Silberstein, *Postzionism Debates*, 179. For the original
Hebrew, see Amnon Raz-Krakotzkin, "Exile in the Midst of Sovereignty: A Critique
of 'Shelilat HaGalut' in Israeli Culture," *Theory and Criticism (Theoria ve-Bikoret)* 4
(1993) 44. See also Raz-Krakotzkin, *Exil et Souveraineté: Judaïsme, Sionisme, et Pensée*

Raz-Krakotzkin argues that the Zionist valorization of a "return to history" accepted the Christian and Enlightenment perception that exilic existence had been an exclusion from history, an exclusion from grace.[63] The Zionist return to history, sadly, has mirrored much of the Christian West's violent and exclusivist practice. Raz-Krakotzkin suggests that "the historical conception of shelilat hagalut, the emptiness of Jewish time that separates the loss of sovereignty over the land and its renewed settlement, is completed in a direct way through the image of the land—the place for the realization and resolution of history—as an 'empty land.'"[64] The distance between conceiving of the land as empty and actually emptying the land of its indigenous inhabitants proved tellingly short.

To counter Zionist discourse and practice of dispossession, Raz-Krakotzkin proposes to recover exile, or *galut*, as a critical concept. Exile as a concept represents an "absence, the consciousness of being in an incomplete present, the consciousness of a blemished world." The absence, moreover, involves a lack of justice for Palestinians. To return from exile, then, must mean justice for the dispossessed. To yearn for redemption is to engage in political activity "that values the perspective of the oppressed, the only perspective from which a moral stance can develop."[65] A recovery of exile as a critical concept demands that Israeli Jews incorporate the consciousness of exiled Palestinians into their own longing for return. As Silberstein explicates Raz-Krakotzkin's position, "By identifying with and assuming responsibility for, attending to, and responding to 'the consciousness of the conquered Palestinian,' the Jew recovers the 'principles embodied in the theological concept of galut.'"[66]

Binationale (Paris: Fabrique, 2007).

63. See Raz-Krakotzkin, "Exile, History and the Nationalization of Jewish Memory." This conclusion bears remarkable similarities to Yoder's critique of Zionism, noted above, as a Jewish assimilation to Christendom.

64. Quoted and translated in Silberstein, *Postzionism Debates*, 178–79; Raz-Krakotzkin, "Exile in the Midst of Sovereignty," 44.

65. Quoted and translated in Silberstein, *Postzionism Debates,* 181; Raz-Krakotzkin, "Exile in the Midst of Sovereignty," 39.

66. Silberstein, *Postzionism Debates,* 181, citing Raz-Krakotzkin, "Exile in the Midst of Sovereignty," 49.

A recovery of exile as a critical concept for political theory or for a theology of the people of God seeking *shalom* for all will be critical not only of exclusivist Zionist practice but also of any narrow nationalism, including Palestinian nationalism, that would threaten to exclude others from sharing in God's gift of landed security. In this critique Edward Said would again be an ally. While typically viewed as a champion of Palestinian nationalism, Said did not view Palestinian statehood as an end in itself, but rather as one potential way for bringing landed security to all in Palestine-Israel. In his later years, in fact, Said became increasingly critical of political arrangements in Palestine-Israel based on separation. "The idea of separation is an idea that I'm just sort of terminally opposed to," Said explained, "just as I'm opposed to most forms of nationalism, just as I'm opposed to secession, to isolation, to separatism of one sort or another."[67] Politics of separation too easily becomes a politics of apartheid, with one group enjoying benefits and privileges denied to the other.[68] As an alternative to the politics of separation, Said offered the model of the binational state in all of Mandate Palestine, a state in which Jews and Palestinians live as equal citizens. In a fascinating interview with Ari Shavit of the Israeli newspaper *Ha'aretz*, Said connected his appropriation of Adorno's critique of home with his support for a binational state. "Adorno says that in the twentieth century the idea of home has been superseded," Said began.

> I suppose part of my critique of Zionism is that it attaches too much importance to home. Saying, we need a home. And we'll do anything to get a home, even if it means making others homeless. Why do you think I'm so interested in the bi-national state? Because I want a rich fabric of some sort, which no one can fully comprehend, and no one can fully own. I never understood the idea of this is my place, and you are out. I do not appreciate going back to the origin, to the pure. Even if I were a Jew, I'd fight against it. And it won't last. Take it from me, Ari. Take my word for it. I'm older than you. It won't even be remembered.

67. Said, *Power, Politics, and Culture*, 425.

68. Commentators of various political persuasions increasingly describe the reality in the occupied Palestinian territories as one of apartheid. For an exemplary analysis, see Oren Yiftachel and Haim Yacobi, "Barriers, Walls, and Dialectics: The Shaping of 'Creeping Apartheid' in Israel/Palestine," in *Against the Wall: Israel's Barrier to Peace*, ed. Michael Sorkin (New York: New Press, 2005) 138–57.

Shavit replied to Said, "You sound very Jewish," to which Said playfully and somewhat provocatively responded, "Of course. I'm the last Jewish intellectual. . . . The only true follower of Adorno. Let me put it this way: I'm a Jewish-Palestinian."[69]

Said and Raz-Krakotzkin both articulate in similar ways an exilic politics of land and return, a politics embracing the challenge of living rightly in the land while nonviolently struggling for a return to the land by the dispossessed, yet maintaining an enduring tension with landedness. The late Palestinian-Israeli writer Emile Habiby summed up the necessary tensions of an exilic politics of land when he spoke of a "freedom of longing for the land within the land."[70] This "longing for the land within the land," suggests Raz-Krakotzkin, can be "a new starting point of all who dwell in the land, a basis for their partnership."[71]

John Howard Yoder, focused as he was on the church's calling to embody a nonviolent politics amidst the Babylons of the world, was wary of attempts to theorize the shape of the ideal state, deeming such efforts as surreptitiously Constantinian attempts to identify the state rather than the church as the primary bearer of the gospel of reconciliation, renewal, and redemption.[72] Yoder probably would have been skeptical of the enthusiasm with which Said promoted the binational state. That said, Yoder did not shy away from ad hoc engagements with the state, encouraging Christians to target particular abuses rather than offering up grand political schemes. Moreover, Yoder's understanding of the people of God as a political body living nonviolently amidst em-

69. Said, *Power, Politics, and Culture*, 457–58. Some Israeli writers share aspects of Said's binational vision. Raz-Krakotzin, for one, believes that *galut* as a critical concept makes possible "a Jewish identity based on the recognition of the potential embodied in the bi-nationality of the land." Quoted and translated in Silberstein, *Postzionism Debates*, 181; Raz-Krakotzkin, "Exile in the Midst of Sovereignty," 49. See also Raz-Krakotzkin, "Binationalism and Jewish Identity: Hannah Arendt and the Question of Palestine," in *Hannah Arendt in Jerusalem*, ed. Steven E. Aschheim (Berkeley: University of California Press, 2001) 165–80.

70. Quoted and translated in Silberstein, *Postzionism Debates*, 182; Emile Habiby, *Ehtayeh*, translated from Arabic into Hebrew by Anton Shammas (Tel Aviv: Am Oved, 1988) 9.

71. Quoted and translated in Silberstein, *Postzionism Debates*, 182; Raz-Krakotzkin, "Exile in the Midst of Sovereignty," 52.

72. See, for example, Yoder, *The Christian Witness to the State* (1964; reprint: Scottdale, PA: Herald, 2002) 77. I discuss Yoder's understanding of the ad hoc character of Christian political engagement in chapter 5 of my *States of Exile*.

pires while seeking their peace and welfare is compatible with the exilic politics of land and return articulated by Raz-Krakotzkin and Said, even as it also operates within an eschatological horizon, a horizon that animates Yoder's vision with more reasons for hope than can be provided by the secular proponents of an exilic politics like Said and Raz-Krakotzkin.

Christians, together with others, must embrace the challenge of living rightly in the land: this can include calling for just distribution of land and working nonviolently for landed security for refugees. However, part of living rightly in the land will mean living lightly. Christians, as citizens of the heavenly city on pilgrimage in the Babylons of the world, will not use violence to establish justice in the land or to bring about a return to the land. Rather than pursue the sovereignty of the sword, they will pray unceasingly and work nonviolently, impelled by a "longing for the land within the land," for the day when all of God's children will dwell securely within the land God so graciously gives.

9

Memory in the Politics of Forgiveness

J. ALEXANDER SIDER

It is part of the psychic and social condition of the victim that he cannot receive compensation for what was done to him. History is still working through that condition, and so above all is the principle of brute force behind it.

—W. G. Sebald[1]

Cain murdered Abel, and blood cried out from the earth; the house fell on Job's children, and a voice was induced or provoked into speaking from a whirlwind; and Rachel mourned for her children; and King David for Absalom. The force behind the movement of time is a mourning that will not be comforted. That is why the first event is known to have been an expulsion, and the last is hoped to be a reconciliation and return. So memory pulls us forward, so prophecy is only brilliant memory—there will be a garden where all of us as one child will sleep in our mother Eve, hooped in her ribs and staved by her spine.

—Marilynne Robinson[2]

1. W. G. Sebald, *On the Natural History of Destruction*, trans. Anathea Bell (New York: Random House, 2003) 147.

2. Marilynne Robinson, *Housekeeping* (New York: Farrar, Strauss & Giroux, 1980) 192.

Introduction

For Christians charitable relations with both non-Christians and other Christians depend upon robustly eschatological conceptions of the faith. Eschatology is the study of whatever is ultimate, and not simply a speculative anticipation of future events, whether imminent or not. Therefore eschatology always entails an account of the place and function of memory within the church. In this essay I argue that the church embodies the memory of God's work in Jesus by institutionalizing processes and practices of forgiveness and reconciliation and thereby activating charity, in both pathic and ecstatic ways. That is to say, the reconciling and forgiving work of God in Jesus helps Christians act charitably, both in the sense of a capacity to receive the other as gift and in the sense of a pouring out of oneself for the other. Eschatology and ecclesiology intertwine as the "conditions of possibility" for practices of charity by creating, sustaining, and shaping the memory of redemption. I examine these claims by bringing the theology of Miroslav Volf into conversation with that of John Howard Yoder. Yoder's eschatology is displayed within an ecclesiology that centrally locates processes of negotiating communal memory as a necessary constituent of peaceable practice. Volf's eschatology, alternatively, is enabled by "a certain kind of forgetting," the primary agent of which is God, which eradicates the persistence of injurious memory in the future consummation of Christ's kingdom.[3] I argue that Volf's hope in a "nontheoretical act of nonremembering" repeats a modernist account of subjective agency that (1) makes forgetting crucial to peaceable practices, (2) applies not only to humans, but paradigmatically to God, and (3) requires radical discontinuities with central elements of the Christian story.[4] For Yoder, on the other hand, reconciliation is doxological in character, and praise is an activity that takes—as well as makes—time. Consequently, Yoder's eschatology is neither static nor grounded in forgetfulness of past injuries, but proceeds precisely as the patient labor of "redeeming the things we can never undo."[5]

3. Miroslav Volf, *Exclusion and Embrace: A Theological Exploration of Identity, Otherness, and Reconciliation* (Nashville: Abingdon, 1996) 131.

4. Ibid., 135.

5. Cf. Paul Wadell, C. P., "Redeeming the Things We Can Never Undo: The Role of Forgiveness in Anne Tyler's *Saint Maybe*," in *New Theology Review: An American*

History and the War of the Lamb

Near the end of *The Politics of Jesus*, Yoder asked about the "meaning-fulness of history."[6] He broached the question in a discussion of con-temporary Christians' obsession "with the meaning and direction of history."[7] Contemporary Christian social ethics, Yoder contended, seeks the "right 'handle' by which one can 'get a hold on' the course of history" precisely to subject it to social engineering.[8] The "handles" approach to history had three characteristics, according to Yoder. First, it isolated one focal point in history that served as a fulcrum for determining the purpose and direction of history. Second, because that handle had to be pursued in order to make history come out right, it justified the sacri-fice of lives (one's own and others'). And third, effectiveness in getting and maintaining control over the handle became the sole criterion in judging the seemliness of human action.

Given these three assumptions, Yoder argued, it is no exaggera-tion to say that moral reasoning in recent centuries has been dominated either by a commitment to pre-Enlightenment stability or by one to post-Enlightenment progressivism. Moreover, these two stances, *prima facie* at odds with each other, share the perspective that the apostolic witness is irrelevant in determining the meaning of history.

Yoder juxtaposed the "handles" approach to history with the an-swer given to the question by the "series of visions and their hymns" that comprise John's Revelation. John's answer was "not the standard answer," because the "image of the sealed scroll in the hand of the 'one that was seated upon the throne'" tells us that the question of the mean-ing of history "cannot be answered by the normal resources of human insight."[9] Instead, to the angel's question, "Who is worthy to open the scroll and break its seals?" (Rev 5:2), all the animals and elders around the heavenly throne, together with myriad angels cry out, "The lamb that was slain is worthy to receive power" (Rev 5:12). John said this,

---

Catholic Journal for Ministry 8:2 (1995) 34–48.

6. Yoder, *The Politics of Jesus: Vicut Agnus Noster*, 2nd ed. (Grand Rapids: Eerdmans, 1994) 232.

7. Ibid., 228.

8. Ibid.

9. Ibid., 232–33.

according to Yoder, not as an "inscrutable paradox but as a meaningful affirmation, that the cross and not the sword, suffering and not brute power determines the meaning of history."[10]

Yoder fleshed out John's "meaningful affirmation" in the following way: history's course is subject to the power of the resurrection rather than to any calculation of causes and effects or to the proportionally greater strength of the so-called "good guys." God's triumph is not caused by the kind of might that justifies the use of violence, but rather is testified to by the *obedience* of God's people *as demonstrated in the exercise of patience*. Moreover, Yoder claimed that the practice of patience embodies the "biblical philosophy of history," which itself is nothing more than the "logical unfolding" of Christ's own work, namely, choosing suffering servanthood, love to the point of death, and faithfulness to God's enemy love over violent lordship, righteousness backed by force, and prudential calculations of effectiveness. In other words, by the very shape of its life the New Testament church related the meaning of history to the incarnation and ministry of Jesus, through whom the will of God is "affirmatively, concretely knowable."[11]

The account of history Yoder offered is eschatological in perspective: what we are doing now not only leads to where we are going, but also makes sense of the present in light of its participation in the future Christ promises.[12] What, however, about the past? I claim that Yoder's eschatology was inseparable from his account of the place and function of memory in the church. In what does that claim consist?

At least in part, memory is a constituent element of Yoder's eschatology in the simple sense of contributing to historical awareness. If cross and resurrection, rather than cause and effect, are the "first principles" for making judgments about the meaning of history, then memory will be deployed just to the extent that we use it to survey past events and make sense of them in light of cross and resurrection.[13] More impor-

10. Ibid., 232.

11. Ibid., 233.

12. Ibid., 241.

13. Yoder did not employ the concept of "first principles" in exactly this sense. I take that concept from its use in Alasdair MacIntyre's "Aquinas Lecture," *First Principles, Final Ends and Contemporary Philosophical Issues* (Milwaukee: Marquette University Press, 1990). In that text, MacIntyre discussed first principles as constituents of practices. He wrote:

tantly for Yoder, however, memory is ingredient to eschatology because without it doxology is rendered impossible. In "To Serve Our God and to Rule the World," Yoder located doxology as central to the Christian task. "To see history doxologically," Yoder said succinctly, is to "describe the cosmos in terms dictated by the knowledge that a once slaughtered Lamb is now living."[14] Doxology for Yoder was therefore a way of seeing that is, for example, displayed by participation in liturgy and ethical behavior. By learning to see history doxologically the church comes to understand that its memory is "embedded within a larger life process," a process of praise, a process that "rules the world."[15]

To say that the church's praise is part of a process that rules the world is not quixotic. Instead, it makes a realist claim out of the confession, "the lamb that was slain is worthy to receive power and wealth and wisdom and might and honor and glory and blessing." The doxologies in John's Revelation are therefore not primarily statements about a future hope, though of course they are that as well. Neither is the force of praise in the first place metaphorical. No, the crucified Jew Jesus is identified as the slain lamb—and it is not the lamb's qualities of innocence, purity, and blamelessness that render praise meaningful, though again these qualities are more than incidental. Rather, it is the life, ministry, and death of the man Jesus of Nazareth that gives force to *this* Lamb's claim to blessing honor, glory, and power. It is central to the doxological character of the eschatological vision of Revelation

---

> Aquinas . . . uses '*principium*' [Greek "*archê*"] of an axiom furnishing a syllogism with a premise . . . and speaks of a principle as composed of subject and predicate . . . . But Aquinas also uses '*principium*' in speaking of that to which such principles refer, referring to the elements into which composite bodies can be resolved and by reference to which they can be explained as the '*principia*' of those bodies. In fact, '*principium*,' as used by Aquinas, names simultaneously the principle (in our sense) and that of which the principle speaks, but not in a way that gives to '*principium*' two distinct and discrete meanings, although it can be used with either or both of two distinct references. (4)

That, however, Yoder did not use "first principles" nevertheless does not mean that the concept is unrelated to his use of the New Testament terms "powers" (*dunameis*) and "principalities" (*archai*), which, in his work, name both rebellious agencies in creation and human structures for making sense out of experience.

14. Yoder, *The Royal Priesthood: Essays Ecclesiological and Ecumenical*, ed. Michael G. Cartwright (Grand Rapids: Eerdmans, 1994) 128.

15. Ibid., 129.

that Jesus' own situation within the political context of first century Israel is transformed by being remembered and confessed as relevant for Christian faith and practice now. To praise Jesus as the slaughtered lamb is not only relevant as a way of seeing what happened on a hill outside Jerusalem two thousand years ago. It is also relevant as a claim about the church's continuation and revolution of Israel's history. What made the movement of which Christ was the center distinctive was that it shared such crucial characteristics with Israel's own story that it could plausibly be construed as itself a continuation of that story.[16]

Salient among the characteristics shared by formative Judaism and Jesus' own ministry was ambivalence toward majesty and kingship "as instruments of divine rule."[17] Within Israel's story, according to Yoder, this ambivalence was demonstrated time and again, through the wars of the Lord in the Deuteronomistic history to Jotham's fable in Judges 8, the Israelites' rejection of the Lord in favor of a human king in 1 Samuel 8, and the Babylonian diaspora wherein Jeremiah advocated *galuth* as a positive calling rather than merely a negative judgment. Jesus' own rejection of what Yoder called "the Zealot option" stood squarely within this stream of Jewish experience, such that Christians differ from Jews not in their low expectations for what kings can do, nor in their form of life as a minority people persecuted under the powers, but rather (a) in their incorporation of Gentiles into the promises reserved for Israel according to the flesh, and (b) in their knowledge, belief, or faith that the powers to which they found themselves subjected have been placed under the lordship of the Lamb.

Because the life, ministry, death and resurrection of Jesus, called "the slaughtered lamb" by the seer of Revelation, is the major anamnetic focus of a doxological vision of history, Yoder argued, Christians derive their behavior from the gospel of Jesus Christ and not from an *ex ante* concern for justification construed in terms of effectiveness: "That action is right which fits the shape of the kingdom to come."[18]

But interpreting history as praise comes laden with a risk, namely, of generating tremendous complacency in the face of injustice, vio-

16. Cf. Robert Jenson, *Systematic Theology*, 2 vols. (New York: Oxford University Press, 1996–1999).

17. Yoder, *Royal Priesthood*, 133.

18. Yoder, *Politics of Jesus*, 137.

lence, suffering, and death. Christian ethics in America, from Walter Rauschenbusch to Stanley Hauerwas, could be depicted as the history of Christians confronting just such complacency. How does Yoder's doxological vision fit or fail to fit that story? Moreover, is construing doxology as the definitive form of Christian participation in history not to give up on the place of other voices in scripture? Does it drown out with "praise before the throne" intonations of penitence, intercession, and lament? Does seeing history doxologically reproduce Marx's claim that religion is the opiate of the people by encouraging complacency under the conditions of oppression? In a word, does praise silence the insistence of cries for justice? In recent theology, few have asked these questions with more incision than Miroslav Volf.

The Rhetoric of *Exclusion and Embrace*

Volf's *Exclusion and Embrace* offers a complex picture of salvation, as even the most cursory reading will suggest. Throughout his inquiry, Volf introduces many of his reflections and themes with questions to the reader: "Could I be serious in suggesting 'forgetting' as the final act of *redemption*?" "Do not the victims have excellent reasons for *never forgetting* the injustices suffered and hurts endured?" "What 'right' does God have to forget all the brutalities done to so many human victims? Would not a loss of *this* memory amount to an embrace between the perpetrator and God . . . ?"[19] Characteristically, Volf's answer to this kind of question is, "Not exactly—a good answer will be more complex than simply 'yes' or 'no.'" In what follows I will not pretend to deal with every aspect of Volf's work, nor will I attempt to summarize *Exclusion and Embrace*. Rather, I will probe the role memory plays in Volf's picture of salvation. Before that, however, a few comments regarding the rhetoric of *Exclusion and Embrace* (the book) and exclusion and embrace (as focal concepts) need to be made, because if Yoder was right that the gospel is gospel only if it can be received as such, then Volf's picture of salvation and reconciliation might not be as charitable as it first appears. So, what do questions of the form I have just sampled do rhetorically? At least two things deserve noting.

19. Volf, *Exclusion and Embrace*, 131–37.

Take, in the first place, a question like, "Do not . . . victims have excellent reasons for never forgetting the injustices suffered and hurts endured?" Volf often uses this form of question at a point in the text where he has piqued his reader's sense of moral outrage. *Of course* those who have suffered the most brutal atrocities have excellent reasons for never forgetting. *Of course* God's forgetfulness of victims in some sense sanctions the perpetrator of violence. The very form of the question promotes a nearly visceral response from the reader. And well it should; put so starkly, these questions evoke strongly polarized reactions, only one of which seems a genuinely moral response.

But ingredient in Volf's method is the conviction that starkly binary moral alternatives are rarely helpful. At the beginning of his third chapter, entitled "Embrace," Volf asks whether "the inner logic of exclusionary polarities [is] irresistible?" He answers:

> There may indeed be situations in which "there is no choice," though we should not forget that to destroy the other rather than to be destroyed oneself is itself a choice. In most cases, however, the choice is not constrained by an inescapable "either us or them." If there is will, courage, and imagination the stark polarity can be overcome. Those caught in the vortex of mutual exclusion can resist its pull, rediscover their common belonging, even fall into each other's arms.[20]

This is a vision of moral heroism. The implicit assumption behind both Volf's question and his answer is that stark dualisms like "forget or remember," "us or them," are the natural responses to tough questions. Behind that assumption, moreover, lies a second assumption, namely, that only a well-trained moral imagination will be able to envision an alternative to binary and dualist logics. But both of these assumptions are questionable. In the first place, seeing the world in terms of hard choices or "exclusionary polarities" itself requires moral training and can as easily be characterized as a way to avoid the pluriformity of human perceptions as it can be described as part and parcel of an acknowledgment that people have competing and even contradictory interests and accounts of the world. In Yoder's terms, the kind of rhetoric could be described as a way to get a handle on history.

20. Volf, *Exclusion and Embrace*, 99.

Secondly, the assumption that it takes moral training to resist cutting the world into opposing pieces needs to be challenged because it fosters notions of ethical expertise, that is, the idea that only the very willful, courageous, or imaginative will be able to know how to negotiate such a stark moral landscape with a truly human appreciation of complexity. But this is still an engineering approach to ethics: the world is not cut into neat halves, so in order to manage it you need a conceptual apparatus that can take stock of just how complex things really are.

Volf's similarity to Yoder should not be overlooked. Both resist answering questions in ways that allow dualisms to go unchallenged. Volf resists polarities by demonstrating how binary thought often masks the complexity of the issue at hand. Yoder's characteristic move, however, was to suggest that the very impulse to answer the question positively or negatively ignores the possibility that the question itself is ill-formed. He did this as a way of reminding the reader that questions have histories that are themselves political. If a theological question is asked in a way that elicits a "yes" or "no" answer (and often "both" or "neither" answers as well), this typically means that the voices that say "that's the wrong question to be asking in the first place" have already been silenced. One example of this kind of reasoning in Yoder's work was his critique of the book *Christ and Culture* in "How H. Richard Niebuhr Reasoned."[21] Niebuhr assumed that "Christ" and "culture" named distinct categories, such that the perennial question before the church is always about how to relate Christ, on the one hand, to culture, on the other. Yoder noted that the very way Niebuhr set up the categories ruled out *a priori* the possibilities that (a) Christ was himself "cultural" and that (b) the church in fact embodies its own culture, no doubt distinct in some ways from other cultures, but not *categorically* different from them.

Even within a generally similar approach, then, Volf and Yoder are not entirely in accord on why or how one should resist simple oppositions. Indeed, the *prima facie* similarities foreground a deeper set of rhetorical differences between the two. Whereas Volf renders the *answers* given to standard questions more complex, Yoder persistently changed the very *questions* asked. The effects of this difference can be

---

21. Cf. Glen Stassen, Diane Yeager, and John Howard Yoder, *Authentic Transformation: A New Vision of Christ and Culture* (Nashville: Abingdon, 1996).

seen by considering a second function of Volf's rhetoric in *Exclusion and Embrace*, namely, the way it harnesses fear of the other.

In a part of the book entitled "The Politics of the Pure Heart," Volf excerpts a powerful story from Željko Vuković's book, *The Killing of Sarajevo*. Volf writes:

> One of the most distressing stories from the war in former Yugoslavia comes from a Muslim woman. Here is how she tells it:
>
>> I am a Muslim, and I am thirty five years old. To my second son who was just born, I gave the name "Jihad." So he would not forget the testament of his mother—revenge. The first time I put my baby at my breast I told him, "May this milk choke you if you forget." So be it. The Serbs taught me to hate. For the last two months there was nothing in me. No pain, no bitterness. Only hatred. I taught these children to love. I did. I am a teacher of literature. I was born in Ilijaś and I almost died there. My student, Zoran, the only son of my neighbor, urinated into my mouth. As the bearded hooligans standing around laughed, he told me: "You are good for nothing else, you stinking Muslim woman. . . ." I do not know whether I first heard the cry or felt the blow. My former colleague, a teacher of physics, was yelling like mad, "Ustasha, ustasha. . . ." And kept hitting me. Wherever he could. I have become insensitive to pain. But my soul? It hurts. I taught them to love and all the while they were making preparations to destroy everything that is not of the Orthodox faith. Jihad—war. This is the only way. . . .[22]

Commenting on the story a number of pages later, Volf continues:

> One could object that victims should no more repent for what the perpetrators have done to the moral makeup of their souls than they should repent for what the perpetrators have done to the integrity of their bodies. Have not "the Serbs . . . taught" the Muslim woman to hate, as she put it? In an important sense, they did; the kind of violence and disgrace she has suffered creates hate. And yet even under the onslaught of extreme brutality, an inner realm of freedom to shape one's own self must be defended as a sanctuary of a person's humanity.[23]

22. Volf, *Exclusion and Embrace*, 111.
23. Ibid., 117.

The Muslim woman's story, combined with Volf's commentary, not only exemplifies the first characteristic of Volf's rhetoric, namely, asking a question in polarizing terms and then suggesting that the standard answers to the question are insufficiently complex. But by offering a nuanced answer to the question, "Have not the Serbs taught the Muslim woman to hate?," rather than contesting the very assumptions constitutive of the question itself, Volf also activates the fear, disgust, and outrage generated by the question. Not only does he allow the fear to remain, but, more importantly, he harnesses its energy. The Muslim woman's story is harrowing; a receptive response to her will involve tremendous pain and outrage. I contest none of this. What concerns me is the way Volf uses the woman's story. The stark polarity of "either us or them," "Jihad—war. This is the only way," generates a fear of polarity that is answered only in a further dualism, *either* Volf's nuanced answers to standard questions *or* degeneration into irresoluble antagonism. Volf gets rhetorical mileage out of the very dualisms he purportedly contests, but he does not cease thinking in dualist terms. Rather, he rejects purportedly inadequate dualisms by holding out for a more comprehensive alternative. But, crucially: *Tertium non datur*.

From Exclusion to Paradise and the Affliction of Memory

A central argument in *Exclusion and Embrace* involves forgetting as the final "act" in the drama of reconciliation. The argument is based in a number of fundamental premises about the nature of justice and about what it means to be a person. Basically, Volf views reconciliation, for which his dominant metaphor is embrace, as life in a community that resists the exclusionary logic of "either us or them" by making a sustainable peace between the self and its others in a world "threatened by enmity."[24] To learn to live this way, Volf argues, requires repentance, forgiveness, making space in oneself for the other, and the healing of memory as constitutive and "essential elements in the movement from exclusion to embrace."[25] Moreover, these essential elements require that

24. Ibid., 100. This is not to say that "embrace" is merely a metaphor for Volf. As he says, reflecting on a similarity in Hegel's *Phenomenology of Spirit*, in his "analysis of the self and the other . . . metaphor and concept are intertwined" (140).

25. Ibid., 100.

Christians engage in "the struggle for truth and justice" in the context of self-giving love "modeled on the life of the triune God."[26]

Volf claims that if Christians are to engage the struggle for truth and justice in a way consistent with their trinitarian and Christological convictions, then one of the first principles to test is freedom as it has been construed in the dominant political theories of post-Enlightenment Western culture. Liberal and socialist political theory, Volf argues, has helped to ensconce liberation and oppression as the dominant categories for theological reflection on social realities. The picture Volf paints is familiar: Within the liberal tradition, freedom is primarily construed negatively. "All people are equal and all are free to pursue their interests and develop their personalities in their own way, provided they respect the same freedom in others."[27] Liberation is thus being freed from the undue incursions of others into one's own pursuit of freedom, while oppression entails subservience or heteronomy to precisely those same incursions. A socialist conception of freedom, alternatively, considers negative freedom to be empty. Freedom is instead conceived of as capacities to live with dignity. Liberation is whatever cultivates those capacities, and oppression is whatever inhibits them.

Neither the liberal/negative nor the socialist/positive conceptions of freedom is satisfactory for Volf, because neither challenges the polarization between liberation and oppression. Human conflicts are often too messy to admit of an easy classification of oppressors or liberators: liberators often "succeed" just to the extent that they become oppressors. In both its liberal and socialist guises, modern freedom is secured only by perpetuating the cycle of liberation and oppression, which nurtures neither reconciliation nor peace. As an ultimate social goal and good, therefore, freedom must be rejected by Christians.

Rejecting freedom as an ultimate social goal does not, however, mean that Christians must give up on the *project* of inhibiting oppression and working for liberation. Instead, Christians must contextualize that project, Volf says, within a vision of love as the ultimate social goal. Freedom is at most a step in a process of moving toward the kingdom of love, a process that transforms the project of liberation by liberating it "from the tendency to ideologize relations of social actors and perpetu-

26. Ibid., 101.
27. Ibid., 101.

ate their antagonisms."[28] But even as a step in working towards a politics wherein love is the ultimate social goal, freedom as a concept needs to be scrutinized.

For instance, it would be mistaken, Volf thinks, if accepting freedom as a proximate goal in working toward "the kingdom of love" prompted Christians to follow the postmodern critique of "universal emancipation."[29] Such critiques, of which Volf takes J.-F. Lyotard to be a leading exponent, demonstrate how modernity has constructed a single universal history that channels the various competing currents of history into one river that flows toward freedom. Lyotard argued that the cultures out of which universal narratives of emancipation arose were themselves "intrinsically plural, heterogeneous, [and] incommensurable," such that we "need to guard the heterogeneity of language games" as opposed to imposing upon them a hegemonic grand narrative. As Volf notes, Lyotard wrote, "Let us wage a war on totality, let us be witnesses to the unpresentable; let us activate the differences and save the honor of the name."[30] But what, Volf wonders, could be a grander or more totalizing narrative than one which suggests that people always and everywhere must resist totality in the name of preserving the incommensurabilities of language games? Moreover, Volf suggests that not only is a summons to resist the grand narrative of universal emancipation itself a grand narrative, but it is one with deleterious political consequences. By maintaining the political conditions under which differences may proliferate in an unregulated manner, a society also maintains the conditions for the proliferation of violence and oppression. Where incommensurabilities are cultivated, violence is inevitable; or, as Volf puts it, "Unable to settle their differences by reasoning, the gods will invariably fight."[31] The agonistics Lyotard envisions could be playful, but:

> When the play gets serious, when one party breaks what the other party thinks are the rules of fair play and players are be-

28. Ibid., 105.

29. Ibid., 105.

30. Ibid., 107. Quoted from, J.-F. Lyotard, *The Postmodern Condition: A Report on Knowledge*, trans. Geoffrey Bennington and Brian Massumi (Minneapolis: University of Minnesota Press, 1984) 81f.

31. Volf, *Exclusion and Embrace*, 108.

ing carried off the field, would not continuing to play 'in peace' amount to perpetuating injustice?[32]

The use of a game analogy to describe the perpetuation of injustice is potentially misleading, just to the extent that competing players/teams in a game do not exemplify incommensurable sets of discourses. This is so at least in part because the rules of games often make provisions for the presence and arbitrational authority of referees, for the use of penalty shots or their equivalent, and for fouls that sideline players for a determinate amount of time after breaking the rules.[33] In such games these provisions make continuing to play "in peace" after the rules have been broken a logical course of action. This is to say that, precisely because games exist within a larger set of agreements between teams or contestants/players, there is always a background of conversation about the goods internal to and attendant upon playing the game in question that do not characteristically leave the players resourceless to dialogically determine a just result in the face of an infraction of the rules. A game is an institution that creates an analogy between players, and rules are the laws that regulate both the gap between (the "ana" in the analogy) players and the ability for them to play together (the "logy" in analogy).[34] Continuing to play *in any other way* than "in peace" would be, at least in the instance of games of the kind I am describing, to fail to practice the game as a game, to fail to discern the institutions of analogy.

32. Ibid., 108.

33. Volf's use of the game analogy to illustrate incommensurabilities is also misleading in that it is part and parcel of the notion of playing a game that those involved *take themselves to be playing the same game.* Lyotard's account of incommensurable language games is not one in which all speakers of various language games take themselves to be playing the same game as everyone else. The relevant analogy to illustrate a "game" situation in which "continuing to play 'in peace'" would necessarily amount to perpetuating injustice would have to involve players or teams engaged in different games. A soccer team playing soccer "against" a baseball team playing baseball is, for instance, an example. Notice, though, that what it means to play a game "against" someone playing another game is unclear. So, the example will still fail as an analogy to the "postmodern condition" unless the soccer team thinks the baseball team is (or should be) playing soccer and the baseball team thinks the soccer team is (or should be) playing baseball.

34. Cf. Gillian Rose, *Mourning Becomes the Law: Philosophy and Representation* (Cambridge: Cambridge University Press, 1996) 10.

It is, however, the case that there are situations plausibly described as "games" in which players will not have a set of deliberative resources on which to draw when the rules of that game as they have heretofore been construed are broken. Some instances of this kind of game might be a backyard football game, kick the can, or professional wrestling. The incommensurabilities involved in this kind of game will typically be ones having to do with an unclear account of the good involved in playing the game in question, which, I would suggest, is often an indication that the play is an *ad hoc* enterprise in which deliberation about how the game is encompassed within, or reflects a vision of, a more determinative conception of the good achieved by engaging in play has not occurred. Yet Volf describes incommensurabilities as what happens when play "gets serious," which on the account of game playing I am representing, is deeply to misconstrue the nature of "seriousness."

While the preceding paragraphs lodge a relatively minor set of objections, Volf's account of the irresoluble war that follows Lyotard's vision of proliferating difference is a prime instance of the way the rhetoric of *Exclusion and Embrace* cultivates fear. At most, in *The Postmodern Condition* Lyotard offered a plea that people might play in peace amidst our differences. But Volf, far from noting either the invitational quality of Lyotard's vision of postmodern politics or the fact that Lyotard's book was written as an effort to resist the "computerization" (homogenization of all difference in the name of technocracy) of society, Volf pushes Lyotard into a *reductio ad absurdum*: incommensurable language games entail irresoluble war. Consider how Volf glosses his account of Lyotard with a characterization of Jürgen Habermas' objection to in-principled incommensurabilities. Volf writes:

> Consider what happens when one tries to replace the modern schema of "oppression/liberation" with a postmodern model of incommensurable "language games." As Jürgen Habermas has argued, intersecting and sequential language games have the unfortunate characteristic that judgments of validity are not possible *between* them.[35]

Habermas accurately assessed what Lyotard said about strict incommensurabilities (in *Just Gaming*), but as a general assessment of postmodernity's political visions Habermas' argument ignores the fact that

35. Volf, *Exclusion and Embrace*, 108.

incommensurabilities among language games do not rule out the possibility of *any* intelligible commerce or shared value judgments among them. An argument that accommodates incommensurabilities among language games simply affirms that agreements are, in many instances, partial. It does not affirm that those agreements are less constitutive of the social fabric than disagreements, nor does it affirm that all shared judgments between language games that are finally incommensurable are invalid. In many instances shared judgments between language games are possible and provide the constitutive conditions under which, as Lyotard himself hoped, people might learn to "play in peace."

Volf acknowledges as much: "[I]ncommensurability is not universal but always local, temporal, and partial, just as the commensurability is."[36] Instead of using this insight to display the resources within a postmodern account of politics to resist totality without committing oneself to Lyotard's struggle to maintain the purity and incommensurability of different language games, Volf translates Lyotard's conviction of the irreducibility of language games into a judgment in favor of principled incommensurability as itself constitutive of postmodern politics *in toto*. Postmodernism, like the modernism of liberal and socialist dreams of emancipation, thus offers only deficient possibilities for envisioning a future of peace, because:

> What stands in the way of reconciliation is not some inherent incommensurability, but a more profoundly disturbing fact that along with new understandings and peace agreements new conflicts and disagreements are permanently generated.[37]

This claim, however, is unwarranted. According to it, we must fear the possibility of *permanent* disagreements and conflict being generated by partial commensurabilities more than we need to fear total incommensurability. What grounds, given the local, temporal, and partial character of the commensurabilities we encounter, could possibly be given for this claim? Conflicts are perhaps always generated, but they are by no means inexorable or permanent, something Lyotard, Michel Foucault, and Gilles Deleuze have helped us all to see.[38] Neither does

36. Ibid., 109.

37. Ibid., 109.

38. Albeit negatively, with Lyotard, since in his account we must *strive* to keep language games pure and *protect* their heterogeneities. Clearly this means that conflicts

conflict always lead to war; indeed, sometimes exactly the opposite is the case. Conflict can be part and parcel of the patient labors constitutive of any peace worth the name.

To return to Volf's argument: the problems involved in the modern schema of liberation/oppression and the postmodern critique of universal emancipation demand that we resist political programs that attempt to "accomplish the final reconciliation."[39] Indeed, for Volf, when the project of final reconciliation is not left to God, it can be a project only of the anti-Christ. The problem that confronts Christians, then, is not that of finding a way to secure future peace, but rather of searching for the "resources we need to live in peace in the absence of the final reconciliation."[40]

From Volf's point of view, the Christian task is more minimal than securing a peace that cannot be undone. Nevertheless, Christians should not give up hope in a final reconciliation. For what, Volf asks, would Christianity mean if the wedding feast of the lamb were truly a grand illusion? And what could that supper entail if not "a reconciliation that can neither be surpassed nor undone"? If Christianity gave up on this hope, it would also be giving up on itself. Therefore, Volf advocates "the struggle for *a nonfinal reconciliation based on a vision of reconciliation that cannot be undone*."[41] Seeking such a nonfinal reconciliation involves at least two things: (1) it involves backgrounding Christian hope to serve as the animus for, but not the proximate goal of, Christian ethical/political engagement now, and (2) it involves a readjustment of the self "in light of the other's alterity," without assuming that the configurations of power are symmetrical between them. Indeed, in Volf's analysis Christians should assume the opposite, a vision of "nonfinal reconciliation" that readjusts "dynamic identities *under the condition of inequality and manifest evil*."[42]

---

and disagreements, even fairly basic ones, *can* be overcome for Lyotard. His project is to force us to linger with our disagreements, to see in the fact of certain kinds of conflict a set of goods to be preserved from the hegemonic discourses of capitalist economic expansion and computerization.

39. Volf, *Exclusion and Embrace*, 109.

40. Ibid.

41. Ibid., 110

42. Ibid. (emphasis added).

Volf argues that Christians need to accept these conditions because of Jesus' proclamation of the kingdom of God. The masses to whom Jesus addressed his message were in conditions of radical inequality and oppression. His message resonated precisely because it was so rife with the "political, economic, and cultural frustrations and aspirations" that animated Israel in first century Palestine.[43]

That Jesus addressed himself principally to the poor and disenfranchised should not surprise us, Volf insists, because any political leader who desires social power needs to command a movement. But Jesus did not aspire to political leadership; rather, he inspired his hearers and "built into the very core of his 'platform' the message of God's unconditional love and the people's need for repentance."[44] Thus, says Volf, "the truly revolutionary character of Jesus' proclamation lies precisely in the *connection between the hope he gives to the oppressed and the radical change he requires of them.*"[45] In what does that radical change consist?

Essentially, repentance consists in the uncoupling of our desires from the social mechanisms that generate envy and enmity. Jesus preached his message against devotion to wealth and hatred of enemies, not merely as psychological states but as sets of material practices to be dismantled. For the oppressed, however, who have only limited access to the material things that engender obsession with wealth and enemy hatred, Jesus' injunctions criticize the passions, not as disembodied emotive states but as visceral responses to the effects of an economy that blocked people off from the pursuit of abundant life. The oppressed, Volf argues, heard Jesus' message of God's love and repentance for sin as "release from the understandable but nonetheless inhuman hatred in which their hearts are held captive."[46]

This is to say that repentance must have material consequences for Volf. That is, repentance is only effective if it breaks the seductive power of envy and enmity, whose "social impact . . . is to reinforce the dominant values and practices that cause and perpetuate oppression in the first place."[47] For victims of violence repentance entails minimizing

43. Ibid., 112.
44. Ibid., 112–13.
45. Ibid., 114.
46. Ibid.
47. Ibid., 116.

their own oppressive behaviors of exercising reactive violence. Victims, according to Volf, need to repent of what perpetrators do to their souls, for "even under the onslaught of extreme brutality, an inner realm of freedom to shape one's self must be defended as a sanctuary of a person's humanity."[48]

How such an "inner realm of freedom" that is the "sanctuary of a person's humanity" differs from the liberal notion of freedom Volf criticizes as insufficient for Christian practice is unclear. Volf claimed with the socialist tradition that the liberal conception of freedom was substantively empty. He also claimed that the liberal conception of freedom is negative—that is, freedom from undue intrusions into one's own pursuit of the good life. But the notion of "freedom from" presumes that the question "Who is free?" makes sense. In the liberal philosophical tradition following Kant, the "who question" is answered as precisely "an inner realm of freedom" and as "the sanctuary of a person's humanity." Within that tradition, the inner realm of freedom or "higher faculty of desire" allows the subject to step back from its substantive commitments and engage the question "What ought I to do?" in the light of reason alone. So, while beginning his account of reconciliation with a critique of freedom as construed in modernist inquiries, Volf ends up reproducing exactly the conception of freedom that is foundational for the enterprise he meant to critique. This is important because the "sanctuary of a person's humanity" makes forgetting both possible and necessary as a constitutive moment in the movement from exclusion to embrace. How so?

For Volf, both repentance and forgiveness, if they are genuine, are truly free activities because they allow people to transcend the normal dynamics of the social fabric. Repentance and forgiveness are practices that uncouple us from our desires for self-justification and revenge, desires that foment envy and enmity. Repentance and forgiveness so uncouple us from misdirected desires precisely because they short-circuit the normal channels and expectations of justice. Given repentance and forgiveness, justice cannot be represented as simple retribution, since retribution is what the claims of forgiveness and pleas of repentance ask us to forego. Neither, however, can justice be construed as strictly restorative. There is no way to undo the past, which is, Volf argues, what

48. Ibid., 117.

a consistent account of restorative justice demands. Instead, repentance and forgiveness illumine the shortcomings of retributive and restorative justice alike, while nevertheless making the claims of justice all the more pressing.

Volf's conception of justice is bound up with his conception of freedom, just to the extent that justice requires heteronomy. While in repentance one "becomes free from alienation and the determination of his actions by others; he comes to himself, and steps into the light of a truth which makes him free," and in forgiving one "breaks the power of the remembered past and transcends the claims of the affirmed justice and so makes the spiral of vengeance grind to a halt," on the issue of justice Volf writes, "every act of forgiveness enthrones justice," because it "draws attention to [justice's] violation precisely by offering to forego its claims."[49] So, while repentance and forgiveness contribute to autonomous self-determination, in the process they foreground the demands of justice even while not satisfying them. And this is no anomaly in Volf's account because in considering what justice requires we are always in a heteronomous relationship with the past. We forgive and are forgiven, but justice must nevertheless be done lest autonomous activity have no purchase in the realm of social reality.

Forgiveness is thus but a momentary uncoupling from the spiral of vengeance that determines the demands of justice. As momentary and fragmented, forgiveness nevertheless echoes the activity of Christ on the cross, where Christ prayed for the pardon of his torturers and so created space in the divine life for the other to come in. Thereby he fulfilled the conditions for a determinative peace to take hold and transform the relation between victims and perpetrators.

The forgiveness Christ prayed for and extended on the cross expressed "the *will* to embrace the enemy," according to Volf. "Christ is the victim who *refuses* to be defined by the perpetrator, *forgives* and *makes* space in himself for the enemy."[50] But this construal of Christ's activity on the cross is monological (*he* wills, *he* forgives, *he* makes space) and, as such, is paradigmatic of the sovereign subject of modern critical inquiry, secure in his identity, with nothing to risk or lose by magnanimously engaging the enemy. As, however, a model of vulner-

---

49. Ibid., 120–23.

50. Ibid., 126 (emphasis added).

able engagement appropriate to a savior who was "emptied of himself," Jesus the victim can be in no position to refuse to be defined by his oppressors—his relationship to them on the cross was not one of sovereign transcendence, but rather of abject humiliation; it was not one of autonomous detachment from his subjective commitments, but from beginning to end heteronomous and other-determined. Yet God raised him up and used Christ's abjection both therapeutically and pedagogically, not to teach Christians a strategy for making space in oneself for the other, but as a demonstration of the extent to which living in a way consonant with the coming kingdom requires giving up on all social controls, being ready to disavow the handles approach to history, even when doing so seems certain to spell only disaster.

It is certainly important to affirm, as Volf does, an ethos that invites engagement with the stranger and the enemy. But it is equally important to disavow the cultivation of dialogical receptivity as itself one more in a cache of power moves deployed to ensure that I retain control over whatever engagements in which I happen to find myself enmeshed. Thematizing forgiveness as an act of ultimate sovereignty, however, is just such a power move. Moreover, it presents Volf with a nearly insoluble problem.

If, on the one hand, the demands of justice refuse to go away, and if, on the other hand, strict justice is a practical impossibility, such that forgiveness is the only way to get uncoupled from the spiral of vengeance, then the proposed solution is not an answer to the problem at hand. Forgiveness in Volf's account does not redeem unrequited justice—the memories of wrongs done and of unrecoverable pasts of wholeness persist even when forgiveness has been extended and received. A sovereign act of autonomy does not overcome the chains of determination that bind us to our histories. Therefore Volf writes:

> After we have repented and forgiven our enemies, after we have made space in ourselves for them and let the door open, our will to embrace them must allow the one final, and perhaps the most difficult act to take place, if the process of reconciliation is to be complete. It is the act of forgetting the evil suffered, a certain kind of forgetting, I hasten to add. It is a forgetting that assumes that the matters of "truth" and "justice" have been taken care of ... that perpetrators have been named, judged, and (hopefully) transformed, that victims are safe and their wounds healed ... a

forgetting that can therefore ultimately take place only together
with the creation of "all things new."[51]

For Volf this divine forgetting is the object of Christian hope. It secures
final reconciliation. But it is also important to note what this act of forgetting is not. Forgetting the memory of past wrongs is no substitute
for justice or forgiveness. Nor does forgetting change the "truth" of the
past. But forgetting is a way of redeeming the past, or so Volf claims:
"Since memories shape present identities, neither I nor the other can
be redeemed without the redemption of our remembered past."[52] Or,
and this is subtly different: "As long as we remember the injustice and
suffering we will not be whole, and the troubling and unanswerable
'open question' that craves resolution in an impossible harmony will
keep resurfacing."[53] In the first quote Volf affirms that redemption of us
requires the redemption of our memories. In the second, however, the
redemption we require is non-remembering.

In sum: for Volf divine amnesia is the final component in a me-
chanics of reconciliation that encodes in its center a lapse between
the demands of justice and the social transformation attendant upon
forgiveness, understood as an autonomous act. Forgiveness cannot
change the past, and since the past is precisely where the history of
pain that requires justice lies, complete reconciliation requires "a stage
of nonremembering."[54]

Volf's argument moves from heteronomous relationships to history, configured in terms of the insatiable demands of justice, to an act
of subjective sovereignty (repentance, forgiveness, making space in
oneself for the other) that uncouples people from their heteronomous
relationships. This act of self-sovereignty is, moreover, secured only by
the further act of a higher sovereignty, the "grace of nonremembering."[55]
For if it is difficult to imagine how victims might become so free in
themselves to forgive those who have wronged them and forego the demands of justice, it is impossible to imagine, Volf says, an autonomous
activity capable of securing a reconciled and non-tragic future between

51. Ibid., 131.
52. Ibid., 133.
53. Ibid., 134.
54. Ibid., 135.
55. Ibid., 138.

victim and perpetrator if the memory of wrongdoing persists. Thus, the affliction of memory can only be healed by the grace of nonremembering, a grace not grounded in subjective sovereignty, but found in the arms of God, at the center of whose "all-embracing memory there is a paradoxical monument to forgetting, the cross of Christ."[56] God alone is able to erase the memory of the "unredeemed past that un-redeems every present," and so lets former enemies, now "separated only by the boundaries of their identities," "embrace each other within the embrace of the triune God."[57]

If, however, the past has not been redeemed, and if the present memory of the past is not being redeemed and cannot be redeemed without being forgotten, such that God must drown "my sinnes black memorie" in "a heavenlie Lethean flood," as John Donne once put it, then salvation ceases to be temporal, the analogy between creation and salvation has been stretched to the point of breaking.[58] Or, in a somewhat different register, to argue for reconciliation only on the basis of a radical discontinuity with the past is another way for Christians to put "handles on history." How so?

The central question, "Who is to be redeemed?" depends on the analogy between creation and salvation. This question interrogates the limits of redemption both christologically and ecclesiologically. Christologically, because it assumes Gregory Nazianzen's dictum: "Whatever would not have been assumed, would not have been healed." Ecclesiologically, because the question requires an account of the church as the body of Christ. Put most boldly, any account of redemption that does not involve our negative memories of past violence and our histories of loss is inadequate, in that who is saved is less than the entire person. If Volf is right about forgetting, it turns out that Augustine was wrong: the God who created us without us will, after all, save us without us too.

To say this presupposes an account of the person as an embodied story. What makes a person a person is precisely that her life can be construed as at least part of a drama, which, as Aristotle said, character-

---

56. Ibid., 140.

57. Ibid., 138.

58. John Donne, "Holy Sonnet 9," in M. H. Abrams, ed., *The Norton Anthology of English Literature*, 6th ed., vol. 1. (New York: Norton, 1993) 1116.

istically consists in beginnings, middles, and ends. Given Volf's account of personhood and personality as notions fundamentally valenced by the Trinity—nonstatic relations that have their "being" in the conversations among the very same relations—Volf has no *prima facie* reason to object to an account of personhood as being part of an embodied story. But Volf's picture of salvation and reconciliation has human persons redeemed precisely from their stories: the memory of justice undone is a memory that cannot continue if people are to regain their integrity and be reconciled to each other. The "creation of all things new" is a radical discontinuity with the old precisely in that it is the beginning of a different story from the story of injustice, oppression, and exclusion that we currently inhabit.

Volf could perhaps argue that in construing his account of redemption as radical discontinuity with the past I am overdrawing the distinction between the here and the hereafter. To be reconciled with each other we need not forget our stories *in toto*; we need only forget the fragments of our stories bound up in the injuries of past violence. Arguably, this is not radical discontinuity, but only partial discontinuity, the constitution of a new language game, to return to Lyotard's idiom, with at most partial incommensurabilities to the language games of which we are currently parts. But, I wonder whether the claim— and it is a claim that must hold if Volf's response to the objection of radical discontinuity is to be sustained—that there are memories not bound up in the violences of the past can be plausibly validated. I confess I have no idea how one might test this question in general, but for Christians perhaps a general inquiry is unnecessary. At least we can say that one memory, that of Christ's crucifixion, is a memory both inescapably bound up in violence and, as such, is also central to our stories as Christians. Without the memory of the cross, no Christianity. Without the memory of Jesus' crucifixion and our violent collusion in it, the "creation of all things new" entails a radical discontinuity with a story that claims no less than that this violence at least, the violence that nailed Jesus to the cross, is essential to the story of our salvation.

It is not that Christ's crucifixion was unavoidable. The violence that culminated in Jesus' death was contingent, not categorically different from any other act of violence. But apart from the crucifixion, the story of Christianity would cease to be the same story. Moreover, an account of hope in a final reconciliation that requires the forgetting of this set of injurious memories cannot be Christian hope, at least in part because it secures our future against contingency at the cost of erasing the past that gave that future a possible coherence in the first place.

The very reasons that led us to question Yoder's doxological vision of history—the persistence of the past's injuries, the place of rage before God, the concern that praise might drown out cries for justice—the very questions Volf addressed, remain in his argument deeply problematic. Justice goes unrequited, and reconciliation is possible only at the expense of the central elements of the story that makes Christians who they are. What if, at this point, we turn back to Yoder? Can he offer an account of history as praise that does not, on the one hand, require radical discontinuity with key elements of the Christian story, and, on the other, addresses the persistence of cries for justice? In the final portion of this chapter, I argue that he can, and indeed does, offer just such an account, by making communal processes of negotiating memory part and parcel of the praise the people of God render before the throne.

Yoder's Politics of Memory

"What would not have been assumed would not have been healed." In some senses it is odd to claim Nazianzen for Yoder, since the statement can be read to presume the kind of incarnational Christology that makes Jesus' obedience to "the one who sent him" merely incidental to Christian theology. What matters about the Incarnation, theologians have claimed by citing sources just like Gregory, is that it represents the infinite capacity of Christ to absorb the failures of humanity and transform them "without impairing his own majesty," as Leo the Great put it.[59] To the kind of incarnationalist theology that demands "a full concept of the prior exalted status which [Christ] forsook," for which Jesus' human career and its results were simply an unveiling mecha-

---

59. Leo the Great, Sermon 28 in J. –P. Migne, ed., *Patrologiae Cursus Completus*, Series Latina 54 (Paris: J. –P. Migne, 1846) 221–26. The relevant lines are 97–98: "Deus enim Dei Filius, de sempiterno et ingenito Patre unigenitus, et incommutabiliter atque intemporaliter habens non aliud esse quam Pater est, formam servi sine suae detrimento majestatis accepit, ut in sua nos proveheret, non se in nostra dejiceret."

nism, Yoder strongly and persistently objected.[60] But in another important sense it is only natural for Yoder's Christology to resonate with Nazianzen's, for both invite a strong interpretation of Jesus' solidarity with those he came to save. Indeed, solidarity is too weak a word, since precisely what Christian tradition affirms is that Christ was one of those whom he saved, not different from them in any respect, except that he was without sin. In this claim, that of the strongest affirmation of Christ's full humanity, both Yoder and Nazianzen locate Jesus' claim to divinity. That he did not consider "equality with God something to be grasped," but saved us as one of us, is "the profoundest proof of his condescension, and thereby of his glory."[61]

The theological sense of Nazianzen's statement can be elucidated by reference to Yoder's Christology. The story of Christ's life would be incomplete without the memory of unjust suffering. Or rather, it is not Jesus' story apart from the suffering of his body. Divested of the memory of unjust suffering, it will not be the same Jesus to whom Christians bear witness. And then what would it mean for Christians to praise him, or to say that praise truly is embedded within a process that "rules the world"? Yoder's Christology pushes these ecclesiological points, namely, that the church's memory loops back to *this* Jesus, "handed over . . . according to the definite plan and foreknowledge of God . . . crucified and killed by the hands of those outside the law" (Acts 2:23). In so doing, it continues his memory, but not just as a memory of the past, but as a mode of being now, for this same Jesus remains relevant as present and future to a people whose life is shaped by praise of him. When Yoder wrote, for instance, that the primary social meaning of eucharist is economic sharing, he was affirming the church's continuation of the story

60. Cf. Yoder, *Preface to Theology: Christology and Theological Method* (Grand Rapids: Brazos, 2002) 86; see also *Politics of Jesus*, 7–8.

61. This is to quote Yoder somewhat out of context. See *The Priestly Kingdom: Social Ethics as Gospel* (Notre Dame, IN: University of Notre Dame Press, 1984) 62. I think it is, however, not to quote Yoder unfaithfully. Nazianzen, for his part, says Christ "honors obedience by his action, and proves it experimentally by his passion. For to possess the disposition is not enough, just as it would not be enough for us, unless we also proved it by our acts; for action is the proof of disposition." See Gregory of Nazianzus, "Fourth Theological Oration," paragraph 6, English translation in *Nicene and Post-Nicene Fathers*, 2nd ser., vol. 7, ed. Philip Schaff and Henry Wace (Grand Rapids: Eerdmans, 1996) 311.

of Jesus' earthly presence.[62] The church's Eucharist announces the body of Christ—the social process of eating together publishes Christ's body, it makes it present for and available to the world. When the church eats and drinks together in Christ's name it "proclaims the Lord's death until he come." The anamnetic focus of the meal is clear. But, precisely in continuing the visible and material dynamics of Jesus' earthly career, this anamnetic activity is encompassed within a wider process than that of a "mere" memorial to a savior now gone and seated far away in heaven. For in repeating and imitating the dynamics of Jesus' earthly ministry, the church continues the story of that ministry, and, as the continuing story of Jesus, continues so also to embody his person here on earth. Memory thus becomes the mode by which Christ's body is made present and available in and for the world.

For Yoder, this was no less true of the practice of forgiveness than it was of the celebration of the Lord's Supper. He argued, "A process of human interchange combining the mode of reconciling dialogue, the substance of moral discernment, and the authority of divine empower-ment deserves to be considered one of the sacramental works of the community."[63] Why? Because a process of reconciliation and moral discernment, just like processes of economic sharing—of eating and drinking together as a way of "looping back" to Jesus—continues the story of Jesus here and now by making that story available in and to the world.

What is crucial to see is that the story of Jesus the church is called to incarnate is not the same story without the memory of unjust suffer-ing. Concomitant upon this claim is the further claim that the church's practice of forgiveness and moral discernment cannot be ordered to-wards a vision of reconciliation, holiness, or redemption that sanitizes the past by erasing it. Since the church remembers Jesus and claims to continue his story, the church's work for reconciliation between victims and perpetrators proclaims the very same work as the work of God in Jesus Christ, the story of which cannot be forgotten if the story is itself to be continued.

"Protestants," Yoder wrote, "have for centuries been arguing that 'only God can forgive,' and that the believer receives reassurance of for-

62. Yoder, *Royal Priesthood*, 365–66.
63. Ibid., 362.

giveness not from another person but in the secret of his or her own heart."[64] While Volf is perhaps not quite as blunt as this, his argument for "nonfinal reconciliation" secured by hope in a final reconciliation enacted by God and grounded in the "grace of nonremembering" in fact repeats the thrust of this Protestant position. The scandal of justice undone and the irrecoverability of the past requires a radical disjunction between the church's work for reconciliation now and the eschatological reconciliation God will effect with "the grace of nonremembering" and "the creation of all things new." But this, according to Yoder, is to misidentify the nature of the scandal in question:

> The heat and vigor of this old Protestant-Catholic debate points us to the difficulty we have in conceiving, and in believing, that God really can authorize ordinary humans to commit him, that is, to forbid and to forgive on his behalf with the assurance that the action stands "in heaven." How can it be, and what can it mean, that such powers are placed in the hands of ordinary people the likes of Peter? The jealous concern of religious leaders, and of all religion, for the transcendence of God, for his untouchablility and his distance from us, might have been able to adjust, or to make an exception, for arrogant claims like this made on behalf of some most exceptional person, a high priest or a grand rabbi, a prophet or king. But the real scandal of the way God chose to work among humans—what we call the Incarnation—is that it was an ordinary working man from Nazareth who commissioned a crew of ordinary people—former fishermen and taxgatherers—*to forgive sins.*[65]

How indeed can a crew of ordinary people be given God's power to forgive sins? How can the process be integral to a doxological vision of history? I have three suggestions to make.

In the first place, forgiveness and reconciliation is a process that *takes* and *makes* time. Forgiveness does not secure us against the contingencies of our past or against the contingencies of our futures. Nor should we insist that reconciliation can occur only if and when our pasts have been sanitized. If forgiveness is a way of continuing the story of Jesus, then it takes the shape, not of a moment in the drama of embrace—with whatever expansive conception of moment we might wish

64. Ibid., 330.
65. Ibid., 330–31.

to adopt—but of an ongoing conversation. As conversation, and by this I mean simply, even if not merely, the desire of victims to talk with perpetrators, forgiveness is not an activity whose primary purpose is to achieve a goal external to the conversation itself. The overriding interest is not with the appropriate punishment for offenders, with reparations for victims, or even with creating a neutral space from which each party may be free to choose to go her or his own way. Rather, forgiveness names the possibility of and desire to continue conversing with the one who has offended, without assuming that one can predict in advance the shape that conversation will take. Moreover, relinquishing control on the shape of forgiveness as conversation requires patience. The needs of the victim and the demands of justice are not self-evident, nor are they assumed to be discrete possibilities that must be "taken care of" before reconciliation can occur. Rather, justice is a good that inheres in the shape of the conversation itself.

Yet, secondly, to insist that forgiveness take the shape of an ongoing conversation whose particular nature is not specifiable in advance of or apart from the engagement itself is not to counsel radical situational-ism. For Christians this is the case at least because forgiveness is a way of continuing the story of Jesus. This means that that story, recorded in the gospels and interpreted within the church, always requires a set of ongoing deliberations about how the current conversation does or does not plausibly continue the story of Jesus. These ongoing deliberations, too, are open-ended; the concern is with making Jesus' story available in the world, and not with a set of *ex ante* rules and procedural justifications.

Finally, forgiving conversations that are partly constitutive of a doxological vision of history require hope. Not hopefulness as such, or hope in final reconciliation, subjective wholeness, or the grace of nonre-membering. Some reconciliations will not prove durable, or will not be effected in certain settings when certain persons are involved because of dynamics like willful stubbornness, trauma, or deep elements of mis-trust—all of which are inescapably bound up in memories of the past. Some notions of subjective wholeness are terrifying; others are merely chimeric, but each is beholden to the fantasy that "I" am fundamentally other than the stories, deployed through time and so composed of the stuff of memory, of which I find myself a part. Some forgetting is no doubt merciful; but where mercy, truthfulness, constancy, and patience embrace in the arms of God, nonremembering can only be a terrible parody of grace. Seeing forgiveness as part of a doxological vision of history affords none of these hopes. Rather, forgiveness as conversation requires hope that, in the midst of, through, and by tarrying with the ruins of memory, by being committed to the patient labor of giving voice to violent pasts precisely as part of the patient labor of crafting a new future, we may again make the story of Jesus available in the world.

10

Traumatic Violence and Christian Peacemaking

CYNTHIA HESS

As someone who was raised in the Church of the Brethren and in Lancaster, Pennsylvania, I have long been interested in learning about religious nonviolence and its potential to foster social change. In studying the Anabaptist tradition, I have found particularly striking its claim that nonviolence is not just an ethical principle but a way of life. As a way of life, nonviolence entails attempting to shape one's whole existence in such a manner that one not only opposes violence but also does not contribute to the very conditions that lead to violent harms. While critics often charge Anabaptists with advocating passivity in the face of violence, many Anabaptists respond that in their view, nonviolence as a way of life is an active enterprise that involves participation in the struggle for social justice. Moreover, they insist not only that action for social justice and nonviolence are compatible, but also that nonviolence necessarily entails seeking to build a more just, and therefore peaceful, world.

Although the Anabaptist tradition offers powerful understandings of nonviolence, it is my contention that this tradition has not fully taken into account the multifaceted ways in which violence marks our existence. Historically, Anabaptist peace theology has focused on pacifism and the refusal of military violence; in this context, nonviolence involves transforming and extricating oneself from external, physical violence. Recent accounts of violence and the self, particularly in the fields of trauma studies and feminist theory, challenge this view of nonviolence by expanding the term "violence" to include forms of violence that are internal to the self, such as the ongoing psychic effects of direct and indirect harms that can take place both inside and outside the church.[1] Feminists and trauma theorists shed light on internal violence by developing conceptions of the self as socially constructed, as coming to be in and through social and cultural relations over time. They argue that when the social contexts and events that form us are violent, this violence does not remain external to our selves. Instead, it becomes internal, an integral part of our identities. As a result, human beings are not just *agents* but also *sites* of violence.

In this essay, I explore traumatic violence—violence that leads to patterns of psychic wounding—as one form of harm that can become internal to socially-constructed selves and communities. Scholars and clinicians who study trauma ("trauma theorists") describe it as an overwhelmingly stressful event that assaults a person and then moves into their body, mind, and soul. This internalization of traumatic violence manifests itself in a variety of ongoing effects, which themselves can be experienced as traumatic. For example, people who have endured traumas such as war and physical assault often remain haunted by these events long after they have ended, reliving them in nightmares, intrusive memories, and flashbacks. Their bodies and minds continue to hold within them the reality of this violence as ever present, even as they move through time.

The prevalence of trauma reveals the need to reconceive nonviolence to address internal violence. If traumatic violence can become internal to selves and communities, then nonviolence must involve not only active resistance to external, physical violence but also the transformation of internal violence through healing. While Anabaptist peace theology has not explicitly addressed this dimension of nonviolence, it does offer resources for an expanded understanding of nonviolence that takes it into account. In particular, Anabaptist views of the nature of Christian community, especially as articulated in the work of John Howard Yoder, lay the groundwork for reconceiving nonviolence

1. The field of trauma studies is made up of scholars from many disciplines who all address trauma and, therefore, are engaged in what many scholars in the humanities call "trauma theory." The use of the phrase trauma theory does not imply that all trauma scholars share a unified view of trauma and its effects. Rather, those who study trauma present a diversity of views, which taken as a whole constitute the field called trauma studies or trauma theory.

to include the transformation of internal violence. Trauma theorists maintain that healing from trauma involves a reconstitution of selves that have been shattered by trauma; Yoder's theology suggests that in Christian community, people's identities are re-formed in Christ as they perform specific practices derived from the biblical narratives of his life, death, and resurrection. In conversation with trauma studies and Yoder's work, I argue that this communal construction of a new identity may help some persons to heal from violence by placing their traumatic experiences in a broader narrative framework that both recognizes the violence and offers the promise of redemption. Christian nonviolence, then, includes the creation of a context in which traumatized persons can heal from traumatic violence through the narrative construction and communal enactment of an eschatological identity and through participation in the revealed but still incomplete new aeon.

Nonviolence in Yoder's Theology

In the twentieth century, John Howard Yoder presented the most well-known argument for the centrality of nonviolence to the Christian faith. Yoder maintains that Christian nonviolence is not an ethic for a few isolated individuals but a way of life for the entire Christian community. Basing his view on a particular reading of the gospel narratives, Yoder argues that throughout Jesus' life and ministry he continually encountered social conflict and a variety of ways to respond to this conflict. Again and again, Jesus rejected the option of countering hostility with sheer force. Instead, he chose an alternative response: the creation of a new social reality, a voluntary and covenanted community of mixed composition in which all persons could live in peace.[2]

This kind of community that Jesus created, Yoder contends, is precisely what the church today is called to be. The church is called to be a new social reality that challenges the wider social order but does not impose its new ways on this order. Rather, the church challenges the surrounding society by refusing to support its violent structures and practices and instead embodying the nonviolent way of Jesus. This does not mean that the church should withdraw from all culture, nor

2. *The Original Revolution: Essays on Christian Pacifism* (Scottdale, PA: Herald, 1971) 29.

does it mean that the church should refuse to participate in the pursuit of social justice. [3] Yoder believes that Christians are called to identify and help transform unjust social relations and structures; however, he thinks they are called to do this *"in the way of Christ."*[4]

To understand better why Yoder claims that the church is called to embody nonviolence, we must look at his view of the powers and their relation to the work of Jesus. For Yoder, the term "powers" refers to the material and spiritual structures instituted by God to order human society.[5] Yoder argues that although these structures are part of God's good creation and are necessary to keep our world running smoothly, they are fallen and seek to separate human beings from God's love by demanding our adherence to values opposed to God's will. The powers no longer act "only as mediators of the saving creative purpose of God; now we find them seeking to separate us from the love of God. . . , holding us in servitude to their rules. . . . These structures which were supposed to be our servants have become our masters and our guardians."[6] Human beings are bound to the powers; they are enslaved to "those values and structures which are necessary to life and society, but which have claimed the status of idols and have succeeded in making us serve them as if they were of absolute value."[7] This, in Yoder's view, describes the lost condition of humans outside of Jesus Christ.

Since human beings are enslaved to the powers, Jesus' work involves liberating them from the powers' control. Yoder begins to explain this process of liberation by stating that since the powers are God's creatures, they cannot be simply obliterated. Yet, since they are fallen, they must be resisted. Jesus reveals the form this resistance should take in his life and especially in his death, when he defeats (but does not destroy) the powers by declining to use the violence and power at his disposal to crush them.[8] Yoder considers Jesus' refusal to overwhelm .

---

3. Yoder, "How H. Richard Niebuhr Reasoned: A Critique of *Christ and Culture*," in *Authentic Transformation: A New Vision of Christ and Culture*, eds. Glen H. Stassen, D. M. Yeager, and John Howard Yoder (Nashville: Abingdon, 1996) 69–71.

4. *For the Nations: Essays Public and Evangelical* (Grand Rapids: Eerdmans, 1997) 111.

5. *For the Nations*, 151.

6. *The Politics of Jesus*, 2nd ed. (Grand Rapids: Eerdmans, 1994) 141.

7. Ibid., 142.

8. Ibid., 144–45.

his adversaries with sheer force an act of resistance because it means he has not allowed the powers to make him over in their own image. By existing in the midst of the powers but refusing to be enslaved by them, Jesus provoked the powers to reveal that they work against God.[9] This revelation that the powers oppose God is their disarming, their defeat at the hands of Jesus. However, that Jesus has triumphed over the powers becomes known only in light of the resurrection, which manifests his victory on the cross. This manifestation strips the powers of their uncontested ability to convince us that they are the "divine regents" of the world.[10]

Yoder argues that Jesus' stance in relation to the powers is not only relevant but also normative for the life of the church. Though Jesus has triumphed over the powers ultimately, they still seek to control the existing social order. The church is, therefore, called to remind the powers that their uncontested dominion has ended.[11] It does this by striving to separate itself from the destructiveness of the powers, by striving to form a community that remains "other" than the world, even as it serves the world. Nonviolence and servanthood—the ethical and political stance of Jesus—must therefore constitute the essence of the church. By incarnating this stance in its own life, the church manifests his victory—and in this way continues to remind the powers of their ultimate defeat.[12]

Yoder thus views the church's nonviolence as essential to its identity and mission. To embody the nonviolent stance of Jesus over-against the destructiveness of the powers, one must have a counter-cultural identity, and only community can provide the context in which such an identity is formed. The church, in Yoder's perspective, is thus an "*alternative construction of the world,*"[13] a gathering of those who witness to Jesus through their words and deeds. Through this witness, the church participates in the life of Jesus and in the kingdom, which he

9. Ibid., 145.

10. Berkhof, in ibid., 147.

11. Berkhof, in ibid., 148.

12. Ibid., 150.

13. *For the Nations*, 153.

inaugurates at the cross.[14] It lives as the "first fruits" of what is to come,[15] proclaiming to the powers that their unchallengeable rule has ended.

It is important to note that in describing the church's nonviolence and alternative character, Yoder does not say that the church can embody this stance because it is sinless while the world is not. The church itself is a power or structure,[16] and it is therefore subject to corruption.[17] However, while Yoder recognizes the church's peccability, he maintains that it can still respond creatively to the destructiveness of the powers, in ways that follow the example of Jesus.[18] His belief in the possibility of creative response to the powers is grounded in his conviction that Christians have the support of the community, training in this community's discipleship life-style, the guidance of the Holy Spirit, and a regenerate will.[19] As a result of these resources, Christians are capable of following the nonviolent way of Jesus, of living life as discipleship.

Yoder contends, however, that the church still does not fully embody the nonviolence of Jesus.[20] When he discusses how the church compromises its nonviolent identity, Yoder generally refers to its participation in the world's dominant social and cultural structures. Since such structures are, in his view, opposed to the work of Jesus and often violent, the church's participation in them is a failure to conform to the path of Jesus and thus also a failure to live as an alternative construction of the world.

Trauma and Christian Nonviolence

While Yoder's analysis of how the church compromises its nonviolent identity focuses primarily on its relations with the wider society,

14. Ibid., 234; *Politics of Jesus,* 51.

15. *For the Nations,* 92.

16. *Politics of Jesus,* 158.

17. Nancey Murphy, "John Howard Yoder's Systematic Defense of Christian Pacifism," in *The Wisdom of the Cross: Essays in Honor of John Howard Yoder,* ed. Stanley Hauerwas et al. (Grand Rapids: Eerdmans, 1999) 65. Reprinted as chapter 3 of this volume.

18. *Priestly Kingdom,* 5.

19. *For the Nations,* 112; *Priestly Kingdom,* 139.

20. *Royal Priesthood,* 169.

trauma theory provides a theoretical framework for exploring another way in which the church may be entangled in the violence of the world. At a most basic level, trauma theory makes this exploration possible by considering a different realm of violence than Yoder does. Whereas Yoder focuses on violence that attacks persons from without (external violence),[21] trauma theory concentrates on violence that has injured persons from the outside and then moved into their bodies, minds, and souls (internal violence). Trauma theorists explore internal violence by analyzing the long-term effects on the self of violent traumatic acts, such as physical and psychological assault. They argue that many trauma survivors continue to experience this violence as ever present, rather than as a painful event in the past.[22]

In describing the long-term effects of traumatic violence, trauma theorists begin with an important distinction between "trauma" and "traumatic stress" or "post-traumatic stress disorder" (PTSD).[23] There is no universally accepted definition of trauma, but trauma theorists generally describe it as an overwhelmingly stressful event that elicits an intense sense of helplessness, fear, and loss of control.[24] Although

21. See Lisa Adler and L. H. M. Ling, "From Practice to Theory: Towards a Dissident-Feminist Reconstruction of Nonviolence," *Gandhi Marg: Journal of the Gandhi Peace Foundation* 16 (1995) 462–80.

22. My essay offers only a social scientific analysis of trauma, but one could also develop a theological analysis of trauma and its effects as well. Many theologians have analyzed trauma in terms of sin and its effects. However, the categories of "trauma" and "sin" cannot be simply equated, as some traumas are natural phenomena that do not result from human wrongdoing. In addition, Linda Mercadante notes that sin-talk may not be helpful in contexts of interpersonal traumas. In her work with abuse survivors and addiction recovery groups, she has found that if she ever uses the word "sin" to describe the damage to their selves that survivors experience, victims believe she is blaming them for their problems. Thus, while the language of sin appropriately describes interpersonal traumatic harms such as physical and sexual abuse, it does not best describe the violence once internalized. See Linda Mercadante, "Anguish: Unraveling Sin and Victimization," *Anglican Theological Review* 85 (2000) 285–302. A better theological term for the condition of traumatization is "brokenness," which highlights that things are not as they should be but does not carry the same implications of blame as "sinfulness."

23. For example, see van der Kolk and McFarlane, "The Black Hole of Trauma," in *Traumatic Stress: The Effects of Overwhelming Experience on Mind, Body, and Society*, eds. Bessel A. van der Kolk, Alexander C. McFarlane, and Lars Weisaeth (New York: Guilford, 1996) 6.

24. Ibid., 6.

some persons easily return to psychological health after experiencing a trauma, others develop traumatic stress or post-traumatic stress disorder, which Bessel van der Kolk and Alexander McFarlane broadly describe as "the result of a failure of time to heal all wounds."[25] For those who suffer from PTSD—for those who are "traumatized"—the trauma is not simply an event that happened in the past. It is constantly relived and reexperienced in the present in the form of repetitive phenomena such as nightmares, flashbacks, and intrusive memories.

It is impossible to universalize the effects of trauma on persons because different forms of trauma can produce different effects, and two persons can experience the same trauma and respond differently to it. Nonetheless, trauma theorists have identified certain core symptoms that often occur in individuals who develop post-traumatic stress disorder. One key symptom is hyperarousal, which Judith Lewis Herman describes as a condition in which persons become physiologically aroused in response to different stimuli in their environment.[26] For those who develop this extreme sensitivity to stimuli, even "seemingly insignificant reminders" can evoke memories of the trauma, "which often return with all the vividness and emotional force of the original event."[27]

A second core symptom of PTSD is emotional numbing, a withdrawal from emotions and physical sensations. One form of emotional numbing is dissociation, a splitting of the mind that can occur during a stressful event and in subsequent periods of stress.[28] When people dissociate, traumatic memories are separated from their ordinary consciousness and are not integrated into their personal narrative; unlike other memories, they are stored as sensory perceptions, rather than in verbal-linguistic categories.[29] Van der Kolk explains that when traumatic memories are organized on a nonverbal level, they tend to recur as nightmares, flashbacks, bodily sensations, or behavioral reenactments of the trauma.[30] Thus, after some traumas a dynamic of mimetic replay

25. Ibid., 7.

26. Ibid., 13.

27. Judith Lewis Herman, *Trauma and Recovery* (New York: Basic, 1992) 37.

28. Bessel van der Kolk, Onno van der Hart, and Charles R. Marmar, "Dissociation and Information Processing in PTSD," in *Traumatic Stress,* 306, 316.

29. van der Kolk, "Trauma and Memory," in *Traumatic Stress,* 286–87.

30. Ibid., 87.

is set in motion, in which traumatic memories continue to circulate in the victim's psychic and physical structures but remain unattached to those memories that constitute his or her personal narrative or life story. For survivors, this recirculation of the traumatic memories has a gripping or totalizing force. It dominates their life, which makes them feel "stuck" in the past, disengaged from the present, and unable to anticipate the future with hope.

In addition to hyperarousal, emotional numbing, and dissociation, traumatized persons often lose the capacity to speak of their traumas and, correspondingly, experience diminished agency and a profound sense of alienation from others.[31] Judith Lewis Herman explains that "Traumatic events call into question basic human relationships. They breach the attachments of family, friendship, love, and community. They shatter the construction of the self that is formed and sustained in relation to others."[32]

The picture of the self that emerges from this analysis of trauma is that of the severely fragmented self, which has a fractured sense of self and world. "Traumatized people," Herman says, "suffer damage to the basic structures of the self. They lose their trust in themselves, in other people, and in God. Their self-esteem is assaulted. . . . Their capacity for intimacy is compromised. . . . The identity they have formed prior to the trauma is irrevocably destroyed."[33]

In describing the long-term effects of trauma in this way, trauma theorists point to an important distinction between the self as agent of violence and the self as site of violence. The traumatized self is a site of violence—a site in which the experience of traumatic violence is repeatedly replayed and reenacted.[34] Trauma theorists note, however, that the

31. Herman, *Trauma and Recovery*, 52.

32. Ibid., 51.

33. Ibid., 56.

34. In using the phrase "site of violence," I am not endorsing a "strong" constructivist view of the self which holds that selves have no coherence or stability and that we cannot identify some essential or universal features of the self. Most trauma theorists adopt a view of the self that shares some commonalities with both constructivist and essentialist accounts of identity. They acknowledge that selves are formed in social and historical contexts but also maintain that selves have certain capacities that are developed over time in the context of healthy relationships (e.g., agency, relationality, memory). On the difference between "strong" and "weak" versions of constructivism, see Serene Jones, *Feminist Theory and Christian Theology: Cartographies of Grace*

self as agent of violence and the self as site of violence are not mutually exclusive. Some traumatized persons who are sites of violence also become agents of violence, in relation to both themselves and to others. It is not uncommon for trauma survivors to compulsively reenact their traumatic experiences by harming themselves or others, or by placing themselves in situations similar to their traumas.[35]

If we take seriously this assertion that the self can be a site as well as an agent of violence, then trauma theory points to another way in which the church can be entangled in violence, other than through its collaboration with the world's dominant social and political structures. If traumatic violence can become internal to the self, it can also become part of the church, which is partially constituted by traumatized persons. This does not mean that trauma has an impact only on church members who have directly endured it. In *The Church with AIDS*, Letty Russell argues that the metaphor of the church as a body implies that all members are related and that what affects one person also affects the others.[36] Thus, while people who have experienced traumatic violence first-hand are affected by it differently from those who have not, trauma is a reality with which the entire church body must contend.[37]

In light of this account of traumatic violence and its ongoing effects on individuals and communities, we must rethink the meaning and practice of Christian nonviolence. Whereas Yoder's view focuses on transforming and resisting external, physical violence, trauma theory reveals the importance of addressing internal violence as well. For the church to transform and disentangle itself from the world's violence, it must not only refuse to be an agent of external violence. It must also be a community that can contribute to the transformation or healing of selves that are sites of violence.

(Minneapolis: Fortress, 2000) 2.

35. Herman, *Trauma and Recovery*, 39; van der Kolk and McFarlane, "Black Hole of Trauma," in *Traumatic Stress*, 10–11.

36. *The Church with AIDS: Renewal in the Midst of Crisis*, ed. Letty Russell (Louisville: Westminster John Knox, 1990) 26.

37. In this essay, I am focusing on the communal aspect of the individual's healing. Given the limitations of space constraints, I will not discuss how whole communities that have been traumatized can recover. For an overview of the issues at stake in communal trauma, see Nancy Farwell and Jamie Cole, "Community as a Context of Healing: Psychosocial Recovery of Children Affected by War and Political Violence," *International Journal of Mental Health* 30:4 (2001–2002) 19–41.

Healing in Trauma Theory

To understand, from a theological perspective, what it would take for Christian communities to contribute to the transformation of internal violence, we must first consider how trauma scholars understand healing from trauma. In general, they describe the process of healing as a reconstitution of the self. As Herman notes,

> The core experiences of psychological trauma are disempowerment and disconnection from others. Recovery, therefore, is based upon the empowerment of the survivor and the creation of new connections. Recovery . . . cannot occur in isolation.[38]

The healing of the fragmentation that occurs in trauma involves the reconstitution of the self in the context of healthy relationships.

Although there is no single path to healing, many trauma theorists agree that at least three steps[39] are necessary for this reconstitution of the self to occur.[40] First, a supportive community for the victim must be established. Second, the traumatic event needs to be integrated into the larger context of his or her life story. This happens when nonverbal, dissociated memories are translated into words and thereby transformed into narrative memory. Transforming traumatic memory into narrative memory requires remembering and retelling the violent event in a safe context. For example, in narrating the trauma in a therapeutic setting, the victim interacts with the event but does so in a supportive place and in the presence of an authentic listener.[41] This process of testifying to their experience in a supportive context can enable the survivor

---

38. *Trauma and Recovery*, 133.

39. Here, I follow Herman's account of recovery. Herman notes that not all trauma theorists divide healing into three stages; some suggest that the recovery process includes as many as eight stages. However, as Herman observes, "there is a rough congruence in these formulations" (ibid., 155).

40. Survivors do not move through these stages in linear sequence. Herman writes, "Oscillating and dialectical in nature, the traumatic syndromes defy any attempt to impose such simpleminded order. . . . However, in the course of a successful recovery, it should be possible to recognize a gradual shift from unpredictable danger to reliable safety, from dissociated trauma to acknowledged memory, and from stigmatized isolation to restored social connection" (ibid.).

41. See Dori Laub, "Bearing Witness or the Vicissitudes of Listening," in *Testimony: The Crisis of Witnessing in Literature, Psychoanalysis, and History*, by Shoshana Felman and Dori Laub, M.D. (New York: Routledge, 1992).

to cognitively assimilate the traumatic event and begin modifying the emotions it evokes, lessening their pain.[42]

Third, for healing to be complete trauma survivors need to be re-temporalized.[43] Having placed the trauma in the larger perspective of their lives as an event(s) that happened in the past, they must reconnect with life in the present once again.[44] This does not mean that trauma survivors simply forget their traumas or leave them entirely behind. Rather, persons who have healed from a traumatic experience still carry it with them but do so in a new way.[45] Having been incorporated into their personal narrative, the trauma stays with the victim but no longer retains its power to retraumatize.[46] When this happens, survivors no longer feel stuck in the past, which makes it possible for them to engage the present and view the future with hope.

A Theological Perspective on Healing

Yoder's theology, though it does not address the problem of trauma, nonetheless resonates in some ways with this understanding of healing offered by many trauma theorists. Yoder, too, understands the self to be formed in relationships. If, as his work suggests, the self is social, then its healing must involve its reconstitution in the context of healthy relationships. For Yoder, a reconstitution of the self can take place in the church as the community enacts transforming relationships of repentance, love, forgiveness, and reconciliation. The church, in his view, is

42. Bessel A. van der Kolk, Alexander C. McFarlane, and Onno van der Hart, "A General Approach to Treatment," in *Traumatic Stress,* 430–31. On the benefits for the victim of narrating his or her trauma, see Ronnie Janoff-Bulman, *Shattered Assumptions: Towards a New Psychology of Trauma* (New York: Free, 1992) 108–10; Susan Brison, *Aftermath: Violence and the Remaking of a Self* (Princeton, NJ: Princeton University Press, 2002) 53–59; Dori Laub, "Bearing Witness," in *Testimony,* 57–74.

43. I thank Shannon Craigo-Snell for suggesting this term.

44. Van der Kolk, McFarlane, and van der Hart, "A General Approach to Treatment of Posttraumatic Stress Disorder," in *Traumatic Stress,* 419.

45. Dori Laub, "An Event Without a Witness: Truth, Testimony, and Survival," in *Testimony,* 91–92.

46. Laub, "Event Without a Witness," 91.

called to be a supportive community in which people are bound to one another in covenantal relationship.[47]

Many communities, however, can create supportive relationships. What I find most interesting about Yoder's theology is not this parallel to the first step of healing many trauma theorists describe, but the resources it offers that can help us to theologically understand the second and third steps of healing, the narrative reconstitution of identity and the retemporalization of the traumatized person. For Yoder, the reconstitution of the self that may take place in the church involves the narrative construction of identity: in Christian community, people's identities are formed "in Christ" as they live as his faithful disciples and thereby integrate themselves into his story.[48] This understanding of the relationship between narrative and identity formation differs from trauma theorists' in at least one important way: Whereas trauma theorists concentrate on the role that the individual story of one's life plays in forming one's identity, Yoder's theology points to ways in which communal narratives can be constitutive of identity as well.

In Yoder's view, Christians integrate themselves into their communal narratives not simply by telling these stories but by enacting them. The church builds and sustains its relationships by performing specific practices that the gospel narratives indicate were embodied and prescribed by Jesus, such as breaking bread together and holding open meetings in the power of the Spirit. These practices are social processes that involve both divine and human action; more precisely, they are "actions of God, in and with, through and under what men and women do."[49] Yoder's work suggests that when Christians perform these practices, they participate in the ongoing story of Jesus' life. As they do so, this story becomes theirs as well, an integral part of who they are. More specifically, the story of Jesus comes to shape the ways in which

47. *For the Nations*, 115; "A 'Peace Church' Perspective on Covenanting," *Ecumenical Review* 38 (1986) 318–21.

48. For a helpful account of the role of narrative in Yoder's work, see Chris Huebner, "Mennonites and Narrative Theology: The Case of John Howard Yoder," *Conrad Grebel Review* 16 (1998) 15–38.

49. Yoder describes the church's practices as activities believers do when they "gather for reasons evidently derived from their faith" (*Body Politics*, 71).

Christians perceive and respond to reality: it comes to inform how they think, speak, act, and make decisions.[50]

This account of the self's reconstitution in the church parallels trauma theorists' descriptions of healing in two ways. First, whereas trauma theorists claim that healing from traumatic violence requires integrating the trauma into one's personal narrative, this account of the church provides a larger narrative—the narrative of Jesus—into which one's story can be incorporated and in which it can be transformed. Second, this integration into the biblical narratives is an embodied process—it happens when the church communally performs specific practices that it receives from the narratives of Jesus' life and ministry. This emphasis on performance and embodiment resonates with a point trauma theorists often make: healing involves the body.[51] In Christian community, healing involves both the individual and the social body.

Precisely how it can be healing to place one's individual story in the church's communal narratives, however, is a complicated matter. Some narratives—for example, those that contain only stories of horror and abuse—do not provide resources that can foster the healing and integration of traumatized selves. The integration of one's trauma into a larger narrative can transform internal violence only if this narrative contextualizes the violence in a broader framework that both acknowledges its reality and offers some hope for a better future. The narrative must contain resources that temper the survivor's fear and disillusionment with a sense of hope and renewal, such that their trauma and its effects no longer seem to define the whole of their existence.

Yoder's analysis of the gospel narratives suggests that these narratives have resources that could provide such hope and renewal for traumatized selves. In his view, a central focus of the biblical narratives is Jesus' proclamation and embodiment of a new vision of positive, abundant relationships in which all persons enjoy the benefits of just and peaceful community. When the church conforms (albeit imperfectly) to this way of life, its members become people formed not only

50. *For the Nations*, 153. On the performative dimension of Christian practices, see Shannon Craigo-Snell, "Command Performance: Rethinking Performance Interpretation in the Context of Divine Discourse," *Modern Theology* 16 (October 2000) 475–94.

51. See Patricia Weaver Francisco, *Telling: A Memoir of Rape and Recovery* (New York: Cliff Street, 1999) 144–51.

by their individual past and present but also by a vision that is inherently communal—one that includes Jesus' resistance to the powers, his call to right relatedness, and his love and compassion. In the church, people's identities come to be defined partly by the communal narratives that the church shares—narratives that contain a positive vision of healing and hope.

The understanding of healing that I am proposing, however, may be problematic for some traumatized persons. In suggesting that the reconstruction of identities that takes place through Christian practices may help to heal the traumatized self, we must note that the narrative which the church performs in these practices has the story of the cross at its center. Thus, in their concrete practices, Christian communities enact the identity of one whose life culminates in an event of traumatic violence. What might it mean for traumatized persons to perform this story of one who was tortured on a cross before being raised from the dead? Would this performance be one that heals, or would it be one that induces yet another mimetic replay of the victims' traumas?

Many feminist and womanist theologians point out ways in which the symbol of the cross has functioned to generate mimetic reproductions of violence. The cross, in their analysis, has often been used to create a social environment in which some persons have been forced to bear the violence of their culture; their enduring this violence has then been seen as redemptive for the culture as a whole. In light of this, some feminist and womanist theologians suggest that the symbol of the cross cannot be healing or redemptive. Delores Williams, for example, argues that redemption has to do not with the cross but with God, through Jesus' life, "giving humankind the ethical thought and practice upon which to build positive, productive quality of life."[52] Drawing on her work, one might conclude that performing a narrative that has the cross at its center inevitably contributes to the creation of conditions that produce subjects who suffer violence and mimetically reproduces violence in those who have endured it.

While recognizing the helpfulness of feminist and womanist perspectives that point out ways in which the symbol of the cross has been abused, I want to suggest that the communal embodiment of a story

---

52. *Sisters in the Wilderness: The Challenge of Womanist God-Talk* (Maryknoll, NY: Orbis, 1993) 165.

that has the cross at its center may be healing in certain circumstances. Some Christian theologians begin to describe this healing function of the cross by emphasizing the theme of divine solidarity.[53] Jesus' sufferings on the cross are not only his own; they are also the sufferings of all others, which he shares with them. This view of the cross might enable trauma survivors to see their reality in Jesus' sufferings; their trauma is now not only theirs but also his. For some traumatized persons, this identification of Jesus' suffering with theirs may help to overcome the alienation associated with their traumas, mitigating some of their pain.

In addition to lessening the alienation of trauma, this understanding of divine solidarity may enable survivors to create a narrative reconstruction of their traumas, which is central to the healing process. As trauma theorists note, part of what makes it possible for survivors to narrate their traumatic experiences is to see these experiences symbolized in ways that are both similar to and different from their own stories. The similarity between the images of trauma and the survivor's experience activates the traumatic memory and enables the victim to confront it; the difference allows the traumatic structure of the memory to be transformed.[54] As van der Kolk and his colleagues observe, the most critical difference in modifying traumatic memories is the context in which the survivor confronts the images of his or her trauma.[55] By interacting with these images in a supportive setting, the survivor can begin to modify the emotions the trauma evokes and alter his or her interpretation of the event. In the church, when traumatized persons find dimensions of their own stories in the narratives of Jesus, they may recall (and perhaps tell the story of) their traumas in a different context: the context of a supportive community. This reconstruction of

---

53. On the theme of divine solidarity, see Jürgen Moltmann, *The Crucified God: The Cross of Christ as the Foundation and Criticism of Christian Theology* (Minneapolis: Fortress, 1993). For a critique of this theme, see Johann Metz, "Suffering unto God," trans. J. Matthew Ashley, *Critical Inquiry* 20 (1994) 611–22, and Johann M. Vento, "Violence, Trauma and Resistance: A Feminist Appraisal of Metz's Mysticism of Suffering unto God," *Horizons* 29 (2002) 7–22.

54. Van der Kolk, McFarlane, and van der Hart, "A General Approach to Treatment of Posttraumatic Stress Disorder," in *Traumatic Stress*, 430.

55. Ibid., 430.

their trauma in a supportive environment can help take away the event's power to retraumatize.

While the notion of divine solidarity may be helpful to a certain extent, the concept of solidarity would be more useful for traumatized persons if extended to include the community as well. In the church, the individual's trauma is shared not only by Jesus but also by other church members. When people in the church participate in Jesus' story, they also participate in each other's stories, which are all held within the larger narratives of Jesus. Concretely, this participation in each other's stories can take place through specific aspects of the church's life and worship, such as times of sharing joys and concerns and small group discussions, prayers, and meditations. The covenantal character of the church requires that its members embody such openness to each other's pain; as a covenanted community, the church is called to enact relationships of mutual openness and support. For traumatized persons, the knowledge that the community (as well as God) is with them in their pain might further take away some of trauma's power to alienate and give them a larger, shared narrative into which their stories can be ritually placed, a framework that holds together the shattered fragments of traumatic memory.[56]

As noted above, however, trauma theorists find that healing entails more than placing the trauma in a narrative framework. Narrating the trauma makes possible the third step of healing, the retemporalization of the traumatized person. Christian communities may contribute to the survivor's retemporalization by providing a context in which they are integrated into the narratives of Jesus. By placing their traumas into this larger narrative context, the survivor does not obliterate or deny their personal story but sets this story in a new framework, one that may

56. The solidarity of the Christian community can make just a small contribution to healing from trauma if understood as only empathy and emotional support. As Joanne Carlson Brown and Rebecca Parker note, the idea that Jesus and the community participate in their suffering can give survivors psychological comfort, but it does not change the social conditions that led to their traumas. Solidarity, in this limited sense of the term, can make suffering more bearable but does not take the suffering away. Especially in situations in which the traumas are repeated and still happening, we need a broader view of solidarity that moves beyond sympathetic companionship to include active struggle on the survivor's behalf. See Brown and Parker, "For God So Loved the World?" in *Christianity, Patriarchy, and Abuse: A Feminist Critique*, eds. Joanne Carlson Brown and Carole R. Bohn (New York: Pilgrim, 1989) 17.

transform its meaning and take away its gripping or totalizing force. In the church, the individual's trauma is integrated into a shared narrative that recognizes the woundedness of humanity and proclaims that this woundedness is being redeemed. This proclamation that the redemption of their traumas has begun (and will be consummated in the future) may give traumatized persons a sense of renewal in the midst of their despair, a hope for the future that yet acknowledges the unpredictability of life and the reality of their pain. As trauma theorists note, this re-contextualization of the trauma—its integration into a larger narrative that tempers fear and disillusionment with hope—is necessary for the trauma to lose its totalizing power. Once recontextualized, the trauma ceases to dominate the survivor's life, and he or she is retemporalized: able to live in the present and look forward to the future.

This retemporalization that I am describing, however, differs from the one that many trauma theorists discuss in that it is an *eschato-logical* retemporalization. The Christian traditions often assert that the Christian community not only engages the present and hopes for the future, it also participates in this future now. Yoder, for instance, suggests that the new aeon or eschaton, though not yet fully consummated, has entered history in the incarnation and work of Jesus.[57] The church participates in it by embodying Jesus' nonviolent way; in doing so, the church chooses to be claimed by and to claim as its own the communal future that he inaugurated.[58] The new identity that the church communally enacts is, therefore, an eschatological identity. In enacting this eschatological identity (becoming an eschatological community), persons in the church do not gain a second identity that simply sits alongside

---

57. *Original Revolution,* 58.

58. Eschatological retemporalization thus involves an overlapping of "aeons" that differs from the overlapping of times that occurs in trauma. For the person suffering from traumatic stress, the past continually intrudes into the present against his or her will; an essential part of healing is thus to locate the trauma in space and time through the narration of the event, which stops the trauma from recycling into the present and makes it possible for the victim to live in the now and anticipate the future. In eschatological retemporalization, the future (the new aeon) overlaps with the present; however, it is the community, rather than the individual, that is the site of this overlapping. Moreover, in religious traditions that emphasize the voluntary character of membership, persons consciously choose to participate in this healing simultaneity of the two aeons. This affirms rather than undermines their agency.

the first, nor do they acquire a new identity that erases the old. Rather, the old remains but is being transformed into the new.

The cross, as the convergence of the old and new aeons, can thus be a symbol that heals as well as one that terrifies: it is the inbreaking of the kingdom as well as an event of traumatic violence. In the context of church practices, images of the cross can both evoke traumatic memories and speak of word of hope. As Victor Turner observes, symbols are multivocal;[59] in its multivocality, the cross tells not just of an event of torture but also of Jesus' compassion for victims and perpetrators of suffering. In suffering on the cross, Jesus makes clear that victims do not suffer alone. In loving his enemies, he breaks the link between the self as site of violence and the self as agent of violence. Refusing to be made over into the violent image of the powers, he lives as the first fruits of a restored humanity, as the one who triumphs over the powers and thereby frees others to live apart from their control. Through the communal performance of Jesus' story, the church participates in the life he makes possible and enacts a new eschatological identity: the identity of the risen one who still embodies the wounds of crucifixion.

Rethinking Christian Nonviolence

This theological analysis of healing makes it possible to offer a reconception of Christian nonviolence that includes not only resisting external violence but also transforming internal violence. Nonviolence as the transformation of internal violence entails the formation of a community in which persons may heal from violence through the narrative construction and communal enactment of a new identity, and through participation in the still incomplete new aeon that Jesus inaugurated. In describing Christian nonviolence in this way, I do not intend to imply that the church is merely a community of wounded healers. I am analyzing just one aspect of its ministry: the creation of a context in which traumatized persons can survive and flourish.

While the prevalence of trauma in our world makes it important to explore this dimension of nonviolence, it is equally crucial to recognize that Christian communities often do not enact nonviolence as

59. "Social Dramas and Ritual Metaphors," in *Dramas, Fields, and Metaphors: Symbolic Action in Human Society* (Ithaca, NY: Cornell University Press, 1974) 55.

healing. Throughout history, many Christian communities have been agents of violence against their own members and people outside of their communities. Moreover, even churches that do not actively perpetrate violence often fail to provide a context that facilitates its healing. This failure manifests itself in a variety of ways: through preaching that does not allow the reality of trauma to challenge the church's view of God, grace, sin, and redemption; through the church's failure to create liberating social structures; and through its denial of the frequency with which trauma occurs and extent of its impact. But while nonviolence as the transformation of internal violence is not fully embodied by Christian communities, it is also not entirely disconnected from them. Some individuals do find that faith communities contribute—perhaps just to a small degree—to their recovery from violence. This dimension of Christian nonviolence is, therefore, "already" and "not yet" present in history.

Trauma theory raises questions about how Christian beliefs and practices might contribute to the retraumatization, or to the healing, of survivors of overwhelming violence. These questions are not easy to answer, especially since trauma survivors respond to violence in many different ways and follow many different paths to recovery. But the stakes for Christian communities to address them are high. When the church creates a context in which traumatized persons can survive and flourish, it embodies a powerful dimension of nonviolence: it participates in the formation of communities and individuals who become not only sites of violence, but also sites of grace.

11

The Wild Patience of John Howard Yoder: "Outsiders" and the "Otherness of the Church"

ROMAND COLES

Introduction

Many liberals and Christians share a profoundly impoverished imagination of how people might live well amidst others who are radically different from themselves. Many early liberals, like Locke and J. S. Mill, resisting other odious forms of power, nevertheless proliferated a series of stories that directly or indirectly legitimated the violent exclusion of many peoples and ways of life from the charmed circle of rational beings entitled to a serious hearing in the developing "democratic" spheres of deliberation, governance, and colonization. This basic strategy (though now less violent and more inclusive in *some* important respects) remains strong and finds one of its most powerful articulations in political liberalism's effort to define before the event the general principles that will guide and exclusively limit all legitimate democratic discourse and practice in pluralistic polities. "Public reason" is the mantra of those engaged in this effort, and "comprehensive doctrine" is the symbol for what is morally to be excluded from the voices and ears of all good citizens.

In recent centuries, many Christians, waking up to the violence wrought by their own a priori condemnations of non-believers, have sought to cultivate more charitable relationships with those outside the church. Most often, these efforts are articulated through forms of liberal tolerance of all modes of faith and faithlessness so long as their particularity remains in the nonpolitical sphere, while their voices in the public political sphere are strictly limited in substance to what can be affirmed by the public reason "we all share." Of course, evoking God and scripture is fine, but only insofar as it is done according to the terms and within the limits of the purported basic consensus. Many familiar modes of Christian resistance to these (often unacknowledged) liberal exclusions take the form of resurgent fundamentalisms, which, while they certainly transgress the closures of political liberalism, appear to offer alternatives that would only return everyone to the worst. And so we often witness contestations to and fro between Christians who offer a bland ecumenicism and tolerance according to a liberalism that is often complicitous with—or very weak in its resistance to—odious forms of power and suffering, on the one hand, and Christians who offer fundamentalisms that are violent and eschew all dialogue, on the other.

As a member of no church, I come to questions of other possibilities from the flickering shards of episodic traditions of radical democratic struggles for more generous and receptive heterogeneous communities. Thus *my* effort to discuss outsiders and the otherness of the church will strike many as strange, and my focus on *John Howard Yoder* in this context, stranger yet. I must admit to sharing the first sense of strangeness, for at times in this essay I find myself heralding a Christian body politics that is at once too close to measure and infinitely remote. I remain as puzzled as anyone by this (im)possibility, and astonished by any generous enough to listen. Perhaps I am sublimely drawn in terror and attraction to the utter lack of authority of my voice in this place at these moments. To escape the insufferable authoritative posture of academic writing is no small allure. But surely that is not all.

More importantly, I find in John Howard Yoder's writings a vision of dialogical communities that brings forth very particular and powerful practices of generous solidarity precisely *through* creative uses of conflict and a vulnerable receptivity to the "least of these" within in the church and those outside it. In fact, few today offer as compelling a vision for pursuing justice and political engagements in heterogeneous societies.

Yoder is a Mennonite. When Mennonites emerged as a minority radical reformation denomination in the sixteenth century, many other

Christians agreed upon at least one thing: Mennonites should be killed. They practiced adult baptism out of a sense of the church as in important ways a voluntary community. They practiced dialogical discernment. They were aloof from coercive state power. They dressed plainly, in opposition to the semiotics of power-laden distinctions. They were pacifists. They practiced excommunication of those who violated these and other practices. These people were not good for the dominant machineries of economic, political, military, and religious power of their day.

Today there are Mennonites of many stripes and they believe many different things, often quite different from Yoder. For Yoder, being a Mennonite Christian involves belonging to a church incarnating a politics that proclaims, "Jesus is Lord." This involves, among other things, complex and discerning practices of pacifism, practicing eucharistic sharing of wealth in production and consumption, a refusal to try to "put handles on history" through coercive state power in order to mold the world to one's vision, and a commitment to the church as a community that engages otherness within and beyond its walls in a radically dialogical and vulnerable fashion. Yoder's church engages the work of reconciliation with an imagination oriented toward forgiveness, repentance, and a profound sense of the world as an abundant gift that should be received from God in the spirit of Jesus Christ. What most interests me about Yoder are the ways in which he combines bearing evangelical witness to his confessedly provincial tradition with vulnerable and receptive dialogical practices with others. Indeed, these latter practices are integral to the witness itself. Witness simply and literally makes no sense at all apart from receiving others with a radical vulnerability.

If one reads Yoder through the lens of a Troeltsch, or a Niebuhr, or a Rawls, one will find only a "sectarian" who offers nothing valuable for developing potent resistance to evil in the wider society, nor for engaging with receptive generosity those from deeply different traditions or fragments of traditions. If one reads Yoder through the lens of, say, a MacIntyre, one will do better, but perhaps still miss a lot. Beyond these crafted misreadings there are other possibilities, and I try to trace a few below.

I think it is wrong to understand Yoder's affirmation of "The Otherness of the Church" and his call to "Let the Church Be the Church" as a turn away from engaging the world. I don't mean simply that the church as Yoder understands it is always deeply engaged with the world and (as he put it following Jeremiah), "for the nations" in multiple ways, ranging from critical resistance, to community practices embodying and proclaiming an alternative gospel ethics, to the flexible experimentation of a minority community in ways that often have broader implications and uses, to selective tactical alliances and forms of cooperation with other groups, and so forth. These are, of course, crucial to Yoder, and they reveal the error of the "sectarian" charge. Nor do I simply mean that the church as Yoder understands it, far from pursuing a retreat into sectarian purity, homogeneity, and imposed harmony, engages the "worldliness" of the world—its inchoate aspects, complexity, heterogeneity, discordance—insofar as it is a body of endlessly unfolding manifold differences drawn into cooperation and creative uses of conflict through reconciling dialogical practices. This too is true and important, and it illustrates ways in which the church might be good news for the world precisely because it provides compelling modes of response to the world's murky, multifarious, messiness. Yet it does not quite hit the registers I seek most to engage. Indeed, paradoxically and frightfully, theories that proclaim to be the best possible internally differentiated/differentiating communities have (in Christian, liberal, and many other forms) often been marshaled to bolster an absolute a priori privileging of their own orientations and limits, and a corresponding deafness to all difference outside. The obliteration of difference *in the name of difference* is as familiar as aggressive war in the name of peace. I would even guess—to pronounce a horizon that this essay works largely *with Yoder's* articulations of vulnerability and patience to resist—that all forms of such *invulnerable* privileging of one's own church and community, no matter how internally dialogical and differentiated, no matter how generously "for the nations" they seek to be, no matter how much they eschew practices of warfare—will, finally and in spite of themselves, slide toward postures at war with outsideness *as such.*[1]

---

1. In fact, this suspicion (articulated in my critical reading of John Milbank's totalizing neo-Deleuzianism in *Theology and Social Theory* in Romand Coles, "Storied Others and the Possibilities of *Caritas*: Milbank and Neo-Niezschean Ethics," *Modern Theology* 8 [1992] 331–51) provided the initial horizon of questioning that I brought to my reading of Yoder.

Yoder treads along other richer paths; his vines grow in other ways. Of course, he too writes that the dialogical "church precedes the world epistomologically" and "axiologically." But he understands this stance as the church's condition for engaging the world generously and with a receptive vulnerability. In other words, he interprets the binding centrality of the lordship of Christ as the opening of dialogical relations between the church and the world in which giving and receiving is possible. Thus, I will argue that vulnerable relations with outsiders are integral to the otherness of the church, and that when this understanding of *caritas* is forgotten and unpracticed, the church loses its otherness, it assimilates to the violence of the world. When Christians cease to engage outsiders with receptive generosity, they cease to let the church be the church, they lose sight of Jesus as Lord. With Buber and Heidegger, each in reference to his most famous work, I read the "and" in my subtitle, "'Outsiders' and the 'Otherness of the Church,'" as the most important word for understanding Yoder and the Lordship he heralds.

Anyone familiar with Yoder's writing will already observe the work of translation in my essay. This is, on Yoder's terms and mine, what must occur in any particular encounter and it opens up hopeful possibilities and risks. I have tried to avoid the latter and pursue the former through a variety of strategies. I have tried to let ring throughout the very specific language of Jesus and scripture that provides the root from which Yoder's efforts grow and to which they always return. Simultaneously, I have entwined with these melodies contrapuntal phrasings that translate and *develop* it with terms drawn from the radical democratic struggles, theorizing, and concerns that I bring to the engagement.[2] In translating and developing, I have attempted to let Yoder's work inflect and transfigure the language closest to me with his meanings, and I know I have done the reverse as well—in some ways that I do not know. By juxtaposing these two languages, neither uncontaminated by nor reducible to the other, I have tried to present some of what each might learn from the other. Each voice discovers a new yet strangely familiar sound. At the same time, the juxtaposition of their

2. For my earlier theoretical accounts of these positions, see especially my chapter on Merleau-Ponty in *Self/Power/Other: Political Theory and Dialogical Ethics* (Ithaca, NY: Cornell University Press, 1992), and *Rethinking Generosity: Critical Theory and the Politics of Caritas* (Ithaca, NY: Cornell University Press, 1997).

distinct terms also creates throughout some dissonance, some of which I discuss toward the end of the essay. In this explicit lack of fit, I hope to keep alive a sense of the differences and thus alert readers to damages unwittingly imposed so readers might creatively attend to them in the name of a more receptive generosity, or the body politics of Jesus, or something yet unsung from which we all might learn. In the final section, I sketch some of the differences that most disturb and haunt the positions with which I was more comfortable prior to my engagement with Yoder. Yoderians might well develop some ghosts for Yoderians.

My inquiry here, however, leads me to attend to Yoder *as* ghost, and, as much as possible, not to exorcise him so as to resume a slumber.

To write of ghosts, however, is not identical to being one. And this again raises the question of from where, "as a member of no church," I embark upon this tensional journey with Yoder. People with self-understandings similar to my own will mightily resist affirming a stable and definitive location of authorship. We view our locations as multiple, shifting, and changing—we are uncomfortable nearly everywhere. Yet I do not write from nowhere; and it is, in fact, my engagements in radical democratic coalition politics that greatly shape my interests in, perspectives upon, and questioning with John Howard Yoder. As a member of an enduring progressive grassroots social movement (Peoples' Alliance), as well as an active participant in a broader (Industrial Areas Foundation) multiracial diverse coalition of religious congregations, social movements, community and neighborhood associations in Durham, North Carolina, I am interested in practical and theoretical modes of engagement that can contribute to enriching democratic dialogue and action among groups with many deep differences. Within our coalition, we are diversely striving to create a public space in which heterogeneous community-specific narratives of suffering and hope can be given voice and receptively engaged. Most groups within the coalition seek to fashion their participation in a manner that at once strengthens their particular community and tradition(s), and at the same time enhances their ability to listen better to and learn from the very different narratives of suffering and hope brought forth by other specific communities. Together, we (and similar coalitions across the U.S.) are groping toward a form of urban power that cultivates direction through a combination of heterogeneous voices and powerfully receptive of ears. We are inspired, both by our different traditions and emergent struggles, and by the possibilities of our being in common, to cultivate a more generous and receptive form of democratic power—to cultivate our particular and intersecting histories in directions that will enhance our capacities to engage in this good work and good news. These are, quintessentially Yoderian concerns, and few are more illuminating in this regard. I read Yoder to learn better some of what this project might mean and require. I read Yoder to raise some questions where I think his thinking might impede these tasks. And I read Yoder in an effort to cultivate in myself an appreciation for the distinct powers for such engagement that stem precisely from a tradition that I do not call my own. At the limit, I read Yoder in an effort to hear good powers that may, in some registers, exemplify admirable and even crucial capacities that people closer to me have as yet been unable to match.

These Are a Few of My/His Favorite Things
(To be Sung as if John Coltrane Were a Mennonite)

Eschewing both religious and secular claims to represent with certain superiority a universal movement and meaning in history—a meaning that would continue to progress only if "we" impose upon the future "the good way our recent past has taken," Yoder offers a position that "is most openly and respectfully, repentantly and doxologically aware of particular historical identity."[3] Yoder's Christianity understands itself as "a goal-oriented movement through time." But where Constantinian Christianity and political liberalism would move into the future by delegitimating their others at the outset and then imposing (openly or in ways less visible) upon all who would resist the linear extension of their most "progressive" present, Yoder suggests that there is no worthy directionality that would not repeatedly have to pass through vulnerable encounters with other directions and indirections. There would be no church worth its name without both teleological (directional) and a-teleological (concerning the unanticipatable) virtues and practices.[4] For

3. John Howard Yoder, *The Priestly Kingdom: Social Ethics as Gospel* (Notre Dame, IN: University of Notre Dame Press, 1984) 3.

4. We should note that Yoder sometimes refuses to employ academic terms like "teleology," and not infrequently signals his reluctance when he does use them. See,

beyond the tepid proclamations of a possible fallibility, the posture of radical reformation asserts that: "Any existing church is not only fallible but in fact peccable. That is why there needs to be a constant potential for reformation and in the more dramatic situations a readiness for the reformation even to be 'radical.'"[5] With contemporary Deleuzians he resists the arboreal imagination. "Far from being an ongoing growth like a tree (or a family tree) the wholesome growth of a tradition is like a vine: a story of constant interruption of organic growth in favor of a pruning and a new chance for the roots."[6]

Yoder seeks to renew a Christian "hermeneutics of peoplehood"— a radically dialogical conception of church practices of discernment— in light of a "Protestant perspective," only to note immediately that

---

for example, his sarcastic comments on "teleology" in "To Serve Our God and Rule the World," in *The Royal Priesthood: Essays Ecclesiological and Ecumenical*, ed. Michael G. Cartwright (Scottdale, PA: Herald, 1998) 128–29. I must postpone discussion of this issue for another time, even as it has everything to do with questions of translation that are at work in the present essay.

5. *Priestly Kingdom*, 5. One could say without exaggerating that Yoder's "wisdom of the Cross" is one forever stretched between a faith in a certain sense of the *adequacy* of the believing community gathered around scripture and informed by the Holy Spirit, and a sense of the peccability or epistemological *inadequacy* that will always to some degree somehow be at work. Thus Yoder writes of the discerning community's "morally adequate knowledge," where "'morally adequate' means good enough to work with, sufficient to enable the community process of discernment. It did not mean absolutely clear, immutable, or without exceptions. It means that my brother or sister within the discerning community has a basis for counting on me, blaming or praising me, correcting or commending me as we together proceed through the discernment process in the midst of our being and doing." At the same time, the epistemological effects of sin "poisons . . . even our ability to know [the good]." See "Theological Revision and the Burden of Particular Identity," in *James M. Gustafson's Theocentric Ethics: Interpretations and Assessments*, ed. Harlan R. Beckley and Charles M. Swezey (Macon, GA: Mercer University Press, 1988) 77–82. This affects selves and the church body. While the latter is the locus of the practices of "regeneration" and "change in orientation," it can only be such, as I argue Yoder argues below, through practices of receptive generous vulnerability with outsiders. If Yoder does not always stress the latter, this is due to the context in which his work so often intervenes (namely, to resist dominant church practices of assimilation to the dominant "public reason"), *not* to some intermittent awareness of the centrality of vulnerable receptivity. Yoder resists a neo-constantinian "receptivity" that would receive and govern itself according to "public reason" precisely because it would thus greatly diminish giving and receiving in dialogue. He thus resists the church's reception of hegemonic liberal "receptivity" in the name of radical vulnerability, not to avoid it, as I fear many mistakenly believe.

6. *Priestly Kingdom*, 69.

the latter has no affirmative historical center that might illuminate its discordant manifestations. "Its common marks are negative": a sense that in the history of Christianity "something had gone wrong"; "a fundamental skepticism about what everybody everywhere always thought"; a "challenge." In contrast to narratives that claim to possess sovereignty by securing a continuous relation to an authorizing origin, "Jesus is Lord" is the solicitation to a "perennially unfinished process of critiquing the developed tradition from the perspective of its own roots."[7] The scriptural accountability thus evoked does not signify a naive sense of transparency and a self-righteous possession of a truth that has been or can be completely restored beyond historical contingency. Rather the wisdom of the cross that teaches "*semper reformanda*" calls communities to open to the future by way of a never completed movement of *dispossession*. The church does not possess the origin—Jesus Christ, like a "proposition . . . which we *hold* to be authoritative and to be exempted from the relativity of hermeneutical debate . . . ." Nor can the church escape the "need to be corrected . . . as if our link to our origins were already *in our own hands*."[8] Rather, the normativeness of Jesus works primarily to "deny absolute authority to any later epoch, especially to the present." It illuminates that all is not well and calls for "midcourse correction," "reorienting our present movement forward in light of what was wrong."[9]

But how would this Gospel *root* that illuminates always-particular dissonances, discontinuities, dispossessions, and renewals within the tradition finally avoid being simply another standard (or method) beyond history that would endow with fundamentalist authority those who speak and act monologically in its name to critique the world around them? And if it was conceived simply as such an authority, might it not then more fundamentally close than open Christians' relation to history and all outsiders—thus resembling the very Constantianism (by which he means, in simple terms, all effort to take "control" of history) Yoder has so profoundly taught Christians to resist? If Yoder escapes this trap, it is because he understands the church's relation to Jesus as the very incarnation of practices of becoming vulnerable to encounter

7. Ibid., 15–17.

8. Ibid., 70, emphasis added.

9. Ibid., 87.

to the otherness of history—the exemplary possibility of dialogical liberty. Or, perhaps better, the exemplary breaking forth of the ways and the desirability of such responsive freedom.

To understand Yoder here we must carefully explore his account of the relationship between "reaching back" to Scripture and practices of vulnerable welcoming. As we reach back, he writes, "what we find at the origin is already a process of reaching back again to the origins, to the earliest memories of the event itself, confident that that testimony, however intimately integrated with the belief of the witnesses . . . will serve to illuminate and sometimes adjudicate our present path."[10] Scripture offers "the early communities' recording and interpreting [Jesus'] words in the ongoing process of defining the meaning of obedience" in their time.[11] The meaning of Jesus' teaching does not stand out all by itself but can emerge only in dialogic discernment of those early communities inspired in his memory. Similarly, "the free-church alternative . . . recognizes the inadequacies of . . . Scripture standing alone uninterpreted . . . [and] locates the fulfillment of that promise [of the guidance of spirit] in the assembly of those who gather around Scripture in the face of a given real moral challenge."[12] Thus truth is always a finite historical incarnation. For Yoder, what might endure is a community of vulnerable dialogic practices responsive to Jesus in their reaching back to Scripture for illumination; one that might allow truth to manifest itself ever anew in the specificities of historical encounter and discernment. If the early church was "fallible, divided, confused," the "structural soundness" of its major teachers lay significantly in their elaboration of such practices.[13]

Yoder spent a lifetime discerning this church epistemology of disciplined vulnerability and cultivated "expectation of newness."[14] I shall only very briefly summarize a few of the most important aspects and then flesh them out in light of the concerns raised at the beginning of this essay.

10. Ibid., 70.
11. Ibid., 116.
12. Ibid., 117.
13. Ibid., 129.
14. Ibid., 38.

For Yoder, the good news of Christ's generosity finds expression in the literal body of the church community. But of what sort of unity does this body partake? What unity does it seek? Yoder emphatically rejects notions of church unity based upon extant agreements that would provide a common denominator foundation for identity, direction, and tolerable pluralism. Such understandings tend to construe every serious dispute as a call for division. To avoid the latter, they then often paper over difference in ways that avoid questions and contestations crucial to the vitality and faithfulness of the church. They avoid or purge precisely the differences that might make conversation worthwhile. Such efforts to maintain a "common currency" capable of circulating like lifeblood throughout the body inexorably tend to cheapen the "coins" in ways that "call for less critical perspective, less sacrifice, and less change."[15] Less ongoing critical reflection and reformation in relation to dominant practices. They proliferate "low expectations for dialogue"—both in terms of what each might offer and in terms of what each might receive.[16]

Far better, Yoder argues, to understand church unity as a commitment to dialogical processes of reconciliation—figured by the early churches' gathering discernment around Jesus' wisdom of the cross. This "radicalizes the particular relevance of Jesus, enabling dialogue through the content of his message: the love of the enemy, the dignity of the lowly, repentance, servanthood, the renunciation of coercion."[17] Scripture, from this radical reformation perspective, most profoundly teaches a "hermeneutics of peoplehood." Central to this is that meetings be "an open process," "where the working of the spirit in the congregation is validated by the liberty with which the various gifts [of all the different members of the church] are exercised, especially by the due process with which every prophetic voice is heard and every witness evaluated."[18] The movement of the community through time occurs as "binding and loosening," whereby it seeks to discern afresh the obliga-

15. *Royal Priesthood*, 294.

16. "Theological Revision and the Burden of Particular Identity," 84–86.

17. Yoder weaves other forms of church "body politics" into this account as well, including importantly, eucharistic bread/sharing in economic consumption and production. See *Body Politics: Five Practices of the Christian Community Before the Watching World* (Nashville: Discipleship Resources, 1992) chapter 2.

18. *Priestly Kingdom*, 22.

tory and the nonobligatory, the need to withhold fellowship and the need to forgive: The community literally alters its shape and direction as it binds here and unbinds there; and it thereby participates in bringing forth the temporal continuities and unanticipated discontinuities of tradition*ing*.

Essential to a dialogic process animated by *caritas*, Yoder repeatedly emphasizes, is the multiplicity of gifts within the church and the need for each to remember and witness how "*every* member of the body has a distinctive place in this process."[19] The different gifts will contribute in diverse ways, times, and places to the shape and directions of the living body of the church, in ever-new ways. To guard against the mortification of the corporate body into a static structure of hierarchical normalizing power, Yoder, reading Paul, emphasizes that "all the gifts are of equal dignity" and each should resist conformist pressures, "giving special honor to the less comely members," by offering them our utmost receptive and critical powers.[20] In the same vein, he argues that "prophecy [edifying communication] is both a charisma [gift] distinctly borne by some individuals *and* a kind of discourse in which others may sometimes participate as well."[21] For this reason, "everyone who has something . . . given by the Holy Spirit to him or her to say, can have the floor"[22] and all must listen to the "least of these."

Yoder affirms the need for diverse members of the church to participate in bringing orientation and order to this highly spirited process. Hence there are those with profound prophetic charisma who help bring forth edifying visions of the church and its place in history,[23] but they are subject to "the other members" who are instructed to dialogically "weigh what the prophet(s) [have] said."[24] So too there will be "Agents of memory" who are particularly resourceful at drawing upon the community's past to illuminate the present, but they "don't judge or

19. Ibid., 29.

20. *Body Politics*, 50.

21. *Priestly Kingdom*, 29, emphasis added.

22. *Body Politics*, 61.

23. *Priestly Kingdom*, 29.

24. *Body Politics*, 61.

decide anything"[25]; "agents of order and due process" offer their gifts to ensure that all are heard and the spirit of conversation is conciliatory.

The conviction is that every member of the body will have a nameable gift. With each of these gifts, the expectation is that several members of a church will be particularly gifted and that episodically the gift will emerge from those among whom its manifestation is least expected. The dialogic practices of giving and receiving here are to bind and loose—discipline and release—the expectation and ushering forth of "Spirit given newness" in ways that illuminate previously unperceived problems and possible responses.[26] For this, some ordering is necessary. Yet Yoder emphasizes that for most of history and certainly now, the need is to renew a radically dialogic and multiplicitous "vitality." "Paul *first* said, 'Every-one has a gift'; *then* he said, 'let everything be orderly.' We too need the first truth, as Good News, before the second. In the name of the first truth we need to challenge the concentration of authority in the hands of office-bearers accredited on institutional grounds." Multifarious vitality needs to be "reined in only after it begins to over reach itself" in deaf and selfish forms of "self-validating enthusiasm."[27] Subverting the way body metaphors historically have supported hierarchy by identifying a member as the "head," he notes that "Christ, not one of the other members, is the head," and "Jesus" was "the last priest."[28] There is a "certain functional hierarchy . . . in that understandable prophecy is preferable, if one must choose, to unintelligible speaking in tongues; but Paul said he did not want his readers to have to choose. Both were valid; he practiced both and wanted others to do so."[29] Church disciplines must always aim to cultivate *both* the expectation of unanticipatable and often initially inchoate newness *and* the discerning capacities to renew the orientation, direction, and order of the Gospel tradition that faces and works with it.

Yet if practicing and discerning the meaning of nonviolence, uncoerced community, eucharistic sharing of wealth, and the priesthood of *all* believers is to occur at the dialogical edge between order and

25. *Priestly Kingdom*, 30.

26. Ibid.

27. *Body Politics*, 51, Yoder's emphasis.

28. Ibid., 53, 56.

29. Ibid., 54.

unanticipatable emergence, between the intelligible and the visceral, is there not still a way in which "Jesus as Head" privileges the body of believers in such a way that, however exemplary relations are to be *within* the church, relations with people outside it would be structured around a rigid hierarchical privileging of Christian vision with effects antithetical to the politics of Jesus just described? In other words, might not "Jesus as Lord" constitute a radical deafness to non-believers, and a confinement of prophesy to those within the church, such that the dialogic conditions of *agape* within give way to monological practices toward others outside in a manner likely to proliferate blindness and violence—certainly *not* the careful discernment that might make vital giving and receiving possible? And would not these degraded relations at the borders migrate inward as "members" are suspected of this and that type of "foreignness" and treated accordingly?

To understand Yoder's resources for resisting this charge we must loop back again to his understanding of the looping back to Scripture, through which an intelligent church might move and reform in time. Just as this looping back to the early church's looping back to Jesus has suggested the shape of traditioning practices and relations within the church and between this community and Scripture, it is again in *looping itself*—the dispersion of the gifts that propel and inform its movements and practices of reception—that we find the illumination and genesis of the relations between the church and those of other faiths and reasons.

In the "perennially unfinished process" of reaching back to discern scriptural accountability, the church cultivates a "readiness for reformation": an expectation that "the Lord hath yet more light and truth to break forth from this holy Word,"[30] that the church ought to move through history as "a continuing series of new beginnings,"[31] Christian practical moral reason "must always expect to be at some point subversive" of the common wisdom outside the church and within it.[32] Reaching back to practices of Jesus and the early churches of scripture provides a "considerable principled solidity" for this process.[33] Yet this

---

30. Ibid., 59.
31. *Priestly Kingdom*, 133.
32. Ibid., 40.
33. Ibid., 118.

guidance is to spur and support—rather than spurn and suppress—vulnerable and receptive encounters with those beyond the church.

From Yoder's radical reformation perspective, Jesus and the early communities gathered around his memory teach that *to be possible at all*, practices of *caritas* must be inflected toward vulnerable engagements with those emerging in margins within the church body *and* those *beyond* it. Hence his other-inflected reading of the basic "body practices": for example:

1. Eucharist, rather than simply the giving and receiving of wealth within the church, "is a paradigm for every other mode of inviting the outsider and the underdog to the table"[34] (Note that Mennonites have been leading innovators in establishing emergent networks of "fair trade" around the globe).

2. Nonviolence finds its exemplarity in vulnerable love of the enemy; and this vulnerable love is articulated not just in a refusal to kill or coerce the other, but in striving to extend the processes of reconciliatory dialogue beyond the church even in the most agonistic relations, where "the commitment [is] to hear not only the neighbor but even the adversary"[35] (Note that the Mennonite Central Committee does profound work around the world to aid in reconciling long-standing violent conflicts).

3. Efforts to discern charisma (gift) must reach beyond the church body to scrutinize incarnations of God's "providence" in manifestations of foreignness.[36]

But putting it this way underestimates, really, the renewal to which Yoder bears witness. For it might misleadingly suggest that the ethical nature of the relationship of Christians toward outsiders is known by the body of believers entirely *prior to* the encounter with the others; known, in other words, simply through the relations between those in the gathered community, Scripture, and the Holy Spirit, in a way that

34. *For the Nations: Essays Public and Evangelical* (Grand Rapids: Eerdmans, 1997) 32.

35. *Body Politics*, 69.

36. For example, Yoder elaborates this point throughout "Meaning after Babble: With Jeffrey Stout Beyond Relativism," *Journal of Religious Ethics* 24 (1996) 125–38, which I discuss in more detail below.

rises above and is somehow itself exclusive and independent of vulnerable receptive engagements with others beyond the church. Yet this is decidedly not the case, for in the presence of outsiders, the looping *back* of discerning ethical practice *cannot itself happen* in the absence of a vulnerable and expectant looping *through* engagements with those of other dispositions, faiths, and reasons. While the church has a certain precedence both epistemologically and axiologically as the body of focused dialogical discernment and action in light of Jesus' practices and pregnant wisdom[37] (and thus there can be no "politics of Jesus" that could be coercive, selfish, nondialogical, invulnerable, or cease to loop back to Scripture), it is, as we shall see, even the case that the church has often learned *about these most basic practices* from "outsiders." Of course, what it learns retrospectively in the most "extreme cases" (in scare-quotes to evoke the paradox of the utter normalcy of such extremity in the long history of Constantinian and neo-Constantinian Christianity, as Yoder reads things) where it has gone astray in evil, is of its own unfaithfulness to Jesus and scripture. Yet in other cases, where Christians learn more from outsiders than that Christians are being decidedly "un-Christian," they learn not primarily of their unfaithfulness but of previously unperceived meanings of faith. The outsiders participate in the very "breaking forth of more light and truth from His holy Word."

Yoder writes of "looping back" as "a rediscovery of something from the past whose pertinence was not seen before, because only a new question or challenge enable[s] us to see it speaking to us."[38] In cases where new questions and challenges arise from outside the church body, they often take the form of new developments and events (e.g., the globalization of corporate capitalism, ecological crises, new forms of techno-genocide, consumer culture, etc.) that might solicit and thus help in foregrounding hitherto unrecognized dimensions and implications of Scripture that illuminate what it now might mean for the church to "be church." They incarnate "the need" for scriptural practices "to be selected and transformed transculturally in ever new settings."[39]

---

37. *Priestly Kingdom*, 11.

38. Ibid., 69.

39. *For the Nations*, 92.

However, more interesting in the present context are times when it is precisely through receptive engagements with outsiders who contest hegemonic practices (in the church, in the wider world, or in the relations between the two) that the church is enabled to "loop back" in ways which enable new light to break forth. At these moments of receptive encounter at the discordant edge between the church and outsiders, the latter participate in reconfiguring the edges, the pruning relationships, and the nourishing circulations between the present church and its scriptural roots.

Historically these relations have sometimes re-illuminated practices that are absolutely elemental to the church. Hence Yoder enjoins:

> [The] hermeneutical role of the community is . . . primordial; i.e., we have to talk about it first. It is however by no means an exclusive possession . . . . When the empirical community becomes disobedient, other people can hear the Bible's witness too. It is after all a public document. Loners and outsiders can hear it speaking especially if the insiders have ceased to listen. It was thanks to the loner Tolstoy and the outsider Gandhi that the churchman Martin Luther King, Jr. . . . was able to bring Jesus' word on violence back into the churches. It was partly the outsider Marx who enabled liberation theologians to restate what the Law and the Prophets had been saying for centuries, largely unheard, about God's partisanship for the poor.[40]

Similarly Yoder notes that most "churches" had to learn important lessons about religious liberty and democracy from anti-church proponents of Enlightenment.[41]

When those within the church are not listening to the Bible's witness, the ears with which the church might loop back will have to receive the ears of the others—even when those ears claim to hear another God, or gods, or no God at all. And when have those within the church ever been listening to scripture as fully as they might? When have they been fully attentive? One could even say that this very possibility hinges for Yoder significantly upon the attentiveness they bring to encounters with outsiders. The voices, places, and times of the emergence of God's gifts are not predictable, even as radical Reformation Christians know

40. Ibid., 93.
41. *Priestly Kingdom*, 23.

that the vulnerable and receptive practices of Scriptural engagement are eternally central to our ability to receive them.

Very significantly, these new and deeper senses of *both* the radical unpredictability of God's gifts *and* the vulnerable and receptive politics of Jesus necessary to receive them, might *themselves* most probably break forth for most modern Christians today if a gift, whose most potent forces and articulations are largely outside the church, is somehow recognized and engaged in the deeper ways intimated above. To translate this again: the fullest conditions of possibility for *caritas* themselves might *emerge* historically in ways that exemplify this fullness before it fills the church in the form of disciplined practices or intentional awareness. Yoder's word for this Christian deliverance from what others might see as a question-begging or vicious circle is "grace." Let us look closer.

In "Meaning after Babble," Yoder writes: "from the Gospel perspective, modern pluralism is not a set back but a providential occasion for clarification. It may enable us to see something about the Gospel that was not visible before."[42] If you miss the uncanny element in the way "the Gospel" *breaks forth in these sentences*, you will miss a lot. For the Gospel perspective from which modern pluralism and pluralists might appear to be a God-given occasion for clarification is *already* the Gospel perspective that has *been clarified* (through Yoder's critical and receptive encounter with these outsiders of modern pluralism) and now "clarifies" something about the Gospel that was not visible before—that was *not Gospel* perspective for most moderns (or perhaps any) before, and still is not for most now. The edge of this teleology-ateleology moves too quickly to be caught at rest. It can only be *offered*, by one discerning at the border of the church and affirming this vulnerable discernment, in hopes that there is or can be a body of believers who can weigh and receive it in a manner that will participate in the breaking forth of this gift. Grace: because what ought to be given has already arrived, "at once original and true-to-type, at once unpredictable and recognizable."[43]

Yoder's looping back through the outsiders and otherness called "pluralism" is enacted in a reading of Scripture that is at once radical and strangely compelling. "Babel in the myth of Genesis," he writes,

42. "Meaning After Babble," 135.
43. *Priestly Kingdom*, 133.

"places the multiplicity of cultures under the sign of the divine will." "Restoring his original plan," YHWH scattered them not as an act of angry retribution, but in an "act of divine benevolence," "for their own good," as Paul recognized.[44] The renewed multiplicity of particular languages, the need for discourse dependent upon particular communities and concrete relations between particular communities, was to "save humankind from its presumptuous and premature effort at divinization," by which various particular individuals and groups tried (and continue to try) in myriad ways to enforce uniformity according to their own self-transparent Truth.[45] The possibility of *veritas*, *caritas*, and *agape*, Yoder's reading suggests, hinges upon engagements within and between different communities that are at once evangelical and vulnerable. Or, evangelical in their vulnerability, and vulnerable in their evangelism. It is to this entwinement at the heart of Yoder's "politics of Jesus"—brought forth in precisely such engagements—that we now turn.

Christians cannot, Yoder argues, confine themselves to the private sphere and the secular currencies of public discourse that many liberals have insisted upon from Locke to Rawls. There is no Christian ecclesiology that could forego the evangelical proclamation to others that Jesus is Lord—that he calls us to peace, voluntary radically dialogical communities, witnessing the wild heterogeneity of giftedness, the cessation of coercive hierarchies, generous sharing of wealth in both production and consumption, and attention in every sense to the "least of these." The church must be a body striving to give as it has received. "The calling to witness to the Other has been a constitutive component of the self-definition of Jewry at least since Jeremiah and of Christianity since Pentecost"[46]—not a "choice." "Jesus is Lord" is the Good News that the practicing church as pulpit and paradigm brings to the world. In discerning, practicing, and offering to others this gift, the church remains true to His word, oriented by His moral substance. It remains faithful that it "learns more from Scripture than other ways" about how to practice a receptive generosity, how to cultivate criticism of self-ag-

44. "Meaning After Babble," 127.
45. Ibid., 132.
46. "Meaning After Babble," 138.

grandizing modes of power, how to maintain a stance of "revolutionary subordination,"[47] and how to engender a readiness for reformation.

But how is this witness to occur? For Yoder, this has to be discerned in each particular case. The church must always strive toward disciplined practices that incarnate and exemplify the Good News. Yet this "letting the church be the church" is never conceived simply as an inward turned sectarian practice, but is at once, "for the nations," the outsiders.[48] As such, exemplifications of Good News must find incarnation in the church's modes of witness to the world. Christians must reject imposing their faith upon others, and also renounce foundational claims to have reached "some kind of transcultural or preparticular ground."[49] Rather they are called to validate their faith repeatedly, in one vulnerable encounter after another.

Crucial to this project is translating "our Word into their words," "one particular community at a time."[50] This is not a call to trim the gospel to whatever "public discourse" claims to be sovereign in the surrounding world. Rather, faithful to their scriptural roots, Christians should contest the discourses and powers that govern the world when the latter contradict the politics of Jesus. But this means that far from simply bearing witness in their "own" idioms, they must also communicate in "terms familiar to particular outsiders," like the messianic Jews did, when they openly "seized [the world's] categories, hammered them into other shapes" that often radically reformed or reversed their meaning.[51] In so doing they bore witness such that the others who were in-

---

47. For an extended discussion of "Revolutionary Subordination," see chapter 9 in *The Politics of Jesus*, 2nd ed. (Grand Rapids: Eerdmans, 1994). It is beyond the scope of this essay to engage the questions raised in that text and responses to it concerning women and revolutionary subordination. I think Yoder aims to articulate a radically post-patriarchal vision, in lines with his reflections on women in the church in *Body Politics*, 60 (and also 61–62). He also seeks to resist certain forms of feminism that would seek liberation simply by opening to women patriarchal institutions such as the role of exclusive priest, or masculine sovereign subjectivity. That said, I am skeptical about whether Yoder's work engages feminist theology and theory as deeply as it should and we must.

48. It goes without saying that this does not mean for the nations as sovereign sources of meaning and state power.

49. "Meaning After Babble," 134.

50. Ibid., 132.

51. *Priestly Kingdom*, 54.

vited to respond could truly hear it. "Interworldly grammars" are often generated in these encounters,[52] but none should "renew the vain effort to find assurance beyond the flux of unendingly meeting new worlds, or to create a metalanguage above the clash."[53] The church's assurance and the other's acceptance are the stuff of ever-renewed challenges.

· To grasp the radical depth of this truth for Yoder we must return to his understanding of translation. Transcultural witness requires that "we must enter concretely into the other community . . . long enough, deeply enough, vulnerably enough, to be able to articulate our Word in their words."[54] This vulnerable renunciation of violence *required for* discerning how to bring good news to the other also "is good news for the Other."[55] Hence Yoder claims, with Martin Luther King and Gandhi, that nonviolence "is thereby an epistemology. . . . The truth of our witness needs [it] to let its credibility show."[56]

But it is not simply an epistemology for *the other*. The vulnerability through which members of the church craft the "what" and the "how" of their witness is simultaneously the risky endeavor through which they might—beyond attesting to the church's own (re)newness—discover newness with and from the others. This is absolutely vital to the attitude and practice of engagement that the church must seek creatively to bind and loose into being. Thus Yoder writes, again with Gandhi, that even "the adversary is part of my truth-finding process. I need to act nonviolently . . . to get the adversary to hear me, but I need as well to hear the adversary."[57]

Yoder further elaborates this claim concerning nonviolence as epistemology in essays on interfaith dialogue. I quote at length a passage that captures the spirit of his arguments:

> It may be the Islamicist Kenneth Cragg who for our time has made most poignant the insight that I have only really understood another faith if I begin to feel at home in it, if its tug at me

52. Ibid., 56.

53. Ibid., 60.

54. "Meaning After Babble," 133.

55. Ibid., 135, emphasis added.

56. Ibid.

57. *Body Politics*, 69. Yoder draws here on the outsider Gandhi in part to textually exemplify his substantive position toward engagements with outsiders.

questions my own prior (Christian) allegiance anew. Likewise, I am only validly expositing my own faith if I can imagine my interlocutor's coming to share it. Perhaps the *word* mission has been rendered unusable in some contexts by abuse, but respect for the genuineness of dialogue demands, *in both directions* that there be no disavowal in principle of my witness becoming an open option for the other. Mission and dialogue are not alternatives: each is valid only within the other, properly understood.[58]

One cannot generously communicate one's faith without striving to inhabit receptively the other's world in a manner that challenges one's own faith as well as the faith of the other. Epistemological nonviolence aims toward practices in which the possibility of giving and receiving are inextricably entwined. This is troubling to the core, for there is no mission without dialogue and no dialogue unless one "takes the risk of having his own ideas . . . radically changed" even as one might seek to radically change aspects of or perhaps most of what the other does and believes.[59] For this reason, Yoder claims: "We are all 'nominal' adherents. No one's faith is final in this life."[60] Paradoxically, to seek to radically renew one's faith in the particularity and universal relevance of Jesus is, for Yoder, to be drawn to him (and thus herald others) precisely in the exemplary illumination through which he makes this generous truth break forth and be real. "The gatheredness of the community is the point . . . where kerygma [heralding] and dialogue coincide, where renewed appeal to the biblical Jesus and renewed openness to tomorrow's world are not two things but one."[61] And *this* faith, *this* time, *must* proceed confessedly repentant and actively critical of the triumphalism which has for so long vainly taken his name to justify conquest.

To herald Jesus Christ as Lord is resolutely to cultivate this stance—these directional practices of indirection—in opposition to the dominant subjugative powers of this world and the relentless and mobile structures of assimilation with which they devitalize critique and resist transformation. It is to be convinced that Jesus teaches (and empowers)

58. *Royal Priesthood*, 255.
59. Ibid., 255 n. 22.
60. Ibid., 255.
61. Ibid., 253.

Christians why and how to do this better than the other ways they have encountered thus far.

Yet if the church is resolutely to resist the bad, it must also resist an immodest tendency to conflate otherness and outsideness with badness. These conflations tend to structure encounters in a totalizing "all or nothing" fashion. In contrast, the challenge is to "affirm a particular witness to be good news without being interested in showing that other people are bad."[62] Indeed, only through the integrity of more receptive engagement does discerning judgement of good and bad become possible. Eschewing such conflation means that very often and for the most part, the dialogical encounters with others in which Christian witness is brought to bear, will not directly engage another's faith as a totality (gathered under a negative mark), but rather selectively draw upon those church practices, habituated sensibilities, and theological perspectives that bear upon those aspects of another's faith/faithlessness that are foregrounded by a particular problem or site of contestation.

Witness to Jesus as Lord must *not* be read as a solicitation to strive for a singular and direct knockout victory over outsiders. Instead it calls for multiple particular vulnerable encounters in which the strengths of the church body are little by little brought to light and perhaps themselves radically reformed and renewed. "Maybe [heralding] has to have several [meanings], each fragmentary, but which might severally add up asymptotically to a functional equivalent of a proclamation of lordship."[63] ("Maybe" and "might" themselves articulate the new posture.) The heralding, discernment, risk, and renewal of faithfulness occur to a great extent in contestatory and cooperative work around particular historically situated questions. What and how do those gathered around Jesus as Lord contribute to identifying—and creatively resisting and responding with alternatives to—*this* pattern of violent conflict, *these* practices of economic subjugation and suffering, *this* set of disciplinary practices entwined with an idolatrous relation to productivity, *that* postcolonial practice of subordination, *that* authoritarian police state, *this* group of people's cynicism, *these* stingy practices of (not) caring for the unborn, the very old, or ill, *these* selfish practices of territoriality, *these* parties' incapacity for more generous and receptive

62. *Priestly Kingdom*, 60.
63. Ibid., 57.

dialogue? What is the fruitfulness of Jesus relative to other alternatives *here*?

Yoder calls for vital and disciplined engagement *and* for a certain modesty integral to both: Given an affirmation of historical particularity and peccability, it would be "contradictory to expect that Christian commitment—even less Christian's performance—should be at the top of every scale. What we're looking for . . . is not a way to keep dry above the waves of relativity, but to stay within our bark, barely afloat and sometimes awash amidst those waves, yet neither dissolving into them nor being carried only where they want to push it."[64] This modesty of "what we're looking for," entwined with the dialogical generosity of how radical reformation Christians are looking, creates the possibility of numerous tactical alliances with outsiders whose directions significantly parallel certain goals of the church.[65] In this sense one might even speak of a tentative, selective, partial confusing of some bodily distinctions between church bodies and outside bodies at certain points in the identity markers that constitute a border between one and another. These, of course, are already confused (in a good way) for Yoder, where the church has incorporated and reformed itself through receptive engagements with outside—and now no longer wholly outside—voices and practices. But, here he broaches an additional confusion of bodies, even when reformation is not what is involved or at stake: the confusion along certain segments of borders between bodies that nevertheless remain quite distinct.

Yoder writes with *and* against these ideas of confusion of the body of the church. While he strongly critiques Augustinian notions of the invisible true church body, neither does he reify the visible body in a manner that would wholly identify it with the practiced body of believers. The very vulnerable generosity that constitutes this body confuses its boundaries. It is, I think, no accident that Yoder draws upon outsiders and outsideness to articulate and solicit this "core" vulnerability. In the *practice* of naming and (in varying ways) receiving lessons from Gandhi, Marx, modern pluralism, Yoder *performs* the vulnerable and ambiguous identity of the giving and receiving body of Christ. And, one should remember that the outside is often not purely other in Yoder's

64. Ibid., 58.
65. Ibid., 61–62.

view. Marx read the Bible, Gandhi encountered Jesus through Tolstoy even as he refused to call himself Christian,[66] and modern pluralism has important debts (and differences) to "the Hebrew and Christian intervention in cultural history . . . missionary mobility . . . love of the enemy . . . relativizing of political sovereignty . . . dialogical vision . . . charismatic vision of the many members of the body . . . disavowal of empire and of theocracy."[67]

Yoder's point decidedly is *not* that "it all originates in Scripture"—as I hope is clear. Rather it is that though God's providence requires visible dialogical church bodies in action, it is infinitely bigger, and ambiguously more than the visible body (what it looks like, what it sees) at any point in time. God's gifts are (to borrow from Merleau-Ponty) a "perpetual pregnancy." The church body generously strives to be midwife for these gifts. Though that oversimplifies, because it is often not clear who is pregnant with what, nor exactly what role Christians might have played in the pregnancy, nor exactly what role the others might have played in the development of the midwife's own body and capacities for midwifery, nor exactly whether segments of the church body's borders might not become highly indeterminate and porous as it works alongside other bodies toward the historical reception of particular gifts in response to particular problems. These bodies are confusing. One could even say that a certain vulnerability to the confusing is constitutive of the discerning and patient body of Christ.

In this vein, against the "easy rejection by Westerners of 'syncretism,'" Yoder is sympathetic with many Christians in the "third world" who remind Europeans that "mixing has gone on for centuries in Europe, whereas the task of authentic communication in the forms of any non-Western culture has only recently been tackled. Until we know how faithfully to speak of Christ in some non-Western language, we can hardly know what identifies culpable syncretism."[68]

Yet while Yoder affirms these imaginative dialogic efforts that are "newly open to far-reaching reformulations of the gospel message," he simultaneously signals what he will always *also* renew as a concern that is for him at once a condition of these efforts and at the same time a

66. *Royal Priesthood*, 260.

67. *Priestly Kingdom*, 60.

68. Ibid., 68.

resistance to a certain direction (or indirection) they sometimes (and perhaps always must to some extent) embrace: "It has not been at work long enough for us to determine whether it will develop criteria for defining heresy."[69] The church must renew its generous and receptive hybridizing vulnerability *and* it must renew its capacities to discern the heresy of "genuinely incompatible elements." It must not simply and undiscerningly conform to indigenous ways.[70] Because Jesus is the root of the church's possibility to receive reformation through the wildly placed and timed gifts of God, Yoder will not hesitate to affirm "fidelity to the jealousy of Christ as Lord"[71]—understood as the fundamental cruciformity of the universe and the practices necessary to herald it. This fidelity indicates a certain limit to the confusion it makes possible, and it is a limit Christians are always enjoined to discern.

This jealousy, Yoder claims, calls Christians to—and is their best possibility for—cultivating receptive generosity. And it does so in no small part by resisting the deification of some antithetical value like "power, mammon, fame, efficacy . . ."[72] There are—within and outside Christianity—a lot of *bad* traditions, fundamental error, evil powers. "The need is not that *those* traditions be integrated . . . . They must be uprooted."[73] At a certain point (discerned by a community first and foremost pushed and pulled by the tensional entwinements of this receptivity and this jealousy) when repeated efforts toward reconciliation have failed, this will involve excommunication, or else the body of Christ as disciplined practice will cease to have any meaning.

"The linguistic line between treason and tradition is very fine. Both terms come from the same root. Yet in substance there is a chasm between the two. . . ." The differences between "faithful organic development" and "compatible extrapolation," on the one hand, and "incompatible deviation" and "sell-out," on the other, are often extremely difficult to discern. Thus Jesus calls Christians to radically dialogical gatherings vulnerable to unexpected otherness in order to discern "the chasm." The church would have to ready itself for vulnerably encoun-

69. Ibid.
70. Ibid., 145.
71. Ibid., 86.
72. Ibid., 86.
73. Ibid., 69.

tering the unwonted to have any hope of exercising good judgment. "Yet if the notion of infidelity is not to fade into a fog where nothing is verifiable, the notion of infidelity as a real possibility must continue to be operational."[74] If this church breaks forth with pregnant visibility, it also bears witness to all it sees that is abortive and anti-church. The what and how of this discernment of fidelity, Yoder calls "body politics." Vulnerable relations will, in some form or another, continue even with those who are decidedly treasonous—but not fellowship.[75]

On Yoder's list of what and how fidelity is *not*: "polytheism." *For the church*, the path to reformation with the unanticipatable manifoldness of His gift must pass through the jealousy of the One. But, then, add this qualification: this paradox is too big for any *one* (individual, group, time) to handle or claim to possess entirely. Then add: that "the prophetic denunciation of paganism" will always be "ad hoc," "vulnerable," and "fragmentary."[76] The sum, for Yoder, is that which is beyond a "sum." It is "'Patience' as Method in Moral Reasoning," which Yoder patiently worked upon for fifteen years until death interrupted the unfolding of this most spectacular non-summing list-like exposition of this practice so central to his understanding of Christian ethics. Patience as, among so many other qualities, the *gift of time* as one has been given time: time for vulnerable witnessing and discerning and participating in the unanticipatable breaking-forth. Patience as suspension of the socially and existentially engendered pressures upon time to *summarize* judgement and engage others in *summary* fashion. Yoder calls this gift to the self and the other, the "'modest' patience of sobriety in finitude." This patience offers resistance to the insistence lodged in every teleological "now" that it *contain* within its own horizon of orientation the future to come and the others within that future. "The certainty with which we have to act one day at a time must never claim finality."[77] This

74. Ibid., 68.

75. This, of course, raises numerous important questions concerning punishment, but they exceed the bounds of what this essay can carefully address. One place to begin to explore these issues more fully is John Howard Yoder, "You Have It Coming: Good Punishment, The Legitimate Social Function of Punitive Behavior" (unpublished, 1995).

76. *Royal Priesthood*, 249–50.

77. "'Patience' as Method in Moral Reasoning: Is an Ethic of Discipleship 'Absolute'?" in *The Wisdom of the Cross: Essays in Honor of John Howard Yoder*, ed.

radically modest stance of in-finality is the very temporality of *caritas* that members of the church must bring to reopen each particular *now*.

At its most radical, the modest patience of sobriety in finitude takes the form of a certain slackening—one might almost say suspension—of the pressures lodged in many familiar renderings of fidelity to "the jealousy of Christ as Lord." For example, suspending the finality of the idea that there is no good way for anyone that does not follow Jesus as Lord; the idea that to believe that the "rebellious but (in principle) already defeated cosmos is being brought to its knees by the Lamb"[78]necessarily implies that all *must* eventually submit to Jesus (by coercion or freely—it matters not a bit to me here). These can be read as claims to finality, and they have been deployed as powerfully and as often to render Christians invulnerable as any claims ever have.

Yoder always resists these Constantinian readings of these claims. Hence, for example, the church should not a priori judge outsiders as bad, and the Lamb worthy of worship might only be discerned through vulnerable engagements with those who do not share this faith, never imposition—the choice is theirs. Yet he appears not infrequently to suggest a singular endpoint ("His ultimate victory") brought about by a distinctly cruciform dialectic or, better, eschatology ("His hidden control"), that one might suspect would engender an overwhelming hubris in believers that could radically vitiate the very receptivity he otherwise cultivates.[79]

I confess to having absolutely no idea *what* it would even mean to think and believe with Yoder here concerning victory and control. But I might have an insight into *how* Yoder thought these ideas must function and how they must not. They are to powerfully inspire and orient the church to resist "the *principalities* and *powers*" that would subjugate creation to idolatries of "power, mammon, fame, and efficacy." They call believers to resist as mythical these closures of history, and begin (again and again) to practice an alternative body politics, confident that the future belongs to *caritas*—even in the face of powers that seek to eternalize subjugation and seem to exhibit enormous capacities to assimilate

---

Stanley Hauerwas, Chris K. Huebner, Harry J. Huebner, and Mark Thiessen Nation (Grand Rapids: Eerdmans, 1999) 31.

78. E.g., *Priestly Kingdom*, 54, 136.

79. *Priestly Kingdom*, 136.

or brutally crush opposition and alternative hopes. Its something like this: "We love our neighbor because God is like that. It is not because Jesus told us to that we love even beyond the limits of reason and justice, even to the point of refusing to kill and being willing to suffer—but because God is like that too."[80]

But this opening of the future *as such*, this claim that the future as such *will* open, and *only* will open, *as caritas*, this claim about today and tomorrow based on what has *already* been reported to have happened—this opening that gives time *must not steal it*. And the unrelenting tenacity of Yoder's efforts to negotiate the complexities and risks at this point will always astound.

Hence a (un)certain suspension, a (un)certain patience. In an essay that reads "Jeremiah" to call Jews and then Christians to bear witness to God's sovereignty by heralding diaspora as grace, Yoder writes again of the jealousy of God: "This enormous flexibility and creative force returns us to the question, Is there anything nonnegotiable in the dispersed minority's witness? Anything untranslatable? Of course there is; it is that there is no other God. The rejection not only of pagan cult but also of every way of putting their own YHWH/LORD in the same frame of reference with pagan deities, even not speaking the divine NAME as others would, was tied for the Jews in Babylon with the proclamation of his sovereignty over creation and history. There is no setting into which that deconstructing, disenchanting proclamation cannot be translated, none which can encompass it. The anti-idolatry message is not bad but good news. It can free its hearers from slavery to the powers that crush their lives."[81]

This liberating non-negotiability can free the hearers, and Yoder's church *must* maintain it and invite others to it. Yet if its stance is clear toward "*the powers*," it is radically indeterminate—radically *patient*—in relation to "*other subject peoples*," who find themselves named in the title of the concluding section of this essay, importantly the only one framed as a question: "Is This a Way Other Subject Peoples Might See Themselves?" With a textual maneuver of most pronounced abruptness, Yoder interrupts any and all pressures of finality that might be building

---

80. John Howard Yoder, *The Original Revolution: Essays on Christian Pacifism* (Scottdale, PA: Herald Press, 1971), 52.

81. *For the Nations*, 76–77.

in his essay, by writing: "I close by declaring my complete lack of authority to answer this . . . question." He then modulates and builds the question in a variety of ways, leaving each modulation starkly unanswered:
"Is there something about this . . . that might be echoed or replicated by
other migrant peoples? Might it give hope to other refugees? To other
victims of imperial displacement? . . . Peoples overwhelmed by imperial immigration?"[82] We'll simply have to "wait and see" (a phrase from
other writings); because the meaning and relevance of "His victory"
breaks off into indeterminacy when faced with other subject peoples
"for themselves." Those within the church simply cannot now know if
their good news is the best news for other subject peoples. *Go out there.*
Listen vulnerably. Herald. Listen. Wait.[83]

Yoder's most radical patience here is not simply a "pastoral patience"
rooted in his sense of power dynamics and Christians' poor relations to
many wounded outsiders. Nor is it simply "therapeutic patience," nor
simply "'contrite' patience of repentance" that acknowledges complicity
in Christian unfaithfulness and evil deeds. No, it is more radical than
these forms of patience that are "for *a* time, for *a* reason."[84] In excess of
these, it is for time itself, time as generous opening, time as gift, gift of
time. In *this* sense, this patience is not where "His victory" *breaks off*
into this indeterminacy (as I suggested in the previous paragraph), but
where it *breaks forth as* this generous indeterminacy. Yoder's patience

82. Ibid., 78.

83. Historically, and in a colonial context, Yoder sees an initial and imperfect but
significant practical working out of this stance in William Penn's relationship to Native
Americans: pacifism, friendship, nonviolent discursive dispute resolution processes
with equal representation on both sides, repentance for past settlers' evil wrong doings,
"paying the Indians again for land that according to Imperial law was already his," no
insistence on conversion or condemnation of Natives' paganism. Yoder countenances
the imperative to go further but abstains from condemning Penn when he writes, in
response to a student's comment that " they should have given [the land] back to the
Indians": to have gone further than Penn and "ask the Indian rulers for their autho-
rization to be guests/immigrants under their sovereignty, or to forsake immigration
completely, would probably have been beyond the scope of anyone's imagination at
the time." Penn's radically generous *and* radically presumptuous erasure of theological
differences between the Quakers and Natives would also have to be radically reformed
in light of the Yoder's reflections, but again, was beyond most imaginations at the
time. See chapter 13, in *Christian Attitudes to War, Peace, and Revolution* (Elkhart, IN:
Goshen Biblical Seminary, 1983).

84. "'Patience' as Method in Moral Reasoning," 27, 29, emphasis added.

as *wild patience*: love for the untamed entangled growings of heralding, listening, waiting.

Reaching Back and Breaking Forth/Off/In/Out?

Many questions spring from these soils. In a few closing words I will reach back to a position many will perhaps discern to be more "outside" than the one I have adopted thus far in this chapter. I will reach back to my locations at various intersections in radical democratic movements where Christians, Jews, Muslims, secularists, neo-Nietzscheans, populists, citizens, and those who have come from afar legally and illegally, join in dialogue and action toward more generous and receptive modes of power. I reach back in the hope of an emerging question with which there might break forth not so much new light as a heightened sense of its possibility.

Reading carefully, one might discern in Yoder an intermittent sense of an element of complicity between pre-Constantinian proclamations of the jealousy of Jesus as Lord and the rise of Constantinianism. For though Yoder claims that the early churches were generally "structurally sound in their major teachings,"[85] he nevertheless indicates a flaw that, in light of the reading of Yoder developed thus far, could be called nothing less than "major." Put simply, they did not quite rightly understand traditioning as readiness for radical reformation in the sense of reaching back as the breaking forth of new light, as practiced generosity toward the unanticipatable future. They partly misconstrued the church's mode of being in time too much in the direction of identity— not enough as "excess."

This term is *not* a postmodern translation. Yoder wrote of the "original revolution" as "an ethic of excess," locating the "style of His discipleship" in the question, "What do ye more than others?" which "is for Jesus a fitting question whereas for the common discourse of ethics one measures oneself by others in order to measure up to the average. Here it is the excess, the going beyond what could expected, the setting aside what one would have a right to which is itself the norm. . . . It is the nature of the love of God not to let itself be limited by models or options or opportunities which are offered to it by a situation. It does

85. *Priestly Kingdom*, 129.

more because the very event of exceeding the available models is itself a measure of its character . . . . Jesus would ask, "How in this situation will the life-giving power of the Spirit reach beyond available models and options to do a new thing whose very newness will be a witness to divine presence?"[86] The early church gathered around Jesus' word in Scripture was "sound in its major teachings" insofar as it creatively articulated them in church body practices. What it did not appear to grasp sufficiently, Yoder suggests in the passages which follow, is the way in which Jesus' question was to deconstruct the ethical indolence of even (especially?) those who would interpret Jesus himself more as a static "model" than as the pregnant incarnation of Good News, which has to be received and given *as pregnant* to remain/become good. Jesus, as the questioning solicitation of this ethic of excess, knew that to be received he had to be received excessively. This opens church-time, or traditioning, beyond the logic of identity which otherwise prevails.

Here is a reading of Yoder's sense of a possible erring in this respect. In the face of gradual and problematic "adjustment to other loyalties" which slides into "unfaithfulness" to the body politics of Jesus, Yoder writes: "it would seem at first that the necessary corrective would be to reject all change, restoring things as they had been before. For the early centuries . . . 'renewal' was that simple; it asked for the restitution of the way things had already been."[87] Thus there is a way in which the early church that was reaching back, and to whom Yoder reaches back, did not fully understand "reaching back." Only modern historical consciousness "made it impossible to think that way."[88]

From this mistake emerged a false choice between "movement forward as accommodation" and reformation as "return to go," which has had disastrous effects to this day. The early churches' insufficiently generative (and excessively identitarian) conception of their restoration practices seems to have weakened their abilities to creatively translate Jesus and scripture into forms that might have allowed them to reorient themselves toward speaking to, resisting, and offering more engaging, powerful, and seductive alternatives to the idolatry of the "principalities and powers." There was a weakening of missionary powers to engage

86. *Original Revolution*, 49–50.
87. *Priestly Kingdom*, 86.
88. Ibid.

new situations and new others. It is in this context of a devitalized church traditioning, that Ambrose and Augustine drew problematically from Roman law, "to speak to questions the New Testament did not help them with."[89] Those who recognized the accommodation for what it was withdrew. "It would have been good at that time to have a new prophetic voice to save the church from the no-win choice between separatism and sell-out. Tragically, there was no such prophet."[90] This was no accident. If the "New Testament did not help," from Yoder's stance, this is because those who read it failed to gather together in a manner sufficiently historically dynamic and receptive to the text, each other, and outsiders, to enable prophetic translations through which it might have spoken. The slide toward Constantinianism might be understood in this context—at least if Yoder's suspicions have any merit. My guess is that his suspicions have a certain heuristic value for the present, regardless of their historical salience in the first centuries following Jesus.

Many factors undoubtedly contributed to the early churches' "return to go" sensibility. Here I pursue only one in the form of some questions. Could it be that the *jealousy* of Jesus as Lord—not just as a concept, but as stories, dispositions, habits, practices—is entwined with and works in spite of itself toward the closure of the church's generous and receptive participation in historical generativity? In one sense this is not a true question. History screams: of course this has happened—Jesus has been worked over thus. Yet I aim the question in a different direction, or at least more deeply. Could it be that this Jealousy in *pre-constantinian* forms acts *in part* as a certain gravitational pull *against* the future—against newness *as such*—in a manner that infuses the church's *caritas* toward time and the other with a certain stinginess that erodes its generativity and generosity from within? Could it be that this non-constantinian jealousy might pressure reformation toward identical restitution, such that the church slouches toward separatism (mini-constantinianisms) or sell-out (Constantinianism)? My point here is not to valorize "newness *as such*," but rather to cast suspicion upon pressures to *de*valuate newness *as such*. This suspicion opens spaces and

89. Ibid., 75.
90. Ibid.

times for patient discernment of the new, in contrast to a priori tendencies toward valorization or devaluation of the new.

I know of *no* generosity that is not "peccable in fact." None without congenital defects and damages against which it must struggle. Every extant movement of generosity has limits and these limits both enable and disable the power of giving and receiving. Every movement of the gift must *attend to these limits*, working them ceaselessly and patiently in ways that address and move beyond the stinginess that remains and often emerges anew in every extant form. The call of receptive generosity is to work at these limits receptively with others—to become more capable of this working-with, especially (but not only) with those others who have been on the underside of power, especially those who claim to have been violated by powers in which we are implicated. My suspicion concerns how Yoder's way of affirming a certain jealousy might weaken the good work at the limit, to which he is called and to which he so profoundly calls us. This jealousy, from my vantage point, is not without its power and capacity for good work, but I would suggest that it needs to be inflected differently and reshaped not only for the radical democratic community coalitions in which I am most invested, but for the work that Yoder calls Good News.

If these questions get at something persistently real, they are by no means devastating nor intended as such. But recognizing a perhaps fundamental and undesirable vulnerability within this Christian jealousy might engender different, possibly more perceptive, capacities for discerning strengths *and* weaknesses of these other modes of faith and being, as well as other loci of critical and constructive practice. It might solicit and encourage more receptive engagements with some forms of polytheism, atheism, and post-secular modes of enchantment, as well as a lot of critical work being done by liberation theologians, critical race theorists, feminists, students of postcoloniality, and ecologists, for example. As I read Yoder, while his work often has sympathies and resonances with—as well as much to contribute to—some of what is best in these and other practices of affirmation and critique, his actual engagement with most of them was quite slim. His work would have benefited significantly, I think, from fuller dialogues with these bodies of work.

Of course, the work to which Yoder was called, the work he did, was tremendous and it took all the time he was given. "Should haves" always have a weak and pretentious ring in cases like his. If they have any merit, it is insofar as they bear upon prospective developments. Thus, perhaps those who are inspired by Yoder would do well to develop some of these points of intersection. Perhaps some Christians would then witness certain virtues of polytheisms, atheisms, or post-secularisms precisely at the points where Christians discover certain vices *within* themselves that seem hard to separate from the cross they bear. Perhaps among these would be the virtues that might be found in certain polytheistic, atheistic, and post-secular tendencies to allow and even seek more receptive and generous blurrings of the insistent inside/outside framework that has governed not only constantinian Christianity, but also, in my view some of Yoder's reflections as well.[91] Perhaps Yoderians might then discover in others inspiring capacities for appreciating and responding to multiple sources of inspiration and orientation that aid radical democratic coalitional efforts which might be integral to and exemplary of some of the work Yoderians too seek to accomplish. Perhaps discerning these relative strengths, in juxtaposition with some weaknesses that tend to be engendered by their own jealousy (e.g., reticence to work as often with outsiders, difficulty hearing and very seriously engaging their claims), might lead those inspired by Yoder to slacken, resituate, and differently consider, articulate, and practice the latter. Perhaps it would call them more often to elaborate, as a community, indebted affirmations—which is not to say embraces—of other communities' stories and sources; practices of recounting with

91. As when, for example, in "Meaning After Babble," 132, he assumes too persistently that Babel is primarily about distinct traditions and communities, when in fact almost all known communities are mixtures of different traditions. Yoder acknowledges and works with this latter point very perceptively at times, as I have tried to show. Yet if he were to think it through in this essay, I think he would have to struggle with "babble" in somewhat different and more difficult, and, I think, more fruitful ways. The inside/outside framework also works to elide some important questions in "On Not Being Ashamed of the Gospel: Particularity, Pluralism, and Validation," *Faith and Philosophy* 9 (1992) 285–300, where Yoder's exaggeration of the newsbearers/host culture distinction perhaps weakens his ability to open certain questions and responses to problems of heralding in late modernity. I realize that this essay strains against liberal assimilation, but would this straining be weakened or strengthened by a greater acknowledgment of the discursive hybridities with which most late moderns always already must begin?

a certain awe the stories and deeds of other communities in order to cultivate a more capacious joy in otherness and readiness to listen. Perhaps.

Echoing Yoder, I have absolutely no authority to say whether these reflections ought to influence how Mennonite Christians might begin to see themselves. But in the instant the question opens, before it is framed by an answer, as Derrida might say, there might be found another opening for *caritas*, another unanticipatable yet somehow recognizable breaking forth. Whether this hope is with or against Yoder, whether it is inside or outside, or whether it might help enhance powers to resist that which is evil in these distinctions without which—paradoxically—there is no resistance to evil, I am no longer sure. To Yoder, even as I lean here in another direction, I am indebted not least of all for this uncertainty, among many other things.

Yet let me not end on this note of still too limited discomfort—as if the discords were quite this easy, as if I could stay for the most part on top of them, or where I was before they appeared. If Yoder's Jesus is a great story, it is not simply because it resonates so much with themes of dialogue and receptivity that I embraced long before my encounter with his writing. More importantly, it is great the way the sublime that is unconquered by sovereign subjectivity is great: it mightily calls into question my perception, sense-making, reach, direction, my ethical and political faiths. Yoder haunts me. He is not an easy ghost, but I want to want him with me. I want him opening new doors and windows in my cave, offering new light and air, and occasionally rattling my walls until I feel in my bones "there's no place like home" and find myself engaged in a new thing.

With and in this spirit, let me close this chapter with an undigested and brief list of some interrelated challenges and questions that Yoder poses to radical democrats such as myself, which I might formulate provisionally at present. Some I have responded to elsewhere.[92] Some remain for future works. Many will likely remain long after me.

1. *The church as body.* To what extent and in what fashions can radical and pluralizing democrats theorize and develop enduring corporate practices of resistance and exemplary alternatives?

92. See Romand Coles, *Beyond Gated Politics: Reflections for the Possibility of Democracy* (Minneapolis: University of Minnesota Press, 2005).

2. *The discipline of the church body.* How might we develop en-spirited disciplines that empower without becoming "disciplin-ary" in the pejorative senses of this word we have identified quite well?

3. *The jealousy of the discipline.* Yoder shows compellingly how a certain jealousy might aid resistance to odious forms of power. What are the possibilities of enduring resistance in absence of this or a similar jealousy?

4. *The generosity of the jealousy.* Is there not a jealousy infusing and partly enabling every generosity; certain refusals, certain relatively rigid limits to any "yes"? Has this been sufficiently acknowledged by neo-Nietzschean democrats? Sufficiently ac-knowledged to draw from this condition its highest possibili-ties and respond to its dangers (as Yoder does in his rendering of patience)?

5. *The pacifism of the generosity.* In the critique of a certain "per-petual peace," and in the embrace of a certain agon, have we not avoided more sustained inquiries into war making as such, even as genealogists have contributed in important ways to critical illuminations of numerous specific war making practices? Is any killing congruent with receptive generosity?

12

Laughing *With* the World:
Possibilities of Hope in John Howard Yoder and Jeffrey Stout

JONATHAN TRAN

Introduction

Near the middle of Max Horkheimer and Theodor Adorno's *Dialectic of Enlightenment*, the authors turn to laughter. This is a rather surprising turn. As anyone familiar with *Dialectic of Enlightenment* can attest, it is not a funny book. While *Dialectic of Enlightenment* has its funny moments (for example, its excoriating comments about Donald Duck), in speaking of laughter Horkheimer and Adorno mean something entirely different from laughable things (for example, Donald Duck). Cover to cover, the authors tear into the most basic presumptions and habits of Western civilization to reveal a social imaginary rotten to the core. Horkheimer and Adorno conjure up an incisively vicious alchemy blending Nietzsche's pronouncement of nihilism writ large onto Marx's analysis of systemic brutality. That the authors can utilize the likes of Nietzsche and Marx to uncover the Holocaust's internal *ratio* reminds us that "depressing" does not have the legs to accurately describe this book. Nothing remains in its wake. Nothing, that is, but laughter.[1]

Horkheimer and Adorno bring up laughter in the context of declaring, "The culture industry endlessly cheats its consumers out of what it endlessly promises," and the authors show how this parasitic

1. Theodor W. Adorno and Max Horkheimer, *Dialectic of Enlightenment: Philosophical Fragments*, trans. Edmund Jephcott (Stanford: Stanford University Press, 2002).

ethos relentlessly attaches itself to everything from aesthetics ("the me-
chanical reproduction of beauty") to desire ("the diner must be satis-
fied with reading the menu") to laughter ("an instrument of cheating
happiness").[2] Hence, initially, and perhaps generally, laughter expresses
the hegemony of banality rather than genuine enjoyment: "There is
laughter because there is nothing to laugh at."[3] Within this vein, laughter is respite, a momentary-at-best "release" from an otherwise ubiquitous assault on existence. Laughter here is not so much joy as cynicism:
laughter as a laughing *at*. Laughter abdicates: there is no escape and
hence, one might as well laugh. And then—and this is the surprising
part—Horkheimer and Adorno write, "What is infernal about wrong
laughter is that it compellingly parodies what is best, reconciliation."[4]
By contrasting "wrong laughter" with "reconciliation" the authors are
suggesting that what is most sinister about our society is that it continuously withholds that for which we most long, that the alienation
the authors so vividly portray and we so quietly suffer is inexhaustible.
And by dangling laughter before us, the text does what it says, showing that even in laughter we fool ourselves: our laughing *at* is finally a
laughing *at* ourselves. The culture industry colonizes and profits from
the unbridgeable gap between desire and consummation, profiteer-
ing off the very estrangement it created. Yet ensconced within all this
vitriol is a subtle implication: wrong laughter is parasitic on (right?)
laughter. Beneath all the cultural bloodsucking lies something good,
or at least something better. There might actually be, for Horkheimer
and Adorno, reconciliation and hence authentic uncorrupted laughter.
Can it be? Genuine enjoyment rather than "a sickness infecting happiness and drawing it into society's worthless totality"?[5] Well, not quite;
for as soon as Horkheimer and Adorno offer this passing reference to
something better, they pronounce, "Joy, however, is austere," invoking
Seneca no less: *res severa verum gaudium*. Even the Latin sounds harsh.
Not since Hegel told us the owl of Minerva takes flight only at dusk has
there been such a letdown. "Grey on grey" is right.[6]

2. Adorno and Horkheimer, *Dialectic of Enlightenment*, 111–12.

3. Ibid., 112.

4. Ibid.

5. Ibid.

6. G. W. F. Hegel, *Philosophy of Right*, trans. S.W. Dyde (Amherst, NY: Prometheus,

John Howard Yoder was once asked, "Are you happy?" To which he responded, "I haven't found that to be a very useful question."[7] Such severity would seem to suggest that Yoder wasn't much for laughing, an impression cemented by his rather dour public persona. And yet apparently, John Howard Yoder loved to laugh, and in such a way that would have shown cynicism to be unfaithful on Christian grounds.[8] For reasons I hope to demonstrate, this odd combination of austerity and laughter witnesses to the doggedly joyful strictures of Yoder's account of hope. His theology after all is one of consummation, of completion and reconciliation, of the type of redemption spoken of by Job (19:23–27) such that the Reverend Sam Wells can preach an Easter sermon entitled, "One Day You Will Laugh."[9] Wells contrasts such laughter to the laughter Horkheimer and Adorno reference, laughter as abdication, laughing *at* a world bereft of consummation, completion, reconciliation, and redemption. Laughter, then, is heady stuff; it is, as it were, no laughing matter, for the "rival versions of laughter" differentiate between worlds ruled by either cynics, or, as Yoder would say, the worshipped Lamb:

> Easter is either everything, or it's nothing. Today is either a doomed attempt to overcome suffering and death with lilies and drums and cymbals and brass and a descant of the last verse, or it's a peek through a keyhole into a world completely changed by Jesus. If it's a peek through the keyhole, then the way God changes the world isn't the conventional way, through guns and bombs and war and conquest. It's through something more dynamic than coercion, but something even more irresistible,

---

1996) xxx.

7. Stanley Hauerwas, *Disrupting Time: Sermons, Prayers and Sundries* (Eugene, OR: Cascade, 2004) 163. Hauerwas shared this story during the obituary he offered at Yoder's funeral in 2000.

8. I learned about Yoder's laughter from Stanley Hauerwas, who worked with and knew Yoder very well, proving pivotal in bringing him to Notre Dame and his theology to academic prominence. Specifically, Hauerwas says, "In fact, Yoder loved to laugh, and I loved to make him laugh." Whether Hauerwas, who is genuinely hilarious (especially to himself), remembers Yoder's laughter as much as he remembers his own is less important than his enduring memory of Yoder's laughter as indicative of the best of his theology.

9. Well's unpublished sermon can be accessed at http://www.chapel.duke.edu/documents/sermons/sermon_213.pdf.

yet more subversive, and more infectious. Something, I want to suggest this morning, something like . . . laughter.[10]

As I said, heady stuff. How do we sustain this kind of laughter? In a world so often burdened by unyielding sadness, how might we laugh appropriately? Inevitably, such questions press against hope and the possibilities of forgiveness and what Margaret Urban Walker has aptly called "Moral Repair."[11] As Yoder's theology is a theology of hope, then, his laughter is finally a laughing *with* the world.

In the following, I bring Yoder into conversation with Jeffrey Stout's account of democracy as a way to illuminate how Yoder laughs with hope. If we agree with Nancey Murphy that Yoder offers a "fairly complete, systematic account of Christian theology," though he refuses to speak in the terms of a systematician, then his hope, like his pacifism, inhabits his understanding of God and God's activities in the world, or what we might call history.[12] Similarly, Stout's democracy is beholden to a larger conception of history; or on pragmatist grounds, democracy *is* a view of history as nothing other than the engaged participation of citizens. By showing how hope works for Stout, my larger purpose here will be to underscore Yoder's own peculiar brand of hope, showing why both Stout and Yoder have reasons for hope and thus laugh *with* the world despite its many troubles. I first look at Stout's Hegelian reasons for hope, unpacking through Merold Westphal how such hope and laughter work, and finally turn to Yoder's account of history and hope, borrowing critical insights from Gerald Schlabach.

Hope and Its Reason

The 1970s and 1980s saw several philosophical and theological critiques of contemporary liberal democracy, eventuating in a simmering unease with Christian participation in democratic life. These voices, which

---

10. Wells, "One Day You Will Laugh."

11. Margaret Urban Walker, *Moral Repair: Reconstructing Moral Relations after Wrongdoing* (Cambridge: Cambridge University Press, 2006).

12. Nancey Murphy, "John Howard Yoder's Systematic Defense of Christian Pacifism," in *The Wisdom of the Cross: Essays in Honor of John Howard Yoder*, ed. Chris K. Huebner, Harry J. Huebner, Mark Thiessen Nation, and Stanley Hauerwas (Grand Rapids: Eerdmans, 1999) 45–68. Reprinted as chapter 3 of this volume.

included Stanley Hauerwas and indirectly Alasdair MacIntyre, sought to show that "liberalism" undermined the very moral formations that made common civic life possible; by allying itself with pernicious forms like market capitalism or rugged individualism, contemporary democracy could not help but sow the seeds of its own destruction. Specifically for Hauerwas, the greater consequence was not for America but rather for the Christian church, to the extent that American Christians continuously conflated their commitments to America and their commitments to Christianity. These discomfitures were not helped by the likes of John Rawls and Richard Rorty, who seemed to add fuel to the fire by articulating, rather unapologetically, democratic reasons for the church to stay away. In response, folks like Hauerwas argued that Christian faithfulness did not require a retreat from politics but rather constituted an alternative politics, such that instead of abdicating to demands for conformity, "Let the church be the church."

It is within this rather messy context that Jeffrey Stout seeks to help Christians imagine the church being the church *within*, rather than over against, the contemporary realities of liberal democracy. Since the early 1980s, among professional religious ethicists, Stout has mounted the most sustained and vigorous defense of Christian participation, specifically by defending it against the likes of MacIntyre and Hauerwas. He does so by attending to their critiques and showing how the respective hopes of democracy and Christianity need not be mutually exclusive, rebuking along the way Christianity's cultural despisers and democracy's religious despisers for their lack of hope, their trigger-happy willingness to contrive a political vacuum that would only result in self-fulfilling prophecies. Rather than surrender to hopelessness, Stout seeks to revitalize hope, or at least name that which ennobles his own rather amazing hopefulness. Stout questions MacIntyre's now famous indictments of incommensurability by pointing to the possibilities for genuine dialogue despite seemingly competing "collateral commitments."[13] In *Democracy and Tradition*, Stout utilizes Robert Brandom's Hegelian pragmatism in order to show how recent advances in philosophy of language and

13. Jeffrey Stout, "The Spirit of Democracy and the Rhetoric of Excess," *Journal of Religious Ethics* 35 (2007) 3–21. Stout initially articulated these misgivings in his *Ethics After Babel*, first published in 1988. See Jeffrey Stout, *Ethics After Babel: The Languages of Morals and Their Discontents* (Princeton, NJ: Princeton University Press, 2001), 191–219.

philosophy of religion reveal incommensurability to be greatly exag-gerated.[14] Brandom writes about Hegel, "The essence of modernity is to see that the norms we are bound by are not just there antecedently to and independently of our doings. The characteristically modern insight is that norms are not, as traditional forms of life implicitly took them to be, independent of the subjective normative attitudes of concept users. They are, rather, products of our recognitive practices."[15] For Stout, de-mocracy as a "recognitive practice" is one of the ways we make explicit, at least in a political way, overlapping commitments that remain largely unspoken until dialectical processes of consciousness require articula-tion in order to, as Brandom describes, "make explicit how ordinary empirical concepts work."[16] History, for Stout as it is for Brandom's Hegel, is one way we speak of this dawning self-consciousness, a way of keeping record of our ineluctable dependence on subjective norma-tive attitudes. Stout depicts the substance of democracy as being *with* others, and its procedures as bridge-building piecemeal achievements. What is required are the virtues of charity toward others and humility toward self. Against moral skepticism, Stout holds that moral claims are justifiable; against moral absolutism, he claims that justifications are contextual. The reason charity and humility are required is because of this double claim in favor of justification and context. If moral justifica-tions are context-laden, and the context is conversation, then the prac-

14. Jeffrey Stout, *Democracy and Tradition* (Princeton, NJ: Princeton University Press, 2004). Stout draws from Brandom's *Making It Explicit: Reasoning, Representing, and Discursive Commitment* (Cambridge: Cambridge University Press, 1994), and *Articulating Reasons: An Introduction to Inferentialism* (Cambridge: Cambridge University Press, 2000).

15. Robert B. Brandom, "Untimely Review of Hegel's *Phenomenology of Spirit*," Unpublished manuscript (http://www.pitt.edu/~brandom/index.html, 4). Part of the implication of Brandom's argument, as I take it, is that genealogy speaks to linguistic biography and hence does not undermine but rather affirms truth-claims and their possibilities: "the *genealogy* of a particular set of inferential-and-incompatibility commitments—the way they have arisen through the rational rectification of actual prior commitments—is essential to understanding their *validity*, the bindingness of the norms they embody" (ibid., 11).

16. Robert B. Brandom, *Tales of the Mighty Dead: Historical Essays in the Metaphysics of Intentionality* (Cambridge, MA: Harvard University Press, 2002) 211. Brandom's construal of Hegel derives from work explicitly relating his phenomenol-ogy to pragmatism. See Robert B. Brandom, "Some Pragmatist Themes in Hegel's Idealism," *European Journal of Philosophy* (1999) 164–89.

tice of conversation requires and inculcates humility and charity "in the democratic game of giving and asking for reasons. . . . Democratic discursive practices are designed to hold themselves open this way."[17] Moral justification attempted in abstraction will always fail because asserted a priori, they forget the context of conversation, which makes any moral claim meaningful. As Brandom states, "Talking at all involves acquiescing in and employing *inferentially* articulated conceptual contents. It follows that unless one engages in practices of giving and asking for reasons (rationally integrating commitments), one cannot *mean* anything: one cannot use those meanings to exert power, nor to engage in literary play, without implicitly acknowledging the normative force of reasons, in the form of what is incompatible with what, and what is a consequence of what."[18] Stout's conversational account of legitimation avoids bewitching metaphysical conundrums because it frames the relationship between truth and justification as use, only further elevating the virtues of charity and humility and the requisite practices of "open-ended inquiry." Democracy as dialectic of asking for and giving reasons grounds hope in an enduring possibility. This is how democracy realizes (becomes conscious of) itself. Stout states, "We are fortunate to be able to ask questions" because such discursivity engenders reasons for hope as long as citizens remain in the game. Disengagement kills hope. The promise of democracy gives and hence demands participation, and only as participation remains will history remain open.

Stout chastens the hopelessness of democracy's cultural and religious despisers by retrieving the historical dynamic of hope and critique that fueled the black intellectual tradition, with the obvious implication: African-Americans have reasons for hopelessness and yet remain beholden to democratic possibilities in ways that strengthen, rather than undermine, their most cherished and critical moral traditions. Stout makes his case by presenting the black church and its involvement in American democracy in order to exhibit reasons for his hope in democracy. If former slaves have flourished, then certainly white liberals like Hauerwas and MacIntyre should be slow to beg out, and should instead proffer their critiques within the larger horizon of the civic nation, which includes many ill-treated but critically engaged

17. Stout, *Democracy and Tradition*, 279, 234.
18. Brandom, "Untimely Review of Hegel's *Phenomenology of Spirit*," 4.

citizens. In this way, the despisers have gone, as Stout says, "too far" in their critiques and hence not far enough in their hope: "I take for granted that our condition is always bad enough in some respects to disturb anyone with a conscience—bad enough today, surely, to bring a democrat close to despair. . . . I also take for granted, as a postulate of practical faith, that there are grounds for hope and humor if we look hard enough in the right places. This was true for the survivors of the Holocaust and for the victims of chattel slavery, so it must be true for us."[19]

For Stout, history is not an abstraction, a privileged view from nowhere; rather, just as citizens occupy space as politics, so they occupy time as history. In the dense materiality of democratic participation, history comes to be as citizens birth it into the world. History is made this way. At its best, democracy makes its own history. That is its great promise, the great instillation of hope that a demos can be what it wants to be. The continual straining-to-be of democracy also underscores its fragility and evanescence. Democracy is not an institution, though it often follows the course of institutionalization. Nor is democracy a political system, though it can be found in political systems. Rather, democracy comes to be and is always on the cusp of non-being, and only as such on the cusp of becoming. Political liberalism falls short in describing the civic nation when it fails to pay heed to these desires that animate democracy. Hence, Stout's democracy is the political form of hope, a gathered life between potentiality and actuality that always promises more as witness to an abiding and immanent more-ness. Perhaps better than any other twentieth-century political theorist Hannah Arendt understood this and so employed the biblical language of "covenant," "promise" and "forgiveness" as discourse necessary to emplot the cascading contingencies that constitute political life.[20] Like Arendt, Stout's work wrestles with this fundamental question of hope and offers a way by which hope might be more than wishful thinking amidst dark times, by locating its flowering in a determinative form of life he calls democracy.

19. Stout, *Democracy and Tradition*, 60.

20. Hannah Arendt, *The Human Condition* (Chicago: University of Chicago Press, 1998).

Laughter and History

In his essay, "Laughing at Hegel," Merold Westphal writes, "It is eschatology as such and not just the realized eschatology of the Hegelian system that is the object, not of mirth, but an anguished laughter that sounds a lot like 'Eli, Eli, lema sabachtani?' (Matt. 27:46)."[21] This anguished laughter comes close, I think, to the type of laughter John Howard Yoder invokes, and in turn distinguishes him from Stout. Hegelian laughter comes with the hope that transcendence dialectically unfolds amongst beings while always holding to an ontological difference. Jacques Derrida relates Hegel with the later Heidegger in this way, citing the unexpected use of "spirit" in Heidegger's work, and through this correlation, one can trace the dialectical rationale shared by both.[22] Hegel found Kant's ontological bifurcation unsatisfying, becoming "suspicious of the suspicion" within Kant's transcendental modesty and thus tried to show how within time, realization of the Idea not only would occur but indeed was the only means by which it could occur. And so when Westphal speaks of a "realized eschatology" in Hegelianism, he means all those ontologies that hasten "the self-mediation of totality" because of an unsustainable temporal lack. In contrast to Kant, for Hegel desire must be only *temporally* forestalled for its production. Westphal sees in Hegel both this impatience, with Kant specifically and philosophy generally, and its overcoming through the "*Aufhebung* of the finite in the infinite." Hegel begins exactly where Kant balked, and thus puts to work the polemic between the noumenal and phenomenal toward an energizing polarity that drives history. Hegel needs both, and if he is right so ultimately does Kant: ontological difference produces torsion, while time brings the possibility of realization that produces movement, what Westphal describes as "negativity in the service of positivity." History then can be understood as the material expression of this positive-negative polarity, turning over as the agonistic coming to be of things in the world and indeed the world itself. There is laughter in Hegel but it's always brief and exasperated, more anxiety than joy. Every consummation produces

21. Merold Westphal, *Overcoming Onto-Theology: Toward a Postmodern Christian Faith* (New York: Fordham University Press, 2001) 211.

22. Jacques Derrida, *Of Spirit: Heidegger and the Question* (Chicago: University of Chicago Press, 1989) 32–40.

new tensions, every satiation new dissatisfaction, until laughter speaks less of play than relief, though relief quickly met by more agony to be synthesized. Within the Hegelian system this is the best that can be hoped for. Yet even within this "completion of mediation" Westphal highlights remainders that cannot be sublated; here death and life, as irreducible presence of chance and contingency, endure, and thus one laughs at Hegel's silly and contrived *die Geschichte ist happy geendet* which would be sad if not for Hegel's ambitions. Because Hegel is so drop-dead serious, not knowing to laugh at himself, one can only laugh at him, rather than with him which one might do if Hegel only realized how simultaneously hopeful and hopeless his project is.[23]

Westphal goes on to press Derrida in the other direction as "Derridean thought remains without hope, anticipating no future time in which we will be simply present to a fully just world. . . ."[24] For Westphal, the attempt from Kant to Heidegger to map transcendence within the terms of immanence renders any fabrication of difference reducible to that transcendence, hence to that immanence because within the terms of finitude (immanence without an actual other) necessity reigns. Hegel smuggled in difference only by first foisting a mythic totality, or more precisely by speaking of that difference within the larger terms of pure thought as the realization of freedom. Hegel and Derrida are offshoots of the same metaphysical soil, the Kantian bifurcation of being. Hegel tries to assuage this difference by historical materiality while Derrida tries to sustain it. In both cases, the Kantian problematizing of difference—its modesty rendering it more powerful—sets the terms of the debate.

In differentiating Derrida and Hegel, Westphal states, "Hope. Ay, there's the rub."[25] The question that pushes Westphal's readings of Hegel and Derrida is the same one that press me in this current essay: What hope respectively animates Stout and Yoder? No doubt both are clear about the current conditions of the world in which they write. Both are cognizant of the dire straits that any moral community in its delicateness resides. And yet in both, there remains an inexhaustible hope such that laughter is for each more than laughing *at*, but a laughing *with*.

---

23. Westphal, *Overcoming Onto-Theology*, 201–18.

24. Ibid., 218.

25. Ibid., 207.

Still, my contention is that Stout's hope is more like Hegel's than Yoder's; indeed, he employs Hegelian pragmatism in order to describe democracy and it is within the terms of Hegelianism that Stout's project offers hope. Stout's hope is animated and sustained by a way of seeing, which I have described as Hegelian in that it stretches forward in time and imagines the arrival of possibilities that perdure even amidst the worst of circumstances; according to Stout, we can retrospectively acknowledge that nothing was ever as bad, or as good, as it seemed, because an immanent moreness coheres beyond sublation, an inexhaustible plenitude germane to history's materialization. Thus Stout's history is necessarily hopeful; more precisely his is a way of viewing history as hope, its steadfastness in the past and its possibility in the future. There was always more. This is always more. There always will be more. How else might one live? Of course, like Hegelianism, such animations and endurances are sustained by selective blindness. But then so is all perception and to pin that exclusively on Stout would repeat the same error. Hope always works this way, as it trains a certain kind of seeing, indeed, seeing what others don't see, what history hasn't shown. No wonder the writer of Hebrews speaks of faith as hope in things not seen (Heb 11:1), which we might rephrase as seeing things others don't see. In this way, Stout, like Yoder, is a believer.

Cities of Hope

In "The Spirit of Democracy" where he clarifies some of his arguments from *Democracy and Tradition*, Stout contends against a pacifism that ostensibly inhibits Christian political participation and though he targets Hauerwas, it is at this point that Stout must come to terms with the politics of Yoder.[26] For Yoder, the axiomatic distinction by which Christian ethics is to understand itself is not church and state, a polemic that would certainly warrant accusations of sectarianism. Rather, the primary axiomatic difference lies between church and world: the direction of God's rule as opposed to the direction of sinful humanity. For Yoder, the distinction between church and world can be most directly understood in terms of the larger narrative by which one understands history and by which a moral community envisions its place

26. Stout, "Spirit of Democracy," 13.

in the world. For Yoder, the givenness of God's victory in Christ, what he calls "the war of the Lamb," gives reasons for the church's hope; and in a sense, the church's hope is nothing other than this, all material and historical reasons of hope being simply proleptic of the larger hope of the Lamb's victory.

Yoder states as much near the beginning of *The Christian Witness to the State*, where he claims the "ground" for Christian social ethics as the scriptural claim, "Jesus Christ, ascended to the right hand of God, is now exercising dominion over the world." According to Yoder, this dominion, which overcomes the claims of dominion asserted by the powers, proves the foundation by which Christian claims have relevance for every province, not simply the church.[27] Every "advance" can only be designated to the extent that it can be mapped onto this hope, which can at best be done in an ad hoc and retrospective manner.[28] In other words, for Yoder, hope resides in Jesus' already but not yet victory such that patience becomes the church's most critical virtue, and impatience its most deadly vice. Jesus is the substance of Christian hope and thus the lens through which it orients itself to time and history. Church is that which places its hope for the world in Christ's saving the world. Yoder speaks of "ultimate values," claiming, "What matters most, the real reason that God lets time go on, is his calling together of his own people through the witness of the gospel. Not building and protecting a bigger and better democracy, but building the church is God's purpose."[29] World, in contrast, is that which places its hope in something other than Christ's salvation. This does not mean that the church refuses to pay heed to the real material concerns of time and history; indeed it invests itself in these concerns as the historic completion of what Yoder calls "the other half of the reconciling process." Church/world is Yoder's way of speaking about this hope, a division between saved/unsaved as a fluid reality. Thus, while building and protecting a bigger and better democracy may not be Yoder's "ultimate value," this

27. John Howard Yoder, *The Christian Witness to the State* (Eugene, OR: Wipf & Stock, 1998) 8.

28. See also John Howard Yoder, *The Royal Priesthood: Essays Ecclesiological and Ecumenical* (Scottdale, PA: Herald, 1998) 130–31, and John Howard Yoder, *The Original Revolution: Essays on Christian Pacifism* (Scottdale, PA: Herald, 1998) 64.

29. John Howard Yoder, *He Came Preaching Peace* (Eugene, OR: Wipf & Stock, 1998) 24.

does not mean that within the reconciling process democracy may not be considered a good; indeed, according to Yoder, the reconciling process will include advances like democracy and other practical goods *as* God's material activity. That is why for Yoder, pacifism is internal to God's already consummating activity, not the cause of it—a critical distinction. While democracy and peace may not be the substance of Yoder's hope, they constitute what Yoder calls the gospel's "moreness" as the substance of Christian faith unfolding in the overcoming of tyranny and the articulation and realization of human rights as reasons for hope.[30]

Concluding *The Politics of Jesus*, Yoder reminds his readers that pacifism is not his primary concern. More so, he worries about those who refuse pacifism because they remain wedded to the world, that is, a rationale that remains atheistic in its understanding of history. It is precisely because the world believes that there is no God, or God does not care about the world, that it charges itself with, as Yoder characterizes, "making history come out right" and thus will utilize whatever means, beyond good and evil, to effectuate those right outcomes. In other words, the problem with the world is not that it loves evil and utilizes violence in a wanton manner. Rather, it desires good, but its goods and commitments remain disordered; it wars incessantly not because it loves destruction but because it longs for peace and goodness but does not believe God will bring peace and goodness, so it anxiously takes matters into its own hands through what Yoder calls a "compulsion of purpose."[31] Yoder's *Politics of Jesus* names "world" as that which denies the Lamb's victory, and consequently subjugates creation (time, space, history) in order to save it. Hence, war is wrong because it places hope in the wrong places, and thus finally is not hope on Christian grounds, which has as its object an eschatological belief that the peaceable God has already won. War is the refusal to worship rightly: "Concern for peace, whether Jewish or Christian, is part of the purpose of God for all eternity. God is by nature a reconciler, a maker of shalom. For us to

30. Ibid., 28.

31. Yoder, *The Politics of Jesus: Vicit Agnus Noster*, 2nd ed. (Grand Rapids: Eerdmans, 1994) 228–33.

participate in the peacemaking purpose of that kind of God is not just morality. It is not just politics. It is worship, doxology, praise."[32]

The distinction between church/world for Yoder is construed in this manner. Stout turns to Yoder's pacifism but fails to recognize this. Ironically, in this way Yoder can be said to be anticipating Stout: Christians can certainly be involved in democracy as one form of the state but to the exclusion of a state that refuses to order its loves, fears, and hopes to God because in doing so, it will rely on itself to order history and will utilize violence, or peace (or violence in the name of peace), to secure its order. For Yoder, the delineation is not church/state, but church/world, and that distinction is set in prominent relief when it comes to the question of the state's violence and war. Yoder's pacifism is not against the state, but against a world that refuses to believe in God. So when Stout turns to Yoder's pacifism, he gets to the heart of the issue, but perhaps in a way that finally puts his case for Christian participation in democracy on shaky ground. In "The Spirit of Democracy" Stout highlights biblical reasons that justify war in order to demonstrate how any a priori certainty about the church's non-violence can be held only by ignoring a large amount of scripture, not to mention thousands of years of history. It behooves Stout, in inviting Christian participation in American civic life, to show why pacifism is not necessary to the church. Yet in doing so, he fails to attend to the rationale of Yoder's christological pacifism: the final victory of the Lamb as the ground of the church's hope. If they are to believe Stout, Christians ought to place at least part of their hope in democracy and a view of history that charges them with its success. If Stout is right, democracy better than any prior social imaginary avails resources for peace, justice, and order.

Because Christianity's hope lies elsewhere it attends to those things as expressions for its hope, as reasons for its faith. Yoder writes, "The place of the church in the history of the universe is the place where Christ's lordship is operative. This is where it is already clear that he rules . . . . The church is moving history by her servanthood. Most of us still think that the way to move history is not by servanthood but by some other kind of rule, but the church is the instrument through which God is moving history by servanthood . . . the servant church

---

32. Yoder, *He Came Preaching Peace*, 34.

is the reason for history. This is why time goes on."[33] Again, in turning to pacifism, Yoder turns to that which the church/world divide underscores, but not on which it stands, which is finally the critical role of hope as the practice of faith. So Stout rightly turns to pacifism but fails to contend with its logic. He may be suspicious of the a priori claim that God is non-violent. But that is not the point of Yoder's pacifism, which is nothing less than the biblical view that God, not we or our bigger and better democracies, is in charge of history. The concerns of *Democracy and Tradition*, that democracy's despisers are making things worse, betrays the difference, as subtle as it may be, between Stout's democracy and Yoder's church. Even though the welfare of the earthly city gives credence to the church's hope that God is reconciling all things to himself, the city's seeming success or failure does not determine that hope. Unlike democracy, the church seeks not to make its own history, but attends to a history already but not yet made, a history that evinces the making of one's own history "a doomed attempt to overcome suffering and death with lilies and drums and cymbals and brass."[34] Hence, Stout's democracy and Yoder's church occupy different cities. They imagine time differently. They worship different lords. Their respective hopes have different reasons. Stout's city, time, worship, and hope tempt another hope, and thus can in this way prove problematic to those communities he imagines himself serving. Yoder's church hopes a different hope: "a peek through a keyhole into a world completely changed by Jesus."[35]

Hope as Promise and Fulfillment

Yoder's laughter arises from the life-giving energies of promise and fulfillment, between prophecy and gospel, between all the fecund tensions that germinate in and over time when one sees history eschatologically.

33. John Howard Yoder, *Preface to Theology: Christology and Theological Method* (Grand Rapids: Brazos, 2002) 248. Yoder continues, "This whole pragmatic management/lesser evil/best results approach to being human is challenged to its core when servanthood is made the key to our ethics" (251). By "pragmatic," Yoder means something other than Stout's philosophical pragmatism, but his concerns are apiece.

34. Wells, "One Day You Will Laugh."

35. Ibid.

Gerald Schlabach observes this in Yoder and chides Yoderians to articulate more clearly the heart of what Yoder coined "the Constantinian
temptation."[36] Schlabach underscores a problematic internal to the
Constantinian temptation, which acts as an unarticulated, and often unnoticed, error on the part of those who would decry Constantinianism
only to, as he describes, "overinterpret church history." Schlabach
astutely gets to the heart of Yoder's theology, and as I argue here, his
peculiar mode of laughter.

According to Schlabach, just as there is a greater danger than
Constantinianism so there is a more basic promise than that which
should help Christians avoid the problems of Constantinianism.[37]
Schlabach refers to an inherent "chronological" and "logical" priority often missed, even by Yoder himself, within the terms of Yoder's
Constantinian formulation: "the problem of how to receive and celebrate
the blessing, the *shalom*, the good, or 'the land' that God desires to give,
yet to do so without defensively or violently hoarding God's blessings."[38]
Schlabach points to the Deuteronomic history as the central scriptural
narrative of promise and fulfillment. Accordingly, the Constantinian
temptation is a temptation internal to and thus coherent within the
scriptures' larger story, a reality often missed by those Yoderians who
disparage Constantinianism while succumbing to its core dangers.

The narrative stretched between the Old and New Testaments
constitutes an ongoing story of promise and fulfillment. The danger of
Constantinianism, again a temptation internal to this larger promise-
fulfillment narrative history, is the proclivity to usher in fulfillment
and to effectively obviate history's dependence upon God. One way
theology attempts to name this is the notion of "realized eschatology" but this description often fails to do justice to all that Yoder
meant by Constantinianism. "Constantinianism" highlights the tendency to take the Deuteronomic narrative and effectively end, or at

36. Gerald W. Schlabach, "Deuteronomic or Constantinian: What Is the Most Basic
Problem for Christian Social Ethics?" in *The Wisdom of the Cross: Essays in Honor of
John Howard Yoder*, ed. Chris K. Huebner, Harry J. Huebner, Mark Thiessen Nation,
and Stanley Hauerwas (Grand Rapids: Eerdmans, 1999) 449–71.

37. See Yoder's articulation of Constantinianism's many expressions in John
Howard Yoder, *The Priestly Kingdom: Social Ethics As Gospel* (Notre Dame, IN:
University of Notre Dame Press, 1985) 135–47.

38. Schlabach, "Deuteronomic or Constantinian," 451.

least relieve, the tensions raised by the promise-fulfillment structure of the Jewish-Christian story. Without both promise *and* fulfillment, the Constantinian temptation entices a view of history that makes no distinction between God and time precisely because it asserts the sure realization of God's promises, which in turn allows for any kind of ethical action and concomitant legitimation. By warning against Constantinianism Schlabach sees Yoder as supremely resisting, perhaps more certainly than any other theologian, this proclivity.

Schlabach's point is to highlight a more basic tension that energizes the life of faith by sustaining, rather than overcoming, a central and critical aspect that subtends the relationship, not between Constantinians and non-Constantinians, but between world and church. For Schlabach, the effect of Yoder's theology is to help Christians embrace the reality that one "cannot negotiate the Deuteronomic juncture without retaining a vital sense of eschatological tension."[39] Those who use Yoder in order to raise suspicions of church-state accommodation have often missed this central issue. Equally, those who try to salvage Christian political participation by inflecting their arguments through this concern (i.e., Stout's *Democracy and Tradition*), then, miss a looming and unacknowledged but equally pernicious parallel: imagining promise and fulfillment *without* fulfillment. Schlabach perspicaciously perceives this inclination in many ethicists who follow Yoder (and inversely for our purposes, those who would reject Yoder) but forget the larger coherence of his ethics, and I argue, laughter. It is the irreducible and inexhaustible dynamic of promise and fulfillment that gives life to Israel and, following, the New Testament church, and both as possibility and actuality for fulfillment in the midst of history's rival hopes.

Hence, corresponding to Constantinianism's aspiration to champion Christian hope as prematurely realized, those erring on the other side preclude the possibility of fulfillment altogether, rendering Christianity simply a horizon of promise and incorrectly deploying Yoder's Constantinian caveats in ways that undermine every suggestion of God's historical participation in time. This impossibly long view of history asks Christians to forever defer God's place in time and suffer

---

39. Schlabach, "Deuteronomic or Constantinian," 461. This observation helps us understand Yoder's suspicions of those who would consider themselves "Yoderians" rather than simply Christians.

such a world without end, as if to read the *promises* of the Old and New Testaments without the *fulfillments* of the Old and New Testaments. Schlabach writes, "This means that although Constantine should represent to us the wrong way to embrace God's promise of liberation, *shalom*, and blessings in all of life, we must not forget that God *does* want to free, heal, and bless even if, in blessing, God risks the possibility that God's people will abuse God's gift."[40]

Devoid of actual peace, justice, and order—returning to Horkheimer and Adorno's premonitions of endless promises and endless cheating— we *should* worry about "wrong laughter." Yet this does not mean that such goods can be taken for granted as birthrights of any politics. This is what makes Stout and Yoder so important to their respective publics, for neither posits what Horkheimer and Adorno refer to as reconciliation as more than a possibility, but they also do not underestimate that possibility. They celebrate the critical tensions resplendent in any community that dares to hope. Right laughter in this way is itself fulfillment, the realization of hope. Schlabach writes, "Constantine remains a major temptation and a false answer but is not, finally, our primary problem. Life is our problem."[41] As such laughter may be the greatest expression of hope and the tensions at play in the politics of promise and fulfillment.

40. Ibid., 454.
41. Ibid., 461.

13

Epistemological Violence, Christianity, and the Secular

DANIEL COLUCCIELLO BARBER

Yoder's Breaching Strategy

The political character of John Howard Yoder's thought is well appreciated. Less appreciated—or perhaps less explicit—is the secular character of his thought. Yoder made no attempt to provide a concept of the secular, and a survey of his work would show that in nearly every instance in which he uses the word "secular," it functions within accepted semantic bounds. This is to say that the word "secular," within Yoder's work, generally denotes the world, as that which is distinct from the church. But what is interesting about Yoder and the secular is not the definition he gives the word, whereby it is opposed to the church, but rather the moments in which he breaches this initial and commonplace opposition by affirming the secular nature of Christianity.

We can look at two instances that exemplify this "breaching" strategy. In *The Original Revolution*, Yoder addresses the ambiguity and even misapprehension that revolves around the term "gospel," originally *euangelion*. His proposal of a way out of this dead end requires the reclamation of the initially "secular" sense of the term. "Originally [gospel] is not a religious or a personal term at all, but a secular one: 'good news.'" Yoder continues to expand this secular aspect of gospel by remarking that it is "good news having seriously to do with the people's welfare," and news that tells of an event that "not merely . . . makes some of us happy, but one which shapes our common lives for the better."[1] In this case, if the proper sense of a theological concept is to be understood, the opposition between the religious and the secular must be breached. The purpose of this breach is not to demonstrate the secular aspect or analogue of a religious truth, it is in fact to demonstrate that primacy must be granted to the secular, and that the opposition between religious and secular occludes theological truth. Faced with such an opposition, theology sides with the secular, because at bottom the secular retains—at least in this instance—two qualities that are essential to the gospel: that it is good news for *the world*, and that it is good news for people in general rather than for private individuals (note that when secular is opposed to the "religious," it is likewise opposed to the "personal").

A second instance of the breaching strategy can be found in *The Politics of Jesus*, when Yoder discusses the distinction between the lifestyle of "the community of disciples," i.e., the church, and the lifestyle of "the crowd," i.e., those who lie outside the church. The primary point he wants to convey is that this distinction derives not from a peculiar abnormality, from "arbitrary rules" that make the church distinct from "normal people," but rather from the church's "exceptionally normal quality of humanness." Already it is possible to see Yoder resisting, when faced with the task of explaining the distinctive lifestyle of the community of disciples, the easily-at-hand opposition between the domain of the church and the domain of the secular. He makes this refusal explicit when he continues: "The distinctness is not a cultic or ritual separation, but rather a nonconformed quality of ('secular') involvement in the life of the world."[2] Yoder thus finds it necessary, in order to articulate the proper theological sense of the church's distinctness, to breach the presumed divide between the church (or the religious, which might be implied by predicates such as "cultic" and "ritual") and the secular. Again, the aim of such breaching is not to point out some secular correlate to the church's distinctiveness, it is—much more radically—to affirm that the church's distinctiveness is properly secular,

1. John Howard Yoder, *The Original Revolution: Essays on Christian Pacifism* (Scottdale, PA: Herald, 2003), 15.

2. John Howard Yoder, *The Politics of Jesus: Vicit Agnus Noster*, 2nd ed. (Grand Rapids: Eerdmans, 1994) 39.

that the church's distinctiveness has validity only when it is understood as a manner of secular inhabitation (and not as an opposition to secular inhabitation as such).

We can see, summarizing the predicates involved in Yoder's breaching strategy, that the affirmation of theology's secularity involves, variously, the refusal to predicate that theology is religious, personal (or individualistic), cultic, and ritual. Positively, to say that theology affirms the secular is to say that what matters for theology is the world—though this is not the same as saying that theology affirms the world as it is presently expressed, given that the community of disciples is distinct by way of its nonconformity with preestablished patterns of existence.

What I hope to advance in indicating Yoder's breaching strategy is not that Yoder is an advocate of something already recognizable, whether that is a "secular theology," a "religionless Christianity," or a détente between theology-as-we-know-it and secularism-as-we-know-it. The above instances do not warrant these conclusive identifications. What they do warrant, however, is a Yoderian awareness that the secular, in some presently indeterminate sense, provides a problematic horizon for theology—a horizon, let me again make clear, that would be avoided rather than addressed by the recognizable conclusions just mentioned. We might even say that the secular is a theological problematic, except that this formulation seems to license two inadequate ideas. The first of these is that the problem of the secular is a concern for theology, and not for non-theological domains. While it is true that secularism develops against the background of Christian theology, the problem it presents spills beyond theological boundaries. The second inadequate idea, which presupposes the first, involves the claim that if secularism is the problem, then theology is the solution. Such an idea falls short not only because it precludes the possibility that the secular is less problematic than, or equally problematic as, theology. It also falls short in virtue of Yoder's breaching strategy, which makes theological truth hinge on an affirmation of the secular. According to such a strategy, it cannot be the case that theology holds the key to the secular; it is in fact far more likely that the secular—as a problematic horizon—provides the cipher for theology, which is itself problematic insofar as it tends, by defining itself in religious, private, cultic, or otherworldly terms, to devalue the secular.

We might say, in short, that what is common to these two inadequate ideas about the relation between theology and the secular is a refusal of the breach opened by Yoder. According to this breaching strategy, the secular is a problematic horizon for theology in the precise sense that it problematizes theology. The point of a problem, after all, is its ability to make us think in new ways, to open new paths, to make possible a future worthy of the name. By definition, then, there is no future for theology if, when facing the problem of the secular, it reaches into its back pocket to grasp the answer it has already tucked away. Accordingly, in what follows I want to take up a rethinking of theology in virtue of the problem of the secular. But what is the secular? This question has recently been posed in novel ways, and independently of a specifically theological vantage, by a number of thinkers, most notably Talal Asad. Thus, before advancing to the properly Yoderian horizon of the secular problematic, I will look at the ways in which the secular has been problematized in a non-theological manner.

Epistemological Violence and the Secular

Asad's work is wide-ranging and nuanced, so much so that one hesitates to draw explicit theses from it, lest these theses proceed too telescopically. Nonetheless, I would venture the assertion that what makes his work on the secular[3] so profound is the way it juxtaposes the continuities and discontinuities between religion and the secular. This gives him the ability to avoid the demand posed by an either/or, which would claim either that the secular is defined by its separation from religion, or that the secular is, in the end, merely another variation of religion (even if it is a concealed variation). Asad attends to phenomena that exceed the limits produced by either a sharp demarcation between or a

---

3. I have in mind *Genealogies of Religion: Discipline and Reasons of Power in Christianity and Islam* (Baltimore: Johns Hopkins University Press, 1993), and *Formations of the Secular: Christianity, Islam, Modernity* (Stanford: Stanford University Press, 2003). Asad distinguishes between "'the secular' as an epistemic category and 'secularism' as a political doctrine" (*Formations of the Secular*, 5). While I do not oppose this distinction, my argument lacks the precision necessary to make effective use of it. Therefore I use the terms somewhat interchangeably, and where one is used the other is in the background. Nonetheless, as my point of entry concerns the role of epistemological violence, I will favor the term, "the secular."

hasty identification of the secular and religion. Notable, for instance, is his attention to the role of pain in religious and secular practice, which establishes a significant differentiation in approaches towards pain, but in doing so makes apparent the indebtedness of secular approaches to religious approaches. Similarly, when demonstrating the differentiation between religion's spirituality and the secular's valorization of literature, the development of the former out of the latter also becomes evident.

The prominent virtue of this juxtaposition of continuity and discontinuity is its capacity to articulate the specificity of and break occasioned by the secular, but at the same time to demonstrate the dependence of the secular on a religious past that it tends to disavow. This has important consequences for the universalizing pretensions of the secular. We can say more about this further on, but at this point we can see that the secular's universalizing function—whereby its break from religion is performed in the name of a universalizing capacity precluded by the specificity of religion—is undercut by its dependence on religion.

Equally problematic for an equation of the secular with the universal is the fact that the secular is produced. Asad constantly draws attention to this fact, though this occurs most notably, perhaps, in his emphasis on habituation. If the secular seems "right" or "natural" to subjects, this is not because the secular has finally excluded the differentiations of particular identities in order to discover the essence that all human subjects bear by nature or by right. On the contrary, the semblance of the secular's rightness or naturalness—where it does appear to subjects—is due to the fact that such subjects are, or have been, habituated by the secular. This, in other words, is another juncture of continuity amidst discontinuity between religion and the secular. Just as religious subjects were habituated so as to attain, let's say, the vision of God, so secular subjects are habituated to see the propriety of goods such as human rights and tolerance. Once again, this is a problem for the secular precisely because a universal situation now appears to depend on a particular manner of habituation. The secular thus faces the paradox whereby a universal situation must be produced through the valorization of one particular set of practices, affects, and concepts, and the devalorization of other particular sets of practices, affects, and concepts.

Asad gets at this paradoxical feature of the secular more explicitly when he observes: "Secularism is not simply an intellectual answer to a question about enduring social peace and tolerance. It is an enactment by which a *political medium* (representation of citizenship) redefines and transcends particular and differentiating practices of the self that are articulated through class, gender, and religion."[4] The secular issues a transcendent imperative, for it claims the universal right to redefine "particular and differentiating practices," yet it is at the same time nothing other than one additional set of practices (that are particular, and that differentiate themselves from other practices). In short, the secular is a particular that arrogates to itself the quality of being universal. This means that the secular must take on a prophetic, or futural dimension— for while it claims to be universal by right, it is not universal in fact. It is in fact particular. The secular thus becomes futural because a future is necessary in order to suture the gap between its *de jure* and *de facto* status.

I have already noted that Asad unveils and critiques this universalizing dynamism of the secular by highlighting its continuities with, and thus manifest dependence upon, the particularity of religion, as well as its reliance on habituation. More directly to the point, however, he issues the demand to reverse this dynamism: whereas secularism gives itself a course according to which it would progressively realize its universal imperative and conceal its particular origins, Asad insists on halting the movement towards universality and foregrounding the particularity of the secular. At one point, for instance, he calls for some restrictions on patterns of thought promoted by the Enlightenment, which of course provides the secular with its theoretical milieu. He remarks that anthropologists, when encountering non-western traditions, "should learn to treat some of their own Enlightenment assumptions as belonging to specific kinds of reasoning—albeit kinds of reasoning that have largely shaped our modern world—and not as the ground from which all understanding of non-Enlightenment traditions must begin."[5] Here the secular's particularity is not something to be relativized in favor of

4. Asad, *Formations of the Secular*, 5.

5. Asad, *Genealogies of Religion*, 200. In *Formations of the Secular*, he continues to emphasize the particular or specific (rather than universal or general) character of secular assumptions by proposing the secular as an anthropological object.

its universalizing pretensions. On the contrary, it is the tendency to universalize that must be undone in virtue of the manifest (though often unacknowledged) specificity, or particularity, of the secular.

The focus of Asad's injunction is the epistemological violence that lies at the heart of the secular. This epistemological violence has a peculiar nature, in that it involves something subtler than the sheer insistence by one particular tradition (or set of habits, affects, and concepts) on its right to overpower another particular tradition. It involves not a direct, straightforward antagonism between one particularity and another (as the previous sentence articulates), but rather an antagonism between universality and particularity. In fact, of course, it certainly is an antagonism between particularities, but this aspect of antagonism is masked because the particularity-that-claims-to-be-universal casts the antagonism as one between universality and particularity. Epistemological violence is set forth by this latter move, whereby one particularity demands that conflict be *understood* not as a conflict between particularities, but as a conflict between universality and particularity. It is, then, precisely this movement, this epistemological framing of conflict, that Asad opposes when he insists that secular assumptions be treated as nothing more than "specific kinds of reasoning," and in no way as "the ground" of understanding.

The fact that the secular functions as the particularity-that-claims-to-be-universal provides the background for the duplicity of its claim to provide "enduring social peace." Even where it does manifestly provide such peace—a factually questionable claim in itself—it can do so only by first establishing itself as a universal paradigm, an establishment that requires the enactment of epistemological violence (if not other, "less epistemological" kinds of violence). What we have with the secular, then, is a peace made possible by violence. Of course, from the vantage of the secular, such violence must be understood as "right"—that is, as justified, or at the very least as tragically necessary, given that this violence enables the establishment of social peace.[6] But when we justify violence in this way, we fall into a vicious sort of circularity: we know that the violence involved in the secular enactment of peace is neces-

6. For an original and sophisticated account of the relationship between secularism, violence, and religion, see Brian Goldstone, "Secularism, 'Religious Violence,' and the Liberal Imaginary," in *The Politics of Religion-Making*, ed. Markus Dressler and Arvind Mandair (New York: Columbia University Press, forthcoming).

sary, because only in this way is it possible for the secular to establish peace. One might fairly ask, in response, why it is that peace must be found by way of the secular? The answer of the secular, it seems, is that the sheer diversity of particularities leads to unending violence, and thus the universal framework of the secular—as that which outstrips particular perspectives—is necessary in order to make peace possible. But in this way the secular merely falls back into direct epistemological violence, given that it once again presents itself not as the particularity that it is in fact, but rather as the universal that it claims to be by right.

If the secular appears as the only answer to the question of how to secure enduring social peace, this is because it has already framed the parameters of the question; if the violence of the secular seems justified in view of the peace consequently made possible, this is because it has already enacted an epistemological violence that frames the possible ways by which we might conceive of violence and peace. The problem of the secular concerns this intrinsic circularity between particularity and universality, this epistemological violence, which is essential to the secular. Epistemological violence is the secular's condition of possibility. To problematize the secular, to call it into question, is to oppose this epistemological violence.

Epistemological Violence and Christianity

It is very important, now, to emphasize a key point of continuity-with-in-discontinuity between the secular and religion—understood here as Christianity. (The determination of religion as Christianity is legitimate here not simply because the category of religion is itself produced by Christianity,[7] but also because historically Christianity is the religion that provides the background out of which the secular emerges.) Let us not overlook the discontinuity, for the claim that the secular provides the universal ground for understanding the world is certainly not identical to the claim, advanced by Christendom, that Christianity provides the universal ground for understanding the world. Nonetheless, it is

---

7. For an account of Christianity's "invention of religion" that is of special relevance to my argument (given that it relates this "invention of religion" to the Jewish-Christian schism), see Daniel Boyarin, *Borderlines: The Partition of Judaeo-Christianity* (Philadelphia: University of Pennsylvania Press, 2006) 10–13.

apparent that something remains continuous throughout this historical transition from a Christian to a secular epoch. In each case, a particular tradition arrogates to itself the right to proclaim itself as universal. Just war, of course, is not identical to humanitarian intervention, and the Crusades are not identical to the promotion of global democracy by means of regime change, but in all of these cases we see the same sort of formal operation: certain kinds of violence are justified, or tragically necessitated, by their capacity to effect the peace or good of the universal (though, again, this operation deflects attention from the fact that such a universal is produced by a particular tradition). Whether we are dealing with Christianity or the secular, we encounter the enactment of epistemological violence.

I have framed this continuity according to a formal operation, but it is equally visible in concrete terms. The particularity-that-claims-to-be-universal has a territory. Broadly speaking, this territory remains continuous from the emergence of Christendom up to the present dynamism of the secular. It includes, roughly, Europe and eventually North America, and it has developed according to the historical processes of colonization. For most, colonization conjures up images of the direct violence involved in the physical act of conquest. This conjuration should not be avoided, but recent work has highlighted the additional—more indirect and sophisticated—ideological modalities by which Europe and North America gave sense to violence. This sense hinged upon the capacity to define simultaneously the identity of the particularity-that-claims-to-be-universal (concretely, the European, and eventually the North American) and the particularity-that-falls-short-of-the-universal (concretely, non-European races). J. Kameron Carter, for instance, has established that the process of becoming-Christian has, for the most part, historically amounted to the process of becoming-white.[8] Furthermore, Gil Anidjar has incisively and forcefully made the point that European identity, in its Christian as well as secular modality, was produced by way of its—ideologically Orientalist—opposition to the Semite, in its twofold manifestation as the Jew (Europe's internal other) and the Arab (Europe's external other).[9]

8. See J. Kameron Carter, *Race: A Theological Account* (Oxford: Oxford University Press, 2008).

9. See Gil Anidjar, *Semites: Race, Religion, Literature* (Stanford, CA: Stanford

Putting it concretely as well as formally, then, the continuity of Christianity and the secular lies in the epistemological violence whereby Europe–North America sets the conditions of possibility for understanding the world, for establishing peace, for justifying violence. One can see the peculiar conjunction of Christianity, the secular (as reason's "philosophical inquiry"), and European hegemony in a recent statement by Pope Benedict XVI in his so-called "Regensburg Address":

> This inner rapprochement between Biblical faith and Greek philosophical inquiry was an event of decisive importance not only from the standpoint of the history of religions, but also from that of world history—it is an event which concerns us even today. Given this convergence, it is not surprising that Christianity, despite its origins and some significant developments in the East, finally took on its historically decisive character in Europe.[10]

We might clarify three points here. First, Christianity emerged out of a "convergence" between the biblical and the philosophical, so much so that this convergence appears to belong more to the providential than to the accidental. "The encounter between the Biblical message and Greek thought," he adds, "did not happen by chance"—it was, he continues, an "intrinsic necessity."[11] Second, this convergence is important not only for Christianity, but for world history—indeed, it was Europe that enabled Christianity to assume its "historically decisive character." Third, the territorial essence of Christianity is Europe, not the East (or the "Orient," the Europeans once would have said), despite the fact that the—Jewish, though he leaves this term unspoken—"origins" of Christianity were, and are, Eastern. Benedict seems to be asserting, in short, that Christianity is Europe. But, he observes, "We can also express this the other way around: this convergence, with the subsequent addition of the Roman heritage, created Europe and remains the foundation of what can rightly be called Europe."[12] So, it is not only that Christianity is Europe, but that Europe is Christianity.

University Press, 2008).

    10. Pope Benedict XVI, "Papal Address at University of Regensburg," at http://www.zenit.org/article-16955?l=english.

    11. Benedict, "Papal Address."

    12. Benedict, "Papal Address."

Benedict's assertion would not be amenable to partisans of the secular, in fact it is in one sense a polemic against Europe's self-conception as secular. But how deep does this conflict between Christianity and the secular run? If we replaced "Christianity" with "Secularism" in Benedict's statement, such that it read, "Secularism is Europe, and Europe is Secularism," would advocates of the secular be displeased?[13] I propose that the battle between Christianity and the secular can be understood as a civil war. Or, we could imagine it as a conflict between brothers who hold in common the belief that their house should rule over others, it is just a question of which brother will rule the house. It does not matter whether we are dealing with Christianity or Secularism, the content is still European and North American dominance, and the form still involves the epistemological violence of a particularity-that-claims-to-be-universal. Anidjar, at one point, clearly pronounces the syllogistic chain of equivalences: "Secularism is Orientalism. And Orientalism is Christianity. It is Christian Imperialism."[14]

All of this poses some severe difficulties for Yoder's breaching strategy. Is the aim of this strategy to affirm the secular character of Christianity? If so, then Yoder would merely be adding a footnote to the history of "Christian Imperialism," one that might provide, at most, the missing theoretical link between two discontinuous yet homologous epochs of domination. Yet I contend that something entirely different is going on in his breaching strategy. I claim, in fact, that Yoder's Christianity is not Christianity (as it has been articulated above), and that Yoder's concept of the secular is not the secular (as it has been articulated above). I claim, furthermore, that Yoder's account of Christianity and of the secular is aberrant, in the sense that it conceives of a Christianity and a secularity that depart from and oppose the his-

13. According to Slavoj Žižek, "What makes modern Europe unique is that it is the first and only civilization in which atheism is a fully legitimate option, not an obstacle to any public post." Atheism, he says, is not only "one of Europe's greatest legacies," it is also "perhaps our only chance for peace." One reason atheism is so valuable is that "it creates a safe public space for believers." Universal peace, then, is made possible by the secularism produced by the particularity of atheist Europe. See "Defenders of the Faith," his op-ed in *The New York Times*, March 12, 2006, at http://www.nytimes.com/2006/03/12/opinion/12zizek.html?_r=1.

14. Anidjar, *Semites*, 52.

tory developed by the continuity of Christian and secular epistemological violence. In what follows, I will try to substantiate these claims.

Against "History"

The first point to address, with regard to Yoder's opposition to the continuous history of Christian and secular epistemological violence, is
his axiomatic opposition to universalism. This is important because,
as I argued above, the particular arrogation of a universal ground of
understanding lies at the heart of, and provides an essential point of
commonality between, Christianity and the secular. Yoder, speaking as
an advocate of what he calls "messianic Christian faith," contrasts his
own particular approach to universality with approaches that would
adopt a universalistic perspective:

> Medieval European imperial Christendom, or Imperial Russian
> Orthodoxy, or the Enlightenment claims of the French encyclo-
> pedists, or the arbitrage today of the news media, or the pro-
> fessional historians, or university academics, have all claimed
> and can consistently claim that the place where they stand is in
> some sense *more reasonable, more universal*, than other places.
> *The missionary messianic community renounces such claims in
> principle.*[15]

Yoder thus rejects, "in principle," the adoption of a position whereby
one particularity, one "place," could claim the right even to be "more
universal" than other particularities or places, much less the right to
bear the universal itself. Already, then, we see Yoder refusing the possibility of the sort of epistemological violence necessary for Christianity
and the secular.

Yoder's principled anti-universalism has some significant consequences for the way in which history is approached. It is possible to
tell history in a way that shares in the same epistemological violence
required by the logic of universalism. In fact, history is often told in this
way, as is recognized by the banal veracity of the claim that history is
written by the victors. History, in other words, does not often tell what
happened as such, much less what could have happened but did not,

---

15. Yoder, *The Jewish-Christian Schism Revisited* (Grand Rapids: Eerdmans, 2003),
114. Emphasis added.

or what some wanted to happen but did not. It tells what happened in such a way that what happened is understood as necessary; it tells what happened from the vantage of those whose existence is made possible by this happening.

Similarly, in the logic of universalism, a particularity does not explain itself—it does not "tell" itself—as one particularity among others, it explains itself as the universal horizon for all particularities. In this sense, such a particularity's happening-to-be-universal is not a description of what is happening so much as it is a projection of what must happen, of what is universally necessitated. When the particularity-that-claims-to-be-universal talks about itself, it is producing what is necessary, that is to say, it is demarcating what is possible and impossible for itself and for other (less-than-universal) particularities. The epistemological violence so enacted is of a piece with that enacted by history, at least insofar as history tells what happened as what necessarily had to happen. When history proceeds in such a manner, it too demarcates the possible and the impossible.

Yoder has this last sort of history in mind in the following description: "Studying history is then the process of showing how what had to happen did happen. The 'had to' is an intellectual construct *ex eventu*. The historian demonstrates his expertise by making that necessity evident."[16] That Yoder is critical of this sort of history-telling is made clear by his remark elsewhere that "perhaps there are few errors more damaging in the reading of history, than the assumption that events had to go the way they did."[17] This is in many respects a difficult assumption to resist, given that any attempt to make sense of what has happened seems to require some kind of intellectual assent to its having happened. It is, in other words, difficult to go about explaining what has happened at the same time that one resists the idea that it had to happen, given that any explanation consents, at least incipiently, to the logic of what has happened.

Yoder seems to be aware of this difficulty, for even as he proclaims, as a critique of historical necessity, that "*It did not have to be*," he also acknowledges that this is "the historian's axiom."[18] The proclamation

16. Ibid., 31.
17. Ibid., 43.
18. Ibid.

that is critical of historians is the proclamation already spoken by historians. It is therefore important to distinguish the alternative directions in which this axiom is taken. The "historian" must presuppose that an event or course of events did not have to be, for it is precisely the non-necessity of the event that necessitates an explanation of the event's occurrence. If the event were necessary, if it had to be, then there would be no need for explanation. However, taking this axiom in an alternative direction, a direction more in line with Yoder's criticisms of history-telling, we should add that while the historian presupposes that the event did not have to be, he does so in order to then explain why it had to be. Yoder thus radicalizes the historian's axiom such that it undermines the possibility of any finality to the telling of history.

It may be helpful, at this point, to summarize my argument so far. Yoder, in virtue of his conjoint opposition to universalism and to history as the production of necessity, is a radical critic of epistemological violence. Since this epistemological violence is the condition of possibility for Christianity and for the secular, his relation to these two traditions will be fundamentally, irreversibly antagonistic.

But if he is against all of this, then what is he for? Thus far, we can say, first, that he affirms the alternative possibilities of history. The possibilities of history are irreducible to "History," understood as that which is told from the vantage of necessity. Furthermore, these possibilities may emerge—they themselves are understood as possible—only insofar as History is opposed. Genuinely historical possibilities of history are, by nature, aberrant departures from History. We can say, second, that he affirms particularity. To be against universalism in principle is also to be for the possibilities opened by the excess of particularities to the universal. I noted earlier that universalism's epistemological violence presumes that universalism is necessary to peace. But this sort of universalism amounts to an *a priori* commitment to violence, a commitment to which the *a posteriori* risk of irresolvable particularity is preferable. The only sort of peace worth having is one that is capable of assuming this risk. As Chris Huebner, in a reflection on Yoder, has remarked, "Peace is itself an agonistic reality."[19]

19. Chris Huebner, *A Precarious Peace: Yoderian Explorations on Theology, Knowledge, and Identity* (Scottdale, PA: Herald, 2006) 142.

I will now examine how the above affirmations—of historical possibilities outside of History, and of particular possibilities outside of universalism—are articulated by the irreducibly apocalyptic and diasporic character of Yoder's thought.

Apocalyptic

It is relatively uncontroversial, within Christian theology, to point to the apocalyptic character of the kingdom established by Jesus. It is, however, less apparent that the consequences of this apocalyptic character have been pursued. This can be seen if we begin with the proposition that what is at stake in apocalyptic is the relationship between the emergence of Jesus's messianic kingdom and the history thereby occasioned. The apocalyptic emergence of this kingdom introduces a shift in the way history is understood, for history must now pivot around the apocalyptic emergence. This seems straightforward enough. What is less straightforward is the degree to which, or the style in which, history may be understood by way of this apocalyptic emergence. And it is here that the error of Christianity—or of Christianity as "Constantinianism," as Yoder would put it—becomes manifest. Constantinian Christianity moves from the straightforward premise, that understanding of history is altered by the apocalyptic emergence of Jesus's messianic kingdom, to the conclusion that this grants humans the ability to know how history ought to develop. In other words, Constantinian Christianity identifies the apocalyptic emergence of the messianic kingdom with the ability to tell a universal history—or, in the nomenclature I am using, the ability to tell "History."

Nevertheless, apocalyptic is not History. As I said above, the consequences of the apocalyptic character of Jesus's kingdom seem to remain unpursued. If they were pursued, it would become necessary to admit that it is impossible to tell a History based on apocalyptic, for the nature of apocalyptic is to crack the continuity of History. There is, in other words, an irreversible disjunction between apocalyptic and History. Certainly it is the case that Jesus cracked the History that Rome sought to tell, so why would it be assumed—as it is by Constantinian Christianity—that Jesus came to inaugurate yet another History? Some might remark that the content of Christian History differs from the content of Roman History. This is a fair, but superficial, point, for it makes the novelty of Jesus's messianic kingdom insubstantial. It leaves out the much more substantial possibility that the novelty of Jesus's messianic kingdom lies not in a new content of History, but rather in a new form of telling History—a form that would, in fact, amount to the refusal of "History" (whether Roman or Christian or Secular). It is in view of this latter possibility, which I take to be correct, that the import of apocalyptic becomes clear: it is because of the apocalyptic character of Jesus's messianic kingdom that there can be no History (Christian or otherwise), and it is because of this apocalyptic character that it becomes imperative to crack History.

This does not mean apocalyptic is ahistorical. It means, on the contrary, that it is more historical than History. To understand history apocalyptically is to understand that history is not continuous, that it is marked by discontinuities that are unpredictable. Such an apocalyptic approach is foreclosed *a priori* by History, which seeks to project continuity over historical discontinuities. Here we can see what I am arguing is the irreducibly apocalyptic character of Yoder's proclamation that "it did not have to be." The historical continuity produced by the telling of History did not have to be. This should be taken not only in the plain sense, according to which History fails to envision the contingency of an event. There is a deeper sense, for such an assumption—that what took place had to be—facilitates an understanding of history that proceeds in terms of continuity rather than discontinuity. This assumption produces not only the false certainty that what took place had to take place, but the equally false (and more insidious) certainty that history is continuous. The assumption errs, in other words, not only factually but also transcendentally—theologically speaking, it is a denial of apocalyptic. It is worth noting, furthermore, that the History produced by this theological failure (Christendom, or Constantinianism) must be utterly opposed. As Yoder remarks, "Christendom does not merely need improvement around the edges; it has become disobedient at heart."[20]

Apocalyptic, then, denies History (including Christendom), but in doing so it affirms historical possibilities, the possibilities to which History fails to attend. Included among these possibilities are those of the past—i.e., those possibilities that exceed what History assumes "had

20. Yoder, *Jewish-Christian Schism*, 137.

to be"—but they are also those of the future. It is important to recognize that History, by producing a transcendentally continuous understanding of the historical, denies the possibility not only of a discontinuous past, but also of a discontinuous future. Here we can see how the telling of History involves the same epistemological violence enacted by the particularity-that-claims-to-be-universal: just as History retroactively projects a transcendental continuity over the past, so the particularity-that-claims-to-be-universal proactively projects a transcendental continuity over the future. History and the particularity-that-claims-to-be-universal are the two complementary faces of the present.[21] Their aim is to turn the past as well as the future into analogous moments of the present, such that nothing ever has been or will be significantly discontinuous with the present. Apocalyptic cracks this present, and in doing so it opens properly historical possibilities—possibilities of the past that could have been, possibilities of the future that may yet be.

Diaspora

I argued, in the previous section, that Yoder's approach to history is fundamentally apocalyptic. This approach involves the claim that Christianity, in becoming "Constantinian," in assuming the epistemological violence of History and of the particularity-that-claims-to-be-universal, abandons the apocalyptic character by which Jesus's messianic kingdom emerges. If Jesus's kingdom is apocalyptic, then Christianity—properly speaking—is possible only by a repetition of this apocalyptic emergence. This has important consequences for thinking about the church, i.e., Jesus's messianic community. It means that the messianic community must emerge historically in the same manner by which Jesus emerged historically—that is, apocalyptically, as the antagonist of History. But how is this possible? In what way can the messianic

21. The present that History and the particularity-that-claims-to-be-universal constitute accord with the logic of Chronos, which Gilles Deleuze describes in *The Logic of Sense*, trans. Mark Lester (New York: Columbia University Press, 1990) 162: for Chronos, "only the present exists in time. Past, present, and future are not three dimensions of time; only the present fills time, whereas past and future are two dimensions relative to the present in time. . . . There is always a more vast present which absorbs the past and future."

community imagine itself as historically apocalyptic, as the enemy of History and the friend of alternative historical possibilities?

We must, in light of these questions, turn to Yoder's insistence on the diasporic character of the church. Obviously, the task of being diasporic is abandoned by the Constantinian form of Christianity. To insist on the diasporic character of the church is to oppose Christendom, which made Christianity into a religion marked by the establishment of territorial sovereignty rather than by the creativity of exilic deterritorialization. But if diaspora is, negatively, a critique of Christendom, what is it positively? The positive model of diaspora, Yoder says, is embodied by Judaism (though he also points to its analogies with the Anabaptist "free church" model). Its specific origination lies with the Jewish exile in Babylon, where, according to Yoder, the claim was made that exile is a normative rather than exceptional, and permanent rather than temporary, mode of existence. Yoder asserts that diasporic existence is centrally characterized by: the synagogue, "a decentralized, self-sustaining, non-sacerdotal community life form"; the Torah, "a text around the reading and exposition of which the community is defined"; and the rabbinate, "a non-sacerdotal, non-hierarchical, non-violent leadership elite whose power is not civil but intellectual, validated by their identification with the Torah."[22] A community thus characterized is one that refuses the sedimentation of identity in favor of the transformations of mobility. Its identity is not centripetal but centrifugal, not territorialized but deterritorialized, not predetermined but discovered through novel encounter, not continuous but discontinuous.

Keeping in mind the Jewish origination of this diasporic model of existence, it becomes clear that the Jewish-Christian schism—which was the specific occasion for Yoder's more widespread claim that "it did not have to be"—was especially detrimental for the historical development of Christianity (indeed, the schism belongs to the "History" of Christianity). Christianity, in separating itself from Judaism, separated itself from diasporic existence. As Yoder notes, "The 'apologetes' like Justin Martyr, who re-conceived the Christian message so as to make it 'credible' to non-Jewish culture, detached the message of Jesus from its Jewish matrix." By developing in this direction, he adds, the church lost not only "its Jewish rootage" as such, but also some key Jewish modes

22. Ibid., 171.

of existence, including the "readiness to live in the diaspora style of the Suffering Servant."[23] Given that Yoder deems this diasporic character to be central to Christian existence, we can say that Christianity abandoned its own essence when it came to define itself in opposition to Judaism. This denial of Judaism, and of diaspora, made possible the failure known as Christendom.

Bound up in Yoder's insistence on the fundamentally diasporic character of Jesus's messianic community is an affirmation of particularity. This is, to be sure, an affirmation that the apocalyptic emergence of Jesus's messianic kingdom happened in a particular manner, but it is also—importantly—an affirmation of something much more substantial. Yoder is claiming not simply that Jesus's messianic community has a particular emergence, but that it must exist in such a way that it is able to affirm the possibilities of particularity. Putting it otherwise, we can say that Jesus's messianic community is possible only insofar as it refuses the move towards universality. It is thus necessary to understand not just that the church is particular, but even more that it is one particular among other particulars. This understanding founds resistance to any attempt, by the church, to claim that it is the particular that realizes or incarnates the universal. In short, the church, if it is to be the church, cannot become the particularity-that-claims-to-be-universal.

If being-diasporic is an essential feature of the church, this means that the church's condition of possibility is a relationship between particularities—which is precisely the sort of relationship that is refused by the particularity-that-claims-to-be-universal. Jesus's messianic community finds its identity, therefore, not in the intersection between particularity and universality, but in the intersection—the encounter—between particularities. Accordingly, the church's identity must not be fixed. On the contrary, it must *become*, for encounter is becoming. Nathan Kerr has made this point, with regard to the church's "liturgy," quite lucidly: "'church' no longer names either a stable site of production, nor does it possess a proper place of its own. Rather, . . . liturgy is precisely the practiced *loss* of a historical 'place' or 'identity.'"[24]

23. Ibid., 152.

24. Nathan Kerr, *Christ, History, and Apocalyptic: The Politics of Christian Mission* (Eugene, OR: Cascade, 2009), 179–80. This important text by Kerr, and my conversations with him, have happily influenced and significantly improved my thinking about Yoder, ecclesiology, and apocalyptic.

The identity of Jesus's messianic community cannot be localized—not because it belongs to the universal, but rather because it belongs to the incessant affirmation of particularity, of the discontinuous encounters between particularities.

Just as apocalyptic cracks History, so diaspora cracks identity. Diaspora also joins the apocalyptic in its insistence on the discontinuous. To say that the church is diasporic is to say that its identity is constituted *by* scattering, *by* entering into particularity without reserve and without reduction. There is, in fact, a kind of convergence between the themes: the apocalyptic affirmation of discontinuity is the affirmation of novel historical possibilities, but these possibilities take place by way of the diasporic affirmation of the discontinuous possibilities of the particular.[25] In this sense, diaspora is to space as the apocalyptic is to time. It is by being-diasporic, i.e., becoming-discontinuous, that the church, or the messianic community, becomes capable of repeating, and thus remaining faithful to, the apocalyptic character by which Jesus instituted it.

25. Yoder claims, for example, that the meaning of the gospel cannot be decided outside of its encounter with a particular culture: "Evangel has to submit—wants to submit—vulnerably to the conditions of meaning of the receptor culture." See "On Not Being Ashamed of the Gospel: Particularity, Pluralism, and Validation," *Faith and Philosophy* 9 (1992) 285–300, at 291. This is in notable contrast to Benedict, who, while willing to grant some value to particular cultural difference, claims that the universal relationship between gospel and reason—that is, the condition of possibility for thinking about the relationship between the gospel and meaning-in-general—has already been determined by a particular, European culture: "In the light of our experience with cultural pluralism, it is often said nowadays that the synthesis with Hellenism achieved in the early Church was an initial inculturation which ought not to be binding on other cultures. The latter are said to have the right to return to the simple message of the New Testament prior to that inculturation, in order to inculturate it anew in their own particular milieux. This thesis is not simply false, but it is coarse and lacking in precision. The New Testament was written in Greek and bears the imprint of the Greek spirit," and since Benedict identifies this "Greek spirit" as the representative of reason, it follows that "the fundamental decisions made about the relationship between faith and the use of human reason are part of the faith itself; they are developments consonant with the nature of faith itself." See Benedict, "Papal Address."

A Yoderian Secular

Diaspora and apocalyptic provide complementary ways of conceiving the otherness of God to the present—to History and to the particularity-that-claims-to-be-universal. For this reason, once again, Yoder is the enemy of "Christianity" and "Secularism." We have seen, above, the sense in which Yoder can be Christian at the same time that he is the enemy of Christianity (or Christendom). But in what sense can he be secular, if he is also the enemy of Secularism? What is at work in his breaching strategy?

I contend that the central point of this breaching strategy is to open a space between a properly Christian affirmation of God's otherness to the present (whether in a diasporic or an apocalyptic guise) and a properly secular affirmation of the world. By affirming the secular, I noted, Yoder is denying any identification of Christian theology and that to which the secular is opposed—religion, for example, or the cultic. The secular, at the very least, names that which exceeds the scope of religion, or of the cultic. It names, more directly, the world. To affirm the secular character of Christianity, then, is to affirm Christianity's "thisworldly" nature, precisely where this world exceeds—is other than—the forms that religion or the cultic imposes on the world. It is important, if we are to grasp the link between God's otherness and the world's otherness, to understand that the otherness of God to the present, or to given reality, is not a matter of the transcendent (where the transcendent means the otherworldly). As Yoder remarks, "It would be wrong . . . to explain the otherness in terms of some metaphysical dualism." It is enough, he continues, to understand that concepts of otherness "relativize the empirical, manipulable 'reality.' They relativize the given in favor of the gift."[26] The given is the present, which is produced by History and the particularity-that-claims-to-be-universal, while the gift is God's otherness, which is produced by diaspora and apocalyptic. This gift is other to the present of the world, but it is not other to the world as such (it is not otherworldly)—in fact, the gift *is* the otherness of the world (the otherness of the thisworldly).

Two important points follow from this. First, we see that Yoder's concept of the secular is fundamentally opposed to Secularism. Yoder's

26. Yoder, *Jewish-Christian Schism*, 162.

secular cracks the present—the world as it is given—in favor of the diasporic discontinuity of the world's radical particularity, the world's otherness to the epistemologically violent present. Secularism, on the other hand, enacts such epistemological violence by participating in the logic of the particularity-that-claims-to-be-universal, and thus by conceiving the world in terms of the continuous present. Second, we can now understand Yoder's breaching strategy as advocating a convergence between the apocalyptic, diasporic character of Christianity and the discontinuous character of the world. There is, in fact, a radical reversibility between the convergent terms. Convergence does not mean that God's otherness tells us how the world should be, nor does it mean that the world tells us how God should be. We cannot fully understand either term of convergence in advance. Convergence demands, on the contrary, that the excess of the world (its historical and particular possibilities) and the excess of the divine be thought in common.

Yoder points to such a convergence when he draws a contrast between "religion" and the category of "history," such that what marks a religion is the inability to affirm history. (It is important here to recall Yoder's earlier claim that one mark of secularity is its opposition to religion—thus history may become another mark of secularity.) Yoder says that "it is possible to distinguish 'religion' as that which sanctifies and celebrates life as it is, things as they are . . . . Over against this understanding of 'religion,' the category of 'history' represents the morally meaningful particular processes, which may not go in a straight line but at least go somewhere."[27] One such example of "religion," he says, is "mainstream Christianity," i.e., Christendom.[28] It is precisely this "religious" approach to history (which I have called "History") that Yoder opposes in his breaching strategy. To say that Christianity is secular rather than religious is to say that it is genuinely historical. It cracks the present ("life as it is, things as they are"), which religion supports, in favor of the discontinuity of history, of the world. This sort of discontinuity "may not go in a straight line," but that is precisely the point, for the world is not continuous, it is composed by particularity rather than

27. Yoder, *The Jewish-Christian Schism*, 108.

28. He adds that if "mainstream Christianity" exemplifies religion, then examples of history may be found in "the Jews, radical Protestants, and (today) the theologies of liberation" (*Jewish-Christian Schism*, 108).

by universality. The only way to move in the direction of the world is to move in the direction of otherness, to move discontinuously. This way allows us truly to "go somewhere," because it allows us to go in the direction of historical and particular possibilities. These possibilities are denied by "Christianity" as well as by "Secularism," but they are affirmed by the secularity of Yoder's Christianity.

14

Fracturing Evangelical Recognitions of Christ: Inheriting
the Radical Democracy of John Howard Yoder with the
Penumbral Vision of Rowan Williams[1]

JOSEPH R. WIEBE

It has gotten to be these days that once you've said "evangelicalism,"
you've already begun a monologue. I am a Mennonite Brethren, and
it is no secret that the Mennonite Brethren church has become more
evangelical than most of its other Anabaptist counterparts. I want to
focus on one corollary of this development—namely, the way it shapes
Mennonite Brethren political identity and its mode of self-articulation.
The Mennonite Brethren slide towards evangelicalism is concomitant
with its political sensibility as being at once a distinct people as well as
the bearers of a message that contains all political orientations within
its teleological horizon. Evangelicalism is, among other things, establishing the scriptural parameters of this message and then foisting its
comprehensiveness on the world. This message is, of course, the gospel,
the Good News that Christ is Lord—something that I think most, if
not all, Christians will want to agree is both scriptural and comprehensive. But as a mode of communication, evangelicalism has become
a totalizing discourse. It advances, multiplies, reproduces, grows, and
impacts;[2] it does not listen, it does not enjoin receptive generosity. Part

1. This paper was originally presented at the conference "Inheriting John Howard
Yoder: A New Generation Examines his Thought," held at Toronto Mennonite
Theological Centre (TMTC) on May 26, 2007.

2. This list of verbs was extracted from the Mennonite Brethren conference of
Canada's website: http://www.mbconf.ca/home/ministries/ (accessed May 10, 2007).

of the reason why the Mennonite Brethren inhabit this discourse is due to its political disenfranchisement. In Canada, before the days of expanded military operations in U.S.-initiated combats like Afghanistan, and before the legality of gay marriages, there was a kind of somnambulism within Mennonite Brethren democratic polity. Canadian multilateralism and social sensitivity lulled Mennonites into a slumber of political complacency. Now there are renewed discussions pertaining to national political matters as well as to the political nature of the church, but the terms of these debates construe disenfranchisement as a concession—something that Mennonites need to "come to terms with." The Mennonite Brethren church still wants influence and privilege; it still wants to be credible according to the logic of political liberalism.[3] Evangelicalism names the identity and discursive technique that enable the Mennonite Brethren church to maintain a sense of its heritage as a distinct community in the world, yet tunes its voice to the sound of certainty and inexhaustion.

The Mennonite Brethren in Canada

The Mennonite Brethren have been interested in missions from their beginning. They were a rapidly growing movement after their detachment from other Mennonites in 1860, stimulating an allure for swelling numbers. During the 1960s, Mennonite Brethren became more programmatic with missions, adopting evangelical models from other (non)denominational and para-churches.[4] "The constituency has usu-

---

3. Several Mennonite Brethren responses to the legality of gay and lesbian marriages in 2003 indicated that they were primarily disturbed by the possibility that same-sex marriage would be "constitutionally embedded in Canada." Though eventually the rhetoric of the Mennonite Brethren church turned inward to discuss how it would deal with the outcome, during the time after the initial court ruling the direction of the debate was toward protecting the hegemony of heterosexual marriages in Canada. It was only after Mennonites—in addition to the other voices within the Evangelical Fellowship of Canada—failed to lobby for the federal government to overturn the court's decision that their focus became establishing a new direction against the movement of Canadian culture. See Dora Dueck, "Ontario Ruling Provokes Shock, Disappointment, Confusion," *Mennonite Brethren Herald,* July 2003. Online: http://www.mbherald.com/42/09/news-9.en.html (accessed May 10, 2007).

4. J. B. Toews, *Pilgrimage of Faith: The Mennonite Brethren Church 1860–1990* (Winnipeg, MB: Kindred, 1993) 247.

ally been liberal in its contributions [to missions], many young people have consecrated themselves for this service."[5] The ecclesiological, theological, and political differences of these influences were rarely taken into account, though their strategies were adopted as the way to bring the gospel to the world. The locus of evangelism subsequently shifted from local congregations to conference boards, which created new initiatives for church growth that focused on church planting. Mennonite Brethrens in the 1980s became increasingly involved with evangelical programs (Evangelism Canada, Vision 2000) to absorb the nation into its escalating purview.[6]

The increased attention to numerical growth confused Mennonite Brethren identity. Both the traditional configuration of the church/ state contrast as well as social concerns were compromised in favor of sharpening evangelism.[7] It seemed as though they were willing to accommodate any aspect of wider society if it could be harnessed as an effective apparatus for proselytizing others. Concern for adopting a persuasive function supplanted the commitment to a distinct lifestyle; abstract belief propositions replaced tradition-informed ethics. In 1986, the perceived threats to a coherent Mennonite Brethren tradition were external—influences such as post-secondary education, individualism, pluralism, affluence, evangelism, and authoritarian leadership models endangered a unanimously applicable Mennonite Brethren character.[8] Nowhere, however, was it questioned that relations with state politics could ever pose a problem to Mennonite Brethren self-articulation, though it was assumed a solid identity was needed to adequately manage any forthcoming changes or new dangers.

Due to new states of affairs, most notably changes in Canadian national policy, the Mennonite Brethren have changed their mode of evangelism. Though still evangelical—including the continued influence of non-Mennonite evangelical programs and strategies—there is no longer the easy accommodation to cultural norms to guarantee numerical results. A renewed priority has emerged for local congregations

5. John H. Lohrenz and Abe J. Dueck. "Mennonite Brethren Church." *Global Anabaptist Mennonite Encyclopedia Online* 1989. Online: http://www.gameo.org/encyclopedia/contents/M4639ME.html.

6. Toews, *Pilgrimage of Faith*, 251.

7. Ibid., 247.

8. Ibid., 213–15.

to root themselves in their social milieu and establish strategies for evangelizing in their particular cultural context. Mennonite Brethren identity is a current interest under investigation within the church.[9] The appeal of results has not evaporated entirely, although a new emphasis has been placed on how Mennonite Brethren articulate themselves in distinction from societal conventions. However, the way in which this uniqueness is expressed communicatively discloses its formal dependency on liberal democracy. The Mennonite Brethren are intent on being protected from external threats, building conceptual and theological barriers to different modes of being (particularly same-sex lifestyles), and preoccupied with expanding the church's scope within these narrow parameters in much the same way as Western nations organize foreign policies. In other words, though there is a renewed sensitivity to being an alternative community to the state, its previous accommodation to mainstream society's presuppositions and way of life has framed the conditions for Mennonite Brethren self-descriptions. The appropriation of evangelicalism into Mennonite Brethren practices and tradition is part and parcel of its political orientation.

To say that evangelicalism is an attendant of political liberalism is to say that the space in which it operates has been configured and subsequently bequeathed to churches like the Mennonite Brethren. The political geography of this space forms a different landscape in which the Mennonite Brethren live and operate in Canada than the American terrain. While the U.S. has seen a rise in an antidemocratic rightwing politics that eschews all things liberal, Canada has somehow avoided a reactionary ascendancy. Whatever other parallels may be made between Stephan Harper's Conservatives and George W. Bush's Republicans, one cannot say that the former is a style of neo-McCarthyism or inverted totalitarianism or any other descriptor that suggests its essential character threatens the basic tenets of democracy. Canadians—Mennonite or otherwise—would not tolerate the politics of a Canadian version of the Bush administration.[10] Thus, it is fair to say, that political liberalism

9. James Toews wrote a five-part series exploring Mennonite Brethren identity, *MB Herald* 47 (2008) 4–8.

10. Polls in Canada have consistently shown a disapproval of Bush and have also revealed the public opinion that Bush has made the world less safe—to the extent that Canadians see Bush as more of a threat than Kim Jong-il. Some thought that Harper would bring some of Bush's policies to fruition in Canada—privatizing portions of

is the dominant ideology and economic practice in Canada. Though this puts Canada in a more democratic state of affairs than its southern neighbor, it nevertheless has the narrow outline of a not-so-generative future. The recent apology, for example, made by the Prime Minister to Aboriginal peoples for Canada's role in the Indian residential schools system acknowledges governmental deficiencies of the past. Such an act displays a vulnerability and willingness for reformation we have yet to see from any U.S. administration. However, given the lack of support for Aboriginal peoples involved in current disputes over land claims—instead favoring housing developments in southern Ontario and increased oil extraction in northern Alberta—it remains to be seen how the penitence of the apology will expand the receptive generosity of Canada's political liberalism. The frustration and aggression of Canada—its government, local authorities, and a large portion of its people—against Aboriginal people's protests, which are not based on economics and capital but tradition and heritage, sketches the marginalization of contestation and the difficulty to generatively resist state initiatives in alternative languages.

Political liberalism deploys a defensive language that closes off vulnerable and critical self-reflection and augments a preoccupation with security and self-preservation. Public discourse—such as the Charter of Rights and Freedoms—is bounded, the rules of the conversation decided in advance, in order to sidestep a cultural slump into fundamental disagreement, yet the structure of this discourse is assumed to transcend differences and hover above the sites of contestation.[11] Thus, political liberalism is characteristically a politics of confinement and exclusion—its language is self-referential (think of its use of descriptors

---

Canada's universal health care, sending Canadian troops to Iraq—but this has not happened, nor does it appear to be on the horizon.

11. The history of the initiation and implication of the Charter in Canada complicates this perhaps too-simplified analysis—though I ultimately think it stands as an accurate description of prevailing public discourse. It is interesting that the defenders of the Charter are judiciaries rather than elected members of parliament, though the notwithstanding clause allows the possibility for the government to have the final word on matters that exceed provincial authority, such as same-sex marriage. Suffice it to say here, despite noble attempts at allowing the courts to have ad hoc authority to vindicate the Charter, the effort to promote democracy by including Canadians in referenda, and the aim to extend liberties and freedoms to marginalized and mistreated groups such as gays, aboriginal peoples, and Quebecers, the continued mishandling of these groups' interests exhibits the inequities of this discourse.

like "terrorist" and "patriotic") and functions as an inflexible mechanism to exclude others prior to engagement. All judgments and procedures of inclusion are made with little-to-no space for adjustment and are employed separately and before other voices are heard. When Stephen Harper carves out a space for evangelical churches to be ethically distinct from a government that legalizes gay marriage and the Mennonite Brethren church subsequently inhabits this space as a political community desiring to be heard and influential, political liberalism furnishes and cloaks Mennonite Brethren identity and language. Put simply, the unquestioned acceptance of political liberalism and the space it allows for the role and language of evangelicalism frames all conversations as closures and all politics as gated. Difference, conflict, translation, disagreement, and uncertainty all get in the way of, are antithetical to, Mennonite Brethren evangelical identity and discourse.

The Politics of Yoder and Radical Democracy

To be clear, my suspicion is not against Mennonite Brethren involvement in or engagement with liberal democracy, but in how it frames conversations—which is why I think it is important to identify evangelicalism as a totalizing discourse to be fractured rather than a problem to be solved. Nor do I assume that this positional identity, located within the framework and logic of political liberalism, can be easily—if at all—extricated. But perhaps there are other ways to appreciate political non-constantinianism and other modes of self-articulation. Exploring alternatives does not negate liberal democratic concerns or conversation partners nor does it mean the suspension of particular faith claims. It just means that there might be ways of seeing Christ beyond our current conceptual horizon, beyond the gates of the church, beyond the language and practices the church uses to proclaim Christ as Lord. The work of John Howard Yoder can be instructive here, yet the way in which his voice is inflected will make all the difference for how he is inherited. I suspect that many evangelical Mennonites who find themselves in a conceded, non-constantinian political position would be more than happy to hear that this is where the church has belonged all along. The confidence to assert that "we do see Jesus" from this space is all too welcomed by a people desperate for a new voice of influence and privilege. Using Yoder in this way—to assert the politics of Jesus as one more form of self-possession, one more way to secure Christian identity and prevent vulnerable engagement with others— is surely a misappropriation, a criticism of certain forms of Yoderian interpretation rather than of what Yoder himself said.[12] Yet perhaps Yoder, in spite of himself, conditions the possibility of a constantinian use of his non-constantinianism. Either way, negotiating the political and theological terrain with Yoder will have to be done carefully. One way to situate Yoder in this conversation between Mennonites and po- litical liberalism is to look at how one democratic form has engaged his work, namely radical democracy. The hope is to deepen the Mennonite connection with radical democracy as a tactical ally in witnessing the politics of Jesus through vulnerable dialogue, critical self-assessment, and receptive generosity.

Radical democrat Romand Coles argues for a politics that vivifies rather than vitiates response and receptivity to others. Far from being a politics of confinement with a totalizing language, radical democracy is a politics that "stretches its listeners between calls to the importance of articulating, mediating, and striving toward the highest values of a community, on the one hand, and painful evocations of the unacknowl- edged suffering often wrought by a community's ideals (or constitutive failure in light of them) and the inextinguishable need to be transformed through receptive engagements with those a community marginalizes and subjugates on the other.[13]" Rather than evoking tension to justify a self-preserving politics, Coles sees politics as articulating the ten- sion between attempts to bring a community's values to fruition and the ways in which others suffer those attempts. A politics borne of this tension would not make preservation and stability the highest ends to meet, but instead opens itself up to the margins, those beyond the limits of its constitutive community. Coles captures this tension as a constant

12. The criticism of using Yoder in this way and the argument for Yoder's meth- odological non-constantinianism, which enables his vulnerable engagements with others, comes from Chris K. Huebner, "Unhandling History: Anti-theory, Ethics and the Practice of Witness" (PhD diss., Duke University, 2002), esp. the chapter entitled "Methodological Non-Constantinianism, Epistemological Peace, and the Otherness of the Church: John Howard Yoder's Hermeneutics of Peoplehood."

13. Romand Coles, *Beyond Gated Politics: Reflections for the Possibility of Democracy* (Minneapolis: University of Minnesota Press, 2005) 2.

negotiation between teleology and ateleology: to listen to and cultivate our cognizance and skills inherited from our traditions and yet critically extend them and be receptive to unforeseeable newness through engagements beyond their reaches.[14]

Coles's politics is "informed" and "energized"[15] by a sensibility based on an ontology of tragedy—a recognition that all attempts of engaging others are laced with violent self-asserting tendencies, which requires the humility to admit that one could be wrong (at best) or violently repressive (at worst) at any time and that a community must be ready to change its form and mode of being at the moment of recognition. Put differently, Coles's political vision is acutely aware that at any moment it might be tragically blind to—or even complicit with—suffering and injustice. Tragedy both "constitutes and challenges democratic tradition," yet is not characterized by loss—either the loss of exceeding and excessive voices or the loss of the ability to assess whether that loss is necessary. A tragic politics continuously receives others, yet recognizes that this receptivity itself is "not unproblematic."[16] Consequently, radical democracy engages views from elsewhere to illuminate the self and overall project. The boundaries of a radical democratic tradition are porous and permeable, its mode of engagement is mobile, all its assurances are unsettled, and the people constituted by it are flexible. Thus, while other forms of political liberalism shore up a perfunctory social space, Coles vulnerably explores and interrogates endless possible encounters within a capacious society.

Coles's engagement with Yoder both supports and displays his politics. The way in which Yoder practices his tradition as a Mennonite is particularly helpful for Coles's attempt to extend and defend liberal democracy insofar as Yoder "combines bearing evangelical witness to his confessedly provincial tradition with vulnerable and receptive dialogi-

14. Ibid., xv.

15. Ibid., 2.

16. I have heard Coles himself describe this politics as "not unproblematic." Coles does not invoke tragedy as a way to escape failure; his use of tragedy is not the unequivocal answer to the problem of political liberalism's tendency to use human finitude as an excuse to keep public discourse restrained lest it fall into an arena for anarchic violence. Coles admits that his tragedy is just as tragic—just as unable to *"escape itself and establish a 'perfect' set of tensions between striving toward our visions and receptively opening to that which challenges us from elsewhere,"* as political liberalism (ibid., 5; original italics).

cal practices with others."[17] Yet Coles admits his encounter with Yoder is a work of translation, which means it will be an encounter fraught with both possibilities and risks.[18] Coles acknowledges that the differences between Yoder's political ecclesiology and his own expansion of political liberalism are significant. However, he sees in Yoder a politics that creatively attends to receptive generosity and simultaneously uses the engagement itself as a practice of the political project for which he strives. Coles's encounter with Yoder delineates his conception of radical democracy as a tradition to the extent that its horizons are stretched ateleologically while it struggles to maintain teleological differences.

Yoder's particularity that stretches radical democracy is "fidelity to the jealousy of Christ as Lord," which is the root of vulnerable dialogue and generative tension with others. Every church is peccable in fact and always responds to its failure to fidelity through extensive self-interrogation of radical reformation, which is more a(n) (uncertain) mode of looking than a (presentable) historical event. Indeed, it is a way of seeing that is neither ubiquitous nor superintends, it does not presume to present its scrutinized objects as clear and usable, but is a practice of recognizing that the truth the church bears is relative to its finite expression. The church that sees the practices of radical reformation—Eucharist as an economical paradigm for sharing resources with both church insiders and outsiders; non-violent love of enemy; discerning gifts of those foreign to the church as possibilities of God's activity—as an acknowledgment of its peccability speaks in dialogues; it needs others to help see Jesus. This need of others for fidelity induces a confusion of bodies (blurring inside/outside distinctions) and discursive conduits (blurring mission/dialogue sensibilities). God's ambiguous providence stirs beyond the visible church community creating the possibility that not all "outsiders" are bad.[19] Christians should be susceptible to this confusion, yet fidelity to the jealousy of Christ as Lord limits the confusion. The limits Christ's Lordship imposes are always to be negotiated and discerned by the body of Christ as historical encounters emerge, disabling attempts at defining the conversation partner prior to the event of dialogue. Body politics name the dialogical practices of radical

17. Ibid., 111.

18. Ibid., 112–13.

19. Coles, *Beyond Gated Politics*, 128.

reformation, through which the church negotiates and discerns its limits as a response to the open yet resistant receptive generosity Christ's jealousy cultivates.[20] All the while, the church never presumes in its knowledge or in its practices a priori the difference between fidelity and treason. Put simply, the jealousy of Christ, the call for people to see the cruciformity of the cosmos, is a call for more, not less, vulnerable engagements.

Yoder's "wild patience" is the condition of possibility for the multiplicity of these dialogues, and is what Coles appreciates for his own politics. Patience is the gift of time that resists "the insistence lodged in every teleological 'now' that it contain within its own horizon of orientation the future to come and the others within that future."[21] This patience relaxes the hold of fidelity as a pressure to close untried relational conduits and waits to hear from any who wish to speak—both inside and outside the church—and waits to see if their articulations and actions are meaningful and effective. Waiting with the trust that the future belongs to Christ frustrates the "closures of history" as it instead gushes out of control into what lies ahead with prodigal irresolution. Yoder's patience—as a virtue that curbs the temptation to escape finitude by seeking security from perceived threats—is key for negotiating and living in Coles's radical democracy, because it waits to see if they are indeed threats to avoid or rather conflicts to creatively inhabit; it dispels the tendency to totalize a community's values by waiting to hear what other communities' values are; it resists the jump to necessitate violence because it listens to those who suffer that violence; and it is crucial for receptive generosity because it allows for excess and unforeseeable newness.

While the jealousy of Christ as Lord enables and sustains this untamed patience, this receptive generosity, it may steal the time it opens, infusing the church's "*caritas* with time and other with a stinginess."[22] Coles offers his own neo-Nietzschean suspicion of jealousy to open up new space at the limits, where Yoder's use of naming the lordship of Christ sharpens the edge. On the one hand, it is no surprise that an atheist would hit his head on this jealousy and call for more recog-

---

20. See John Howard Yoder, *Body Politics: Five Practices of the Christian Community Before the Watching World* (Scottdale, PA: Herald, 1992).

21. Coles, *Beyond Gated Politics*, 130.

22. Ibid., 135.

nition of atheistic virtues and their possibilities. On the other hand, however, Coles discovers in Yoder moments when his articulation of the inside/outside framework could be further receptively and generously blurred.[23] Coles sees, for example, in the essay "On Not Being Ashamed of the Gospel" that Yoder's "exaggeration of the distinction between newbearers [sic] and host culture perhaps weakens his ability to open certain questions and responses to problems of heralding in late modernity" and elides questions of "discursive hybridities."[24]

Coles's suspicion appears to be on the mark, as one can see in Yoder a constantinian use of "methodological" non-constantinianism in the way he homogenizes the just-war tradition, gaining unambiguous access to an imprecise and unsettled discourse in order to present his ecclesiological alternative.[25] Of course more needs to be said: Yoder's list of the just-war criteria is meant to be open and charitable, much like his use of constantinianism as referring to a shift rather than the man was meant to be open to the historical contingencies surrounding the fourth century. Yoder's reconstruction of the just-war tradition is meant to "confirm the integrity of [his non-pacifist] interlocutors," but he says that in order "for me to take them seriously does demand that I ask of them how they are making [just war] operational."[26] Yoder admits that

23. Ibid., 137.

24. Ibid., 276 n. 21.

25. This analysis of Yoder is largely indebted to Alex Sider's discussion of Yoder's use of the constantinian "shift" to bypass a careful investigation of the polemical context in the fourth century, even though Yoder elsewhere argues for attentive historiography. Sider is supplementing the work done in Huebner's "Unhandling History" to consider the "non-Constantinian registers" of Yoder's methodology in order to uncover moments of inconsistency that benefit Yoder's own argument. J. Alexander Sider, "To See History Doxologically: History and Holiness in John Howard Yoder's Ecclesiology" (PhD diss., Duke University, 2004) esp. the chapter entitled "Constantinianism Before and After Nicaea: Issues in Restitutionist Historiography," 134–81. Sider says, "The problem [with narratives that display the past as a monolithic story] is that they disambiguate history in order to justify their investment, or unstated set of contemporary theological polemical concerns. . . . To the extent that Yoder relied on such narratives without explicit attention to the concerns that shaped them, his narrative concerning Constantinianism risks further authorizing theological narratives that do not locate equivocation and difficulty as partly constitutive of what it means to think historically" (141–42). I am saying that Yoder does the same thing with the just-war tradition as what Sider says he does with the historiography of Constantinianism.

26. John Howard Yoder, *When War is Unjust: Being Honest in Just-War Thinking,* 2nd ed. (1996; Reprinted, Eugene, OR: Wipf & Stock, 2001) 5.

the just-war tradition is without an official account or ecclesial authoritative statement, thus he "adds clarity" to the various lists of just-war criteria, "going beyond the tradition" so as to give "credibility" to render his conversation partners morally worthy.[27] But is the primary problem with just war its credibility? Just warriors never wrote clear lists, and Yoder never asks why this is the case. Instead of allowing for the difficulty and equivocation within the tradition to stand, Yoder's synthesis of the deviating criteria gives it the conceptual clarity it needs to be subsequently given the benefit of the doubt. In other words, it appears that the integrity of Yoder's interlocutors depends on first being educated by him, who stands both beyond and within the tradition.[28] At best, it should remain an open question whether educating the other on what/ who they are is indeed respecting the other.

Suffice it to say here, given Coles's suspicion of the possibility of jealousy as inflicting a stinginess in Yoder, there are moments where Yoder himself should have been more uncertain and patient in his historiographical presentation of a dialogue partner—in a word, more Yoderian. Coles shows how Yoder can be instructive for Mennonites whose perception of evangelism is an impatient giving of themselves— impatient because there is no time for receiving the differences of others who appear to threaten the way in which Mennonites currently distinguish themselves in society. Moreover, Coles is instructive not only in what he says but who he is: an outsider who both wants to learn from others as well as push them on their own accounts of a just society's constitution. My consideration of Coles in terms of my Mennonite Brethren heritage is a (small) gesture to acknowledge the activity of God that may be rustling past the perceptual registers of the church. At the same time, however, to take his criticisms of Yoder seriously *as a non-Christian radical democrat* requires a penitential dispossession of my own claims to perceive Christ outside my church—for to claim

---

27. See ibid., 1–7.

28. Yoder appears to endow himself with a ubiquitous stance he elsewhere claims to be an illusion. On the one hand he adds clarity to the structure of the just-war tradition by adding an additional category that does not appear within the existing lists, thus "going beyond the tradition" (*When War is Unjust*, 3n). Later, on the other hand, the clarifications he gives to the tradition "belong to the integrity of the just-war tradition claim. . . . They are the conditions of its credibility *from within*" (*When War is Unjust*, 127; emphasis added).

my ability to recognize Christ in radical democracy in the same way I am saying the Mennonite Brethren recognize him in themselves is to be guilty of the certainty and impatience I want to disturb. I would like to say that Coles "gets" Mennonites more right than they understand themselves, but to do so would only privilege my own voice, my own perception, and render Coles's version of Yoder not "not unproblematic." Thus it is important to point out that Coles's translation of Yoder into a tragic politics leaves remainders.

Despite clear points of connection, it may be that Yoder's politics is not translatable into a framework based on Coles's ontological tragedy. Coles admits that he has "no idea" how to "think and believe" Yoder's declaration of Christ's "victory and control."[29] I suspect that this is because nowhere does Coles investigate the ways in which Yoder's eschatology informs his politics, ecclesiology, and, most importantly, patience.[30] Instead, Coles articulates Yoder's Christianity—as "a goal-oriented movement through time"—through his own category of teleology.[31] Yoder understands eschatology to be "a hope that, defying present frustration, defines a present position in terms of the yet unseen goal that gives it meaning. . . . It is the meaning of the *eschaton* for

---

29. Coles, *Beyond Gated Politics*, 131.

30. When Coles does mention Yoder's eschatology he frames it in terms of a political resistance and hope in *caritas*. Coles understands Yoder's "victory and control" as a function to "powerfully inspire and orient the church to resist the 'principalities and powers' that would subjugate creation to idolatries of 'power, mammon, fame, efficacy.' They call believers to resist as mythical these closures of history and to begin (again and again) to practice an alternative body politics, confident that the future belongs to *caritas* – even in the enormous capacities to assimilate or brutally crush opposition and alternative hopes" (ibid.). Yoder is indeed concerned with both resistance and *caritas*, but they seem to be askew without a more explicit background of *eschaton* and a discussion on how the church is the bearer of the meaning of history as it has been seen on the cross. The church's resistance to the powers is not sustained by a hope in *caritas*, that one day all will live by love and charity, but rather Christian resistance is a practice in recognizing both the createdness and fallenness of the powers and that the future—the horizon of the church—belongs to Jesus.

31. Coles does acknowledge in a footnote that his use of teleology to describe Yoder's project may be a problematic translation, but goes no further than that. See *Beyond Gated Politics*, 273 n. 4. It would have been interesting, given that the entire chapter on Yoder is centered on the theme of translation, for Coles to expand on this particular case of translation. The quote comes from John Howard Yoder, *The Priestly Kingdom: Social Ethics as Gospel* (Notre Dame: University of Notre Dame Press, 1984) 3.

present history."[32] The hope that Christians name is peace, which has come and will return in the form of a person, Jesus Christ, who orients and illuminates Christian action and politics. Yoder's eschatology both informs the character of patience (it gives the thing for which we wait) and instructs the politics that practices patience (it is a peaceful politics). By translating this sensibility into a teleology, the thing for which Yoder hopes and where his hope comes from become unclear.[33]

Christian hope, according to Yoder, depends solely on God. Part of what may be going on in Coles's read of Yoder is a misunderstanding of providence. Coles argues that for Yoder, "though God's providence *requires* visible dialogical church bodies in action, it is infinitely bigger and ambiguously more than the visible body (what it looks like, what it sees) at any point in time.[34]" However, Yoder himself says, "to know that the Lamb who was slain was worthy to receive power not only enables his disciples to face martyrdom when they must; it also encourages them to go about their daily crafts and trades, to do their duties as parents and neighbors, without being driven to despair by cosmic doubt."[35] In other words, it is not that Christian hope is in a providence that requires a certain form or mode of church, but rather Christian hope is in the paradoxical victory of God's weakness that works *even when* the church fails to be what it is called to be. God's providence comes as a surprise beyond the boundaries of the church—Coles understands this well—but also comes at its most decisive when the church fails, namely on the cross. Put simply, it is the cross, and not tragedy, that is the ground of reality.[36] To put it in Coles's terms: the cross is what *informs* and *energizes* Christian political judgment and action.

32. John Howard Yoder, *The Royal Priesthood: Essays Ecclesiological and Ecumenical* (1994; Reprinted, Scottdale, PA: Herald, 1998) 145.

33. I do not want to be misunderstood here: I am not suggesting that Coles does not see Yoder's politics as crucially peace-centered. I am rather wondering if Coles has investigated adequately the intrinsic hopefulness of Yoder's patient peace.

34. Coles, *Beyond Gated Politics*, 128 (emphasis added).

35. Yoder, *Priestly Kingdom*, 61.

36. Part of the ontological difference that I am suggesting separates, to some degree, Yoder and Coles may be seen in a quote to which Coles only partially refers. Coles writes that for Yoder "the dialogical 'church precedes the world epistemologically' and 'axiologically'" (*Beyond Gated Politics*, 111). Coles uses this quote to argue that for Yoder "this stance [is] the church's condition for engaging the world generously and with a receptive vulnerability." The full quote reads: "The church precedes the world

The corollary question to put to Coles is: where does hope come from in an ontology of tragedy? Coles's politics creates a diverse community that cultivates a sense of dignity within the suffering of the world through receptive generosity and vulnerable inclusivity. Coles's hope appears to come from within this tragic sensibility to receive and be vulnerable to others, even though at any moment this politics could fail. It may be fair to say that Coles's hope is in the ongoing and polymorphous (not univocal) process of radical democracy. That Yoder's hope comes from a person and not a process, that he is able to see the cross not as tragic but as the instantiation of providential hope, allows him to catch glimpses of the end of tragedy—namely, the *eschaton*, which does not reside solely in the future. Such a posture and vision, I think, makes a difference in how one describes one's situation and how one then acts in that world. At the very least, Yoder is not committed to a process the same way Coles puts all his faith and hope in democracy.[37]

If I were to leave the conversation here, however, it would sound as though I were repeating the refrain so familiar and comfortable to Mennonite Brethrens—we do see Jesus. There are ocular differences between Coles and Yoder, and *because* I find myself within Yoder's Mennonite tradition these differences do not prompt me to choose the familiar over the disparate as much as it darkens my perception. Summarily stated, Christ is both at home in and in exile from both Mennonites and radical democrats, and their deviations are mutually illuminating, dimming. Inheriting Yoder, then, will also be inheriting

---

epistemologically. . . . The church precedes the world as well axiologically, in that the lordship of Christ is the center which must guide critical value choices, so that we may be called to subordinate or even to reject those values which contradict Jesus" (Yoder, *Priestly Kingdom*, 11). Coles's observation of the "church's condition" is not wrong, but the point Yoder is making is that Jesus comes prior to all—such that all knowledge and politics find their reality in his being. Thus, when Christians act in light of the cross (not tragedy), they work with the grain of the universe.

37. Yoder is very critical of those who see democracy as necessary, as it can become a constantinian preoccupation. Coles may be more committed to discussions on the best form of government than Yoder is willing to allow for the church. Yoder says, "Perhaps 'democracy' is not univocal or not always good. Our interest is rather to reach behind those 'Christendom' assumptions to ask whether they are necessary, or what we would learn by no longer assuming them" (Yoder, *Priestly Kingdom*, 213 n. 4.). Coles would definitely agree that democracy is not always univocal, but I think his commitment to the (radical) democratic process may leave him answering the constantinian question, "What is the best form of government?" (ibid., 154).

his deficiencies as Coles sees them. To continue reading Yoder after listening to Coles is to be torn between being simultaneously for and against Yoder, for and against Coles. Given the emphasis that both give to the importance of continually accepting new interlocutors to both stretch and deepen one's inherited tradition, perhaps a third voice could reflect on the possibilities residing within this being torn-between. And so I take up Coles's call for Yoderians to inflect Yoder with other voices in new intersections of dialogue to blur the boundaries further and develop more work at the limits, dulling the edges of the church. All of which is to say, Coles's engagement with Yoder reframes political conversations through fidelity to the jealousy of Christ's lordship in order to be more receptive and generous. To push on the excessive creativity of this mode of engagement is to push for more church, more Christ, at the margins; to fracture a settled center.

Williams's Political Theology of Non-Recognition

It should be an open question whose voices our discourses intersect with, and, given the practices of a radically dialogical community, it is not a matter of sitting back and choosing conversation partners. In light of the current privileged political position of the Mennonite Brethren and the concomitant desire to be influential, the reception of Yoder's voice in dialogue with radical democracy still may sound limiting and certain to the ears that hear his conviction that we do see Jesus. Put differently, Yoder, even through Coles, may be heard to be more victorious and controlling than it would be if it were heard from the underside of history. Yoder pushes the uncertainty of all our claims and practices of Christ's Lordship but rarely if at all mentions the tragedy of these circumstances—that others suffer these conditions, that we need to cultivate a penitential capacity for flexibility, that we all share the wounds of one another's mistakes. Yoder more frequently refers to the Anabaptist church that suffers constantinian handles on history, though it too is often, if not always, complicit in strategies of control. The Anabaptists, like other marginal Christian communities, are the martyred community that, despite violent persecution and seeming defeat, can indubitably proclaim Christ's victory over the powers that kill them. Thus, Yoder articulates the way the history of Anabaptism is identified with the crucified Christ.[38] But considering the evangelical temptation to use this cruciformity as a way to insist upon and hunker down, it may help to have our culpability weigh down our visual aplomb.

Delineating obedience as remembering guilt rather than as an exclusionary presupposition may slacken the pressure to tighten fidelity into a stingy confidence. Rowan Williams reminds us that the resurrected community is a victimizing people; those who claim that salvation is only found in Jesus comprise the court that murdered him.[39] Conversion is recognizing the victim and turning to her to be transformed. This turning is complicated not only because it requires a penitential capacity for standing under the pressure of our own unbending judgment, but also because every relationship blurs easy distinctions between victim and oppressor. We are all victimizers and victims. Turning to Christ as the only pure victim, the only victim who was never oppressor, will equally not be easy but is the tension that contains the generative possibility of transcending the "master/slave" binary. This turning determines our relationship with others. The confidence of the church's service to Jesus is not rooted in its particularity *per se*, especially if it means an obsession with safeguarding tradition. Hope is found in the enemy, in those who have been excluded by virtue of their threatening presence. Turning to Christ as the paradigm for these kinds of encounters with our victims/enemies also conveys that the prerequisite of establishing the moral worthiness of the interlocutor is uncalled for. The conditions for reception are not based on first confirming the integrity of others, but are rather guided by "a willingness to receive from those we have imagined have nothing to give."[40] Christ's forgiveness constitutes the transformation of memory—that though we have and continue to oppress we should not despair, for this tyranny of violence does not have the last word—thereby commissioning a discipleship marked by hopeful penitence. If there is an "only" in the salvation in Christ, then it is retrospective and recognized through remembering one's guilt and receiving from unpredicted others.

38. Yoder, *Royal Priesthood*, 87.

39. Rowan Williams, *Resurrection: Interpreting the Easter Gospel*, rev. ed. (Cleveland: Pilgrim, 2002) 6.

40. Ibid., 11.

Christ as the pure victim forestalls our attempts at identifying our victimhood with him; the resurrected Jesus appears to us as a stranger. While a martyred people can, in a sense, empathize with the mangled body on the cross, no one can have such a quick rapport with the resurrected crucified. Any articulation of a God who is revealed in the risen Christ must include an apophatic sensibility. Williams's expression of Christ's non-competitive presence is darkly poetic, making it worthwhile to recite his descriptions that pour out like a swirling haze over our assurances of recognition: Christ is "utterly unsusceptible to definition," "an obstinate and restless dimension of unclarity," "eluding identification and control."[41] The strangeness of the risen Christ hampers the familiarity of Jesus suffering on the cross. But even when he is recognized as the crucified resurrected, his "strangeness and his recognizability are both *shocking*."[42] The risen Jesus upsets our descriptions and disturbs the certainty of our knowledge. The reverberation of the shocking collision of strangeness and recognizability destabilizes the image of the crucified, and yet his hospitality gestures a renewed fellowship. We are held close and held off; we do see Jesus, but asymptotically—as he is an "endlessly receding horizon." Through Christ we can address God, but all our designations, our very language, is entangled in "lostness, darkness, and alienation." Naming Christ as Lord may not be translatable or negotiable, but our utterances of it merely speak attempts at distinguishing calls "addressed to us from beyond the limits of everyday understanding, from outside 'the world.'"[43]

Put simply, as Williams does, "there are points when recognition fails."[44] All victims and adversaries have their own perceptions that are beyond the other's grasp; both offer gifts without which the other's sight is deficient. Part of the witness of the church is living in conflictual relationships with those who "decide differently." Conversations of this kind "risk an unresolvedness" without the concern for reaching agreement or conformity.[45] It is risky as the convictions, the pacifism, that enables

41. Ibid., 83.

42. Ibid., 84 (emphasis added).

43. Ibid.

44. Rowan Williams, "Making Moral Decisions," in *The Cambridge Companion to Christian Ethics*, ed. Robin Gill (Cambridge: Cambridge University Press, 2001) 13.

45. The phrases in quotes come from ibid., 14.

the possibility for nonviolent inclusion of unforeseeable newness might be challenged by being vulnerable to those others who suffer injustice. Williams, like Yoder, claims that these vulnerable and contentious relationships require a visual exchange of one another's attempts to see Christ. There is a moment, a provisional pause, in these struggles, when we "turn from our confrontation in silence to the Christ at whom we all *try* to look."[46] The breaks are frightening and agonizing but offer the hope that perchance we can descry a light both of us can acknowledge.

The cross is a glimpse of God that silences, and our striving to reflect its light can only be shadowy illuminations of an uncontainable light source that arrives from elsewhere. All our encounters and dialogues formed by the cross are mere "glimpses at utter difference" that "strain our language to breaking point."[47] The negativity of theology depends on the illuminations of other uncertain gazes on the world that each in their own way tries to discern meaning. The church renews its vision, its reflective capacity, not by converging what little light it has, gathering its crepuscular twilight into a centre of clarified radiance and totalized articulation, but by exploring the shade of its edges. All the church is, in its uncertainty, is a series of edges—the church as light to the world is shade all the way down. This is a shade that blurs the inner/outer framework, encouraging confusion and hybridities insofar as the jealousy of Christ draws the church further and further into the world's own uncertain light to stimulate new conflicts as the possibility for renewal. Of course there is still a distinction between church and world, although it isn't basic and only names the two ways that God works. Williams's use of church/world, as with Yoder, is beyond interior/exteriority, and names a limit the world often draws from the outside rather than by the church well in advance.[48] Williams tells a story that was told to him of a convent that put up a sign facing inward that said "private."[49] The reversed sign is a reminder that it is the "world" that withdraws into privacy, away from conflictual reformation and critical self-reflection.

46. Ibid., 14 (emphasis added).

47. Rowan Williams, *Christ on Trial: How the Gospel Unsettles Our Judgment* (Grand Rapids: Eerdmans, 2000) 137.

48. Cf. Williams, "Making Moral Decisions."

49. Rowan Williams, *The Truce of God* (New York: Pilgrim, 1983) 62. See the chapter entitled, "Illusions of Peace."

Whereas the church is a tensional dwelling of people united to struggle together in the attempt to collaborate and embody God's will. Williams calls the church a protesting body, the character of the protest is a vulnerable stance that Christians take as those people who endlessly strive to *try* to see Jesus in new horizons and diversity. That monastery life acknowledges the absolute incompleteness of life-together and allows for an honest wrestling with what it means to be a witness, which thus necessitates openness to others—even those who inhabit what the church calls world. We are silenced by the shock of the risen Lord, a silence that beckons us to listen, which will make conversation more difficult, not less. All of which is to say, faith within the church is always provisional, incessantly searching for heterogeneous openings that go beyond presuppositions of a dichotomous church/world limitation.

Conclusion: Penitential inheritance

To be sure, the penumbral vision that Rowan Williams has of the church is not all that different from Yoder's uncertain suspension and patience. Both want to stress the creativity of a tensional indeterminacy to ease our hold on the world. Patience and opacity both frustrate our attempts at totalization, problematizing the desire to flee from the edges to the centre in order to panoptically look out at the world trying to see everything at once. But I see more in-between these two theologians than a basic agreement. Williams's inflection on Yoder's fidelity pushes the silence within our witness, the penitence within our uncertainty, and darkens the recognizability of Christ. He enjoins us to patiently inhabit the provisional pauses in our discourses. And yet I can already feel Yoder pushing back, resisting a politics that only fractures. Yoder gives an ecclesiology for the forgiveness that constitutes the transformation of memory. *Body Politics*, for example, pronounces the institutionalization of practicing the forgiveness witnessed on the cross that constitutes the church as a structured social body. It is not just that the silences, interruptions, and breathing spaces of conversations unclench methodological seizures, but that *Body Politics* is about imagining non-competitive spaces for speaking. The rule of Paul—that every person who has something to say gets the floor—shows the generosity of a gathering that waits for the speech of neighbors and adversaries. Here, Yoder understates the distinction between insiders/ outsiders or worship/deliberation, consenting to a truth of Christ found by acknowledging the "healing resources of his ministry [which] can by the nature of things reach farther than the knowledge of his name."[50] Authority is yielded, the registers of language relinquished, in this discursive practice that confesses the limitations of local congregations. This pragmatic acceptance of the limitations of knowledge is neither a totalized discourse nor a mode of fracturing, but a possible moment of constructive transformation that enables speech—and evangelism by extension.

Inheriting Yoder as a radical democrat beckons us to listen to Williams's uncomfortable whispers that remind us of our own guilty acts of victimization, which makes Yoder's words of recognition—his evangelism—sound other than triumphant. At the beginning of this essay I suggested that even though Mennonite Brethrens look distinct from state politics on the surface, the way they evangelize shows their subterranean accommodation to political liberalism. I then argued that the inheritance of Yoder within this political orientation might contribute to certain delusions of grandeur attributable to a false clarity of Christ. The link between evangelicalism and political liberalism is weakened through Yoder's connection to radical democracy, which Coles initiates by pushing the uncertainties within Yoder's patient fidelity to Christ. To inherit Yoder within a radical democratic context rather than a more perfunctory political liberalism includes responding to Yoder's deficiencies as Coles sees them, viz., the need to mix Yoder with other voices. Hence, I claimed that Rowan Williams's emphasis on the church's guilt and its interference with any consistent recognition of Christ changes the intonation of Yoder's declarations to be even more penitentially uncertain. Where Mennonites go from here depends on whether we let the link between evangelicalism and political liberalism be problematized by the darkness of Christ. Or, perhaps to hybridize Yoder and Williams, the mode of evangelism changes if our witness communicates that we do see Jesus but we don't always recognize him. Moreover, even when we do recognize Jesus—when we do see the practices and have the language to witness his alternative kingdom in this world—our words are wreathed in tendencies to dominate. Perhaps

50. Ibid., 69.

there is no way to fully rectify this problem, but perhaps one way to initially address it is to see how one aspect of the domination within Mennonite Brethren evangelism is received from the language of liberal politics. The concomitant theological problem is that this makes the presence of God in the world—the politics of Jesus—look similar to the way in which the world organizes itself, namely in terms of territorial competition.

For Mennonites to use their cruciformity, the martyr stories in their histories, as a privilege that resists penitential practices turns witnessing the politics of Jesus into just one more instance of the world's "endless struggles for advantage, where success lies always in establishing your position at the expense of another's."[51] I am arguing that Mennonite Brethren adoption of evangelicalism is one occasion of a rivalrous mode of engagement that morphs witness into a conquest over non-Christian positions. Even our best-intentioned conversations—such as Yoder's attempt to make just war credible in order to help it become a more convincing argument—employ language that overstates the line between what we are arguing for and what we are struggling against, making our dialogues seem overly uncomplicated. Encouraging a more penitential sense of our history is not meant to deemphasize evangelism *per se*, it just makes encounters with others a lot less sensational and more prosaic. Ordinary conversations generally do not advance, multiply, reproduce, grow, and impact, rather they are usually plodding and quotidian. The urgency for dramatic confrontation reverberates in the tone of evangelical speech, outlining discussions as territorial battles where people are either won or lost. But the activity of God's providence is neither determined nor assured by the same standards of power that adjudicate success in the world's current arrangement. The stake in evangelism is not winning potential converts simply because we do not need to make room in this world for God. Evangelism and discipleship are not about increasing numbers or bolstering social services if these things are meant by us to assure God's presence according to what we mean as success. Thus, evangelism should be informed and energized by absence and invisibility; God is not located in the structures of the current political system nor is the success of witness something that can be easily seen. Church and state—Mennonite Brethren and politi-

51. Williams, *Christ on Trial*, 45.

cal liberalism—neither practice identical politics nor compete for the same territory. Perhaps evangelism names the conversations that enable Mennonites to imagine new possibilities for life together as a way to offer new relationships, allowing us to hear the word in fresh ways. Mennonites will be different not because we have a handle on Jesus or more information that others lack, but only because we are open to various relations—with memories we would rather forget, with enemies we would rather not talk to, with strangers we would rather not listen to.

The difference Williams makes to Yoder's political theology is the constant reminder that we fail to embody the politics of Jesus and that others suffer our failures. An evangelism animated by a penitential sense of history will witness a power that is active in this world yet beyond human perception, not captured by our descriptions or identity. Putting Yoder and Williams in conversation here can and should be reframed by the ambivalences and deconstructive moments Williams brings, but should not be understood as just one more dialectical leap to the next framework. Put differently, I am not suggesting that Coles or Mennonite Brethrens should accept Williams as doing everything that Yoder does and more. Rather, Williams's emphasis on the shocking events of our encounters cadences Yoder's modes of communication and begins inchoate gestures and murmurs of response from within Yoder's texts—both in what he does and does not say. It is grappling with the incessant pushes back and forth between Yoder and Williams that I think we can start to descry shades of Christ in the world, in movements like radical democracy. The generative struggle to learn new ways of listening and speaking includes a politics that cultivates an opaque sensibility, appreciating the shadows cast by the intermingling illuminations of others, tactical allies, and the church.[52]

52. Thanks to Romand Coles, Stanley Hauerwas, and Isaac Villegas for their generous aid in this essay. This essay was written before Stanley Hauerwas and Romand Coles published *Christianity, Democracy, and the Radical Ordinary: Conversations Between a Radical Democrat and a Christian* (Eugene, OR: Cascade, 2008), but after I took a class on radical democracy and Christianity co-taught by Stanley Hauerwas and Romand Coles in the spring of 2006.

15

Communio Missionis:
Certeau, Yoder, and the Missionary Space of the Church[1]

NATHAN R. KERR

"The present situation in church and theology can be summed up in the form of the following question: Does the church take up a space within the world, and if so, what kind of space is it?"

—**Dietrich Bonhoeffer**

"The [Christian] community is as such a missionary community or it is not the Christian community."

—**Karl Barth**

Throughout his life and work, John Howard Yoder sought to recover the visibility of the church as a distinct political community in the wake of Christendom, and against the backdrop of contemporary Constantinian Christianity. The church's primary visibility just *is*, for Yoder, a certain form of political witness; the church, we might say, precisely by way of its practices of worship, takes up *space* in the world, and that space is irreducibly political. At the same time, however, and closely related to this concern for concrete political visibility, is Yoder's insistence that the

1. I am grateful to Joshua Davis and Stanley Hauerwas for reading and commenting upon an earlier draft of this essay.

church's existence is fundamentally *missionary*. It was primarily a missionary concern that from the beginning to the end of his life animated Yoder's insistence upon the church as a concrete ethical, political, and communal reality. The church, for Yoder, is political precisely *as* a missionary people, insofar as this peculiar peoplehood, this lived communion, is itself the mission. The visible political community that we call "church" is thus what one might call a *communio missionis*.

In this essay, I want to explore the conditions according to which the church might exist in this world as just such a *communio missionis*; that is, I should like to ask after what it would mean to say that the church takes up a *missionary space* in this world. I will do this by bringing Yoder into conversation with the French theological and socio-cultural theorist Michel de Certeau. By drawing upon Certeau's theorizations of "place" and "space," of "strategies" and "tactics," and of "culture," "*habitus*," and "practice," from within the context of his reflections on contemporary Christianity, I will argue that the Christian community is only a "community of mission" insofar as it is a community that lives its true life not by demarcating its own proper "place," but rather by way of living within that "space of encounter" with the other that is opened up in the world by way of the identity of Jesus Christ as "the Other." At the same time, however, I hope to show that Certeau's analysis opens onto the need for this space of encounter to be conceived otherwise than on his exact terms if it is to be a space of genuinely political transformation. As we shall see, Yoder's own work here serves as a critical supplement to that of Certeau, as it demonstrates how this need forces us into a deeper understanding of the missionary community as the community of *Jesus Christ*—because the nature of Jesus Christ's own identity is missionary, our own relationship to Jesus occurs by way of a communal participation in *his* missionary movement. It is at this point that Yoder's own conception of the church as a missionary community gives way to a better understanding of its properly *theological* political visibility.

While he is best known for his groundbreaking work in the fields of historiography and social theory, perhaps the most extraordinary of Michel de Certeau's contributions to modern intellectual discourse was the boldness with which he sought to negotiate the difficult task of articulating a genuine Christian "space" or praxis in and for a world that increasingly leaves Christianity or the church with little or no room for its own definitive "place." "No longer to know whether God exists, but to *exist* as Christian communities"—*that*, Certeau insists, is the first question confronting theology today; and it is a question answerable not so much by way of new theoretical constructs, but rather by way of a concrete and embodied *action*, a lived practice, by which alone the living God is discovered ever-anew in our world.[2] In seeking to articulate how it is that we are so to exist, Certeau presents us with his seminal notion of the Christian community as a "non-place," a non-territory, in virtue of which the Christian community exists within the missionary "space of encounter" with the other that is opened up by the work of God—indeed, of Jesus Christ himself—in the world. For Certeau, this space of encounter opens up as a particular "way of proceeding" that is specific to Christianity,[3] and according to which alone Certeau considers Christianity genuinely to be "thinkable" today.

The boldness with which Certeau articulates the possibilities for a contemporary Christian space rest upon his incisive and penetrating analysis of modernity, one of the chief hallmarks of which is the eclipse of the church as a central locus of meaning, and as the exemplary form of human community.[4] By way of a secularism coterminous with modernity itself, the various human sciences have proceeded to script the social body in a manner that displaces the religious or theological: "modernity is characterized precisely by the fact of having been inaugurated, not without them [i.e., Christians] nor even essentially against them, but in terms of revolutions of which religion was no longer the principle."[5] Given this eclipse of theological and religious hegemony in the modern West, Christianity is now faced with the manifest impossibility of "identifying faith with a site," or "place" (*lieu*).[6] Indeed, what Certeau is concerned with here is the possibility of thinking Christianity

2. Michel de Certeau, "How is Christianity Thinkable Today?" in *The Postmodern God: A Reader*, ed. Graham Ward (Oxford: Blackwell, 1997) 154–55.

3. Michel de Certeau, *La faiblesse de croire*, ed. Luce Giard (Paris: Seuil, 1987) 264.

4. See Frederick Christian Bauerschmidt, "Introduction: Michel de Certeau, Theologian," in *The Certeau Reader*, ed. Graham Ward (Oxford: Blackwell, 2000) 212.

5. Michel de Certeau, *L'étranger; ou, L'union dan la différence*, 2nd ed. (Paris: Desclée de Brouwer, 1992) 137. See also, *La faiblesse*, 193–201.

6. Certeau, *La faiblesse*, 296.

"after Christendom," in which that institutional authority according to which Christianity claims to be "the center of the world and the place of the true" no longer holds.[7]

While Certeau's probing analyses of the various hegemonizing logics and practices of modernity are all of critical importance, what interests me here is his analysis of the particular logic that he calls "place" and of the bearing this has upon his understanding of contemporary Christian practice. In *The Practice of Everyday Life*, Certeau articulates "place" as that which operates according to the logic of the "proper"; to live according to the logic of place is thus to "locate" the world with respect to that which is one's own, one's property, for the sake of producing and maintaining as far as possible a stable identity, language, and culture.[8] Where there is place, one is assured of an identity and stability, along with a certain authority, and, not least, a home.

It must be understood, however, that the idea of "place" functions for Certeau as a kind of "operational concept." That is to say, for Certeau, to have identified one's own proper "place" is by definition to have committed oneself to living in relation to that place and its surrounding world by way of a certain "strategic" calculus. Hence, Certeau says that "a strategy assumes a place that can be circumscribed as *proper* (*propre*) and thus serve as the basis for generating relations with an exterior distinct from it."[9] This strategic "economy of the proper place," as Certeau calls it,[10] thus depends upon a certain cultural process whereby the interior can be distinguished from the exterior for the sake of maintaining and propagating the identity of place. This cultural process of interiorization/exteriorization is what Certeau calls, following Pierre Bourdieu, a *habitus*.[11] The point here is that the very identification of one's own "proper place" not only depends upon but is also in some sense a function of a "concentric" structuring of interiority to exteriority, whereby the external proliferation of cultural practices and identity

7. Ibid., 126.

8. Michel de Certeau, *The Practice of Everyday Life*, trans. Steven Rendall (Berkeley: University of California Press) 117–18.

9. Ibid., xix.

10. Ibid., 55.

11. Ibid., 57.

structures is itself the basic means of sustaining the identity of one's own internal cultural place.

Furthermore, and perhaps most important for the purposes of this essay, this strategically concentric construction of place (which throughout his *oeuvre* Certeau associates with the modern fetishization of "writing" or of "scriptural reproduction"—the paradigm for him of an "operation organized around a center"[12]) functions as a distinct kind of "hermeneutics of the other."[13] This hermeneutics functions according to a dynamic of "instrumentality," of "utility"—"or, rather, that of *production*, at least insofar as this voyage which increases the initial investment is, analogically, a productive labor."[14] To put this another way, we might say that the economy of place is just such an economy of production: insofar as the habitual interiorization of a given identity requires the exteriorized practice of that identity, the *habitus* of place requires the ongoing identification and cultivation of analogous places, points of contact external to one's own "proper" place, at which points this given identity is reproduced and represented back to itself for the sake of its own stability and solidification. In terms of this economy of place, then, and in relation to the subject who acts as habituated by this concentric dialectic of interior/exterior, "*the other is extension*, where understanding delimits objects."[15] The logic of place, in the end, turns out to be functionally totalitarian, imperialistic, and colonizing. The "other" comes to name and to refer to the "entire circumference with respect to a center which generates it" (to invoke a formula deployed by Certeau in another context).[16] To speak of "the other" is to speak of the extension of the whole horizon of intelligibility that the languages and practices of a given cultural place necessarily require. In the end, the economy of place is that of a language that "sets out to find a world; at stake is a mission."[17] And what is at stake in this externalizing mis-

12. Michel de Certeau, "Ethnography: Speech, or the Space of the Other: Jean de Léry," in *Certeau Reader*, 133. See also "The Scriptural Economy," in *Practice of Everyday Life*, 131–53.

13. Certeau, "Ethnography," 134–39.

14. Ibid., 137, 138.

15. Ibid., 139.

16. Michel de Certeau, "The Gaze: Nicholas of Cusa," *Diacritics* 17 (1987) 2–38, at 29.

17. Certeau, "Ethnography," 138.

sion is nothing less than the self-reflexive production of a given internal identity.

It is against this backdrop that Certeau wants to ask what it means to think and to live as a Christian today. For it is in precisely these terms that we have to speak of there no longer existing a decisively Christian "place"; indeed, what Christians have to do with here is precisely "the death of our ideological reassurance and our missionary totalism."[18] "Christianity" no longer names either a stable site of production, nor does it possess a proper place of its own. As Certeau well realizes, the implications of this are profound: "If one accepts that there is no longer any Christian place, and hence neither are there any tasks which are proper to it, then Christian experience can no longer be a system or a language."[19] Bereft of its capacity to found a "place," and so of the opera-tive criteria for the production of a "proper" Christian identity, by what logic is it then possible to go on *existing* as Christian communities? Certeau's conclusion is that apart from any *theoretical* construct with which definitively to locate a proper Christian identity, we are left only with a mode of *action*—what he elsewhere calls "the movement of per-petual departure"[20]—by which we "follow after" the risen Jesus Christ in the world as we are "converted" ever-anew toward the other.[21]

This double movement of "discipleship" and "conversion," by which Christian faith is *enacted* in the world, is perhaps best under-stood in terms of Certeau's brilliant analysis of Jesus as "La rupture instauratrice."[22] For Certeau, "Jesus" is identified by way of the singular event of an "inaugural rupture" within history, by which Jesus "is" as that one who opens up a space of genuine encounter with the other, which encounter is alone the "condition of truth" of this event itself.[23] This space of encounter operates according to what Certeau calls the "not without," meaning that the "truth" of that which we call "Christianity" occurs *neither* apart from the instaurational event of Jesus himself in

18. Certeau, "How is Christianity Thinkable Today?" 150.

19. Certeau, *La faiblesse*, 278.

20. Michel de Certeau, *The Mystic Fable*, trans. Michael B. Smith (Chicago: University of Chicago Press, 1992) 299.

21. Certeau, *La faiblesse*, 293–95.

22. Certeau, *La faiblesse*, 183–226; see also "How is Christianity Thinkable Today?" 142–58.

23. Certeau, *La faiblesse*, 213–15.

his otherness, *nor* apart from the plurality of others to whom Jesus is identifiably bound in the kenosis of his "person."[24] To put it in terms of the relationship of discipleship and conversion, we might say that we respond to the call of Jesus as we are continually turned outward in conversion to the other, for Jesus just *is* that one who makes space for the testimonies of multitudinous others. By way of this double movement, Jesus is thus "named" for Certeau *as Other*: "Jésus est l'Autre."[25] It is important to emphasize, however, that Jesus is "Other" for Certeau only as the possibility of a *praxis*; Jesus is "Other" precisely as that one whose work is to "give space to"—or, "to permit" or "make room for"[26]—an ongoing encounter with *other* others, by being and making us receptive to "other places to come."[27] As such, the "work" of Christ-as-Other is to be identified with that very praxis by which we ourselves are given over to the "encounter with others, elusive brothers," by which encounter alone we truly are and become "Christian."[28] We might thus speak of the "space of encounter" opened up by the inaugural rupture of Jesus as the space of a praxis—discipleship—by which we are delivered over to the believing testimony of another; one is "Christian" only in being continually *converted* to an encounter with the other as other (whose "otherness" as such *is* her testimony to Jesus as "the Other"). This space of encounter is thus itself the "missionary space" within which alone the Christian community is thinkable and livable today. "Church" itself comes to name that double movement of discipleship and conversion— the movement of *mission*—by which we pass on to communion with an irreducible plurality of others, and in which we come to encounter ever-anew that Other—Jesus—who authorizes that communion.[29]

It is precisely as constituting such a missionary "space" in the world that we might best understand Certeau's insight that the Christian community exists as a "non-place," or "non-site" in this world. And it is precisely as such a practiced "non-place," furthermore, that the missionary praxis of encounter occurs for Certeau as a kind of political operation.

24. Certeau, "How is Christianity Thinkable Today?" 146–47.

25. Certeau, *La faiblesse*, 225.

26. Certeau, "How is Christianity Thinkable Today?" 142–45, 149–50.

27. Certeau, *La faiblesse*, 225.

28 Certeau, *L'étranger*, 69; cf. *La faiblesse*, 305.

29. See Certeau, *La faiblesse*, 225.

Borrowing again language that Certeau develops in *The Practice of Everyday Life*, it might thus be said that the Christian community exists not by way of the "strategic" logic of "place," but rather according to the "tactical" calculus of what he calls "space," or "*practiced* place." A "tactic," as Certeau defines it, lacks a "place" of its own (*propre*), as well as its own panoptic view of the whole within which to locate the other.[30] As opposed to a strategy, then, by which one's own "proper" place is identified and organized by the postulation of a certain form of power, a tactic is "a calculated action determined by the absence of a proper locus," as well as by "the *absence of power*"[31]; a "tactic" is a way of working on and within the places of power for the sake of opening up "a space," in which the other might be lived and encountered *as* other independent of her "placement" by the strategic technologies of the "proper." Instead of the "hermeneutics of the other" deployed by the economy of place, then, the tactics of the non-place, or space, operate according to the mode of what Certeau calls a "heterology." A Protean and elusive term for Certeau, "heterology" might best be defined with Michael Barnes as "the deconstruction or uncovering of unavowed forms of closure,"[32] that is, as the fracturing of the totalitarian logic of place by the opening up of spaces within which the other might appear and speak as genuinely other.

In light of this, it might be possible to speak of the missionary movement that is the Christian community as constituting for Certeau the politically heterological project par excellence.[33] Indeed, as Certeau puts it, "The irruption of Jesus does not found a new place [*lieu*]. . . . It introduces the non-place [*non-lieu*] of a difference in a system of places."[34] In following after Jesus by being converted and "delivered to the voice of the other and dependent on his coming or response," the Christian community's "way of proceeding" is precisely the perpetual losing of its property, a perpetual "exile out of identity," a "movement of perpetual departure" that can only rightly be described as the work

30. Certeau, *Practice of Everyday Life*, xix.

31. Ibid., 7–38.

32. Michael Barnes, *Theology and the Dialogue of Religions* (Cambridge: Cambridge University Press, 2002) 62.

33. See Graham Ward, "The Voice of the Other," *New Blackfriars* 77 (1996) 526.

34. Certeau, *La faiblesse*, 294.

of "diaspora."[35] And yet it is just by way of "losing its property" in this movement of exile in response to the call of the other that the church "appears"—is rendered politically *visible*—as an executed "cut in the social body," as a living in the "'moment' of the break" with every identifiable social and institutional "place."[36] The Christian movement of perpetual departure thereby exists as "the perpetual insinuation of alterity in established positions,"[37] by which alone it appears as that "space of encounter" with the other that exists independently of the ideological protection guaranteed by the "economy of place."

It turns out, then, that Certeau's articulation of the Church as a "non-place," as a "space" of missionary encounter with the other in the world, is not only constitutive of but turns upon a certain mode of political "movement" for its visibility in the world. And it is at this point that Certeau's work is most illuminative of these same themes as they appear in the work of John Howard Yoder. Indeed, what I want to suggest above all is that Certeau's seminal understanding of the Christian community's "way of proceeding" as a missionary "movement of perpetual departure" serves nicely as a guiding hermeneutical lens through which to read Yoder's ongoing struggle to articulate the idea that "dispersion is mission,"[38] in a manner that is constitutive of the Christian community as a diasporic peoplehood, without reserve. Yoder's unfailing commitment to remaining true to the Jeremianic call to "seek the peace of the city" could very well be understood as his own mode of simultaneously refusing the temptation to assume and to privilege the existence of Christianity's own "proper" place, as well as articulating positively the sense in which the church's political life, its very peoplehood, is inconceivable and untheorizable apart from its lived encounter with other.[39]

And yet just as important is the way in which Yoder's articulation of these very themes might serve as a kind of supplement to Certeau's

35. Ibid., 295–96.

36. Ibid., 279.

37. Ibid., 285–86.

38. John Howard Yoder, *For the Nations: Essays Public and Evangelical* (Grand Rapids: Eerdmans, 1997) 52.

39. Cf. Chris K. Huebner, *A Precarious Peace: Yoderian Explorations on Theology, Knowledge, and Identity* (Scottdale, PA: Herald, 2006) 125–26.

heterological account of them. Apart from this supplement, Certeau's heterological account of Christian homelessness, diaspora, and exile might just leave us with a merely reactionary politics, a politics of tactical *resistance* that is yet still dialectically determined as over-against the dominant matrices of the status quo.[40] What is needed rather is the articulation of a politics of mission whose content is not simply the conversion to the other as such, but rather conversion to the other as sign and sacrament of God's new creation, in which the other can be seen as liberated *from* her bondage to the ideological structures of this world as she is liberated *for* participation in God's coming Kingdom. The rest of this essay will thus be given to articulating in outline the way in which Yoder's vision of the church as a diasporic peoplehood "fills out" the shape of the politics that Certeau's account of the Christian community as a missionary "space of encounter" calls for.

What is perhaps most important about my reading of Yoder by way of Certeau is not just the way in which Certeau helps us to make sense of Yoder's claim that the Christian community is from the outset and without remainder to be a missionary community, but that such a community exists only as it issues from the event of Jesus Christ. In an important early essay on the nature of the church as a missionary people, Yoder eschews just the kind of concentric and insularly strategic articulation of Christian existence that Certeau is critical of, when he insists that the question of mission has to do fundamentally with coming to "see the church in relationship to the world rather than defining ecclesial existence 'by definition' or 'as such.'"[41] "Peoplehood" and "mission" are thus in this way each "the condition of the genuineness of the other."[42] In making this association of peoplehood with mission so strongly, Yoder's concern is precisely to combat the association of the church with the notion of politics that coincides around the "establishment of a total society"[43]—which establishment is precisely the upshot

40. See Graham Ward, *Theology and Contemporary Critical Theory*, 2nd ed. (New York: St. Martin's, 2000) 156; F. C. Bauerschmidt, "The Abrahamic Voyage: Michel de Certeau and Theology," *Modern Theology* 12 (1996) 15–19.

41. John Howard Yoder, "A People in the World" [1967], in *The Royal Priesthood: Essays Ecclesiastical and Ecumenical*, ed. Michael G. Cartwright (1994. Reprinted, Scottdale, PA: Herald, 1998) 65–101, at 78.

42. Ibid., 78.

43. Ibid.

of the logic of "place," as Certeau defines it. And it is just in making the church the bearer of such a total social identity that mission is fundamentally "compromised."[44] All of this leads Yoder to the important conclusion that the only way properly to conceive the church politically is to conceive the church *as* mission. In an important passage that bears quoting in full, Yoder puts it thus:

> The political novelty that God brings into the world is a community of those who serve instead of ruling, who suffer instead of inflicting suffering, whose fellowship crosses social lines instead of reinforcing them. This new Christian community in which the walls are broken down not by human idealism or by democratic legalism but by the work of Christ is not only a vehicle of the gospel or only a fruit of the gospel; it is the good news. It is not merely the agent of mission or the constituency of a mission agency. *This is the mission.*[45]

The thing I want to point up here is not only the way in which this passage resonates with our conclusion above—that the church is an irreducibly missionary community—but that its very existence as such a community is a uniquely Christic operation, "derived from the man Jesus."[46]

It is precisely at this very point of convergence, however, that we find a marked distinction of emphasis between Certeau and Yoder as regards the relation of Jesus to this community. This point of distinction has to do with the fact that whereas for Certeau Jesus is generative of the community as a kind of historically foundational event—an "instaurational rupture" that inaugurates Christianity by a distinct originary act—for Yoder Jesus is constitutive of the community as one whose very *life* apocalyptically irrupts into history as the inbreaking of the Kingdom of God; Jesus bears the Kingdom, and so the meaning and orienting point of the church, in his very *person*.[47] Where Certeau is concerned, Jesus founds the church as a kind of formally representative point of departure, whose "withdrawal" by which he "makes

44. Ibid., 89.

45. Ibid., 91 (emphasis added).

46. Ibid., 95.

47. See Nathan R. Kerr, *Christ, History and Apocalyptic: The Politics of Christian Mission* (London/Eugene, OR: SCM/Cascade, 2008) 127–60.

room" for the other is dialectically coincident with history's ongoing progress, thereby making of the Jesus the founder of the church as "the degree zero of a series," to borrow Certeau's own phrase.[48] By contrast, for Yoder, Jesus is constitutive of the church as the community that it is—the *communio missionis*—insofar as Jesus does not exist in a mode of withdrawal but as the one who is the eternally *sent one*—sent *into* the world to love the other in the concrete, self-giving mode of radical *agape*, which *agape* is the way of the coming Kingdom of God. God's Kingdom comes, that is, by way of a concrete "conferring of a mission in history,"[49] and *Jesus* is not simply the condition of possibility for that mission, in a founding mode of absence or withdrawal, but is himself *present* as the embodiment of that mission in his singular way of life.

There are two key implications that follow from this christological point of distinction between Certeau and Yoder. The first of these implications has to do with the double movement of discipleship and conversion by which we relate to and follow after Jesus as "the Other" by way of our ongoing conversion to *other* "others." As to Certeau, it is not unfair, I think, to suggest that insofar as Jesus is foundational for Christian existence in a formalized mode of absence or withdrawal, then to "follow after" him as Other by way of "conversion to" the other's witness to him as Other is to risk the formalization of "otherness" and "the other" as such. If Jesus as Other is constitutive of Christian community as fundamentally signifying a foundational "lack" or "loss,"[50] then the question is raised as to whether my ongoing conversion to the other is not merely a function of the Christian's always having dialectically to posit the other as that which she is "lacking" in order to be herself; "otherness" becomes a function of the logic of identity, and the dual movement of discipleship and conversion becomes conceptually mediatory of a certain kind of excessive self-reflexivity.[51] To be fair to

---

48. Certeau, *La faiblesse*, 121. See Bauerschmidt, "Abrahamic Voyage," 21.

49. John Howard Yoder, *The Politics of Jesus: Vicit Agnus Noster*, 2nd ed. (Grand Rapids: Eerdmans, 1994) 24.

50. Certeau, "How is Christianity Thinkable Today?" 150.

51. Of course, as Bauerschmidt remarks, the specter of Hegel is definitely lurking here. Bauerschmidt, "Abrahamic Voyage," 18–19. This is the case as regards both the constitutive relation of Christ's withdrawal to the ongoing processes of history, as well as Certeau's deployment of the Heideggerian "not without" (which is rooted in an Hegelian logic) as constitutive of Christian "identity." See Certeau, "How is

Certeau, he is indeed seeking to escape this logic by insisting that the double movement of discipleship and conversion is only thinkable as a concrete praxis, a lived practice that is not "theorizable" as such apart from such lived practice. But one wonders if, given the way in which Jesus-as-Other is operative for him as a formal "lack," this practice can be conceived otherwise than as a merely negative, perhaps even "content-free" praxis of the "perpetual insinuation of an alterity within established positions."[52] This would itself be to render the Christian community's practical visibility by way of perpetual flight into theoretical invisibility. Insofar as the Jesus which the disciple follows after is present by way of a perpetual absence, so the perpetual departure by which one is converted to the other would thus have to occur as a movement of perpetual withdrawal, which movement would in turn render the missionary space of the Christian community operative in terms of its own formalized socio-political "lack" with respect to every proper "place."

The double movement of discipleship and conversion appears to happen quite differently for Yoder, however. To use Certeau's language Jesus is "the Other"—that is, *God*—for Yoder insofar as he is first of all God's own "self-giving way of love" for the other.[53] Furthermore, if God is other in this way, then the other is encountered as other only insofar as she is encountered as that one who is loved in her concreteness and specificity as this singular other. And it is in being loved as such that the other is freed genuinely to be *other*, that is, to be free to love in the self-giving way of love by which God loves in Jesus as "the Other." The upshot of this is that, for Yoder, the double movement of discipleship and conversion is clearly less dialectical and more concretely participatory, or, we might say "koinoniac." We ourselves only encounter the other as other insofar as we *follow after* Jesus in his "self-giving way of love" as

---

Christianity Thinkable Today?" 146–47. For a theological reading of Hegel that is thoroughly resonant with Certeau's analysis here, see Eberhard Jüngel, "The Effectiveness of Christ Withdrawn: On the Process of Historical Understanding as an Introduction to Christology," in *Theological Essays*, ed. John Webster (Edinburgh: T. & T. Clark, 1989) 214–31.

52. Certeau, *La faiblesse*, 280. See Arthur Bradley, *Negative Theology and Modern French Philosophy* (London: Routledge, 2004) 52–61.

53. See Yoder, *Royal Priesthood*, 217–18.

God.[54] But to love in this way in the mode of *discipleship* is to say that we are indeed *converted to* the other in her transformative witness to Christ's work, which witness is her freedom to love, especially to receive and to love *me* as other in my participation in Christ's prevenient love for *her* as other. And so the self-other dialectic is overcome by way of a mode of discipleship in which we participate in God's eternal, outgoing love for the other in Christ, by continually being converted *by* Christ and *to* one another in the freedom to love *each* other as the *concrete* other that she is. In sum, for Yoder, discipleship is thinkable only as a mode of *participation* in Christ's self-giving way of love,[55] and such participation happens as I *go out* to the other and am converted to and join her in the particular way in which she has been given, in the concreteness and contingency of her singularity, to love Jesus as Other.[56]

The second key implication follows upon this, and it has to do with the nature of Christian existence as diasporic. To Certeau's important insight that the Christian community exists in a perpetually dispossessive and non-territorial mode of "losing its property" (what Yoder would call the "unhanding" of history and of "strategic effectiveness" as a matter of "accepting powerlessness"[57]), we can now add the Yoderian insight that such a mode of existence is itself the positive upshot of our participation in Jesus Christ's own singular way of life, which is a way of living *independent* of the "powers and principalities"—the structural mechanisms of territory and control—as the embodiment of the Kingdom of God, as sign and sacrament of the New Jerusalem

---

54. Ibid., 218.

55. Yoder, *Politics of Jesus*, 113–14, and 112–33 *passim*.

56. Though we cannot go into detail here, the differences between Certeau and Yoder on this point may very well turn on a doctrine of the Holy Spirit. This can be seen in their different logics of "excess" according to which Jesus is operative as Other in history. For Certeau, this "excess" is the function of the "lack" of Christ's presence that is filled by the emergence of innumerable believing others. See Certeau, *La faiblesse*, 277–86. For Yoder, however, this excess is unequivocally identified with "the life-giving power of the Spirit, by which power alone Jesus' person and work of outgoing love to the other are identifiably at one with the coming of God's Kingdom. See John Howard Yoder, *The Original Revolution: Essays on Christian Pacifism* (Scottdale, PA: Herald, 1971) 49, 51. For more on this "logic of excess" at work in Yoder's Christology, see Kerr, *Christ, History and Apocalyptic*, 144–58.

57. Yoder, *Politics of Jesus*, 228–41.

to come.[58] The movement of exile, of "perpetual departure," that Jesus' independence and that our participation therein thus embodies is not simply conceived negatively as a mere "cut in the social body," as a mere "break" with every identifiable social and institutional "place." It certainly is that. But Yoder rather helps us to emphasize that this negative judgement "upon the present order" is the inevitable ricochet of living in *this* world according to the "imminent promise" of a new order[59]; the reason that the Christian community is "utopic," living in this world as having no "place" of its own, is not simply because it is founded upon a moment of perpetual withdrawal at the point of its origin, but because it lives by belief in the promise of Jesus that "the world to come is the real world."[60] This world to come is indeed the fullness of love by which we are bound to Jesus as Other through that transformation of grace by which we are given to love *each* other, in Christ, *as* other. As opposed, then, to a praxis whose content is that of a kind of "formal" departure and withdrawal, we have rather in Jesus "the creation of a distinct community with its own deviant set of values and its coherent way of incarnating them."[61] And it is just our participation in Jesus' singular, independent outgoing love for the other that is constitutive of this community, this "deviant set of values." "Peoplehood" *is* "mission" by way of our participation in the singular *mission* of Christ; and "exile" is our positive participation in the lived independence of Jesus from the logic of what Certeau calls "place," and of what Yoder names "the powers."

Yoder's diasporic vision is thus premised upon a *positively* political understanding of exile *as mission*. The Christian community is without a "provincialized" place or a "stable or autonomous identity,"[62] as well as without its own presumed linguistic framework,[63] precisely *because* it is

58. Yoder, *Politics of Jesus*, 134–61. On the "independence" of Jesus from the powers and the "logic" of his singular historicity, see Kerr, *Christ, History and Apocalyptic*, 134–44. See also Daniel Barber's essay, "The Particularity of Jesus and the Time of the Kingdom: Philosophy and Theology in Yoder," *Modern Theology* 23 (2007) 63–89, upon which my account is heavily dependent for some of its terminology.

59. Yoder, *For the Nations*, 168.

60. Ibid., 134–39

61. Ibid., 175.

62. John Howard Yoder, *The Jewish-Christian Schism Revisited*, eds. Michael G. Cartwright and Peter Ochs (Grand Rapids: Eerdmans, 2003) 150, 151.

63. Yoder, *For the Nations*, 24.

sent into the "place" of the other so as to work for the other's liberation *from* the powers of this world and *for* the coming Kingdom of God, as now bound up with its own liberation as the Christian community, as such. Thus it is that Yoder takes as paradigmatic for the Christian community of mission the Jeremianic command to "seek the peace of the city where I have sent you into exile, and pray to the Lord on its behalf, for in its peace you will find your peace" (Jer 29:7). As Yoder remarks, however, "'Seek the peace of the city' is too weak a translation for Jeremiah's command. It should be translated 'seek the salvation of the culture to which God has sent you.'"[64] It is precisely by way of not possessing a cultural-linguistic "place" of its own that the Christian community exists as it is given over to and for the transformation of the culture and language of the other.

Here the important point is that Yoder is articulating a positive *politics of diaspora*; this is not mere political deviation, but rather a politics of working and praying for the *political transformation of this world* as sign and sacrament of the coming Kingdom. Furthermore, this salvation, this political transformation, is bound up with Yoder's alternative logic of otherness. "Those people are qualified to work at the building of the city who build it for others, who recognize it as not their own turf but God's."[65] For the same reason, Yoder speaks of the sense in which the earthly Jerusalem has itself always functioned within Judaism and Christianity both as "more than a place," as a sign and sacrament here below of "the other Jerusalem" to come, and as a sign of *God's* own "extraterritoriality."[66] It is precisely this "otherness of Jerusalem" on earth, the extraterritoriality of God's Kingdom here below, that "points us away from possessiveness . . . so as to favor the outsider."[67] In short, for Yoder, it is God's very own extraterritoriality that binds us to the other in mission, and that liberates the Christian community to be that "utopic" people—that "non-place"—for whom the political transformation of the city to which it is sent in mission is constitutive of its visibility as God's people in the world. But it is also God's extraterritoriality that is itself definitive of the city's liberation and transformation, insofar

64. Yoder, *Jewish-Christian Schism*, 202 n. 60.

65. Ibid., 164.

66. Ibid., 161–64.

67. Ibid., 162.

as that city's salvation is precisely its liberation *from* the logic of "place" and its liberation *for* participation in and the enactment of the extra-territoriality of God's own *agape*; the true "space" of mission is one in which we are freed from the logic of place by being caught up in God's own mission of eternal, outgoing love for the other in Christ.

Finally, then, we are in a position to state clearly that which we have so far only been alluding to in the previous paragraphs. It is precisely as the embodied sign and sacrament of God's coming Kingdom, as the sacrament of this world's conversion—indeed, of the conversion of *place* itself—to this coming Kingdom, that the utopic and diasporic Christian community is rendered concretely *visible* as the missionary space of encounter that it is. Here I should like to suggest that Yoder's account of "sacrament as social process"[68] gives us to think the political visibility of the church positively in a manner that Certeau's logic of perpetual withdrawal does not, while still allowing us to avoid the kind of fetishization of ecclesiastical sacramentality that insists upon conceiving the Christian community in itself as "the center of the world and the place of the true," which would be to reinscribe the concentric logic of place with respect to the Church's sacramental structure. If the "social process" which the church "is," is irreducibly and perpetually a diasporically *eccentric* movement of mission, then the Christian community is *sacramentally* visible precisely by way of those concrete practices—paradigmatically baptism and Eucharist—by which God acts perpetually to give it to work for the "salvation of the culture"—the conversion of the "place," the "city"—to which it has been sent.[69] To say

68. See Yoder, "Sacrament as Social Process: Christ the Transformer of Culture," in *Royal Priesthood*, 359–73.

69. There is not space here to enter into the debate as to whether Yoder's account of "sacrament as social process" in the essay already mentioned and in *Body Politics* served to reduce the sacramental life to ethics and to sociology, as some have argued. I can only suggest that if we are to take seriously Yoder's affirmation that God is always at work to act "in, with, and under" these human acts, in such a way that "the community's action is God's action" (see John Howard Yoder, *Body Politics: Five Practices of the Christian Community Before the Watching World* [Scottdale, PA: Herald, 1992] 1, 3, and *passim*), and if I am right that this social process is to be conceived as irreducibly missionary, such that the church only "is" by way of participation in the self-giving love of God that is the sending of Jesus Christ, then the trajectory of Yoder's thought, as I have argued in this essay, itself forbids the kind of sociological rendering of the church-as-place that would make such a reduction possible, whatever else Yoder might have meant by his accounting of these practices at various points.

this is to say that the church is visible as a missionary space that is a non-place, precisely insofar as the church's sacramental life *is* the sign of the truth of the fact that it need not exist by way of the logic of place, with its own sovereign center, but rather exists only by way of that eccentric "social process" by which it is given ever anew to receive and to love the other—the "outsider"—in her own singular conversion to the coming Kingdom of God. And yet, for the church to be given sacramentally to receive and to love the other as other in this way, is for the church to be visible as a social process of being *bound* to the other as other by way of the other's own sacramental participation in the missionary life of Christ-as-other, whose self-giving way of love makes of Christ himself "the transformer of culture."[70] To say this is to say that the church's sacramental practices are themselves only sacramental *as* practices of mission, as visible practices of that very *love* by which members of the Christian community are bound to one another and to every other *qua* other in Christ.[71] That is to say, the church's sacramental practice—its "social process"—is its very participation in the sending of Jesus Christ that is God's own self-giving way of love. To speak of the church's sacramental visibility as "social process," then, is just another way of saying that "mission makes the church."[72]

And so, to conclude: To read Yoder in light of Certeau's work is indeed to affirm with Certeau that the Christian community exists as a "non-place" in the world, and so lives as a "way of proceeding" whose "movement of perpetual departure" opens up a "space of encounter" that is conceivable precisely as a "missionary space." And yet to supplement Certeau with Yoder is to accentuate all the more clearly and positively the sense in which to accept dispossession, to accept this movement of perpetual departure, is not merely to "accept 'not being in charge' as a lesser-evil strategy of mere survival, nor as a mere tactic," as Certeau

---

70. Yoder, *Royal Priesthood*, 360.

71. Perhaps this point is best articulated in Yoder's discussion of "The Fullness of Christ," the fourth practice discussed in *Body Politics*, which is the reconciling gift-relation between human beings that is miraculously "achieved by Christ alone," in the power of the Spirit, and which happens as the visibility of that "trans-ethnic people" of which eucharist and baptism are consitutively the sign and sacrament. See Yoder, *Body Politics*, 48–50, 52–53, 58–59.

72. Cf. Kerr, *Christ, History and Apocalyptic*, 173–75.

would seemingly have it, but to accept this *as* mission from the outset.[73] Missionary dispersion is not the formal by-product of Christ's original disappearance and perpetual withdrawal; it is rather *constitutive* of the Christian community, as our mode of participation in Christ as that *one* who is himself *sent* to embody God's own eternal, outgoing love for the other as the way of the Kingdom, the new world on its way. Existing in this way, the Christian community, as bound to the other by its missionary participation in Christ's own sending love, is indeed given to be lived and to be seen as that "space" from within whose movement God's active reign in the world can be not only discerned and perceived,[74] but sacramentally lived and visibly enacted. And yet, as Yoder would be quick to remind us, the Christian community only is such a "space" insofar as she lives *in* and *for* the transformation of *this* "place," the place—the "city"—in which she finds herself here and now, *this* place which is not and can never be "her own."[75]

73. Ibid., 171.

74. See Yoder, *Politics of Jesus*, 154–55.

75. I should like to state here, in a final note, that to live diasporically in this way in relation to a "place" that is not one's own, for the sake of that place's transformation and conversion to the coming kingdom of God, is not necessarily to privilege exile and dispersion as over-against land and return. To live in this way rather requires the development of what Alain Epp Weaver, drawing upon the work of Daniel Boyarin, calls a "diaspora consciousness in the land," the development of a mode of faithful living in the land in which the land itself is conceived not as a "place" to be possessed, but as a kind of "space" of dispossession, a "shared space" of encounter with and conversion to the other. See Alain Epp Weaver, "*States of Exile: Visions of Diaspora, Witness, and Return* (Scottdale, PA: Herald, 2008) 2–3, 44–66, esp. 60–64 (a portion of which is reprinted as chapter 8 of this volume). My thanks to Michael Cartwright and Stanley Hauerwas for pressing me to confront this issue of land and return in relation to the idea of dispersion-as-mission as developed in my own work.

Contributors

Daniel Colucciello Barber teaches in the Department of Philosophy and Religious Studies at Marymount Manhattan College.

Peter C. Blum is Professor of Philosophy and Culture and director of the Sociology and Social Thought program at Hillsdale College.

Daniel Boyarin is Professor in the Departments of Near Eastern Studies and Rhetoric at the University of California, Berkeley.

Romand Coles is the McAllister Chair in Community, Culture, and Environment at Northern Arizona University.

Peter Dula is Assistant Professor of Religion and Culture at Eastern Mennonite University.

Cynthia Hess is Study Director at the Institute for Women's Policy Research in Washington, DC.

Chris K. Huebner is Associate Professor of Theology and Philosophy at Canadian Mennonite University.

Nathan R. Kerr is Assistant Professor of Theology and Philosophy at Trevecca Nazarene University.

P. Travis Kroeker is Professor of Religious Studies at McMaster University.

Nancey Murphy is Professor of Christian Philosophy at Fuller Theological Seminary.

Gerald W. Schlabach is Professor of Theology and Director of Justice and Peace Studies at the University of St. Thomas.

J. Alexander Sider is Assistant Professor of Religion at Bluffton University.

Jonathan Tran is Assistant Professor of Theological Ethics at Baylor University.

Alain Epp Weaver, a doctoral candidate in theology at the University of Chicago, works as an international program director for Mennonite Central Committee (MCC).

Joseph R. Wiebe is a doctoral candidate in Religion and Politics at McMaster University.